SARAJEVO, 1941–1945

SARAJEVO, 1941–1945

Muslims, Christians, and Jews
in Hitler's Europe

EMILY GREBLE

CORNELL UNIVERSITY PRESS
ITHACA AND LONDON

First published 2011 by Cornell University Press
Printed in the United States of America

Library of Congress Cataloging-in-Publication Data

Greble, Emily, 1978–
   Sarajevo, 1941–1945 : Muslims, Christians, and Jews in Hitler's
Europe / Emily Greble.
      p. cm.
   Includes bibliographical references and index.
   ISBN 978-0-8014-4921-5 (cloth : alk. paper)
   1. World War, 1939–1945—Bosnia and Hercegovina—Sarajevo. 2.
Sarajevo (Bosnia and Hercegovina)—History. I. Title.

   D766.62.S37G74 2011
   940.53'49742—dc22
                                                    2010029823

Cornell University Press strives to use environmentally responsible
suppliers and materials to the fullest extent possible in the publishing of its books. Such materials include vegetable-based, low-VOC
inks and acid-free papers that are recycled, totally chlorine-free, or
partly composed of nonwood fibers. For further information, visit our
website at www.cornellpress.cornell.edu.

Cloth printing   10 9 8 7 6 5 4 3 2 1

FOR MY SISTER, JULIA

CONTENTS

MAPS AND ILLUSTRATIONS

ACKNOWLEDGMENTS

I owe thanks foremost to three extraordinary scholars and mentors, Norman Naimark, James Sheehan, and Robert Donia, whose guidance and support over the past decade have helped me excavate Sarajevo's stories from the archives and turn them into this narrative. The support and confidence of Norman Naimark has been vital at every step. His assiduous mentoring gave me clarity, perspective, and confidence to see this project through. James Sheehan challenged me to expand my intellectual horizons and find the right voice to capture my ideas. Recognizing my love of Sarajevo's stories, he also introduced me to Mack Walker's *German Home Towns*, a book that deeply shaped the kind of scholarship I wanted to pursue. Robert Donia read the manuscript for this book far more times than he bargained for, each time sharing more of his seemingly bottomless insight into Balkan history. His guidance through the complex worlds of Bosnian archives and historical polemics has left an inestimable imprint on this work.

Among the many other scholars to whom I am indebted is Husnija Kamberović, director of the Institute of History in Sarajevo, whose sponsorship of various forums helped me to develop my ideas, and whose historical objectivity and integrity has been inspiring. Gilbert McArthur's early encouragement was instrumental. Ivo Banac offered invaluable advice on the pursuit of Yugoslav history, always provoking rigor in my analysis. István Deák sparked my interest in the dark and complicated history of Hitler's Europe; he and Gloria Deák have been a wealth of academic and personal support. Aron Rodrigue encouraged me to think of this book as a part of post-Ottoman studies. Katherine Jolluck taught me the value of seeking out women's stories in crafting the complexities of everyday life.

The keen eye and insightful critiques of my reading circle—Malgorzata Fidelis, Irina Gigova, Katherine Lebow, and Andrea Orzoff—enriched this book and strengthened its arguments. Ravit Reichman's perceptive readings of the introduction and conclusion pushed me to make more explicit theoretical and conceptual ideas; her clever ability to distill complex concepts into a few words left a particular imprint on the headings in the pages to follow. Years of friendly debate about genocide, nationalism, and Bosnian history with Paul B. Miller, who dissected parts of this work, was instrumental in its development. James M. Ward astutely criticized the earliest drafts of these chapters, becoming the rare reader who could state bluntly when a chapter was boring. Chinnie Ding's laborious clarification of my prose brought out its subtleties. Rebecca Reich has proven herself time and again a loyal friend and sounding board, coming through in every emergency—academic, personal, and melodramatic.

As I finished this book, I was lucky to come into a wonderful history department at The City College of New York. I am especially grateful to Cliff Rosenberg, my chair, who read the manuscript and helped me clarify some of its arguments. Beth Baron, Craig Daigle, Greg Downs, Danian Hu, Andreas Killen, Anne Kornhauser, Adrienne Petty, Darren Staloff, and Judith Stein have given critiques of parts of this work; they and Susan Besse, Barbara Brooks, and Barbara Naddeo have offered essential assistance as I navigated the vagaries of a new institution amid pressing manuscript deadlines. The financial and institutional support provided by deans Fred Reynolds and Geraldine Murphy was invaluable. Finally, I offer a special thanks to my students, especially those in my courses on comparative empire and minorities in Europe, for broadening my perspective on concepts of empire and identity.

This book would have been impossible to research and write without the generous financial support from Fulbright-Hays, IREX-IARO, the American Council of Learned Societies, the Mellon Foundation, and both the Center for Russian, East European, and Eurasian Studies and the Department of History at Stanford University. A two-week summer fellowship at the U.S. Holocaust Memorial Museum helped me hone my ideas on wartime confessional politics; Vicki Barnett and Suzanne Brown-Fleming were especially supportive. I am grateful to Steven Miller and Robert Rotberg at the Belfer Center for Science and International Affairs for giving me a home and a support network for two years of writing, and to Tony Judt, who provided a fellowship at the Remarque Institute at New York University, during which I completed this book.

Historians of Bosnia learn quickly that archivists do not simply act as gatekeepers, but as research advisers and advocates of objectivity. This project would have been impossible to complete without the assistance of the wonderful people who work at the archives and libraries in Sarajevo and Zagreb. While there are far too many individuals to mention by name, I want to extend special thanks to Muhiba Kaljenac and Alma Leka at the Historical Museum of Bosnia and Herzegovina; Milena Gašić, Huso Hodžić, and the late Mustafa Dervišević at the Historical Archive of Sarajevo; and Sandra Biletić, Amira Hujdur, Mina Kujović, and Šaban Zahirović at the

State Archives of Bosnia and Herzegovina. I am especially indebted to Se-jdalija Gušić, director of the Historical Archives of Sarajevo, who welcomed me into the archive community, supporting my research unconditionally at every step.

The professionalism and commitment of Cornell University Press has made this process unequivocally positive. John Ackerman gave his support to this book with enthusiasm and graciousness. Jamie Fuller's smooth copy editing and Susan Specter's production expertise proved instrumental in making the final hours productive and enjoyable.

Portions of chapters 3 and 4 are reprinted from "When Croatia Needed Serbs: Nationalism and Genocide in Sarajevo (1941–1942)," *Slavic Review* 68, no. 1 (Spring 2009).

This book would not have found itself without the guidance, support, and encouragement of friends in the Balkans and the United States. In Sarajevo, my dear friend Milena Gašić and her family—Dule, Marina, Saša, Irina, Tea, and Lea—made sure I always had a home away from home. They spent countless evenings helping me decipher nearly illegible, fad-ed Cyrillic handwriting and talking through my historical interpretations, while stuffing me full with *sarme* and *princez krofne*. Irfana Softić and Indira Telegrafčić ensured that I was immersed in every facet of Bosnian cultural life, from May Day in Maglaj to Thursdays at Slogo. Asim Guhdija chal-lenged me to think about Bosnia more provocatively. My two talented re-search assistants, Aleksandar Gašić and Željka Poloni, were my eyes and ears in Sarajevo when I could not be there. In New York and Stanford, Anita Škara and Sanja Medić patiently taught me to speak Croatian. In Split, the Balić and Singolo families were an incredible support system as I learned the language and customs of the region. The late Ante Balić cared deeply about history, encouraging my work even when my narratives challenged his truth. Through Vlatko Balić I fell in love with the Balkans; his support made this book possible in many ways.

I am also grateful for the conversation and friendship of Julia Cohen, Liz Cohen, Erin Dillon, Kevin Cusick Dix, Scott Ebner, Jake Gamage, Christopher Johnson, Jesse and Lena Kauffman, Tiffany Mercer, Elise Molinelli, Karen Rob-bins, Sharron Silvers, Ashley Simone, Tammy Smith, and Ted Weesner. Sandy Silverman's guidance helped me to keep track of the big picture. My spirited extended family—Derek Stensby, the O'Donnells, the Knox/Koestenblatts, and the Worsnicks—ensured that I left the library from time to time.

My family deserves a special note of recognition for their selfless sup-port. Though we did not know it at the time, my father, Thomas Greble, spent his final hours talking with me about the title of this project. He im-parted an intellectual curiosity and passion for storytelling, without which I would not have become a historian. My mother, Diane Greble, has been there constantly, even when this meant avoiding land mines in Herzegovina or carrying boxes of documents through the snowy streets of Sarajevo when the frigid wind had stopped every tram in the city. She nourished me with steadfast support and love, not only encouraging, but enabling me to pursue my dreams. Through my brother, Matthew Greble, I learned how to empathize without fully understanding. Emily Weltman, kindred spirit and lifelong friend, has always made life more manageable. Matthew Worsnick's confidence in me and patient support transformed the anxious final stages of writing a book into a delightful experience. He has given me countless reasons to relish the interstices as much as the highlights; for this I am eternally grateful.

Finally, my sister, Julia Stensby, has lived this book with me since its inception in our childhood, when we played "hide from the Nazis" in the crawl space of our house and furtively laid awake hours past bedtime reading *Winds of War* and *Mila 18* under the covers. As we grew up, she became my late-night editor, confidant, and mediator. Throughout our family's intellectual and personal challenges in the past decade, her emotional and editorial support often went hand-in-hand. I dedicate this book, with love, to her.

MAJOR ARCHIVES

ABiH   Arhiv Bosne i Hercegovine (Archives of Bosnia and Herzegovina)

ARIZBiH   Arhiv Rijaseta Islamske Zajednice Bosne i Hercegovine (Archives of the Islamic Religious Community of Sarajevo)

HDA   Hrvatski državni arhiv (Croatian State Archives)

HM   Historijski Muzej Bosne i Hercegovine (Historical Museum of Bosnia and Herzegovina)

IAS   Istorijski Arhiv Sarajevo (Historical Archives of the City of Sarajevo)

USHMM   Archives of the United States Holocaust Memorial Museum

Hoover Institution Archives

NOTE ON LANGUAGE AND
FOREIGN TERMS

The South Slavic language spoken in Sarajevo has had many names over the past century. Rather than engage with the political debates that surround the naming of language, Sarajevans often refer to their mother tongue vaguely as "our language." During the Yugoslav eras, the language was called Serbo-Croatian, a hybrid of Serbian, the eastern variant written in the Cyrillic alphabet, and Croatian, the western variant that used the Latin alphabet. Today Bosnia has three official languages: Bosnian, Croatian, and Serbian (commonly referred to as BCS). For consistency, I defer to the historians, governments, and individuals in my sources. I thus use "Serbo-Croatian" when discussing Yugoslav historiography and "Croatian" when referring to the policies of the Ustasha regime.

Throughout this work, I have kept all personal names and place names in their original forms. Whenever possible, I use standard anglicized words for the names of groups, such as in the case of Chetnik, Ustasha, and Partisan. This is the model adopted by Jozo Tomasevich in *War and Revolution in Yugoslavia, 1941–1945: Occupation and Collaboration* (Stanford: Stanford University Press, 2001). In a similar vein, I adapt Ivo Banac's system set out in the seminal work *The National Question in Yugoslavia* (Ithaca: Cornell University Press, 1984), using the adjectives "Croat" and "Serb" to refer to people (e.g., Croat nation, Serb politician), and "Croatian" and "Serbian" to refer to language and concepts that assume a long history (e.g., Croatian language, Serbian Orthodox Church).

SARAJEVO, 1941–1945

CITY LINES

Multiculturalism and Sarajevo

Since that fateful day in June 1914 when a teenage boy shot Archduke Franz Ferdinand, setting off a chain of events that triggered the First World War and razed Europe's empires, Sarajevo has stood for the death of the old European order. And lest the city's importance be overshadowed by the tumultuous decades that followed, the international spotlight returned to Bosnia's capital in the 1990s, when the siege of Sarajevo stunned the world and shattered illusions that Europe's violent past had been laid to rest. The brutal siege, like the assassination, signaled the end of an era.

But Sarajevo has come to embody more than these violent bookends of a short twentieth century. In one of history's many ironies, during the breakup of Yugoslavia the city earned a reputation as a unique place of tolerance, diversity, and peace in Europe's dark century. Indeed, Sarajevo became the hallmark of all that worked in Yugoslavia, a symbol of multiculturalism at its best. The city was a center of Muslim, Catholic, Orthodox Serb, and Jewish communities, each with a rich local history and strong connections throughout the region. The city's international reputation was cemented through popular culture, travelogues, films, and most important, the spectacle of the 1984 Winter Olympics—when images of snow-kissed mosques, churches, and synagogues evoked hope in plurality and the promise of a multicultural future.

In his epic history of post–World War II Europe, Tony Judt rejoiced in the fact that while multicultural Europe had been "smashed into the dust . . . thanks to war, occupation, boundary adjustments, expulsions and genocide," a remnant had survived in Yugoslavia, especially Sarajevo. "On its restricted scale," Judt wrote, "the Bosnian capital was a genuinely cosmopolitan city: perhaps the last of the multi-ethnic, multi-lingual, ecumenical urban centers that were once the glory of central Europe and the eastern

Mediterranean."[1] That Sarajevo's distinct pluralist culture survived the devastation of the First World War is noteworthy; that this culture persisted
and even thrived despite war and genocide in the Second World War is
extraordinary. This book sets out to understand how this multicultural idyll
survived the calamities that overwhelmed Europe in the 1940s.

In April 1941, the Axis partners invaded and occupied Yugoslavia. Sarajevo, like all of Bosnia, was incorporated into the Independent State of Croatia (Nezavisna Država Hrvatska)—commonly referred to as the NDH—one
of the most notoriously brutal Nazi satellite states. The NDH was run by
the ultranationalist Croat Ustasha regime; its capital was Zagreb.[2] Although
generally associated with Roman Catholic reactionary politics, the Ustasha
regime adapted a version of national ideology that viewed the Croat nation
as composed of two faiths—Catholicism and Islam. This had important
consequences for Sarajevo. As the traditional seat of the Islamic Religious
Community (Islamska vjerska zajednica) in Yugoslavia and the High Sharia
Court (Vrhovni šerijatski sud), Sarajevo was designated the cultural, political, and religious capital of the Muslim community in the NDH. Moreover,
as a regional hub for the German occupation command, the city became a
center of debates on Bosnia's position in the European system of states and
the place of Islam in Hitler's Europe. And as the major crossroad for Bosnia's transportation and communication systems, Sarajevo became a prime
target of the armed insurgencies fighting for power in the Yugoslav civil
conflicts—most famously, Tito's Communist Partisans, who liberated (or
conquered) the city in April 1945.

Sarajevo's wartime geopolitical position thus offers a perfect starting
point for an investigation into the clash that occurred as different kinds of
communities and traditions interacted with the ideological forces of Fascism, nationalism, and Communism. Indeed, as a multiconfessional city
caught in the midst of a many-sided war, it offers a privileged vantage point
from which we can evaluate how world war and civil war transformed society
and how local civic, political, and cultural codes shaped national wartime
dynamics.

Beginning with a portrait of Sarajevo on the eve of war, this book examines how a city shared by Muslims, Catholics, Orthodox Serbs, and Jews
experienced the wartime crises. To this end, it responds to Omer Bartov's
call for historians to integrate state and local agendas of the war—and
thus capture the "big picture"—by writing "community studies" that take
into account "the personal interaction between people, their prejudices,

1. Tony Judt, *Postwar: Europe since 1945* (New York: Penguin, 2005), 8–9 and 684.
2. For the plural of the term "Ustasha," I adopt a nontraditional approach in academic
writing and use "Ustashas" instead of one of the Croatian-language plural forms of the word—
Ustaše or *Ustaši*. This choice fits grammatically with the anglicized forms of the other well-
known political movements functioning in Bosnia during the war, the Chetniks and Partisans.

needs, and urges, as well as their memories, traditions, and perceptions."[3] In probing the local dynamics of the war from political, cultural, religious, social, and economic standpoints, this book seeks answers to the following questions: How did local leaders navigate the war in order to assert their own agendas? In what ways did ideas of nation, race, religion, and civic community influence decision making and alliances? And ultimately, what lessons can be drawn from studying Sarajevo? Was multiculturalism a vestige of an imperial past doomed to a cruel death at the hands of the twentieth century? Or was it a different path to modernity, a different European model?

In the chapters that follow, I argue that Sarajevo's leaders responded to the challenges of the war by clinging to two aspects of the city's traditional culture: (1) a system of confessional identities that persisted in the private sphere and (2) a local solidarity—or what I call civic consciousness—rooted in Sarajevo's Ottoman and Habsburg traditions of political pluralism and cultural diversity. The combination of these two central values created a set of local codes that mandated treating members of the "community" in particular ways.

The Making of a Multicultural City

Sarajevo's experiences in the Ottoman, Austro-Hungarian, and Yugoslav eras molded the city's demographics and forged its distinct social and political culture.[4] When the Ottomans founded Sarajevo in 1463, they aimed to build a great Muslim city on the frontier of Christian Europe. Choosing a small Catholic merchant village along the Miljacka River as the center point of the new city, the Ottomans constructed mosques and established religious orders and an administrative headquarters. Conversion to Islam was gradual but widespread among Bosnia's Christians.[5]

Although Muslims dominated politics and society from Sarajevo's earliest days, large communities of Sephardic Jews, Roman Catholics, and

3. Omer Bartov, "The Roots of Modern Genocide: On the Macro- and Microhistory of Mass Murder," in *The Specter of Genocide: Mass Murder in Historical Perspective,* ed. Robert Gellately and Ben Kiernan (New York: Cambridge University Press), 79–80; 85–87.

4. Two good English-language general histories of Bosnia and Herzegovina are Robert Donia and John Fine, *Bosnia and Hercegovina: A Tradition Betrayed* (New York: Columbia University Press, 1994), and Noel Malcolm, *Bosnia: A Short History* (New York: NYU Press, 1996).

5. The foundational works on Sarajevo's early history are Hazim Šabanović, *Bosanski pašaluk* (Sarajevo: Svjetlost, 1982), and Behija Zlatar, *Zlatna Doba Sarajeva* (Sarajevo: Svjetlost, 1996). Conversion to Islam is a highly contentious subject in the historiography and among the Balkan communities. The nature of these conversions, including who converted, when, and why, has been used to fuel Serb and Croat nationalist claims that Bosnia's Muslims belong to their national group. For an overview of recent scholarship, see Markus Koller's bibliographical essay in Marcus Koller and Kemal Karpat, eds., *Ottoman Bosnia: A History of Peril* (Madison: University of Wisconsin Press, 2004), 4–8.

4 ~ CITY LINES

Orthodox Serbs lent the city a multiconfessional character. Some Roman Catholics and Orthodox Serbs migrated from rural Bosnia; others lived in villages that became incorporated into the expanding city. The Sephardic Jewish community sought refuge in Sarajevo and other parts of the Ottoman Empire after the expulsion of the Jews from Spain in 1492. All three religious communities developed administrative centers in Sarajevo, a legacy that would carry through the twentieth century.

In the Ottoman social system, people were defined and governed by their religious communities. Education, socioreligious matters (marriage, inheritance), and internal legal affairs fell exclusively within the religious domain. Marriage to someone of another faith required conversion and was extremely rare. As in the rest of the empire, the Ottomans had separate laws and governing arrangements with the city's non-Muslims. The Ottomans permitted only the Franciscans, a Roman Catholic monastic order, to minister to Catholics in the Ottoman Balkans, and they disallowed the Roman Catholic diocese from working in the empire.[6] They acknowledged the authority of the Sephardic Jewish rabbis in a 1622 statute.[7] Sarajevo's Orthodox Serb community was placed under the Patriarch of Constantinople.[8]

The city's physical structure further contributed to its social and cultural development. Sarajevo was organized into numerous *mahalas*, segregated residential neighborhoods, each of which surrounded a religious institution. Kemal Karpat, an Ottoman historian, describes how the separation of these religious communities and the absence of vertical social mobility outside one's community strengthened their "internal cohesion."[9] It also reinforced local loyalties and the power of neighborhood elites.[10]

Despite being integrated into the Ottoman state structure, Sarajevo's Muslim elite gradually acquired a philosophy of autonomy. By the seventeenth century, they dominated the city's political, military, and commercial classes and dictated the terms of the city's relationship with Istanbul. They eschewed Ottoman Turkish in favor of the local dialect, a cultural practice

6. John Fine, "The Medieval and Ottoman Roots of Modern Bosnian Society," in *The Muslims of Bosnia-Herzegovina: Their Historic Development from the Middle Ages to the Dissolution of Yugoslavia,* ed. Mark Pinson (Cambridge, Mass.: Distributed for the Center for Middle Eastern Studies of Harvard University by Harvard University Press, 1996), 12–13.

7. A. Sućeska, "Položaj Jevreja u Bosni i Hercegovini za vrijeme Turaka," in *Spomenica: 400 godina od dolaska Jevreja u Bosni i Hercegovini,* ed. Samuel Kamhi (Sarajevo: Oslobođenje, 1966), 47–48.

8. *Serbian Orthodox Church, Its Past and Present,* vol. 1, Belgrade: Serbian Patriarchy, 1965), 16–17.

9. Kemal Karpat, *An Enquiry into the Social Foundations of Nationalism in the Ottoman State: From Social Estates to Classes, From Millets to Nations* (Princeton University Center of International Studies Research Monograph no. 39, July 1973), 7.

10. Alija Bejtić, "Ali-pašina Mahala u Sarajevu," *Prilozi Institut za Istoriju* 2 (1966): 25.

that employed linguistics to strengthen regional loyalty.[11] At a few points in the city's history, local Muslim leaders even restricted how often official Ottoman representatives could visit their town. Such autonomous inclinations resonated throughout Bosnia. For example, unlike their peers in other parts of the Ottoman Empire, Bosnia's class of Janissaries (Ottoman military elite) took wives, acquired property, and developed close ties to the city's guilds and crafts.[12] Like Janissaries everywhere, they were known to feel greater allegiance to local Muslim nobles than to the sultan.[13] In Sarajevo, this legacy of political isolation and autonomy cemented certain attributes of the city's identity, particularly the feeling among members of the local elite that they alone were responsible for the communities under their care.

Although Sarajevo's ruling Muslims enjoyed substantial political and social autonomy, they also grew accustomed to sharing the city with people of other faiths. Members of Sarajevo's communities mixed as merchants and consumers in the bazaars. Consequently, by the nineteenth century Sarajevo's civic culture blended aspects of its diverse confessional traditions; while rooted in Islam, it nevertheless reflected and incorporated other identities. The economic legacy of the early Ottoman centuries also helped to prepare the city for political plurality, which the Ottomans cultivated in the nineteenth century in a series of reforms known as the Tanzimat. Faced with the challenge of European modernization and expansion into its territories, the Ottomans sought to modernize, centralize, and strengthen the empire. A central goal of these reforms was to equalize the position of Muslims and non-Muslims by creating equal opportunities in government, developing mandatory conscription, removing mediating religious and political bodies, and establishing secular, civil laws for all citizens. Sarajevo's Muslims protested this reduction in power and rebelled several times in the first half of the nineteenth century. Ottoman troops crushed the rebellions and implemented the reforms by force in the 1850s. In 1865, the Ottomans established a regional council in Sarajevo composed of both Muslim and non-Muslim representatives. They assigned seats on the basis of religion, guaranteeing that Muslim, Jewish, Catholic, and Orthodox Serb leaders each had a voice in the local government.[14] Gradually this council became understood as the centerpiece of the town's political pluralism; it

11. Ivo Banac, *The National Question in Yugoslavia, Origins, History, Politics* (Ithaca: Cornell University Press, 1984), 41.

12. John Lampe and Alan Jackson, *Balkan Economic History, 1550–1950: From Imperial Borderlands to Developing Nations* (Bloomington: Indiana University Press, 1982), 27. On the autonomous Bosnian military culture, see Markus Koller, *Bosnien an der Schwelle zur Neuzeit: Eine Kulturgeschicthe der Gewalt, 1747–1798* (Munich: R. Oldenbourg, 2004).

13. Following a Janissary uprising in Istanbul, Sultan Mahmud II abolished the empirewide Janissary Corps in 1826.

14. Robert Donia, *Sarajevo: A Biography* (Ann Arbor: University of Michigan Press, 2006), 32–35.

was the bedrock of representative municipal government that would exist in some form through the Second World War. Four centuries of Ottoman rule thus endowed Sarajevo with a distinct civic and social culture and introduced a new path toward political plurality. Indeed, the Ottoman legacies of local autonomy and representative government created a foundational culture of multiconfessionalism, as both an idea and a set of practices.

Starting in 1878, four decades of Austro-Hungarian rule under the Habsburgs would give Sarajevo's diverse population time to modify these local customs to address the challenges and demands of the modernizing era.[15] In contrast to the experience of other Balkan cities such as Skopje and Novi Pazar, which found themselves the objects of competing Ottoman, Greek, Bulgar, and Serb claims, and to that of Belgrade and Sofia, which became capitals of emerging nation-states, the citizens of Sarajevo were encouraged by the Austro-Hungarian authorities to strengthen their religious piety and imperial loyalty and discouraged from expressing national identities. To accomplish this, the imperial authorities codified some aspects of Sarajevo's civic culture and challenged others. For example, although Vienna sent delegates to govern the city, the new rulers sought to continue certain Ottoman traditions, such as that of designating seats on the town council for representatives from each of the religious communities. The town's multiconfessional culture acquired the bureaucratic and legal institutions it would need to solidify its local character through the twentieth century.

With the importation of Viennese arts, architecture, and ideology, many of Sarajevo's elite began to think of their city as a special cosmopolitan enclave. In 1883, the monarchy formally made Sarajevo the capital city of Bosnia and Herzegovina, which sparked a new wave of investments in the city's economy, culture, and communication structures. From 1889 to 1904, Sarajevo was the only city in Bosnia and Herzegovina with a telephone line. This fed into the notion of a distinctive Sarajevo culture that stood apart from the poorer, less civilized areas of the former Ottoman world and also from the rest of Bosnia and Herzegovina—where literacy rates were only 13 percent.[16] The Habsburgs also catered to Muslim desires for autonomy, winning support from members of the Muslim elite who still felt angry about the Ottomans' abrupt and radical social leveling earlier in the century. Sarajevo thus assumed a complex new imperial and civic identity at the same time that it was being exposed to national ideologies. These parallel

15. On Bosnia during the Austro-Hungarian era, see Robert Donia, *Islam under the Double Eagle: The Muslims of Bosnia and Hercegovina, 1878–1914* (Boulder: East European Monographs, distributed by Columbia University Press, 1981), and Robin Okey, *Taming Balkan Nationalism. The Habsburg "Civilizing Mission" in Bosnia, 1878–1914* (Oxford: Oxford University Press, 2007).

16. Iljas Hadžibegović, *Bosanskohercegovački gradovi na razmeđu 19. i 20. Stoljeća* (Sarajevo: Institut za Istoriju u Sarajevu, 2004), 24, 67, 78.

developments profoundly shaped political dynamics during the Habsburg era and left an imprint on the city's politics in the coming decades.

Despite the Habsburgs' attempt to suppress nationalist sentiment within Bosnia's borders—and partly as a result of such efforts—fin-de-siècle Bosnia saw the rise of radical politics and the spread of nationalism. The ideas of South Slavic reciprocity, prevalent since the 1830s, went through different phases. Some versions endorsed a unified linguistic platform that could bridge the Serb and Croat nations, some advocated self-determination for southern Slavs living in the Habsburg Monarchy, and a final group promoted a cultural program that would unite South Slavs using the Italian or German model of nation-state building.[17]

While the seeds of nationalist ideologies had been planted in Sarajevo in the late Ottoman era, earlier nationalisms had maintained a more inclusive character. For example, although some of the city's Orthodox Serbs embraced the nationalist ideology being espoused in neighboring Serbia, many retained strong connections to the Muslims, Jews, and Catholics with whom they shared a hometown. They thus sought to adapt a national ideology to include members of other faiths. Similarly, the Franciscans, the leaders of Catholic intellectual life in Sarajevo, rejected rightist Croat nationalism in favor of a civic-based national identity. Such an urban, ecumenical concept of nationhood stood in contrast to the firebrand movements developing in the countryside, which preached separatism, hate, and intolerance.[18]

Demographic changes sparked by industrialization and immigration helped to fuel the spread of new political ideas and the fractionalization of the city's confessional communities.[19] As the population more than doubled in the first decades of the Habsburg era, divisions deepened along every imaginable fault line: generational, gender, confessional, national, political, and class. Exacerbating these local tensions, the Austro-Hungarian authorities decided to reorganize aspects of the city's religious life. Among the most significant changes was the foundation of a Roman Catholic archdiocese, which aimed to restore Bosnia's Catholics to a regular hierarchy, and the establishment of the Islamic Religious Community, which administered Muslim religious life. In sanctioning the latter, the Austrians hoped to reduce the sultan's influence over Muslims living in their empire while simultaneously catering to requests from a new group of Muslims who looked to Vienna as a model of religious and educational autonomy. The Islamic Religious Community was headed by the *Reis-ul-ulema*, a local

17. On the cultural dynamics of Yugoslavism, see Andrew Wachtel, *Making a Nation, Breaking a Nation: Literature and Cultural Politics in Yugoslavia* (Stanford: Stanford University Press, 1998).

18. Marko Attila Hoare, *The History of Bosnia from the Middle Ages to the Present Day* (London: Saqi, 2007), 57.

19. Peter Sugar, *Industrialization of Bosnia-Hercegovina, 1878–1918* (Seattle: University of Washington Press, 1963).

elected leader who worked with a council of advisers, called the Ulema Medžlis. After the Austrians annexed Bosnia in 1908, Sarajevo's Muslims negotiated a special statute that guaranteed them religious and cultural autonomy, severing their final remaining official ties to Istanbul.[20] Many conservative, observant circles of Muslims greeted this act with hostility.[21] The entire city was politically charged, as both nationalist and confessional groups agitated for autonomy within their communities and influence over the city.

Against this tense backdrop, Sarajevo was propelled into the international spotlight in 1914, when a Serb pupil, Gavrilo Princip, shot the Austrian archduke, Franz Ferdinand, and his wife, Sophie, in their car as it drove through the city's streets. The assassination became known as the spark that ignited the Great War. Sarajevo immediately gained an international reputation as a city of terrorists and a hotbed of nationalism, despite the fact that the assassin, a rural Bosnian Serb youth, was on record as being anti-Sarajevo.[22] Contrary to the city's later reputation, many of its traditional elites—Catholics, Jews, Muslims, and even Orthodox Serbs—remained loyal to the Habsburg Monarchy and to one another throughout the First World War.[23] Certainly wartime tensions existed, and many people felt an affinity to the homogenous national movements then developing. But many city leaders put aside their differences to confront the crises of famine, inflation, and injustices of war. For example, when the Habsburgs persecuted Orthodox Serbs in retaliation for the assassination, a number of important Muslim leaders protested.[24] Language likely played an important role in allowing the city to retain elements of its civic unity. Whereas many

20. The Reis-ul-ulema is the supreme Islamic religious authority in Bosnia; when Bosnia was incorporated into Yugoslavia from 1918 to 1941 and from 1945 to 1992, the Reis-ul-ulema was the highest Muslim figure in Yugoslavia. He is the grand mufti and the head imam, which signifies both a political leader and a Muslim cleric who leads prayer. The position is unique in Bosnia because the Reis is elected by a council of Muslims rather than appointed by the state. A brief overview of the position of the Reis-ul-ulema and a biography on Spaho and his predecessors can be found in Ferhat Šeta, *Reis-ul-ulema u Bosni i Hercegovini i Jugoslaviji od 1882. do 1991. godine* (Sarajevo: Islamska Vjerska Zajednica, 1991).

21. Historically, Bosnian Muslims practiced a version of Hanafi Sunni Islam, which they carried over from the Ottoman Empire and which is most similar to the kind of Islam practiced in Turkey. An excellent (if brief) overview of Islam in Bosnia during the interwar period can be found in Nada Kisić-Kolanović, "Muslimanska inteligencija i islam u Nezavisnoj Državi Hrvatskoj," *Časopis za suvremenu povijesti* 36, no. 3 (2004): 895–1322.

22. Hoare, *History of Bosnia*, 88.

23. When the Austrian authorities imprisoned a number of innocent Serbs after the assassination, local Muslims fought for their release. See Alija Nametak, *Sarajevski Nekrologij* (Zurich: Bošnjački Institut and Nakladni Zavod Globus, 1994), 15–16. On the city during the First World War, see Donia, *Sarajevo*, 127–129.

24. Atif Purivatra, *Jugoslavenska Muslimanska Organizacija u političkom životu kraljevine srba, hrvata, i slovenaca* (Svjetlost: Sarajevo, 1974), 21. An updated comprehensive overview of the Yugoslav Muslim Organization can be found in Zlatko Hasanbegović, "Jugoslavenska muslimanska organizacija u politickom zivotu Kraljevine Jugoslavije 1929–1941" (PhD diss., University of Zagreb, 2009).

multilingual towns became more nationalized during the war, Sarajevo's linguistic cohesion served as an important unifying mechanism. The legacy of collective survival in one brutal war would carry through to the next.

When the First World War ended and the Great Powers redrew the map of Europe, they retroactively ratified an agreement by Serb and Croat leaders to create a hybrid Yugoslav state called the Kingdom of Serbs, Croats, and Slovenes (see map 1).[25] The new state was designed as a democratic royal monarchy under the Serb Karadjordjević dynasty. Belgrade became the state's capital and egalitarian Yugoslavism its centralizing ideology. Local leaders from every Sarajevo community approached peace optimistically after four years of fighting, famine, and disease. Some were hopeful that the city's Austro-Hungarian legacy—a strong emphasis on bureaucratic efficiency and institutionalized equality among the city's religious communities—would help make Sarajevo a leading force in Yugoslav life and culture. They also thought the city had an economic advantage. While the economies in other areas, notably Serbia, collapsed during the war, Sarajevo had remained a center of wartime mining and military manufacturing.[26] Many Sarajevans initially joined the Democratic Party (Demokratska stranka), which aimed to develop a centralized administration within the Yugoslav state and fight against federalist and autonomy projects. There also existed a fairly strong chapter of the Communist Party, as well as a host of other smaller parties seeking a voice in the new government.

But optimism for Yugoslavia was short-lived. Instead of developing a pluralist participatory government, state leaders in Belgrade promoted an increasingly centralized, Serbian, and autocratic agenda. Muslim leaders, the traditional centerpiece of Sarajevo's political life, found their pleas for security and equality ignored. Instead, they felt excluded from decision making and on the defensive in the state's agrarian reform, which sought to redistribute property away from wealthy Muslim landowners to poorer Orthodox Serb peasants.[27] In 1924, Belgrade threw another punch at Sarajevo when it eliminated Bosnia's status as a separate administrative unit, formally ending Sarajevo's role as an official center of politics and culture in the western Balkans.

Members of Sarajevo's political elite also felt excluded from state decision making, voicing their grievances early and often through the city council. The Belgrade government repeatedly postponed local elections, limiting the powers of the municipal government. Law by law, Belgrade stripped Sarajevo's leaders of the autonomy they cherished. Across the city, people began to gravitate toward the nationalist parties that they felt

25. On the creation of Yugoslavia at the Paris peace treaties, see Ivo J. Lederer, *Yugoslavia at the Paris Peace Conference: A Study in Frontiermaking* (New Haven: Yale University Press, 1963).

26. John Allcock, *Explaining Yugoslavia* (New York: Columbia University Press, 2000), 55–58.

27. Purivatra, *Jugoslovenska Muslimanska Organizacija*, 26–27.

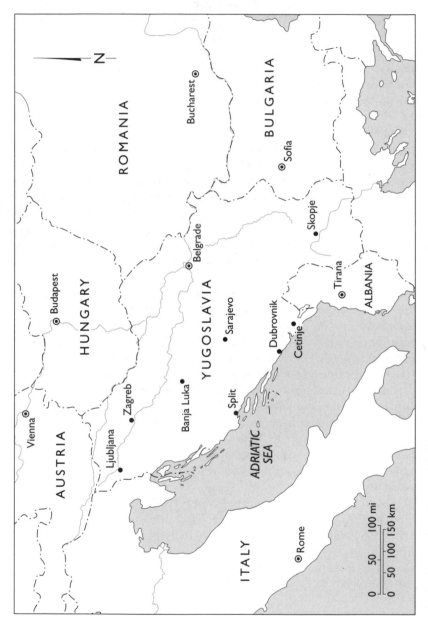

Map 1. Interwar Yugoslavia, 1918–41

supported the particular goals of their ethnic, confessional, or national community. Sarajevo's Catholics joined the Croat People's Party, which was oriented toward Zagreb and sought some form of federalist or autonomous alternative within the Yugoslav structure. Orthodox Serbs supported the Radical Party, which claimed to represent the interests of citizens of Yugoslavia but which became associated with attempts to impose Serb politics on the rest of the country. Muslim politicians formed the Yugoslav Muslim Organization in an effort to gain a larger voice in a political system that excluded their community.[28] These divisions could be seen as early as the 1920 election, foreshadowing a growing disconnect between the political goals of Sarajevo and that of the government in Belgrade.[29]

Class divisions in Sarajevo were also increasingly prevalent in the 1920s and 1930s, particularly as the economy spiraled downhill. But politically, class played less of a role than other categories. In 1921, the Yugoslav government outlawed the Communist Party, thus dismantling the major labor party. As national parties developed, local leaders expected class interests to be resolved within the context of national interests. This proved complicated because many of the parties espoused programs that privileged one class over another.[30] Furthermore, the government was suspicious of efforts to rally the working class, occasionally arresting suspected Communists from labor organizations. Class interest parties thus never formed a serious challenge to confessional and national organizations in interwar Sarajevo.

As Sarajevo found itself on the periphery of the country's politics, it also grew isolated from the Yugoslav economy.[31] The state's disregard for the town does not appear to have been intentional. The Belgrade government was struggling to unify the currency system, integrate institutions and internal markets, and reform disparate regional agrarian policies.[32] By the late 1920s, the economy was in recession. While Belgrade was consumed with the state's major political and economic problems, Sarajevo's textile and crafts industries nearly collapsed, and poverty spread citywide. Increasingly it appeared to many of the local elite that the Yugoslav state was transforming Sarajevo from a Balkan metropolis into a marginalized provincial town beset by economic and social maladies.

28. Some Belgrade officials openly stated their intention to "destroy" dreams of sovereignty in Bosnia. Banac, *National Question in Yugoslavia*, 181. On Sarajevo's relationship with the Belgrade government, see Donia, *Sarajevo*, 141–150.

29. Mustafa Imamović, *Historija država i prava Bosne i Hercegovine* (Sarajevo: Magistrat Sarajevo, 2003), 289–291.

30. For example, Bosnian historian Atif Purivatra underscores that the Yugoslav Muslim Organization claimed to represent all Muslims, but its economic and social goals aided middle-class merchants and landowners at the expense of Muslim peasants. *Jugoslovenska Muslimanska Organizacija*, 444–448.

31. On Yugoslav economic policies in the interwar era, see Jozo Tomasevich, *Peasants, Politics, and Economic Change* (Stanford: Stanford University Press, 1955).

32. Allcock, *Explaining Yugoslavia*, 55–56.

Belgrade's secularizing agenda only made matters worse. Muslim and Catholic religious leaders felt victimized by the Yugoslav government, which preached equality for all religious institutions while in practice deferring on most matters to the Serbian Orthodox Church. The state crippled the Catholic Church and the Islamic Religious Community by progressively revoking their autonomy, subjugating religious laws to secular law, and working to replace religious traditional values with a liberal secular culture. Conservative religious leaders grew isolated from the state and from the progressive, modernizing leaders within their communities, who gave little credence to predictions of civilization's imminent demise.

Complicating these local dynamics were Hitler's ascendance to power in the early 1930s and the outbreak of the European war. After maintaining Yugoslavia's neutrality for two years, on March 25, 1941, the Yugoslav regent, Prince Paul, signed the Tripartite Pact, thus joining Hitler and Mussolini's camp. Two days later, amid public outcry, riots, and protests in Sarajevo and across the country, a military coup overthrew the regent and gave control to the young king, Peter II. The new king immediately abrogated the pact and declared Yugoslavia's neutrality. Overnight, protests against Nazi Germany transformed into state-sponsored celebrations for Yugoslavia. Religious leaders held services in the king's honor; political officials swore public oaths and plastered the town with Yugoslav flags. This enthusiasm was cut short, however, as German troops began to mobilize on Yugoslavia's borders in early April 1941, and every community braced for war.

Community and Communities

When war broke out in Yugoslavia in 1941, Sarajevo had about eighty thousand citizens, a mix that was divided by religious group as 34 percent Muslim, 29 percent Catholic, 25 percent Orthodox Serb, and 10 percent Jewish.[33] In addition, there were smaller populations of Roma, Volksdeutsche, Italians, Czechs, Russians, and other immigrants who had made their way to the city during the Habsburg and interwar eras. Like their European counterparts, the citizens of Sarajevo had assumed multiple identities over the preceding half century as the city changed from an urban crossroads on the Ottoman frontier to the capital of an Austro-Hungarian province, and then again to a seemingly insignificant city in the interwar Yugoslav state. National, political, religious, civic, and local allegiances at times reflected political positions and represented cultural frameworks through which Sarajevans viewed the world around them.

33. I derive these figures by looking at the city's demographic changes from the last official Yugoslav census in 1931 and an estimate by the municipal government in June 1941 that placed the city's population at eighty-seven thousand. See *Popis Stanovnišva, 31. Marta 1931* (Belgrade: Opšta Državna Statistika, 1931), and *Sarajevski Novi List,* June 28, 1941, 4.

Scholars of European history now take for granted that identities are constructed and fluid, that individuals can have many identities simultaneously, and that they highlight the ones that are most salient in particular historical contexts.[34] Moreover, "ethnicity, race, and nationhood," as Rogers Brubaker asserts, "are fundamentally ways of perceiving, interpreting, and representing the social world. They are not things *in* the world, but perspectives *on* the world."[35] The fluidity of identity becomes especially critical in wartime, when the stakes are raised on the local and national levels.[36] Building from these ideas, it would make sense that the definition of "community"—a concept rooted in the dynamic relationships among individuals—is also fluid and contested and that the experience of civil war, genocide, and occupation shifts this definition. In sociology, the concept of community has been recognized as slippery and elusive, which has led sociologists to propose competing, incompatible definitions.[37] Yet defining the community is exactly what local leaders attempt to do in cases of civil war and ethnic cleansing. My intention in probing the nature of community throughout this work is not to assign a definition to the term but rather to illuminate the local debates through which it was negotiated.

A close look at everyday life reveals that despite the modernizing, secularizing trends of early-twentieth-century history, in Sarajevo, religious—or more precisely, confessional—identity remained relatively static: it was acquired at birth and could be changed only through complex conversion processes not commonly undertaken. Official religious organizations maintained birth, death, and (in many cases) property records. Moreover, each confessional community—Muslim, Jewish, Catholic, and Orthodox Serb—had its own rituals and organizations that connected members and strengthened bonds of trust. These were not uniform or homogenous units: each confessional community faced internal conflicts on a range of topics, from theoretical and theological disagreements over the relationship of faith, nation, and politics to policy disputes over mixed gender activities and mixed marriage. Many subgroups of these communities in fact had

34. See, for example, Rogers Brubaker, Margit Feischmidt, Jon Fox, and Liana Grancea, *Nationalist Politics and Everyday Ethnicity in a Transylvanian Town* (Princeton: Princeton University Press, 2006); Jeremy King, *Budweisers into Czechs and Germans: A Local History of Bohemian Politics, 1848–1948* (Princeton: Princeton University Press, 2002).

35. Rogers Brubaker, *Ethnicity without Groups* (Cambridge, Mass.: Harvard University Press, 2004), 17.

36. Among the recent studies that address this issue are Chad Bryant, *Prague in Black: Nazi Rule and Czech Nationalism* (Cambridge, Mass.: Harvard University Press, 2007), and Tara Zahra, *Kidnapped Souls: National Indifference and the Battle for Children in Bohemia, 1900–1948* (Ithaca: Cornell University Press, 2008).

37. Two helpful reviews on the sociological debates surrounding the nature of community—from Marx, Weber, and Durkheim to Tilly, Gellner, and Anderson—are Amitai Etzioni, "Creating Good Communities and Good Societies," *Contemporary Sociology* 29, no. 1 (January 2000): 188–195, and Steven Brint, "Gemeinschaft Revisited: A Critique and Reconstruction of the Community Concept," *Sociological Theory* 19, no. 1 (March 2001): 1–23.

overtly secular agendas, and thus are commonly described as "ethnoconfessional" or "ethnoreligious."

The structure of Sarajevo's civil society encouraged consolidation along confessional lines. Citizens may have mixed in the bazaars, the bureaucracy, and the city's public life, but—as late as 1941—they preferred to socialize with their own. Multiculturalism in this context should not be confused with contemporary Western liberal ideas of diversity, integration, and secularism but should instead be understood as a model of tolerance and coexistence that reflected customary civic codes passed down from earlier generations. Every confessional community had its own cultural and social clubs, choirs, soccer teams, and humanitarian organizations. In the South Slavic languages, such an organization is called a *društvo*, a word that encompasses many different English concepts, including society, community, company, crowd, club, organization, and union. Perhaps it is most similar to the German term *Gesellschaft*, a word that can be used to describe both a specific club and civil society generally.[38] These associations or societies were common throughout the region and became an important means of cultivating separate ethnoconfessional worlds.[39]

From 1918 to 1941, more than thirty societies existed in Sarajevo with memberships that ranged from the teens to the thousands. While they had distinct humanitarian, social, cultural, or political objectives, they often defined their missions (in whole or in part) according to the norms of one confessional community. More than any of the city's political or religious institutions, it was the *društvo* that represented Sarajevans. In different ways, each one catered to local needs and concerns. A few even had affiliated financial institutions—credit unions, in effect—that allowed members to bypass state banks and deal exclusively with their own community leaders. Leaders of the largest societies had power and prestige. When a local problem arose, they sought to resolve it on their own terms. National politicians recognized that alliances with city leaders could be key to expanding their bases of support in the city. The societies also taught Sarajevans what was expected of them as members of the city. By organizing holiday activities, fund-raising drives, and social activities; publishing almanacs and articles; and financing schools, public lectures, and libraries, the societies perpetuated and strengthened the distinct local culture within each community and contributed to a sense of connectedness among them.

National and cultural societies were among the largest and wealthiest organizations in Sarajevo. Many had been founded in the late Habsburg

---

38. Ferdinand Tönnes, *Community and Civil Society*, translated by Jose Harris and Margaret Hollis (Cambridge: Cambridge University Press, 2001), xli.

39. On the social impact of societies in eastern Europe, as well as comparative examples from other cases in the region, see Brubaker et al., *Nationalist Politics and Everyday Ethnicity*, 287–290.

era as a way of developing political consciousness among Bosnians and helping to improve literacy. They set up schools, published books, and developed centers of education, promoting secular, modernizing agendas. Nevertheless, they generally remained limited to a single confessional group. Narodna Uzdanica and Gajret were Muslim societies with Croatian and Serbian agendas, respectively. The Croat cultural society Napredak was predominantly Catholic and the Serb cultural society Prosvjeta predominantly Orthodox. Sephardic Jews congregated around La Benevolencija. Sarajevo's community of Volksdeutsche, a group of around three thousand people of German and Austrian origins, had their own cultural organization called Kulturbund; Slovenes had a society too.[40]

The city also boasted nearly a dozen humanitarian societies, almost all of which had a religious charity slant, such as Merhamet, the largest Muslim humanitarian group, and the Croat Catholic Women's Society (Društvo hrvatskih katoličkih žena u Sarajevu).[41] In the interwar era, the expansion of private, confessionally based societies both raised the moral capital of religious leaders and encouraged the laity to play active roles in safeguarding and reviving confessional culture and social norms.[42]

Uniting these communities was a larger civic identity that had also cemented over several generations: that of the *Sarajlije*—or Sarajevans. Unlike residents of some of interwar Europe's other multicultural cities, where such identities survived mainly in the hearts and souls of minority groups left out of nationalizing programs, in Sarajevo members of every confessional background still felt a personal, almost familial connection to their hometown.[43] For some, this connection was primarily an emotional attachment, whereas for others it was linked to nostalgia for a lost era, a

40. On the development of the *društvo* in the Habsburg era, see Hadžibegović, *Bosanskohercegovački gradovi*, 85–89. For specific analyses of the different societies working in Sarajevo, see Ibrahim Kemura, *Značaj i uloga "Narodne Uzdanice" u društveniom životu Bošnjaka* (Sarajevo: Bošnjački Institut i Institut za Istoriju, 2002); Ibrahim Kemura, *Uloga "Gajreta" u društvenom životu Muslimana Bosne i Hercegovine (1903–1941)* (Sarajevo: Veselin Masleša, 1986); Ismail Hadžiahmetović, *Narodna Uzdanica u kulturnome i društvenome životu Muslimana Bosne i Hercegovine* (Tuzla: Historijski Arhiv, 1998); Tomislav Išek, *Mjesto i uloga HKD Napredak u kulturnom životu Hrvata Bosne i Hercegovine* (Sarajevo: Institut za Istoriju, 2004); Tomislav Išek, "Djelatnost Kulturbunda i Folksdojčera," in *Sarajevo u Revoluciji* ed. Nisim Albahari et al., 4 vols. (Sarajevo: Istorijski Arhiv, 1976–81), 2:284–285; and Avram Pinto, "Jevrejska Društva u Sarajevu," in Kamhi, *Spomenica*, 173–188.

41. Uzeir Bavčić. *"Merhamet" (1913–2003)* (Sarajevo: Muslimansko Dobrotvorno Društvo, "Merhamet," 2003).

42. This process was not dissimilar to what occurred among other oppressed religious groups in Europe. For example, Margaret Lavinia Anderson has argued that the Kulturkampf in Bismarck's Germany "raised the moral authority and the popularity of the clergy to unprecedented heights—just as it delivered the initiative in preserving the church to the laity." "Historiographical Review: The Limits of Secularization: On the Problem of the Catholic Revival in Nineteenth-century Germany," *Historical Journal* 38, no. 3 (1995): 666.

43. In Pressburg/Bratislava, for instance, Jews retained this identity when other communities did not. See Peter Bugge, "The Making of a Slovak City: The Czechoslovak Renaming of Pressburg/Pozsony/Prešporok, 1918–1919," *Austrian History Yearbook* 35 (2004): 226.

feeling commonly elicited by war.[44] For many intellectuals, the connection
to Sarajevo encompassed and reflected the qualities and values associated
with cities generally—cosmopolitanism, sophistication, urbanity, civility,
and modernity.[45]

After decades of immigration to the city from the Bosnian countryside
and central Europe, Sarajevans had come to think of their world through
the prism of their hometown; indeed, the town had distinct ethical, cultural,
and political norms that translated into everyday experience and impacted
human behavior. Whereas such affection for a particular civic place was
common to communities in eastern Europe, in Sarajevo it existed both in
the web of unofficial cultural values experienced in the everyday and at the
level of the official.[46] Unlike national groups, the Sarajevo community was
not an "imagined" one.[47] Being a Sarajevan required action. On a practical level, it often meant submitting an application for *zavičajnost,* a term
that technically means belonging to a certain area but more loosely can be
understood as having citizenship of a place. As opposed to national citizenship, *zavičajnost* was determined by the local city council.[48] Being a Sarajevan also involved abiding by certain ethical codes of the city, "common
life" (*zajednički život*) and "neighborliness" (from *komšiluk,* meaning neighborhood). These terms captured the city's structure as a mosaic of separate
confessional communities united by shared historical experiences, social
customs, and interactions in the pluralist public sphere.[49] Each generation
taught the next a set of learned behaviors, customs, and rituals and passed
down pluralist institutions that had developed in order to accommodate
this local culture.[50]

44. On nostalgia during wartime, see the introduction to Svetlana Boym, *The Future of Nostalgia* (New York: Basic Books, 2001).
45. In this case, the term can be understood as similar to civic nationalism, as explained by Hans Kohn, *The Ideal of Nationalism: A Study in Its Origins and Background* (New York: Collier Books, 1944), and Rogers Brubaker, *Ethnicity without Groups,* 132–146.
46. A good illustration of this contrast between shared cultural values on the individual level and those on the official level is Shimon Redlich, *Together and Apart in Brzezany: Poles, Jews and Ukrainians, 1919–1945* (Bloomington: Indiana University Press, 2002).
47. On imagined communities, see Benedict Anderson, *Imagined Communities: Reflections on the Origin and Spread of Nationalism* (New York: Verso, 1991).
48. See IAS, Gradsko Poglavarstvo, Zapisnik Prezidijalne sjednice gradskog poglavarstva u Sarajevu (February 1, 1940, and November 19, 1940).
49. Donia, *Sarajevo,* 4.
50. Sarajevo was exceptional among the big multicultural post-Ottoman, Mediterranean, and east European cities in that it maintained this strong sense of civic consciousness through the Second World War. As Mark Mazower has shown, Salonica, a city often cited for its similar heterogeneous demographic, had been transformed by 1930 into a nationalized Greek town where only a fraction of the population even remembered life in the Ottoman Empire. See *Salonica, City of Ghosts: Christians, Muslims and Jews, 1430–1950* (New York: Knopf, 2005), 310. In Smyrna (Izmir), Ataturk's army wiped out multiculturalism with the invasion in 1922. See, for instance, Giles Milton, *Paradise Lost: Smyrna, 1922* (New York: Basic Books, 2007). In a less brutal yet no less effective fashion, throughout the interwar era Sofia's identity became anchored to the Bulgarian national project and Bratislava's to Slovak nationalism. On Sofia,

In 1956, a Yugoslav ethnographer, Cvetko Kostić, described the complex relationship between the individual and the city in the Balkans, which he argued had contributed to the development of distinct local mentalities that reflected social customs, economic developments, and the physical domain of the city.[51] Central to a Balkan town's consciousness, Kostić argued, was its *čaršija*, a word that means at once square, marketplace, bazaar, and two sociological ideas: a social group with particular customs and also a distinct mentality.[52] The character of the towns varied across the region, from towns like Novi Pazar that had retained heavy Turkish influences to towns in Herzegovina, which had strong economic and cultural ties to Dalmatia. In Sarajevo, the čaršija served as a physical and symbolic center of the urban collective: it was both a site of economic interaction and socializing and an idea, a term used to refer to the civic community. It was also a site of religious institutions and organizations, highlighting the importance of the town's confessional tradition.[53] Consequently, a wealthy merchant in Sarajevo did not necessarily belong to the same milieu, community, or social group as a wealthy merchant in Novi Pazar, Priština, Mostar, or Dubrovnik. Indeed, the cultural variations of civic identity make it difficult to speak of a collective notion of "urbanity" in this part of the world; rather, they underscore individuals' loyalty to a specific place.

While "civic consciousness" is arguably an elusive concept, the way that Sarajevans responded to the war reveals that, in practice, having a local solidarity and an agreement to abide by certain collective values directly affected wartime policies. For example, in contrast to the experience of many other parts of Hitler's Europe, Sarajevo's religious and political officials teamed together to help more than a thousand Jews convert to Islam and Catholicism. The city's intellectual fathers certified Muslim Roma (gypsies) legally Aryan, a direct challenge to the Ustasha regime's racial policies that placed race ahead of religion. And far from being slaughtered en masse like Serbs in parts of the NDH, many of Sarajevo's Serbs survived the war and even remained involved in the city's public life. Indeed, in 1943,

---

see Irina Gigova, "Writers of the Nation: Intellectual Identity in Bulgaria, 1939–1953" (PhD diss., University of Illinois, 2005); on Bratislava, see Bugge, "The Making of a Slovak City." And Timothy Snyder has shown how in Riga, Vilnius, Lwów, and other cities in eastern Europe, nationalism triumphed over "traditional patriotism" and "local loyalties" as the region became entangled in war. See *The Reconstruction of Nations: Poland, Ukraine, Lithuania, Belarus, 1569–1999* (New Haven: Yale University Press, 2003), 181, 207.

51. Cvetko Kostić, "Postanak i razvitak 'čaršije' (primer čaršije Bajine Bašte)," *Glasnik etnografskog institute SAN-a* 4–6 (1955–57): 139.

52. Ibid., 123.

53. Hadžibegović, *Bosanskohercegovački gradovi*, 12–13. During the socialist era, *čaršija* became a code word for "pettybourgeoisie" among many socialist scholars. This seems to be a deliberate distortion of the term's previous meaning in order to speak to the ideological language of the time. Thus the phrase *čaršijska posla* would later be interpreted as "petty bourgeois business." In the wartime period, however, it did not have this negative connotation. The čaršija was considered a positive attribute of the town.

Orthodox Serbs held a majority of seats in Sarajevo's city council, including the position of deputy mayor. All these examples reveal the persistence of the town's religious and civic frameworks, yet, as I explain throughout the book, they also contributed to a tension between the two. The balance of power between the religious community and the civic collective shifted back and forth as the local elite reacted to legislation or the possibility of another regime change. What is key, however, is that national, political, and racial categories never pulled real weight on this pendulum.

It is important that the Sarajevo community not be understood in normative terms. Exclusion is inherent in any definition of community, which requires a "them" in order to define "us." Deciding *who* to exclude or for what reasons fell to local leaders, and at various points in the war it became a process that united people across confessional lines. While such "othering" is commonly enacted in terms of national, religious, gender, or class categories, the Sarajevo elite had their own ways of determining who belonged to the civic community. In order to strengthen the local urban collective and protect it from outside influences, they emphasized that Sarajevans shared a common moral culture, one that peasants, refugees, and foreign political rulers threatened in different ways. Naturally there existed disagreement over who, precisely, a Sarajevan was, a disagreement that contributed to different policy decisions during the war. Rarely if ever, though, was there disagreement on the need to create some kinds of boundaries around the civic community.

By emphasizing confessional and civic bonds throughout this work, I am not suggesting that nationalism played no part in Sarajevo politics. On the contrary, many nationalist societies and political parties formed during the Habsburg era and remained salient during the interwar years; among the aforementioned cultural societies the most powerful were motivated in part by nationalist ideologies. Nationalism was politics de jure, and it was impossible for city leaders to avoid nationalist inclinations or agendas. They were part and parcel of every political, economic, and cultural discussion in the country. It was possible, however, to be both a fervent nationalist and a fervent supporter of Sarajevo: many Sarajevo Croats believed that in building a Croat nation-state they could restore Sarajevo to the cultural and political position it deserved.

The three main national movements in interwar Bosnia were the Serb, Croat, and Yugoslav projects.[54] Serb and Croat nationalism had developed in the nineteenth century during the height of romantic nationalism that spread throughout Europe. As ideologies, these movements tied together aspects of religion, territory, linguistic unity, and historical myths in order to control people and territory in the Balkans. Although divisions existed

54. Ivo Banac discusses these political and national programs in his seminal work on Yugoslavia's foundation, *The National Question in Yugoslavia, Origins, History, Politics.*

within the movements, both Serb and Croat nationalists claimed Bosnia-Herzegovina as part of their historic land and campaigned to nationalize Bosnians in the nineteenth and twentieth centuries. Moreover, both camps considered Muslims who had converted to Islam during the Ottoman era to be members of their national group. Thus, national identification in Sarajevo was not always tied to ethnicity in the ways that it would be at the end of the twentieth century. Members of every Sarajevo religious community periodically felt connected to or disconnected from those larger national projects.[55] As late as 1941, some Muslims and Jews considered themselves Croats and Serbs. Catholics and Orthodox Serbs did not always identify as Croats and Serbs, respectively, but could cross national lines. Associating with a "nation" was a way of orienting oneself toward a particular political-cultural project but not necessarily a way of understanding one's background and allegiance.

Consequently, ascribing identities to individuals during the war is a complex process. While many Sarajevans were not necessarily pious, I prefer using confessional terms—those assigned through birth or conversion—when it is necessary to categorize individuals, despite the obvious irony of assigning a religious identity to people who may have had little religious conviction. The label "Croat" or "Serb" refers to an individual who expressly identified or is expressly identified in the documents with that national program. Thus "Orthodox Serb" refers to a member of the confessional community, whereas "Serb" denotes an individual who identified with the Serb nation. When possible, I combine terms in order to give a clearer picture of an individual's identity, as in "Catholic Croat" or "Muslim Serb." This is more complicated in the case of Sarajevo's Jews and Muslims, for whom there were not yet separate terms to indicate the split between religious and cultural identities.[56] This system occasionally gives rise to superficially self-contradictory terminology. For example, when discussing conversion during the Holocaust, I refer to some individuals as "Muslim Jews," by which I mean individuals who by religion were Muslim but fell into the state's racial categorization as Jews.

Deciding upon simple descriptive adjectives to define groups is difficult, particularly in studies like this one that aim to deconstruct categories.

55. For an overview of how these national movements developed in Bosnia, see the first chapters of Hoare, *History of Bosnia*.

56. The development of Bosnian Muslim national identity and the complex process of integrating religious and secular understandings of Muslim identity are discussed at length in the introduction to Tone Bringa, *Being Muslim the Bosnian Way* (Princeton: Princeton University Press, 1995), and throughout Francine Friedman, *The Bosnian Muslims: Denial of a Nation*) (Boulder: Westview, 1996). During the late socialist period, Muslims differentiated between *Muslimani* (capital M), a national distinction, and *muslimani* (lowercase m), which signified the religious community. At the Second Bosniak Congress, convened in Sarajevo on May 28, 1993, Bosnian Muslims assumed the term "Bosniak" to differentiate their national identity from their religious one.

The oft-used yet imprecise terms "traditionalists" and "modernizers" are fraught with ambiguity and orientalist assumptions of "backwardness." Thus I prefer the terms "progressive" and "modernizing" to refer to groups that promoted aspects of secular, European ideas of state and society, and I use "conservative," "observant," and "reactionary" to define groups that aimed to employ the principles and ethics of their faith in political life. Like any system of categorization, this one is imperfect. Some conservative religious groups adopted modernizing and even Fascistic practices; some secular groups participated in confessional politics and promoted customary practices. Despite myriad gray areas, the two overarching categories provide useful signposts of how people framed their goals.

The Nation in Peripheral Vision

My approach to questions of identity and community differs from that in many studies of twentieth-century European history, which use the nation and nation-state as the primary paradigms to analyze groups of people and states. At the Paris peace treaties after the First World War, Wilsonian self-determination—the belief that every nation, or people, should govern itself—guided European leaders as they drew state boundaries on maps where European empires had long stood. The nation-state system thus became the definitive way of determining European borders, and it remains so today.

But before the ink had had time to dry on Europe's new maps, the nation-state system was confronted with problems. Europe was a relatively small space where nations overlapped and intermingled, especially in the former Prussian, Habsburg, Russian, and Ottoman lands. The newly created nation-states were hardly homogenous. Moreover, the Great Powers drew borders with an agenda, punishing the losers by awarding contested territories to their neighbors. This created a backlash in countries like Germany and Hungary, where new leaders rose to power with calls to reunite the severed nation. On the other side of those borders, national minorities trapped in "foreign" nation-states—such as Hungarians in Romania and Germans in Poland—along with those national groups denied their own states, like Croats and Slovaks, made claims for autonomy and secession.

Asked to choose loyalties along these externally drawn lines, some people in multiethnic regions found that they did not fit easily into the prescribed national groups; others who spoke multiple languages and enjoyed good relations with neighboring nations found it convenient (and at times necessary) to shift their allegiances and identities depending upon political circumstance; still others tried to carve out space for themselves in the new nation-states in which they lived while retaining elements of their own cultural and linguistic identities.[57] Throughout the interwar era, state leaders confronted hostile minority groups, irredentist neighbors, and ambiguously defined communities, as well as the economic and social crisis of the European Depression, by clinging to the legitimacy of their own national claims. The stakes were high, as many came to believe that the very survival of their nation was at risk.[58]

The advent of Fascism and Nazism radicalized national politics in the 1930s. Different groups hoped to manipulate the political uncertainty to further their own goals, revise state borders, and adapt goals of the Nazi "New Order" to fit their visions of an ideal society. Nazi Germany used its hegemonic position in economic and political affairs to exert influence across central and southeastern Europe, winning support from groups that shared Hitler's ambition to redraw Europe's map and stamp out liberalism, communism, and secularism.[59] The result was the emergence of deadly conceptions of race-based nationhood that encouraged mass violence and wrought a massive social revolution across the continent. Even those multicultural towns that managed to retain their character through the nationalizing interwar era could not withstand these pressures of war and ethnic cleansing.[60]

Nationalism has become so identified with modern Europe, particularly with the era of World War II, that scholars have only recently begun to question whether the breadth of its appeal and uniform application might have been exaggerated for provincial areas and parts of Europe's periphery.[61] This is especially the case for the Balkans, where the emergence of

57. These themes have recently received considerable attention from scholars of central and east European history. See, for example, Bryant, *Prague in Black: Nazi Rule and Czech Nationalism;* Theodora Dragostinova, "Speaking National: Nationalizing the Greeks of Bulgaria, 1900–1939," *Slavic Review* 67, no. 1 (Spring 2008): 154–181; John Fine, *When Ethnicity Did Not Matter in the Balkans: A Study of Identity in Pre-nationalist Croatia, Dalmatia, and Slavonia in the Medieval and Early Modern Periods* (Ann Arbor: University of Michigan Press, 2006); Pieter Judson, *The Guardians of the Nation: Activists on the Language Frontiers of Imperial Austria* (Cambridge, Mass.: Harvard University Press, 2006); and King, *Budweisers into Czechs and Germans.*

58. Rogers Brubaker introduces this triadic nexus among national minorities, nationalizing states, and external national homelands, which defined central and eastern Europe in the interwar era. *Nationalism Reframed: Nationhood and the National Question in the New Europe* (Cambridge: Cambridge University Press, 1996), 5–6.

59. On the spectrum of nationalisms that gradually converged under the umbrella of the radical Right over the course of the nineteenth and twentieth centuries, see Paul Hanebrink, *In Defense of Christian Hungary: Religion, Nationalism, and Antisemitism, 1890–1944* (Ithaca: Cornell University Press, 2006); Brian Porter, *When Nationalism Began to Hate* (New York: Oxford University Press, 2000); and the essays in Ivo Banac and Katherine Verdery, eds., *National Character and National Ideology in Interwar Eastern Europe* (New Haven: Yale Center for International and Area Studies, 1995).

60. See Snyder, *The Reconstruction of Nations.*

61. On the ways that historians traditionally accepted ethnicity as a given, see Jeremy King, "The Nationalization of East Central Europe: Ethnicism, Ethnicity, and Beyond," in *Staging the Past: The Politics of Commemoration in Habsburg Central Europe, 1848 to the Present,* ed. Maria Bucur and Nancy M. Wingfield (West Lafayette, Ind.: Purdue University Press, 2001), 112–152.

ultranationalist movements in the wartime and postwar eras colored histories of the region. But the dynamics in wartime Sarajevo, like those in other parts of central Europe, suggest that history and collective memory have imposed "nationness" on communities where it simply did not exist or existed in competition with other ideological projects.[62] While individuals and institutions frequently invoked national claims in asserting political demands, territorial ambitions, and cultural dominance, such identities often did not resonate beyond elite circles.

Although we have come to expect a vibrant national culture to proliferate in cities at war, in Sarajevo the opposite took place: the idea of the nation proved less useful in fostering local bonds as the war dragged on.[63] Furthermore, in those circles where nationalism did resonate, the national ideology was often different from the one espoused by the leaders of the nationalist movements outside the city. Indeed, being Croat, Serb, or Yugoslav meant something different in Sarajevo than it did in Belgrade or Zagreb. National identities took on a local character that stemmed partly from Sarajevo's heterogeneous demographic makeup and partly from the town's distance from the major political and military decision-making centers.[64]

Traditional theories of nationalism posit that the concept of the nation solidifies first in cities and only gradually spreads to the periphery through a centralized print culture, political rhetoric, public institutions, military service, and community celebrations.[65] The Volksdeutsche (ethnic Germans) living in Czechoslovakia, Yugoslavia, and Poland took cues from Hitler's Berlin (or used the Third Reich as leverage in their countries). The Hungarian speakers in Transylvania had ties with Budapest. Greeks in Bulgaria sought connections with Athens. But nationalism is not just a top-down process; it also develops on the ground, incorporating local customs, values, and goals into a cultural project that is subsequently

---

62. For recent works on the concept and interpretation of national indifference, see Zahra, *Kidnapped Souls*, and James Bjork, *Neither German nor Pole: Catholicism and National Indifference in a Central European Borderland* (Ann Arbor: University of Michigan Press, 2008).

63. Jay Winter and Jean-Louis Robert suggest in their work on World War I that wars have a propensity to "nationalize" cities, in part by linking urban and rural communities in the defense of a single nation-state. See Winter and Robert, conclusion to *Capital Cities at War: Paris, London, Berlin (1914–1919)* (Cambridge: Cambridge University Press, 2007), 2:469.

64. This is not unique to Bosnia. On diverse approaches to German nationhood, for example, see the essays in David Blackbourn and James Retallack, eds., *Localism, Landscape, and the Ambiguities of Place: German-Speaking Central Europe, 1860–1930* (Toronto: University of Toronto Press, 2007).

65. Within the enormous literature on nations and nationalism, some of the studies that have influenced this work include Anderson, *Imagined Communities;* John Breuilly, *Nationalism and the State* (New York: St. Martin's, 1982); Ernest Gellner, *Nations and Nationalism* (Ithaca: Cornell University Press, 1983); Eric Hobsbawm and Terence Ranger, eds., *The Invention of Tradition* (New York: Cambridge University Press, 1992); Anthony D. Smith, *The Ethnic Origins of Nations* (New York: B. Blackwell, 1987); and Eugen Weber, *Peasants into Frenchmen: The Modernization of Rural France, 1870–1914* (Stanford: Stanford University Press, 1976).

transmitted to the center. Ordinary people can have a great impact on their national identity.[66] Thus widespread competition existed *within* purported national groups over how to define the nation and in turn how to frame a nation-state—or even a different kind of state. The entire Nazi empire was riven with such rivalries. In analyzing local dynamics of this struggle in Sarajevo, I explore how the friction between concepts of nation and community shaped wartime experiences as well as national and international policies.

The overemphasis on nationalism and national categories in the study of Balkan and European history has inhibited nuanced analyses of the other kinds of identities that persisted in the region and shaped twentieth-century experiences. Discussions of religious identity, for instance, are usually combined with discussions of nationalism. This has created a misplaced sense that confessional identity was somehow static, as well as an overdetermined link between religion and national identity.[67] European states often conflated the ethnic and the religious in campaigns of nationalization and state centralization: imperial Russia's Russification campaign and Bismarck's Kulturkampf are two of the best known examples. A difference in studies of the post-Ottoman world is that these links are often understood as extensions of Ottoman social relations, particularly the millet system, wherein different ethnoreligious communities had varying degrees of autonomy. Scholarship on the Ottoman Empire, however, has shown that the concept of the millet was actually a *product* of the Ottoman reform movement in the nineteenth century, not the driving force behind it.[68] While relevant to the formation of national identity, there was nothing predestined about certain Balkan religious groups metamorphosing into separate nations. For instance, it would have been impossible for the linguistically and culturally diverse Rum millet (Orthodox Christians) to have yielded a single nation in the modern era. Various Balkan national projects gained momentum at different points in the first half of the twentieth century, representing a broad spectrum of possibilities for defining national communities in the twentieth century.

Just as nationalists used religion to solidify claims to the nation, so religious leaders in the modern era used nationalism to promote religious identity. This is most evident in the case of the Roman Catholic archdiocese

---

66. Michael Herzfeld, *Cultural Intimacy: Social Poetics in the Nation-State*, 2nd ed. (New York: Routledge), 6.

67. On the ways that religion and nation became linked in Bosnian nationalisms, see Mitja Velikonja, *Religious Separation and Political Intolerance in Bosnia-Herzegovina* (Austin: University of Texas Press, 2003). On the region more generally, see the essays in *Religious Quest and National Identity in the Balkans*, ed. Celia Hawkesworth, Muriel Heppell, and Harry Norris (London: Palgrave, 2001).

68. See Benjamin Braude, "Foundation Myths of the *Millet* System," in *Christians and Jews in the Ottoman Empire: The Functioning of a Plural Society*, ed. Benjamin Braude and Bernard Lewis (New York: Holmes and Meyer, 1982).

in Sarajevo, the Vrhbosna archdiocese, which promoted a radical, exclusive Croat nationalism as a means of resurrecting a Catholic-based society. It can also be seen among some Bosnian Muslims who appropriated national identities to advance Islamic agendas. By contrast, there were Muslims and Catholics who viewed confessional bonds as the essential glue of their society but believed that such bonds had the greatest impact when they remained independent of politics and ideology. Analyzing social and humanitarian group activities alongside political, religious, and cultural institutions thus adds another vital piece to this Balkan puzzle.

By disaggregating religion from national identity, I underscore the persistence of faith as a code of ethics and the confessional community as a framework for decision making and political alliances. To borrow from Christopher Clark and Wolfram Kaiser, debates over the relationship between modernity, politics, faith, and national identity represented not "a stand-off between the forces of tradition and those of transformation" but rather a dynamic discussion on the moral and political responsibility of religious leaders, the duties of civic leaders to incorporate or respect religious traditions, and the ways that religious leaders would use their moral capital to shape the political agenda.[69] While segments of the Muslim and Catholic population drew upon some combination of early modern religious and historical customs as the basis for their agenda, many of them were nevertheless progressive in their approaches. They used contemporary political tools to achieve their goals, forging strategic political alliances and relying heavily on media and propaganda to disseminate messages. Local religious leaders had their own visions of what the Nazi "New Order" would mean in their societies. Advocates of tradition wanted a voice in defining the forces of transformation.

Religion is hardly the only facet of identity that has been lost in the mire of national mythologies that pervade Balkan historiography. A host of secular and civic identities also shaped everyday experience, from one's membership in a particular trade or cultural society to an individual's place of birth. Taking Pierre Bourdieu's discussion of "social capital" as a starting point for understanding wartime local politics, I suggest that the wider one's personal network, the more fluidity the individual had to navigate day-to-day crises, make strategic alliances, and avoid the repercussions of bad decisions. By associating with a confessional community and participating in the civic community, Sarajevans expanded their networks of survival. The catch was that what it meant to belong to the local milieu often stood in direct contrast to the community that national and international actors hoped to establish in Sarajevo during the war.

---

69. Christopher Clark and Wolfram Kaiser, eds., *Culture Wars: Secular-Catholic Conflict in Nineteenth-Century Europe* (Cambridge: Cambridge University Press, 2003), 9.

Mapping the New Order in Europe

Friction between center and periphery was apparent in every dimension of wartime politics. In propaganda and practice, the new order promised to revolutionize society and redraw Europe's borders. But the form of the revolution and the face of Europe's future map were poorly defined, creating immense competition between states, as well as within communities, as political leaders jockeyed for power and territory.[70] Sarajevo's leaders recognized early in the war that the borders of the central Balkans were in flux, and they wanted a seat at the table to determine their political destiny. Some dreamed of autonomy for Bosnia with a political capital in Sarajevo; most recognized that Sarajevo's economy was not self-sufficient, let alone capable of sustaining a broader, Bosnian economy without strong networks to neighboring regions and foreign backing. Moreover, while Sarajevo had a strong political tradition of representative government, which had served the interests of the city since the 1860s, this model was not adaptable to rural Bosnia.

Thus when Yugoslavia capitulated to the Germans in April 1941, many of Sarajevo's Muslim and Catholic leaders hoped to negotiate a relationship with the Nazi and Ustasha authorities that would allow them to control local affairs and define the new polity while relinquishing power in larger foreign policy and ideological matters. But in attempting to integrate their notions of community and culture into the new militarist, racist, and secular frameworks advocated by their German and Ustasha rulers, they discovered that local and national expectations of the new order were hopelessly incompatible. By examining competing local goals—goals that the Germans played off one another in their efforts to divide and rule—we may use Sarajevo's story to reassess assumptions about wartime alliances, particularly the collaboration of Balkan Muslims with the Nazis, the partnership of Muslims and Catholics in the NDH, and the relationship between the Communists and Bosnia's communities.

Here Sarajevo's status as a "peripheral" city is critical. By peripheral, I mean that it was not the political, economic, or cultural capital of any state or political entity, though it was situated in central Bosnia. Throughout Europe, merchant towns and provincial centers customarily fostered particular social relations, political cultures, and social norms that shaped their responses to externally imposed agendas. Analysis of the periphery during moments of crisis and transformation illuminate the reciprocity and negotiation that occur between local and national events. In Sarajevo, this dynamic shaped a range of issues, from the implementation of a genocidal

---

70. This draws from the arguments in Mark Mazower, *Hitler's Empire: How the Nazis Ruled Europe* (New York: Penguin, 2008), and Holly Case, *Between States: The Transylvanian Question and the European Idea during WWII* (Stanford: Stanford University Press, 2009).

agenda to the cultural program of the nation-state.[71] Moreover, analyzing local responses on the periphery sheds light on individual motives for supporting or resisting national and international movements. In focusing on the same groups of people in one space, this book reveals how seemingly contradictory behaviors can be based on the same set of goals. In Sarajevo's case, the quest for political autonomy, economic and social stability, and deference to religious tradition led invariably to alliances with the Right and Left, and to the attack on and defense of the same groups at different points in the war.

In crafting the narrative of Sarajevo's wartime experience, I integrate political, religious, social, and cultural standpoints: perspectives *within* the city as well as those *on* the city. Drawing from seven archives in three countries, my research includes diverse materials ranging from letters of Sarajevo's highest Muslim and Catholic authorities, the German consul, and ordinary townsmen to reports amassed by the municipal and national governments, state courts, the Ustasha secret police, the resistance armies, the German consulate, the National Theater, and so on. Weaving together these stories, this book uncovers the motivations behind local decision making and the step-by-step changes in perceptions of community and identity that occurred as Sarajevo experienced war, occupation, genocide, and social revolution. In so doing, it shows how the city's culture endured these crises and how it was irrevocably changed by them.

Broadly speaking, the first four chapters concern how concepts of identity, community, and belonging clashed and changed during Sarajevo's political transition from interwar Yugoslavia to Hitler's Europe. Focusing on 1941 and 1942, these chapters draw attention to the ways that local leaders attempted to preserve their own codes of community, whether civic, religious, or national. The first part of the book thus illuminates the rifts and reciprocity between local issues, national policies, and the radical ideologies prevalent at the time.

Beginning with a portrait of the city on the eve of war, chapter 1 introduces the mosaic of Sarajevo's communities by exploring the links and tensions among everyday human stories, political ideologies, and the civic and cultural processes of the town. The second chapter jumps into the

---

71. Studies in European history that have informed this understanding of the transformation on the periphery include Edward Whiting Fox, *History in Geographic Perspective, The Other France* (New York: Norton, 1971); Charles Tilly, *Vendée* (Cambridge, Mass.: Harvard University Press, 1964); and Mack Walker, *German Home Towns* (Ithaca: Cornell University Press, 1971). Fox's work analyzes how merchant cities on the periphery of France fostered different kinds of social relations than did cities in the state's core. Tilly examines the behavior and motivations that led a group of French towns to oppose the French Revolution, exploring the social transformation that occurred within the context of the crisis. Walker explores German towns that resisted incorporation into the Prussian Empire when they realized that the empire would force them to abandon their local political and social norms. In each case, the story of the periphery significantly challenges historical assumptions drawn from the narrative of the core.

hectic months of war and political transition: the collapse of Yugoslavia in April 1941, the arrival of the German occupation, and the establishment of the NDH under the Ustasha regime.[72] It exposes the inner workings of the NDH from Sarajevo's perspective and introduces the irreparable rift that occurred among local (city), national (Ustasha), and international (German) agendas. Chapter 3, an examination of the local process of genocide, reveals that the ensuing discord between the city and ideas of the new order was not just a power struggle with the Ustasha regime but, more fundamentally, an ideological battle to define and protect the values and basis of community. The chapter exposes local debates over the categorization of "non-Aryans" and "foreigners," uncovering the everyday interactions of victims, bystanders, and perpetrators. As a counterpart to this discussion of ethnic cleansing, which focuses on the treatment of individuals slated for expulsion from the national body, chapter 4 examines how Sarajevo's remaining Croats and Aryans came to understand their own identities. In particular, it underscores two simultaneous processes: the city's fragmentation along national lines and its integration along civic ones.

From 1942 to 1945, Sarajevo's leaders gradually came to terms with the harsh reality that the political entity they envisioned had no place in Hitler's expanding empire, let alone in twentieth-century Europe. They spent the final years of the war in a desperate, if at times futile, attempt to secure a stake in the future political order and preserve aspects of their local culture amid an emerging civil war and Axis military losses and retreat. Nineteen forty-two marked a critical turning point in the transformation of the psyche of many Sarajevans. In translating aspects of their local culture into the modern political system, many local leaders, particularly Muslims, started to reframe their ideal visions of society. Some began to see ethnocultural diversity as a good in itself and not simply as an unfortunate byproduct of their heterogeneous composition. Others became convinced that without a strong nationalist or ideological stance, their voice would be lost.

The final chapters of the book turn to the ways that local leaders attempted to manipulate the disjunction between international, national,

---

72. A brief overview of the Independent State of Croatia and the Ustasha regime can be found in Sabrina P. Ramet, "The NDH—An Introduction," *Totalitarian Movements and Political Religions*, 7, no. 4 (December 2006): 399–408. More exhaustive discussions are provided in Jozo Tomasevich's tome *War and Revolution in Yugoslavia, 1941–1945: Occupation and Collaboration* (Stanford: Stanford University Press, 2001), and in Stevan Pavlowitch, *Hitler's New Disorder: The Second World War in Yugoslavia* (New York: Columbia University Press, 2008). On the way that the Independent State of Croatia functioned in Bosnia, see Enver Redžić, *Bosnia and Herzegovina in the Second World War* (London: Frank Cass, 2005). For a historiographical review of the Serbo-Croatian literature, see Nada Kisić-Kolanović, "Povijest NDH kao predmet istraživanja," *Časopis za suvremenu povijest*, 34, no. 3 (2002): 679–712. Classical works on the subject include Fikreta Jelić-Butić, *Ustaše i Nezavisna Država Hrvatska, 1941–1945* (Zagreb: Liber, 1977); Bogdan Krizman, *Ustaše i Treći Reich* (Zagreb: Globus, 1983); Bogdan Krizman, *Ante Pavelić i Ustaše* (Zagreb: Globus, 1986); and Ladislaus Hory and Martin Broszat, *Der kroatische Ustascha-Staat, 1941–1945* (Stuttgart: Deutsche Verlags-Anstalt, 1964).

and local prerogatives in order to further their own goals. Although a broad consensus of Sarajevans came to detest the existing system under the Nazis and Ustashas, they remained apprehensive about the political choices available. Instead of participating in the civil war, leaders in Sarajevo attempted to create new movements to compete with the three dominant factions. Chapter 5 presents the dynamics of the Yugoslav civil wars, focusing especially on how discrete groups of Muslims began to craft autonomous and future-oriented policies in the midst of civil and world wars, policies that contributed to the creation of the Bosnian Muslim Waffen SS unit. This discussion of resistance and civil war continues in chapter 6, which investigates the city's growing political and social crisis after the capitulation of Italy in September 1943. The last chapter examines how city leaders attempted to hold the city together during the terror and chaos of the Ustasha and German retreat and the political transition to Tito's Yugoslavia.

Sarajevo, 1941–1945 ultimately contends that by adapting local concepts of community and civic responsibility to the wartime social and demographic transformations, town leaders were able to protect the values and ideals associated with multiculturalism while acquiescing to some political and ideological demands at the national and international levels. In this way, Sarajevo's multicultural character survived the war even when many of its citizens did not.

1

PORTRAITS OF A CITY ON THE EVE OF WAR

"Sarajevo has a soul like a village, though it is a town," a poet named Constantine relayed to Rebecca West during her visit in 1937. He continued,

> Here Slavs, and a very fine kind of Slav, endowed with great powers of perception and speculation, were confronted with the Turkish Empire at its most magnificent, which is to say Islam at its most magnificent, which is to say Persia at its most magnificent. Its luxury we took, its militarism and its pride, and above all its conception of love. The luxury has gone. The militarism has gone. . . . But the conception of love is still in the city, and it is a wonderful conception, it refreshes and revivifies.

As the British novelist and her husband pressed him to elaborate—no doubt trying to determine whether the poet spoke nostalgically of a time long since passed—Constantine concluded, "How far this tradition exists today I cannot tell. . . but I am sure that the conception gives the town a special elegance."[1]

Despite the nationalist tensions that were escalating across the region in 1937 and the looming specter of war, visitors were nonetheless struck by Sarajevo's utterly special character. While the profusion of mosques, churches, and synagogues contributed to this character, as did as the blend of Ottoman, Habsburg, and Yugoslav signifiers, the town's quiddity was not merely the product of its architecture and landscape. More important for

---

1. Rebecca West, *Black Lamb, Grey Falcon: A Journey through Yugoslavia* (New York: Viking, 1941), 383–386. "Constantine" was actually Stanislav Vinaver, an Orthodox Serb of Jewish heritage who was a Belgrade writer and head of the Press Bureau. West and her husband traveled throughout the Yugoslav lands in 1937. She recorded her impressions about life, society, food, customs, and politics in what has become one of her most famous books, one that redefined the travelogue genre.

this story, it was seen in citizens' everyday interactions and institutionalized through the public and private spheres.

This happened in two distinct ways. First, a civic, social, and cultural concept of Sarajevo formed gradually between the Ottoman and Yugoslav eras, developing into an understanding of what it meant to be a member of Sarajevo society. This civic consciousness was on display in the public sphere and entrenched in the political and cultural institutions of the town. Complementing this civic identity was a rich confessional tradition, which had evolved through the interwar era to reflect a combination of religious and secular characteristics. Although the relationship between civic and confessional identity was always in flux, Sarajevo's multicultural character depended upon the consistent presence of some degree of political plurality and a mutual respect for confessional traditions. Although Constantine's poetic description of Sarajevo's social fabric lacked this sociological nuance, it is clear that he, like most people in the city, understood that something about the town's civic and social structure formed the essence of Sarajevo's soul.

This chapter seeks to demonstrate through the portraits of local community leaders how these two central concepts of community and social organization were lived in Sarajevo on the eve of the Second World War. The four men chosen—two religious leaders and two representatives of the cultural milieu—are not intended to parallel one another or to serve as microcosms of the communities they represent in this story. Instead, by presenting the complex relationship of local, national, and international dynamics through their personal experiences, they provide a window into the world of interwar Sarajevo. These stories illuminate the city's political and cultural dynamics, linking Yugoslav political events to broader European developments. In so doing, each portrait highlights the conflicting allegiances to one's state, confessional community, national group, family, and city—conflicts that would carry through the war. Each man thus represents one of the four confessional pillars of Sarajevo's society; yet his story simultaneously reveals the difficulties of using one person to represent an entire community. For when the war began on April 6, 1941, issues of identity, religion, and nationalism became so entangled with the politics of state building, world war, and ethnic cleansing that it is only by understanding the human stories that we can now grasp how the city responded to crisis and how the war changed the landscape of everyday life and society.

Fehim Spaho: The Grand Mufti's Last Letter to Belgrade

When Sarajevo's grand mufti, Fehim Spaho, awoke on Saturday, April 5, 1941, the future looked grim. War loomed just around the corner, Sarajevo's four religious communities had fallen into discord, and Yugoslav military preparations threatened the integrity of Islamic institutions. As there was nothing he could do about the war and as Sarajevo's divisions were too great for one man to resolve, Spaho concentrated on one of his principal duties as Reis-ul-ulema, the leader of Yugoslavia's Muslims: managing relations between the Muslim community and the Yugoslav government. He sat down that morning and penned a letter to the Yugoslav Ministry of the Army and Navy in Belgrade, complaining that too many of Sarajevo's Muslim clergy had been drafted into the military. Religious and educational institutions were short-staffed, and Muslim students were idly "wandering around with nothing to do."[2]

Spaho was not ignorant of national security concerns. Like the rest of his countrymen, he had watched with dismay as the Belgrade government had nearly collapsed the week before. Nevertheless, he felt it his religious duty to reject Belgrade's efforts to draft men who were vital to the sustenance of Islamic life in Sarajevo. To Spaho, the military draft of Muslim clergy was another grievance in a long list of affronts to Islam. Since 1918, the government had steadily usurped the autonomy of the Islamic Religious Community and restricted the jurisdiction of Islamic law (Sharia) and the Islamic religious courts. The Yugoslav king, Aleksandar, was said to be staunchly anti-Muslim. In addition to stripping Muslim landowners of property, under his watch the government had offended Muslims by shutting down mosques, turning some Islamic religious institutions into military warehouses, and curtailing Muslim marriage laws. After the establishment of a royal dictatorship in 1929, matters had further deteriorated. Since 1909, the Islamic Religious Community had had autonomy over Muslim religious life, religious endowments (*Vakuf*, Bosnian; *Waqf*, Arabic), educational institutions, and the administration of the Islamic Religious Community itself. Now the Belgrade government planned to take over these functions, reorganizing the internal structure of the community and transforming some of its customs. Most insultingly, the government had moved the seat of the Reis-ul-ulema from Sarajevo to Belgrade.[3] In 1930, the highly respected Reis-ul-ulema Džemaludin Čaušević had resigned to protest the government's intrusions into the affairs of the Muslim community, especially the administration of the Vakuf.[4] Furious, members of the Muslim elite fought to have their leader returned to Sarajevo, finally succeeding in 1936. They nevertheless remained wary of the government's intentions.

Before becoming Reis-ul-ulema in 1938, Fehim Spaho had been the president of the High Sharia Court in Sarajevo. He was thus intimately

2. IAS, Ostavština Fehima Spaha, box 3, document 693 (April 5, 1941).

3. All of these initiatives are discussed in Imamović, *Historija država i prava Bosne i Hercegovine*, 315–317. They are also discussed in the context of Bosnian Muslim history in Mustafa Imamović, *Historija Bošnjaka* (Sarajevo: Preporod, 1998), 491.

4. The authoritative study on the relationship of the Reis to the Belgrade government is Enes Karić, ed., *Reis Džemaludin Čaušević: prosvjetitelj i reformator*, 2 vols. (Sarajevo: Ljiljan, 2002).

acquainted with the tensions between religious and secular law and worked closely with political leaders and religious advisers to try to reach a compromise that would preserve the fundamental laws and values of his religion while accommodating the state. The threat of war and the enthronement of a new king, however, gave Belgrade new excuses to infringe on Spaho's authority. He had to react now if he hoped to retain any influence under the new Yugoslav government. As a precautionary measure, he maintained good relations with the local German consulate and with advocates of Croat autonomy.[5] Spaho knew that no matter who ruled Yugoslavia, he would be burdened with the difficult task of synchronizing the expectations of the Islamic Religious Community with the demands of the state.

Such a task would have been easier if Muslims had stood as a united front. Spaho's brother, Mehmed Spaho, had attempted to achieve Muslim unity through the political system, leading the nonnational Yugoslav Muslim Organization (Jugoslavenska Muslimanska Organizacija, or JMO) throughout most of the interwar era. Initially a collection of meetings held by Muslim civic and religious leaders voicing the community's grievances and asserting collective demands, the JMO gradually emerged as a formal organization, assuming the character of a political party in its demands for Muslim representation in the state government. The movement underwent numerous political transformations throughout the interwar era as it sought to mitigate the state's agrarian policies, integrate Muslim voices into the political system, and demand autonomy. Zlatko Hasanbegović argues that because of its "confessional features" and "agenda of autonomy," Serbs believed that the organization was a conservative religious group that represented only Muslim landowners deprived of their property by the new agrarian reform. In reality, the organization had all the characteristics of a secular, civic political movement.[6] While it succeeded in creating a fairly unified voice of Muslims in Belgrade during the 1930s, it failed to prevent secularism and nationalism from further fragmenting local Muslim communities throughout the state. Indeed, the schism widened within the Muslim community as religious leaders and politicians struggled to assert control over the administration of the Islamic Religious Community.

In Sarajevo, certain groups of progressive, Western-oriented Muslims hoped to transform Islam into a religion that was compatible with a secular state by reducing the autonomy of Muslim religious leaders and relaxing Islamic laws. Others strove to protect the Sharia and even strengthen Islam as a system of life, law, and politics. Fehim Spaho's election as Reis-ul-ulema in 1938 was deeply controversial because the fact that he was Mehmed Spaho's brother suggested to religious Muslims that the community's

5. IAS, Ostavština Fehima Spaha, box 3, document 683 (January 2, 1941), and box 2, document 590 (January 7, 1940).
6. Hasanbegović, "Jugoslavenska muslimanska organizacija u političkom životu Kraljevine Jugoslavije 1929–1941," 6–7.

political and religious spheres were merging in an uncomfortable manner.[7] After the death of Mehmed Spaho in 1939, a political crisis plagued the Yugoslav Muslim Organization and left Muslim leaders deeply divided over the best political solution for the community.

Reis-ul-ulema Spaho tried to use his religious position to unite the different parties through the central religious administration, but neither the progressives nor the Islamists—as I will refer to them—were pleased with this balancing act. The former viewed him as too conservative, the latter as compromising the faith. The rift within the Muslim community steadily widened, a continual problem for Spaho's administration. To complicate matters, by 1941 there were multiple factions within each camp. The "progressives"—those who embraced some combination of modernization, nationalism, and European political ideas—had formed several movements. One group supported Yugoslavia and hoped to work with the existing government, another called for Muslim autonomy within Yugoslavia, and the third advocated a union of Muslims and Croats. All three groups wanted to help Muslims assimilate into Europe and, in the words of the Muslim intellectual Hamdija Kreševljaković, "to save the Muslim masses from illiteracy and poverty."[8] They disagreed, however, on the best way to achieve these goals. Because Muslims did not yet have a clearly defined national movement of their own, they divided among Serbs, Croats, and Yugoslavs— descriptions they used to define their political and cultural attitudes rather than their ethnic identity. Muslims could view themselves as members of the Muslim religious community and simultaneously hold certain political or cultural roles that identified them with the Serb or Croat camp. In Spaho's family, Fehim aligned with the Croats, his brother Mustafa declared himself a Serb, and Mehmed remained adamantly unaligned.[9]

Opposing the Muslim progressives were conservative, reactionary imams and religious scholars who abhorred compromise and fought rigorously against secularization. While the term "Islamist" is problematic in its ambiguity and its diverse contemporary variations, I use it in this context to define Muslims in Bosnia who based their political and social reform projects on Islamic tradition and law. Like the progressives, the Islamists formed many camps, ranging from those that simply sought the separation of religion from state politics to those that looked to develop a new political system that respected the Sharia tradition. Fed up with liberalism and the political polarization of Muslims, in 1936 a group of "dissatisfied ulema"— imams, religious judges, and religious scholars—formed an association called El-Hidaje, which means "the true path."[10] The group believed that

7. Ibid., 288–289.

8. IAS, Ostavština Hamdije Kreševljakovića, box 1, document 32 (January 14, 1939).

9. Banac, *The National Question in Yugoslavia*, 375.

10. Background on El-Hidaje can be found in Redžić, *Bosnia and Herzegovina in the Second World War*, 86–87.

the Islamic Religious Community should function parallel to the state and that Islamic institutions should independently govern Muslims. Many of their leaders embraced ideas similar to those circulating among the Egyptian Muslim Brotherhood.[11] El-Hidaje criticized the "ignorance" of the Yugoslav government, which made decisions on behalf of Muslims "without consulting religious officials, theologians, or Sharia legal experts."[12] The association's leader was Mehmed ef. Handžić, a Cairo-educated Sarajevo Muslim who taught at Sarajevo's medresa (Islamic religious school) and served as the first librarian at the Gazi Husrevbegova biblioteka (GHB), the largest and most important Islamic library in Bosnia. By 1941, El-Hidaje had grown to 1,500 members. Many of the ulema refused to accept Fehim Spaho as their legitimate leader, viewing him as a political pawn who was too willing to sacrifice the principles of Islam in order to appease the secular government. Spaho knew, however, that El-Hidaje's notion of Islamic society was incompatible with civil law and a democratic nation-state.

Starting in March 1941, Spaho also had to deal with a new movement called the Young Muslims (Mladi muslimani). Founded by forty male students who sought a voice in reshaping the relationship between Islam and the state, the Young Muslims argued that Islam was not simply a religion but rather "a system that solved every component of human life."[13] Like their elders in El-Hidaje, the young men rejected the secular state and sought the return of Islamic values. However, they did not embrace El-Hidaje's clerical side, instead arguing that the Muslim laity and intelligentsia should lead the effort to revitalize Islam in Sarajevo and all of Bosnia. They advocated building rigid divisions around Muslim identity, and they opposed working with Serbs and Croats. Many of the students worked closely with Sarajevo's foremost Muslim humanitarian organization, Merhamet, thus combining their political views with a tangible social mission. This alliance would help create important grassroots social networks among Muslims during the war.

Given these deep fractures within his community, Reis-ul-ulema Spaho should have been elated when in the course of the riots and celebrations that broke out in Sarajevo between March 25 and March 29, 1941, Sarajevo's Muslims put aside their political and religious differences and worked together as a united front. Unfortunately, the price of this unity

11. On the interwar origins and development of the Muslim Brothers in Egypt, see Lia Brynjar, *The Society of the Muslim Brothers in Egypt: The Rise of an Islamic Mass Movement 1928–1942* (Ithaca: Ithaca Press, 2006). On the ideological influences from Egypt, see Hasanbegović, "Jugoslavenska muslimanska organizacija," 306–307. Several leading members of El-Hidaje had studied in Egypt and other parts of the Middle East, thus acquiring direct knowledge of global trends in Islamic politics.

12. *Sarajevski Novi List,* June 2, 1941, 3.

13. Omer Behmen, ed., *Mladi Muslimani 1939–1999* (Sarajevo: Bošnjački Institut, 2001), 1:23. On the Young Muslim movement generally, see also Zilhad Ključanin, ed., *Mladi Muslimani* (Sarajevo: Biblioteka Ključanin, 1991), and Sead Trhulj, *Mladi Muslimani* (Zagreb: Globus, 1992).

was the severing of close relations between Sarajevo's Muslims and their Jewish neighbors, communities that had lived and worked side by side for centuries. On March 29, 1941, a prominent Muslim organization, Gajret, summoned representatives from the important progressive and Islamist institutions to an urgent meeting to discuss the "destructive work" of the Jews, who they alleged had spread defamatory rumors that suggested Muslims would compose a fifth column if the Germans invaded. Gajret was a society that strongly supported Yugoslavia, which lent the meeting a certain political clout. Forty elite Muslims, representing diverse segments of the city's Muslim population, responded to the invitation. At the conference, the men agreed that the Jews had "gone too far" and "must be stopped once and for all." They then drafted and signed a statement that accused Sarajevo's Jews of slandering Muslims, "agitating and provoking" anti-Muslim sentiments, and destroying the city's interreligious peace. They called the Jewish provocation an "insult" to Muslims, who had graciously provided Jews with a safe home for centuries.[14] Spaho did not attend the meeting or publicly sanction it, although he was invited and received a copy of the minutes.

Although the Muslim leaders were unwarranted in blaming the city's Jews for these rumors, their concern over being labeled a fifth column was well founded. In the days following the military coup in Belgrade, public unrest and uncertainty over Yugoslavia's future had fueled tensions among all of Sarajevo's communities. Rumors spread rampantly from the cafés to the bazaars about which groups were participating in the Yugoslav rallies and which were not. Many of the rumors questioned the loyalty of Sarajevo's Muslims, who did not participate as actively as other communities, partly because many religious Muslims disliked engaging with the public sphere and partly because many of them did indeed support Germany. Nevertheless, Muslim leaders were dismayed to have their allegiance questioned, especially at such a critical time. Although everyone knew that there were multiple culprits behind the anti-Muslim rumors, including the Yugoslav government, blaming the Jews was the easiest way for Muslim leaders to assert their community's loyalty and challenge the hostile rumors without attacking Serbs, the dominant political group in Yugoslavia.[15]

This was not the first time that Sarajevo's Muslims had resorted to antisemitic rhetoric in their efforts to develop a united Muslim front. In the 1920s, Sarajevo's Sephardim had voted overwhelmingly for a nationalist Serb party, which tailored its agenda to include Jewish issues and even held local campaign rallies in Ladino, a Judeo-Spanish language spoken

14. The summons to the meeting can be found in ARIZBiH, Ulema Medžlis, document 1689/41 (March 29, 1941). The meeting's minutes are located in IAS, Merhamet, "Zaključak," box 4, (April 1, 1941).

15. La Benevolencija refers to this in its response, also found in IAS, Merhamet, La Benevolencija's response to the Muslim Conference, box 4 (April 1, 1941).

by many of the town's Sephardim. Many Muslims perceived this as Jewish disloyalty to the city. To punish the Jews, the Yugoslav Muslim Organization had sponsored a boycott of Jewish stores in 1925, but the boycott failed to resonate with the majority of Muslims in the city. During the economic recession of the 1920s and 1930s, some Jewish entrepreneurs fared better than their Muslim counterparts, a situation that bred resentment. Although the city's traditional Jewish craftsmen and artisans suffered alongside their Muslim townsmen, Muslim merchants blamed Jewish competition in the marketplace for their economic decline. Some of these merchants joined a small group that circulated an antisemitic pamphlet, *Svoj svome* (*To each his own*) in the winter of 1940–41, which promoted a European-wide effort to encourage people to boycott Jewish businesses.[16] Muslim political leaders also grew suspicious of the emergent local Zionist movement and the development of left-wing and Communist Jewish organizations among the Sephardic working class. As the Muslim community came under attack in late March 1941, many found it easy to believe the fabricated story that Jews had instigated the rumors.[17]

Upon receiving a copy of the Muslim conference's allegations on April 1, La Benevolencija, Sarajevo's foremost Jewish cultural society, formally responded. The society denied that Jews had spread any rumors and argued that they had exhibited enormous "patience" and "discipline" during this difficult time. Far from being agitators, Jews had actually been victims of antisemitic attacks during the riots. Jewish leaders objected to this blatant attempt to pin responsibility for citywide tensions on the Jews and argued that Muslims had no evidence to back up their accusations. Admitting that there might have been a single incident, they were still astonished that the Muslims would blame the entire Jewish population for one alleged act. Citing the "unfortunate" development of a "psychosis" in the city, the society appealed to Sarajevo's Muslims to work with Jewish leaders to foster peace in both the nation and the city.[18]

Fehim Spaho had many Jewish acquaintances and may have used his position to reconcile the two communities. Before he had a chance to respond, however, the Yugoslav army drafted dozens of Islamic instructors, jeopardizing the entire system of Muslim education in Sarajevo. Because of his position as Reis-ul-ulema, Spaho's primary responsibility was to Yugoslavia's Muslims, not to intercommunity relations. So on April 5, he wrote to the Ministry of Defense in a last-ditch effort to seek military exemptions for

16. Aleksandar Stajić and Jakov Papo, "Ubistva i drugi zločini izvršeni nad Jevrejima," in Kamhi, *Spomenica*, 214.

17. On Jewish-Muslim relations in the city, see Harriet Pass Freidenreich, *The Jews of Yugoslavia, A Quest for Community* (Philadelphia: Jewish Publication Society of America, 1979), 19, 173–175, 183–184. On the rise of Zionism in Sarajevo, see Paul Benjamin Gordiejew, *Voices of Yugoslav Jewry* (Albany: SUNY Press, 1999), 64–65.

18. IAS, La Benevolencija's response.

important religious figures and in doing so to assert his religious authority before his divided Muslim flock as well as the Yugoslav state.

Leon Finci: A Plea from the Sephardim

There are two signatures at the bottom of La Benevolencija's heartfelt plea that Muslims join the group in promoting intercommunity cooperation. The first name, signed in the Cyrillic script, is illegible.[19] The second, signed in the Latin alphabet, belongs to Leon Finci, the vice president of the organization and a well-known humanitarian and patron of the arts.[20] Together the authors formally addressed the city's Muslims on behalf of "every Jewish religious institution and social organization in Sarajevo." But the letter had a distinctly Sephardic tone in its plea to restore historic Muslim-Jewish relations. It argued that it was "well known" that the "religious-moral customs," "civic consciousness," and "local loyalties" of Sarajevo's Jews had been vital in sustaining good relations between Sarajevans of the Muslim and Jewish faiths for centuries.[21] In reality, however, only one part of the Jewish community really shared that tradition.

Leon Finci, like most of the city's Sephardim, could trace his family's Sarajevo lineage to the sixteenth century, a legacy that few of the city's Catholics and Orthodox Serbs shared.[22] In 1941, the Sephardim comprised 85 percent of Sarajevo's ten thousand Jews and were an integral part of the city's social fabric. They spoke primarily Ladino and had a rich musical and literary life. Of the city's eight synagogues, seven were Sephardic. The Sephardim maintained a distinct local culture that centered on their religious and linguistic-cultural traditions. In the four hundred years since their arrival in Sarajevo, they had never been persecuted for religious reasons. Many Sephardic families actually lived in the Muslim residential neighborhoods and owned shops adjacent to their Muslim neighbors in the bazaars. Moreover, Sephardic culture had become an important part of Sarajevo's heritage. In the 1920s, a group of non-Jewish intellectuals praised Sarajevo's Sephardim for their "noble, rich, and necessary cultural work," which had benefited the entire city. The Sarajevo Haggadah—a colorfully

19. I believe it belongs to Rabbi Albahari.

20. Avram Pinto, "Jevrejska Društva u Sarajevu," in Kamhi, *Spomenica*, 173–187.

21. IAS, La Benevolencija's response. Ironically, today in the twenty-first century, it is once again a Finci who leads Sarajevo's struggle for peaceful relations and reconciliation in the postwar environment. Jakov Finci, a founding father of the Interreligious Council of Bosnia and Herzegovina and the president of La Benevolencija, has spearheaded several international projects that promote reconciliation and equal rights. He has published on the topic in *Transitions Online*.

22. Leon Finci's ancestors could be traced to a migration from Florence in the sixteenth century and were listed in the Ottoman census of 1725. For references to the family, see Isak Levi, *Jevrejska Opština, Jewish Community in Sarajevo* (Sarajevo: Jevrejska Opština, 1984), 7; Moritz Levy, *Die Sephardim in Bosnien* (Klagenfurt, Aus.: Wieser Verlag, 1996), 31.

illustrated Jewish book of rites brought to Sarajevo by the Sephardim—was an immense source of pride to Sarajevans, who considered it the "most precious" artifact in the city's museum.[23]

Although small groups of Ashkenazim had lived in Sarajevo during the Ottoman era, the city's community of Ashkenazim was formed in the 1880s, when a wave of Ashkenazi immigrants arrived from other parts of the Austro-Hungarian Monarchy.[24] The new Jewish immigrants tended to speak German, and they built their own administrations, graveyards, synagogues, and organizations, completely disconnected from those of the Sephardim. The Sephardim disliked the foreign intrusion, and the two communities existed completely separately until the 1920s. Moreover, the Ashkenazim interacted differently with Sarajevo's other communities. They did not share the legacy or traditions of Ottoman life and quickly dominated many aspects of modern society: the bureaucracy, medicine, education, and industry. From their arrival, the Ashkenazim functioned like a European national group rather than a religious-based community. Consequently, Sarajevans often perceived them as different or, even worse, as outsiders. The rigid division between these two communities started to relax in the early 1920s when a handful of young progressive Sephardim joined a group of Ashkenazim who hoped to foster a single Yugoslav Jewish identity. The group founded Sarajevo's first unified Jewish club in 1927 and began publishing a local weekly paper, the *Jewish Voice* (*Jevrejski Glas*), in 1928. Legally, however, the two communities remained separate, and many Sephardim preferred it that way.[25]

It is hardly surprising that when antisemitism first emerged in Sarajevo, it had a distinct anti-Ashkenazi slant. Immediately after the First World War, local authorities in Bosnia and Croatia began a campaign to remove the "foreign," German-speaking Ashkenazim on the grounds that they supported the Habsburg monarchy or the Communists.[26] Foreign literally meant just that: immigrants from abroad. Concepts of racial foreignness were not yet salient in the town. Furthermore, in the late 1920s and 1930s, Sarajevo's lower classes blamed German, Slovene, and other central European immigrants for the city's high unemployment, low salaries, and failed crafts industry.[27] This group included many Ashkenazi Jews, who seemed to

23. On the cultural position and legacy of the Sephardim in Sarajevo, see Alija Bejtić, "Jevrejske Nastambe u Sarajevu," in Kamhi, *Spomenica*, 31, and Pinto, "Jevrejska Društva u Sarajevu," 176.

24. On Sarajevo's Ashkenazim, see Julije Hahamović, "Aškenazi u Bosni i Hercegovini," in Kamhi, *Spomenica*, 142–152.

25. The divisions between Sarajevo's Ashkenazim and Sephardim are discussed in Freidenreich, *The Jews of Yugoslavia*, 15–24, and in Moni Finci, "O socijalnoj i političkoj diferencijaciji među sarajevskim jevrejima u razdoblje 1918–1941," *Prilozi Institut za Istoriju* 18 (1981): 291.

26. Freidenreich, *The Jews of Yugoslavia*, 182.

27. On the development of postwar xenophobic attitudes and the onset of antisemitism, see Avram Pinto, *Jevreji Sarajeva i Bosne i Hercegovine* (Sarajevo: Veselin Masleša, 1987), 186–188, and Donia, *Sarajevo*, 159–165.

prosper at a time when the rest of the city was suffering from an economic depression. The idea that Jews were foreigners to the city was reinforced when a new group of Ashkenazi refugees arrived in Sarajevo from Austria after the Anschluss (annexation by Germany) in 1938.

While antisemitism was significantly less prominent in Yugoslavia than in other east European states, a broader-based movement appeared in the 1930s.[28] An underground antisemitic press even published the Protocols of the Elders of Zion in the Serbo-Croatian language in 1936. In 1940, Belgrade passed several national laws that limited Jewish participation in public life. As the government began treating "Jew" as a uniform category, Sarajevans started to overlook the fact that their Sephardic neighbors had lived in the city far longer than they had (and thus could hardly be considered foreigners). On the eve of war, various local and national papers started identifying Jews as an "unwanted or foreign element" (*nepoželjan*) in Yugoslav society. Both the Muslim and Catholic presses introduced antisemitic references. Even the local Orthodox Serb leadership alluded to the negative influences of Jews, republishing articles from a well-known Orthodox bishop in Serbia who blamed Jewish propaganda for the decline of Western civilization.[29] Although many authors borrowed the contemporary racial language, they overwhelmingly conceived of Jews as comprising a religious or cultural-national group, not a biological category. This would have a deep impact on their wartime policies. The vast majority of Sarajevans continued to believe that a Jew could convert out of that identity.

Sarajevo's Sephardim had been patient through each of these developments, blaming national and economic pressures instead of their townsmen. But the Muslim conference was the last straw. Jewish community leaders found the meeting especially distressing because it had been organized by Gajret, a society composed of pro-Yugoslav and pro-Serb Muslims.[30] After two decades of state propaganda that welcomed them into the Yugoslav national group, Jews felt hurt that in the city's most dire hour, a Muslim group that aligned itself with the Yugoslav ideal could unashamedly jump on the antisemitic bandwagon. Jewish leaders realized that antisemitism was no longer limited to small, powerless groups. It had become mainstream. In a few short months, Leon Finci had been transformed from a leader of the Sephardim, one of the pillars of Sarajevo's social order, to an unwanted Yugoslav Jew.

---

28. Antisemitism in Sarajevo was never as widespread as in Belgrade or Zagreb. For comparison with other parts of the country, see Ivo Goldstein, ed., *Antisemitizam, Holokaust, Antifašizam*, (Zagreb: Židovska općina Zagreb, 1996), and Ženi Lebl, *Do "Konačnog Rešenja": Jevreji u Beogradu 1521–1942* (Belgrade: Čigoja štampa, 2001).

29. Nikolaj Velimirović, "Opozicija Boga," *Kalendar Bratstvo*, 1941, 4.

30. Gajret's inner circle had thirty members; its total membership was about twenty thousand. Kemura, *Uloga "Gajreta" u društvenom životu Muslimana Bosne i Hercegovine (1903–1941)*, 144 and 283.

Yet despite this shifting local rhetoric that adopted external definitions for the local Jewish community, Sarajevo's leaders preserved customary social policy: instead of seeking guidance from national leaders on the question of antisemitism, local Muslim and Jewish leaders dealt with one another. Indeed, they directed their correspondence to one another, and many sought to resolve the dispute through the local network of societies. Thus, following local tradition, Sarajevans recognized Leon Finci—vice president of La Benevolencija and onetime president of Lira, Sarajevo's Sephardic choir—as a legitimate public representative for Sarajevo's Jews. Likewise, Gajret was one of the local societies that sought to speak for Muslims. The truce that La Benevolencija sought was essentially a plea for Muslims to reject outside pressures of radical Right politics, nationalism, and antisemitism and instead abide by the Sarajevo tradition of "common life." The Sephardic leaders wanted to underscore that even now, Sarajevans shared more with each other than with political outsiders. As an overture to their Muslim townsmen, they compared the rumors that questioned Muslim loyalty to the rise of antisemitism, depicting Sarajevo's Muslims and Jews as victims-in-arms who needed to work together to defend themselves from foreigners who did not have the city's best interests at heart.[31] The exchange between the two societies in the days before the war reveals that many members of the local elite still believed they could solve the city's problems in their traditional way.

Although Finci never received a response to his letter—the Muslim conference planned to reconvene on April 3, but I have found no record of that meeting—he would have been pleased to know that a few months later, some of Sarajevo's Muslims realized he was right. But on the Jewish Sabbath, April 5, as antisemitism mounted and generals from four Axis countries prepared to invade his country, Finci could only fear the worst.

Božidar Bralo: One Eye on Berlin

Father Božidar Bralo, the pastor at St. Joseph's Catholic Church, was busy with weddings during the first week of April 1941: young couples across Sarajevo rushed to the altar to get married before the soldiers shipped out. As April 5 fell on a Saturday, the traditional day for Catholic weddings, Bralo no doubt prepared many young couples for the sacrament.[32]

Father Bralo was a priest in the Archdiocese of Vrhbosna and a close friend of his superior, Archbishop Ivan Šarić. Throughout the Yugoslav era,

31. IAS, La Benevolencija's response.
32. On weddings in Sarajevo, see *Jugoslovenska Pošta*, April 5, 1941, 5. Although Božidar Bralo is one of the most infamous Catholic figures from wartime Sarajevo, there is practically nothing written about him before 1941. Everything that we know about his background is revealed in either Ustasha or Communist propaganda published during and after the war.

Bralo was integral to Sarajevo's Catholic life, assuming many public roles from editor of *Katolički svijet* (*Catholic World*) to president of Sarajevo's local Catholic choir, Trebević. He was known for his work with Catholic youths and for his desire to build a more fervent Catholic culture in Sarajevo. For example, he tried to mandate that all Catholic students from the first to eighth grade attend Sunday school. In 1939, Archbishop Šarić rewarded Bralo for his dedication by appointing him to be the first vicar at Sarajevo's newly founded St. Joseph's Church. Both Bralo and Šarić eventually hoped to transform the church into Sarajevo's second cathedral.[33]

In the days leading up to the war, however, presiding over marriages, leading youth groups, and organizing choir rehearsals were not Bralo's only concerns. He also participated in secret meetings with other Croats who supported the Axis cause.[34] Though seemingly on an unofficial level, Bralo appeared to sympathize with a small group of Catholic Croat extremists who rallied for an alliance with Nazi Germany and hoped to use such an alliance to attain Croat autonomy. He passionately despised both the Yugoslav state, which he viewed as a facade for Great Serb nationalist aims, and the Yugoslav national idea, which suppressed Croat nationalism. Bralo believed that the Axis powers could save Catholics in Bosnia from secularization, liberal immorality, and Serbianization. Allegedly he had become especially well known among his fellow clergy for his vehement anti-Serb stance.[35] Such views were not uncommon among the clergy in the Vrhbosna archdiocese, which had strong ties to the Croat national movement, encouraging Sarajevo Catholics to cultivate stronger ties to their brethren in Croatia than to their fellow townsmen of different faiths.[36] The archbishop wanted to unify Catholics under the banner of Croat nationhood. He believed that one could not be a Croat without being Catholic.[37]

The Bosnian Franciscans had a somewhat different approach to the configuring of nationhood and religious identity than was typical of the new diocesan clergy. In part, their approach reflected a power dispute between the order and the diocese. After the Vatican introduced the regular diocesan system, the Franciscans grew resentful of being deprived of their

33. On Bralo's various roles within the church and the Catholic community, see Viktor Novak, *Magnum Krimen, pola vijeka klerikalizma u Hrvatskoj,* 2nd ed. (Belgrade: Nova Knjiga, 1986), 731–742, and Živko Jošilo, "Od Va do VIIIa Razreda," in Albahari et al., *Sarajevo u Revoluciji,* 1:596.

34. *Osvit,* April 10, 1942, 11.

35. See the reference to a report by a Sarajevo Franciscan, Karlo Karin, published in Novak, *Magnum Krimen,* 360.

36. This stance became even stronger once the war began. See *Katolički Tjednik,* April 27, 1941, 1.

37. For an overview of the Catholic Church in the Austro-Hungarian era and a review of the division between the archdiocese and the Franciscan order, see Zoran Grijak, *Politička djelatnost vrhbosanskog nadbiskupa Josip Stadlera* (Zagreb: Hrvatski Institute za Povijest and Vrhbosanska nadbiskupija, 2001), and Berislav Gavranović, *Uspostava redovite katoličke hijerarhije u Bosni i Hercegovini 1881. Godine* (Belgrade: Popović, 1935).

long-standing authority and autonomy to minister in the region, and this resentment exacerbated their differing view of the role of religious leaders in national movements. Because of their deep local experiences and familiarity with the Ottoman system, the Franciscans had promoted strong ties with Bosnia's other confessional communities and questioned deliberate attempts to tie the fate of Catholicism to that of the Croat nation. In the early 1900s, for example, they published a provocative article that argued, "Catholicism would not be ruined if the Croats disappeared, nor would the Croats be ruined if they ceased being Catholics."[38] The animosity between the two Catholic institutions grew steadily in the interwar era during the reign of Archbishop Ivan Šarić, who continued to promote a clericalist brand of Croat nationalism that emphasized the Catholic roots of Croat identity.[39]

Politically, then, the archdiocese opposed any Catholic movements that tried to work with the Yugoslav government. He particularly disapproved of the Franciscans, who maintained private religious work and cooperated with the government. In 1940, Šarić demanded that the minister of justice remove a Sarajevo Franciscan from his staff, but the minister refused.[40] Such opposition to the wishes of the institutional church seemed to exacerbate Šarić's hatred for the Yugoslav government and his irritation at the Franciscans. Arguably as punishment, he censored Franciscan articles, books, and periodicals, excluded the religious order from fully participating in the city's seminaries, attempted to usurp their state funding, and limited their participation in public life. Nevertheless, the Franciscans carried on with their own mission. They continued to work closely with Sarajevo's other religious groups and offered a less national venue for the practice of Catholicism.[41]

The discord between the Franciscans and the archdiocese came to reflect the political divisions among Sarajevo's Catholics: some looked to movements in Zagreb, Croatia's capital, for guidance on the question of Croat nationhood and others looked inward to the city's own traditions as they shaped their cultural ideas. Both sides viewed themselves as Croats, but they preferred different political options. Their local discord was overshadowed by the political rift developing between the Serb and Croat parties in Yugoslavia. Croats felt progressively marginalized in the centralizing state. Political stagnation and nationalist rivalries steadily increased throughout the 1920s. Tensions boiled over in 1928 when a Serb politician gunned

38. As paraphrased by Ivo Banac in *The National Question in Yugoslavia*, 364.
39. On the internal divisions in the interwar era, see Anđelko Barun, *Svjedoci i učitelji povijest franjevaca Bosne Srebrene* (Sarajevo: Svjetlo riječi, 2003), 340–344.
40. On Archbishop Šarić and his reign, see Ignacije Gavran, *Lucerna Lucens? Odnos vrhbosanskog ordinarijata prema Bosanskim Franjevcima (1881–1975)* (Visoko: Nadlada pisceva, 1978), 96–141. For a description of the incident in 1940, see 207.
41. Barun, *Svjedoci i učitelji*, 340–342.

down three Croat representatives on the floor of parliament. Stjepan Radić, the beloved leader of the Croat Peasant Party, was one of those hit; he died from his wounds six weeks later.[42] Before Croats had time to absorb fully what had happened, King Aleksandar dissolved parliament and established a royal dictatorship. He then divided the country into new administrative units, called *banovine*, most of which fell under Serb control. In response to the king's action, a small group of radical Croats fled into exile and formed a terrorist organization known as the Ustasha revolutionary movement. The Ustashas worked underground throughout the 1930s, helping Macedonian terrorists in the Internal Macedonian Revolutionary Organization (IMRO) plan the assassination of King Aleksandar in 1934. The assassination destabilized the Yugoslav state but failed to destroy it. Tensions between Croats and Serbs remained high throughout the 1930s. Croats across Yugoslavia began to look for political alternatives. Some factions made overtures to Mussolini's Fascist government in Italy, which encouraged dissolving the Yugoslav state so that it could annex some of its territories. Others looked to Hitler's Germany as a potential ally and savior.[43]

Fearing the implosion of the country, in 1939, the government hoped to resolve its domestic situation with the Cvetković-Maček Agreement, commonly referred to as the Sporazum, a compromise between Croats and Serbs that decentralized the federal government. The compromise created a larger district (*banovina*) of Croatia, which included large chunks of Bosnia. For many Croats, the reforms were too little too late. In Sarajevo, radical Croat nationalists were angry. Although it never articulated such a goal, the agreement essentially assigned Sarajevo to a Serb sphere of influence. That same year, Father Bralo was appointed to his new position at St. Joseph's, thus becoming a more public moral guardian for the oppressed Catholic Croat population.

Since anti-Yugoslav and pro-German sentiments were also on the rise in Sarajevo's Muslim community—which in addition to complaining that the state was infringing on its religious autonomy also felt slighted because the Yugoslav government had excluded Muslim representatives from the Sporazum in 1939—members of the Catholic and Muslim elite developed a wary partnership. Some progressive Muslims believed that Muslims and Catholics could work together as Croats; many Muslims living in Zagreb had completely integrated into the national movement, seeing themselves as both Muslims and Croats on the eve of war.[44] However, many of Sarajevo's

42. On the Croat Peasant Party's development in the 1920s, see Mark Biondich, *Stjepan Radić, the Croatian Peasant Party, and the Politics of Mass Mobilization, 1918–1928* (Toronto: University of Toronto, 2000).

43. The most comprehensive study of the development of the Ustasha movement in exile is Mario Jareb, *Ustaško-domobransko pokret: Od nastanka do travnja 1941. Godine* (Zagreb: Školska Knjiga, 2006).

44. On Muslims in Zagreb, see Zlatko Hasanbegović, *Muslimani u Zagrebu, 1878–1945* (Zagreb: Institut društvenih znanosti Ivo Pilar, 2007).

Muslims were skeptical of the long-term objectives of their Catholic allies. They feared Bralo's radicalism and the archdiocese's history of clerical nationalism. They also worried about the Catholic Church's response, or lack thereof, to anti-Muslim behavior. In early 1941, a local Croat journal published an article that ominously referred to Muslims as "Turks" who had torn Bosnia away from its Catholic roots.[45] Moreover, on several occasions, Catholics had attacked and killed Muslims in towns near Sarajevo for what appeared to be ethnoreligious reasons.[46] Muslim skeptics wondered how much control they would be expected to relinquish in exchange for a political alliance with the Catholic Croats. They would soon find out. In the meantime, Father Božidar Bralo would have been keeping one eye on Berlin and the other on St. Joseph's.

Borivoje Jevtić: The National Theater's Curtain Call

Amid the city's escalating tensions and the peril of war, on the evening of April 5, Borivoje Jevtić prepared for an opening at Sarajevo's National Theater. Days before, the theater's manager had been inducted into the Yugoslav army, appointing Jevtić to serve as acting manager until he returned from the front.[47] Jevtić had been the theater's dramaturge, so he knew the company well. Despite the threat of war, he planned to premiere a new show, a Saturday evening tradition. Tonight it would be the comedy *Porodica Blo* (*The Family Blo*) by the Serb playwright and actress Ljubinka Bobić. Jevtić's cast and crew included Muslim men and Orthodox, Catholic, and Jewish men and women.[48]

Jevtić, a well-known intellectual, author, and playwright, was an Orthodox Serb born and raised in Sarajevo. He had become famous in 1914 at the age of twenty as a member of Young Bosnia (Mlada Bosna), a movement involved in the assassination of Franz Ferdinand. Although the assassination has been interpreted as an act committed by advocates of Great Serbia, Mlada Bosna itself was a diverse movement that sought to overthrow the Habsburg Monarchy.[49] To many Sarajevo youths at the turn of the century, such an ideology seemed to have been conceived with Sarajevo in mind.

After spending most of the First World War in an Austrian prison, Jevtić returned to Sarajevo in 1918 when Yugoslavia won her independence. He immediately became a public spokesperson for the Mlada Bosna movement,

45. Gabrijel Cvitan, "Sjećanje na Bosnu," *Napredak Kalendar,* 1941, 34.
46. IAS, Ostavština Fehima Spaha, box 2, document 566 (January 27, 1940, and April 10, 1940).
47. IAS, Ostavština Borivoja Jevtića, box 4, document 50 (March 29, 1941).
48. *Narodno Pozorište u Sarajevu* (Sarajevo: Muzej književnosti i pozorišnje umjetnosti Bosne i Hercegovine, 1998), 133.
49. For an overview of Mlada Bosna and its members, including Jevtić, see Predrag Palavestra, *Književnost Mlade Bosne* (Sarajevo: Svjetlost, 1965).

which he, and many other Sarajevans, viewed as instrumental in the foundation of the Yugoslav state.[50] Although he had strong ties to Belgrade's intellectual community and supported the national government, Jevtić's primary loyalties were to Yugoslavia and Sarajevo. He held Bosnia's multi-confessional tradition in high regard, often incorporating characters of different faiths into his stories and plays. He published in Muslim, Croat, Serb, and Yugoslav periodicals and edited Sarajevo's Yugoslav literary journal *Pregled (Review)*.[51]

While supporting the government, Jevtić shared his neighbors' concern about Sarajevo's demotion in the hierarchy of Yugoslav cities, which he chronicled in various articles in the late 1920s and early 1930s. In 1929, for example, he expressed fear that the city was entering a cultural crisis, citing as proof the rising rate of illiteracy.[52] In 1931, he grew angry when a theater critic dared to compare Sarajevo's National Theater to that of Skopje, a city in Macedonia. He noted that "the heterogeneous audience in Sarajevo is much larger than in Skopje; the cultural tradition is stronger; and the artistic demands for the theater are far more refined and rigorous." Furthermore, he subtly suggested that the Skopje theater was an agent of Yugoslav propaganda, while Sarajevo's theater was a true art house.[53] His irritation underscored a key theme that Sarajevo's intelligentsia would continue to emphasize through the wartime era: Sarajevo should be looked upon as a cultural center, not a provincial appendage to some foreign national agenda.

But unlike the many Muslim and Catholic intellectuals who began to sour on the idea of Yugoslavia as the crises of the interwar era intensified, Jevtić clung to the Yugoslav legacy. In the late 1930s, he wrote his best-known play, *Revenge*. This play, like many of Jevtić's works, focused on Mlada Bosna. Instead of romantically glorifying a few of the movement's heroes, however, he portrayed the movement as the collective action of ordinary Sarajevans who had come together on behalf of the Yugoslav nation to ward off the Austrian enemy.[54] The timing of the play's premiere in 1939 was hardly coincidental: a new German enemy was slowly conquering Europe, once again threatening the security and independence of South Slavs. With *Revenge*, Jevtić subtly staked his position on the war.

Jevtić's commitment to Yugoslavia was not unique. Many Orthodox Serb intellectuals in Sarajevo remained strong supporters of Yugoslavism through the 1930s. Like many of their townsmen, they too grew frustrated

50. See, for example, his play on the assassination: Borivoje Jevtić, *Sarajevski Atentat* (Sarajevo: Štamparija i izd. Petra N. Gakovića, 1924).

51. Borivoje Jevtić, *Izabrana Djela*, vols. 1–3 (Sarajevo: Svjetlost, 1982). See also "Iz crvenog Hafiza" (Smrt Muhameda Hadžijamakovića)," *Gajret Kalendar*, 1941, 108–124.

52. *Pregled* 3, no. 4 (1929): 293.

53. *Pregled* 5, no. 7 (1931): 373.

54. Wayne Vucinich, "Modern Yugoslav Drama," *American Slavic and East European Review* 5 (May 1946): 5–6.

by Belgrade's autocratic centralism, wanting Sarajevo to gain more control over its own affairs.[55] Their attitudes did not go unnoticed by other Serb nationalists in Bosnia, who periodically accused Sarajevo's Serbs of being too Yugoslav and not Serb enough—indeed, some Serb nationalists from other parts of the region suggested that the movement "abandon" activism in Sarajevo because the "character" of the city's population prevented its Serbs from becoming active nationalists.[56] This did not mean that the city was devoid of Serb nationalists. Some local Serb journals promoted a steadfast nationalist agenda, arguing, for example, that Bosnian Muslims were ethnically Serbs and that Bosnia had greater historical and cultural ties to Serbia than to Croatia.[57] Moreover, as Muslims and Catholics transformed their desires for political power to ambitions for autonomy, the Orthodox Serb population grew closer to Belgrade.

Sarajevo's Serbian Orthodox Church appears to have been less of a political force than its counterparts in the Muslim, Catholic, and Jewish communities. The church overwhelmingly welcomed the foundation of Yugoslavia in 1918, which reunited the Orthodox Church in Bosnia with the Serbian Holy Synod.[58] Unlike the crises developing in the Muslim and Catholic religious communities, which suffered from internal rifts and a marginalized public status, the Serbian Orthodox Church benefited from its new privileged status in a state governed by Serbs and went about its business seemingly united. Church organizations, choirs, and committees served as the centers of cultural, social, and political networks.

Sarajevo's Orthodox leaders struggled with the same concerns about Communism and secularism as did leaders in the other religious communities. They expressed these concerns through discussions of the tragedy that had befallen the Orthodox Church in the Soviet Union, suggesting that the fall of Russia was reverberating throughout the Orthodox Christian world.[59] In the dramatic events of late March 1941, the church stood firmly behind the Yugoslav king, opposed the Tripartite Pact, and resisted any alliance or agreement with Hitler's Germany.

Jevtić, like the vast majority of Sarajevo's Serbs, did too. The community had much to fear from a German invasion. Memories of Austrian brutality against Serbs in the First World War were still fresh in the collective memory, especially among Jevtić's generation. Moreover, they knew that a German invasion would reverse their community's status in favor of Muslims and Catholics. Serbs had dominated the regional government, the military, and

55. Donia, *Sarajevo*, 132 and 165.
56. Hoare, *History of Bosnia*, 137–139.
57. *Novi Istočnik*, March 1940, 78–80.
58. Since the Ottoman era, the Orthodox Church in Bosnia had fallen in the jurisdiction of the Orthodox Church of Constantinople. See Donia, *Sarajevo*, 163.
59. On local concerns about the fall of Russia and the future of the Orthodox Church, see *Novi Istočnik*, March 1940, 73–77, and "Pobeda Hrišćanstva u sovetskoj Rusiji," *Bratstvo*, September 1939, 166.

the bureaucracy for two decades, and anti-Serb feelings ran strong in some Muslim and Catholic circles. Nevertheless, many of Sarajevo's leading Serbs still believed that they could overcome the city's ethnoreligious and political tensions. By raising the theater's curtain that Saturday night, Jevtić publicly renewed his commitment to Yugoslavia and his belief in Sarajevans.

Jevtić was hardly alone in this endeavor. Throughout the riots and the army's mobilization in the first week of April, many of Sarajevo's public figures tried to quell the onset of a citywide panic and heal the divisions between the city's communities. Town officials, police, journalists, and intellectuals tried to give Sarajevans the impression that they, the city's leaders, had everything under control. This mentality had become ingrained in the city's public culture. At every important transitional juncture—the Austro-Hungarian occupation in 1878 and subsequent annexation in 1908, the onset of the First World War, and the founding of Yugoslavia—Sarajevo's leaders showed remarkable flexibility, tolerance of one another, and resilience in the absence of national laws. April 1941 was no different. Belgrade offered Sarajevo's leaders little advice beyond empty pleas for national unity. Local leaders had to fend for themselves, calling on Sarajevans to "forget everything that was between us, for we are one nation." As bar fights broke out after political debates, they beseeched Sarajevans to respect the spirit of city bequeathed to them by their grandfathers and to honor Sarajevo's "great tradition" of peaceful interconfessional relations. At the same time, the city council asserted its control over local affairs. The town police congratulated citizens for keeping their demonstrations "peaceful" but also prepared for an increased need in law enforcement.[60] On April 5, the city council announced price caps, warned civilians to limit their use of gas, water, and electricity, and began to build air-raid shelters. Sarajevo's courts postponed cases because of the "uncertain times."[61]

Meanwhile, Borivoje Jevtić—ever the dedicated Yugoslav—began rehearsals for the following week's premiere of *Na Božjem Putu* (*On God's Way*): a play written by a Muslim Croat, Ahmed Muradbegović, directed by a Serb, and featuring, as always, a multiconfessional cast.

The Streets of Sarajevo, circa 1941

It is unlikely that Fehim Spaho, Leon Finci, Božidar Bralo, or Borivoje Jevtić crossed paths on the Saturday before the war. Each man had his own part of the city, just as he had his own concerns and his own community. Although the boundaries between the city's communities had become more porous in the preceding decades, the town retained physical characteristics of its multiconfessional mosaic. The old city in the east, known as Baščaršija, was

60. *Jugoslovenska Pošta*, March 28, 1941, 4, 5.
61. Ibid., April 5, 1941, 5.

Place Names

A. railroad station
B. military camp
C. Land Museum
D. St. Joseph Church
E. Ali Pasha Mosque
F. state government buildings
G. Evangelical Church
H. National Theater
I. New Jewish Synagogue
J. New Serbian Orthodox Church
K. Roman Catholic Cathedral
L. Old Jewish Synagogue
M Gazi Husrev Bey Mosque
N. Old Serbian Orthodox Church
O. Emperor Mosque
P. St. Anthony Church
Q. old Town Hall

Notes

[1] Woodrow Wilson Street (interwar and postwar)
[2] Field Marshal Putnik Street (interwar), Red Army Street (postwar)
[3] King Aleksandar Street (interwar), Marshal Tito Street (postwar)
[4] Prince Petar Street (interwar), Vaso Miskin Street (postwar)
[5] King Petar Street (interwar), Yugoslav Army Street (postwar)
[6] Field Marshal Stepa Stepanović (interwar and postwar)
[7] Mis Irbina Street (interwar and postwar)
[8] Trumbić Street (interwar), Golubić Street (postwar)
[9] Vuk Karadžić Street (interwar and postwar)

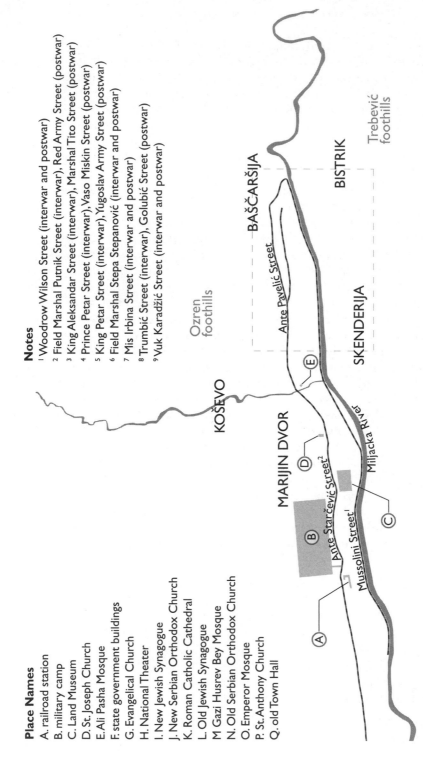

KOŠEVO

MARIJIN DVOR

Ozren foothills

BAŠČARŠIJA

BISTRIK

Trebević foothills

SKENDERIJA

Ante Pavelić Street

Miljacka River

Ante Starčević Street[2]

Mussolini Street[1]

Map 2a. Sarajevo, circa 1942

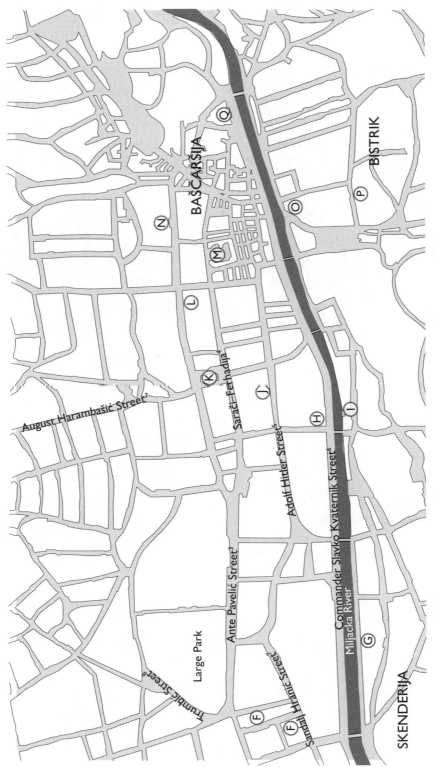

Map 2b. Central Sarajevo, circa 1942

Figure 1. Postcard from wartime Sarajevo. Original is in author's possession.

Spaho's realm. It was a picturesque Ottoman town. Stone mosques stood proudly on every corner, their courtyards filled with people greeting one another or drinking from the fountains. Small craft shops glistened with the copper goods of local artisans. Towering above the bazaar were dozens of white and green minarets, from which the muezzin called Muslims to prayer five times each day. Cobblestone streets wove around one- and two-story houses and shops where women in brightly colored veils and head scarves carried groceries to their homes in the predominantly Muslim neighborhoods.[62] The city's oldest Christian churches and Jewish synagogue blended in with the stone and wood buildings, just as those communities had lived unobtrusively in Ottoman Sarajevo. Muslims and non-Muslims gathered in the old town's coffee shops, although often at separate tables, to whisper about the war and sip thick Turkish coffee, which they poured from small bronze coffee pots (*džezva*) handcrafted in the bazaar. Small eateries served traditional spinach and minced-meat pastries in phyllo dough. Alcohol and pork were nowhere to be found. Visitors like Rebecca West could not help but feel the historic presence of Islam and the prevalence of religious ties, even in this era of nationalism.

A hundred meters west of the center of Baščaršija, the Ottoman quarter ended and Sarajevo's Habsburg quarter began. Everything from the architecture to the pavement beneath one's feet seemed to change in one fell

62. Women's attire in the early 1940s is discussed in Muniba Korkut-Spaho and Safija Šiljak, *Mlade muslimanke, Svjedočenja i Sjećanja* (Sarajevo: Mladi Muslimani, 1999), 26.

Figure 2. Panorama of Sarajevo, circa 1941. Courtesy of the Historical Museum of Bosnia and Herzegovina.

swoop. While the division between the two quarters was hardly absolute, it was certainly apparent. Pedestrian promenades, Secessionist-style government buildings, and European shops with pork chops and wine reminded visitors that this was a central European city. The Habsburg quarter was marked by the New Serbian Orthodox Church and the Roman Catholic cathedral, symbols of Christianity's increasing public presence in the late nineteenth century. The National Theater, where Borivoje Jevtić was busy with rehearsals, was here as well, directly between the New Serbian Orthodox Church and the river. A few blocks to the west, also along the river, Leon Finci's office at La Benevolencija was nestled in the midst of parks, fountains, shops, businesses, and residences. It was right around the corner from the New Sephardic Synagogue, one of a handful of buildings constructed during the interwar era. The mixture of religious and civic structures served as a visible reminder of the merger of identities in the first part of the twentieth century. This was now a city of faiths and nations, a town where confessional politics mixed with those of the secular state, creating a conspicuously local way of negotiating policy.

Father Bralo's parish at St. Joseph's was a good twenty-minute walk from Finci's office, on the far western end of Sarajevo in a neighborhood called Marijin Dvor. This part of the city was less dense. In place of markets, shops, and office buildings it had extended lawns and paths along the river. The quarter was dominated by St. Joseph's, an impressive stone church intricately decorated with stained glass, and by the Austrians' architectural marvel, the Land Museum (*Zemaljski Muzej*, bos.; *Landesmuseum*, ger.)—four buildings laid out in a square to resemble the architectural plans of state museums in Vienna and Budapest. In the center of the museum was a courtyard with a lavish botanical garden, a curious appendage to a city that spent half the year covered in snow but a source nonetheless of great pride for Sarajevo's intellectuals. Across from the museum one found the train station, which marked the end of the city. Beyond it were villages and farms where peasants raised livestock and grew vegetables to feed the burgeoning urban population. Outside of Sarajevo lay a world not yet governed by the codes of the city, a place that did not share its self-conceptions as a center of cosmopolitanism, of "civility" and "urbanity."[63]

To get from Spaho's office in the eastern tip of the city to Bralo's rectory in the west, a traveler in 1941 had three options: walk along the pedestrian paths that followed the Miljacka River, ride the rickety old tram that encircled the city, or drive in a private car along Sarajevo's thoroughfare, known at the time as King Aleksandar Street. Only a few prominent Sarajevo citizens, like Fehim Spaho, had their own cars, so most people traveled by foot or tram. When leaving the city, civilians usually traveled by train. Since Sarajevo was surrounded by mountains on three sides, many of which were covered by snow until the first days of summer, leaving by foot was an arduous task that only the most desperate attempted.[64] It would be only a matter of days before such labors would become commonplace.

• • •

When Borivoje Jevtić left the theater, when Božidar Bralo closed the parish doors, and when Leon Finci and Fehim Spaho went to bed on April 5, this was their city. Perhaps before falling asleep, Finci and Spaho reflected on how to foster reconciliation between Muslims and Jews. Jevtić possibly wondered where his friend and predecessor had been stationed with the army. Bralo may have been preparing his homily for Sunday mass the next morning. Although they all had vastly different perceptions of the impending crisis their communities faced, they unquestionably shared a fear of the unknown on the eve of war. They could hardly have imagined

63. These are terms that sociologist John Allcock uses to describe Sarajevo's culture in *Explaining Yugoslavia*, 305.
64. I have based my physical description of Sarajevo on my own impressions of the town, as well as on the descriptions offered by West in *Black Lamb, Grey Falcon* and by Donia in *Sarajevo: A Biography*. I also relied on pictures from the nineteenth and early twentieth centuries found in H. Tahmiščić, *The Measure of Sarajevo* (Sarajevo: Zavod za izdavanje udžbenika, 1970), the postcard collection in I. Huseinović and Dž. Babić, *Svjetlost Evrope u Bosni i Hercegovini* (Sarajevo: Buybook, 2004), and various wartime maps of the region.

that within days Sarajevo would become a small urban island embroiled in a fierce war that would leave hundreds of thousands homeless and dead. Occupation, genocide, and civil war would challenge each of their concepts of community and force them to draw lines around us and them in new ways. Together with their townsmen, they would soon confront the irreconcilable clash between the needs of the city and those of the confessional community and between the demands of racial and neighborhood politics.

2

AUTONOMY COMPROMISED

Nazi Occupation and the Ustasha Regime

German bombs struck Sarajevo on April 6, 1941. The bombardment continued sporadically for nine days, destroying several residential buildings, warehouses, and factories and killing ninety-three people.[1] During that time Sarajevo was isolated. The city's telephone and telegraph services worked only intermittently; few newspapers arrived from outside the city. Most residents received their information from refugees and Yugoslav troops fleeing before the German army's advance into Serbia. King Peter II issued proclamations calling on Sarajevans to stay strong and unified. But people panicked anyway. The train station was overwhelmed as Sarajevans fled the city and refugees arrived from the countryside, neither group quite sure where it would be safest.[2]

Sarajevo's municipal government remained intact during the attack. On April 7 the mayor's office formed an air-raid committee, which encouraged civilians to stockpile food and water and strictly enforced new blackout laws. Local police prohibited public meetings, enforced a city-wide curfew, and forbade residents to listen to enemy broadcasts.[3] At the same time, however, city leaders made a tremendous effort to keep life as normal as possible. *Jugoslovenska Pošta* (the *Yugoslav Post*) published the little news it received, focusing mainly on patriotic activities within the city. Rain and heavy fog sheltered residents from the attack for several days during the first week. The weather cleared up by Saturday, April 13,

---

1. ABiH, Društvo Crveni Križ, box 21, document 1373 (May 6, 1941).
2. See reports in *Narodno Jedinstvo*, Sarajevo, April 7, 1941, and in the city's main newspaper, *Jugoslovenska Pošta*, April 11, 1941, 4.
3. *Jugoslovenska Pošta*, April 7, 1941, 4, and April 9, 1941, 4. See also the minutes of Jediler from April 10, 1941, in IAS, Jediler, box 1, Zapisnik. The society appears to be one of the few that continued to meet during the bombings.

however, and bombing resumed, striking the National Theater along with other parts of the city.[4]

The first troops of the German army (Wehrmacht) arrived in the city on April 15. The Yugoslav army was ill prepared for them and withdrew into the mountains, leaving Sarajevo's local officials to fend for themselves.[5] Sarajevo's small community of Volksdeutsche eagerly met the arriving German troops and joined them in pillaging the city.[6] Serbs looked on with alarm as the Germans haughtily removed the plaque commemorating Gavrilo Princip's assassination of Archduke Franz Ferdinand in 1914, a gift they sent to Hitler. The Jews kept a low profile while the Germans destroyed the new Sephardic Jewish synagogue, burned its libraries and archives, and seized prime Jewish real estate to house the German military and administration.[7]

The mayhem that accompanied the German army's arrival died down quickly. German officers wanted to get Sarajevo under control—not that difficult a task given the pro-German attitudes of many of the city's Catholics and Muslims. The German command ordered civil servants and local law enforcement to return to their jobs and granted them the power to govern and police the city. They in turn opened factories, banks, and public institutions and established an exchange rate. Together with local authorities, German soldiers patrolled the city, confiscated private weapons and vehicles, and enforced the curfew. They suppressed resistance and sabotage with threats of execution.[8]

After the invasion of Yugoslavia, Germany, Italy, and their Axis partners partitioned the country, annexing regions on their borders and establishing separate occupied protectorates in Serbia, Montenegro, and Macedonia. In the division of the spoils, they combined parts of Croatia and Bosnia-Herzegovina to form a new ally. The Independent State of Croatia (NDH) was thus founded on April 10, 1941. Hitler and Mussolini tried to persuade mainstream Croat politicians to collaborate with them in the creation of the NDH but failed to win their support. They then awarded leadership of the newest satellite to the Ustasha Party, a small, ultraradical pro-Nazi group with a history of terrorism (including a role in the 1934 assassination of King Aleksandar). The Ustasha leaders had lived in exile in Italy since 1929,

4. ABiH, Narodno Pozorište Sarajevo, box 2, document 735 (May 12, 1941). On the weather, see Safet Šefikić, "Stradanja stanovništva od prvih bombardovanja," in Albahari et al., *Sarajevo u Revoluciji*, 2:89.

5. For a detailed military overview of the German invasion and occupation of Yugoslavia, see Mladen Colić, *Takozvana Nezavisna Država Hrvatska 1941* (Belgrade: Delta-Pres, 1973).

6. Tomislav Išek, "Djelatnost Kulturbunda i Folksdojčera," in Albahari et al., *Sarajevo u Revoluciji*, 2:284–285.

7. Descriptions of the German army's arrival can be found in Redžić, *Bosnia and Herzegovina in the Second World War*, 6–12.

8. The German army issued a series of proclamations and orders to the city, which were translated by local offices and can be found in ABiH, Poglavnikovo Povjereništvo Sarajevo/ Upravni Odjel, box 1, document 4 (April 22, 1941).

Figure 3. Destruction of the Jewish synagogue during the German bombing, April 1941. Courtesy of the Historical Museum of Bosnia and Herzegovina.

during which time they had trained a small militia and made preparations for a future Croat nation-state. They were vehemently anti-Serb, anti-Semitic, and anti-Communist and had little support in Yugoslavia.[9] Ustasha leaders often based their political fervor on their Catholic faith, especially when seeking support from the Catholic hierarchy in the region, but they promoted a version of Croat national ideology that recognized Muslims as Croats. Sarajevo was the second largest city, exceeded in size only by Zagreb, which was designated the capital of the NDH (see map 3).

Thus Hitler's "New Order" was imposed on Sarajevo. Because of their isolation during the German invasion, however, most Sarajevans did not actually know for another week that a new state had been formed or that they belonged to it. This chapter explores the transitional period, examining the negotiations that occurred between local and national leaders in the political, cultural, and religious spheres. I suggest that although many of Sarajevo's Muslims and Catholics ostensibly supported regime change, the transitional months left them confused about the ideology and practice of the new order because the local understanding of autonomy was in fundamental discord with the Ustasha and German programs. Gradually

9. Less than 10 percent of the state's Catholic population supported the Ustasha movement, and only a handful actually belonged to the Ustasha Party. See John R. Lampe, *Yugoslavia as History: Twice There Was a Country* (Cambridge: Cambridge University Press, 2000, 208).

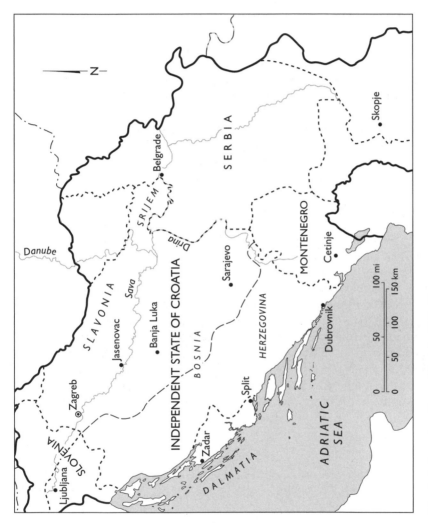

Map 3. Independent State of Croatia, 1941–45

Sarajevans realized that the Germans and the Ustashas were looking out for themselves—the needs and wishes of Sarajevo's citizenry were important only to the extent that they secured support for the Axis partners.

Political Sphere: Invasion of a State

Upon the foundation of the NDH, the Ustasha leader Ante Pavelić, a Catholic Croat from Bradina, a small village in western Herzegovina, assumed the title *poglavnik*, the Croatian equivalent of führer or duce. Since Pavelić had not yet returned from exile when the country was founded on April 10, a small cadre of his supporters established a government in Zagreb on his behalf.[10] The Ustasha core imagined themselves as liberators of a Croatia that had been occupied for eight hundred years by various foreign rulers. Accordingly, they promised to restore the Croat nation to its medieval glory by cleansing the country of foreign elements and influences, a goal that led to discriminatory and genocidal policies.[11]

The diverse population of Croatia and Bosnia posed a problem for the Ustasha leaders. The core national group—Catholic Croats—comprised only about 50 percent of the population of the NDH. The other half was divided among Orthodox Serbs, Muslims, Volksdeutsche, Jews, and Roma (gypsies).[12] This diversity was more pronounced in Bosnia, which contained an even smaller percentage of Catholic Croats. The Ustasha leaders realized that their state's survival depended on alliances between Catholics and Muslims. Thus they actively courted "Croats of the Muslim faith" with promises of autonomy for the Islamic Religious Community and equality for Muslims. Ustasha propaganda referred to Muslims as the "flower" of the Croat nation, while history books emphasized that Muslims were Catholics who had converted to Islam centuries before. Ante Pavelić even appointed a few Muslims to top positions in his government. In exchange for their support, Muslims expected a degree of political and religious autonomy. Sarajevo, the home of the Reis-ul-ulema and the Islamic Religious Community, became the unofficial center of Muslim Croatia.

10. These men included Marshal Slavko Kvaternik, the minister of defense; Mile Budak, minister of religion and culture; Mirko Puk, minister of justice; and Andrija Artuković, minister of the interior.
11. Jelić-Butić, *Ustaše i Nezavisna Država Hrvatska*, 74–83.
12. In *War and Revolution in Yugoslavia, 1941–1945*, Tomasevich deals with this briefly on page 335 and in his chapter "Alleged and True Population Losses," 718–750. The most recent census of the region was in 1931. Estimated population growth for the entire Yugoslav state was roughly 12 percent during the 1930s. With this in mind, I reviewed the census data from 1931 by county (*srez*), including all the counties that fell into the Independent State of Croatia and excluding the cities and islands annexed by Italy. This is by no means a scientific approach but offers a general estimate of the population.

From the foundation of the NDH on April 10 to the arrival of the German troops on April 15, Sarajevo had no concrete information on the status of the Yugoslav government in Belgrade. Rumors of Croatia's independence reached the city before news of Yugoslavia's capitulation. On April 17, the German commander, Colonel Becker, met with five city delegates, of whom two were Muslim and three were Catholic. The Catholic priest Father Bralo was among them. Colonel Becker confirmed that Yugoslavia had capitulated and that Sarajevo was now a part of the NDH. He gave the delegates permission to travel to Zagreb to meet with their new government, equipping them with vehicles, guns, and passports for the daylong journey. When Sarajevo's delegates arrived in the new capital, they met with a top Ustasha minister, Mile Budak, and gave him a letter describing how the city's Muslim and Catholic elite had been "caught unprepared" by the establishment of the NDH. They sought guidance and support, complaining that Sarajevo had no central leadership and was completely "disoriented."[13] A handful of men claiming to work for the Ustasha had started to arrive in Sarajevo in the days before the delegation arrived in Zagreb, but they brought no instructions from the new regime and were more interested in looting and vandalizing than in political transition.[14] Meanwhile, the poglavnik temporarily suspended all of the state's judges and attorneys, and he assigned public employees a probationary status.[15] Many local leaders were unclear about who was supposed to be running the city. The local German occupation (Stadtkommandant) exacerbated the problem by censoring domestic communication between the city and state leaders.[16] Although the Germans had gradually relaxed their control over the city by June, their authoritarian presence in the first two weeks signaled to city leaders that the Ustashas were under supervision.

While technically independent, the NDH was not treated as a completely sovereign state by its Axis partners, a reality that left an imprint on Sarajevo's leaders throughout the war. In a series of treaties, the Italian and German militaries divided the country into two zones of occupation, which they retained until the Italian capitulation in 1943, when the Germans occupied the entire state. Although the senior Axis partners put the Ustasha regime in charge of domestic affairs, they dictated foreign affairs, controlled military operations, and exploited the economic resources of the NDH. Sarajevo's local leaders thus served two masters: the Ustasha regime in Zagreb and the German occupation command. The Germans

13. Atif Hadžikadić, one of the Sarajevo delegates in Zagreb (and the city's first wartime mayor), described this meeting in "Prva Veza Sarajeva sa Zagrebom u NDH," *Osvit*, April 10, 1942, 11.

14. Ante Džeba, "Mačekova zaštita u sprezi sa Ustašama uspostavlja vlast," in Albahari et al., *Sarajevo u Revoluciji*, 2:117–118.

15. Tomasevich, *War and Revolution in Yugoslavia*, 382–383.

16. ABiH, Vrhovni Šerijatski Sud, box 195, document 281 (May 1941).

kept a small garrison, an active police force, some Gestapo agents, and several SS units in the city, as well as a local consulate office that reported to the main German embassy in Zagreb.[17] On all military matters, city authorities prudently deferred to the German command. In civil matters, the Germans expected the municipality to cover their living expenses and handle a range of tasks from laundering army uniforms to fixing the asphalt for German vehicles.[18] (That Zagreb did not compensate the municipality for these expenses would amplify tensions between the city and the regime as the war progressed.) At times the Germans catered to the Sarajevo leadership; at other times they enforced the regime's agenda. One observer tried to capture the extent of German involvement in Sarajevo by comparing it to the German occupation of France—another case where the Nazi occupiers relied heavily on a local administration while making decisions about security and economic issues.[19]

Top Ustasha leaders finally arrived in Sarajevo on April 24, eight days after the Germans. Marshal Slavko Kvaternik, the minister of defense of the NDH, and General Glaise von Horstenau, the head of German operations in Croatia, accompanied by a troop of Ustasha soldiers, police, and politicians, resolved to take control of the city. Just as the Germans had done the week before, they marched into the city with all the pomp and circumstance befitting a victor but also an occupier. Kvaternik and his officers set up a political and military headquarters, then turned to deal with Sarajevo's municipal government. Acknowledging the importance of strong local leadership for maintaining order, they kept the city's basic political infrastructure intact. They appointed Atif Hadžikadić, a Viennese-educated Muslim Croat who had been one of the delegates in Zagreb, as mayor and Petar Jurišić, a Catholic Croat, as deputy mayor. Both men were well-known Croat enthusiasts.[20] Hadžikadić had been among the first Muslims in 1918 to emphasize that Yugoslavia represented Serbs, not Muslims; he viewed interwar Yugoslavia as a period of Serb occupation of Bosnia.[21]

17. Muharem Kreso, "Sarajevo–Sjedište okupacionog sistema u Drugom svjetskom ratu" in *Prilozi historiji Sarajeva*, ed. Dževad Juzbašić (Sarajevo: Institut za istoriju and Orijentalni institut, 1997), 360.

18. See a report from the city council in IAS, Gradsko Poglavarstvo, box 842 (May 29, 1941); a note to the mayor from the local German command in ABiH, Poglavnikovo Povjereništvo Sarajevo/Upravni Odjel, box 1, document 84 (May 29, 1941); and a letter from Feldgend Trupp 219 to Sarajevo's Railway Department in IAS, Gradsko Poglavarstvo, box 849 (June 11, 1941).

19. Report from Dr. Vasilije Vojnović, filed with the archives of the Federal Secretariat for Foreign Affairs (SSIP), Belgrade, Ministarstvo Unutrašnjih Poslova Kraljevine Jugoslavije London-Kairo (1941–45), F-1, pov. Br. 496. I received a copy of this document from the personal archives of Muhidin Pelješac, who copied the material from the Yugoslav archives before the war in the 1990s. I do not know the current location of the original document.

20. Jelić-Butić, *Ustaše i Nezavisna Država Hrvatska*, 99–100.

21. Hasanbegović, *Jugoslavenska muslimanska organizacija*, 429.

Ante Pavelić appointed several deputies to oversee the transition. He appointed two deputies (*poglavnikovi povjerenici*) to serve as liaisons between Sarajevo and his regime in Zagreb: Father Božidar Bralo and Hakija Hadžić, a prominent Muslim professor. Although these men considered themselves supreme authorities in Sarajevo, they essentially served as middlemen and mouthpieces for Zagreb. They announced national laws, made public speeches, appointed commissioners to oversee institutions and businesses, and developed the city's network of propaganda, the centerpiece of which was a new newspaper, *Sarajevski Novi List* (*Sarajevo's New Daily*). Pavelić also appointed a deputy in charge of consolidating the Ustasha regime in Bosnia and Herzegovina: Jure Francetić, a Catholic Croat from Otočac, a town in the heavily Serb part of Croatia called Lika. Francetić was a die-hard Ustasha Party man and a member of Pavelić's inner circle. He, too, arrived in Sarajevo with Marshal Kvaternik on April 24, ready to overhaul the city.[22]

After two weeks of uncertain and sparse rule, Sarajevo suddenly had a complex political, military, and police structure stitched together by Ustasha ideology. Predictably, the entire government was fraught with problems. Pavelić's regime announced laws before creating an infrastructure to implement them. Many state officials lacked the political expertise necessary to run a country and often contradicted each other. Moreover, they squabbled, leading to awkward situations in which, for example, the Ministry of the Interior evicted the Ministry of Religion and Education in a fight over office space.[23] Communication between Zagreb and other cities was poor. It was unclear to local officials in Sarajevo who was responsible for doing what. For example, on April 26, Sarajevo's post office sent Deputy Hadžić a letter inquiring about its status. It had heard that "some" ministry was responsible for it, but nobody had informed the office directly.[24]

Sarajevo's military personnel were also in the dark on questions of jurisdiction. The military of the NDH was divided into two discrete forces: the Home Guard (*domobrani*), composed mainly of officers and soldiers who had been part of the Yugoslav army (or had fought previously with the Habsburg army), and the Ustasha army, a party militia that modeled itself on Himmler's SS and Fascist Italy's Blackshirts. One Croat historian argues that the separation of the armies led the Ustasha leadership to favor the political army over the regular army, which in turn "led to disagreements over how to prosecute the war, as well as competition, military confrontations, and numerous other problems."[25] In August 1941, the regime added

---

22. Rafael Brčić, "Okupacioni sistem i ustaška Nezavisna Država Hrvatska u Sarajevu (1941–43)," in Albahari et al., *Sarajevo u Revoluciji*, 2:259–262.

23. HDA, Ministarstvo pravosuđa i bogoštovlja NDH, Odjel bogoštovlja, box 1, document 2370 (May 3, 1941).

24. HM, Ustaška građa, document 1127 (April 26, 1941).

25. Zvonimir Jelinović, "Hrvatska vojska (domobranstvo) i obrana," *Časopis za suvremenu povijest* 27, no. 3 (1995): 571–573.

a third enforcement agency to handle domestic matters, the Ustasha Surveillance Service (Ustaška nadzorna služba), which included secret police and intelligence units.[26] Like the Home Guard and the Ustasha militia, the surveillance service established a regional headquarters in Sarajevo. Each of the three agencies worked separately and reported to different ministries in Zagreb.

Despite the presence of the German occupation command, Ustasha political leaders, and an array of police, military, and militia groups, Mayor Hadžikadić and Deputy Mayor Jurišić were often left to their own devices in running the city. Although the mayor was adamantly pro-Croat and had been appointed by the Ustasha leadership, he was inspired by the Habsburg bureaucratic system under which the mayor of Sarajevo had influence in shaping municipal affairs. He sought autonomy over his offices—perhaps because he was loyal to Sarajevo, perhaps because he craved power—and preferred to staff the city's agencies with his local cronies instead of men from Zagreb. He leaned heavily on a circle of Croat Muslims and Catholics who had been friends and colleagues since the 1920s.[27] The mayor, like many of the men surrounding him, had belonged to the Yugoslav Muslim Organization.

On Hadžikadić's first day in office, he distributed a memo to town employees announcing that the mayor's office would assume control of every aspect of the city's government until "normal conditions" resumed. His office encouraged departments to hire German-speaking employees, developed a commission to assess war damage from the bombing, established a temporary public kitchen for the poor (which included a group responsible for "comforting" the unemployed), delegated departments to handle traffic and road cleanup, and set food prices at prewar levels. On April 29, as Ustasha soldiers roamed the streets, the mayor's office requested pistols from the Germans to arm its own patrols.[28]

In April, city and state authorities shared the perception that this was a transitional period. After about a month, however, it became clear that the political and military organs in Sarajevo were not resolving their jurisdiction issues or formalizing relationships with one another. As the weeks dragged on with little improvement, the mayor's office grew frustrated with the absence of a central authority or a governing framework. Many town bureaucrats instinctively decided that the best way to deal with the regime

26. Tomasevich, *War and Revolution in Yugoslavia*, 341.
27. For a list of these men and a brief discussion of their relationship with Croat politics in the 1920s and 1930s see Muhamed Hadžijahić, *Od tradicije do identiteta* (Zagreb: Islamska Zajednica Zagreb, 1990), 210–211. For political background on Hadžikadić and Hadžić, see Imamović, *Historija Bošnjaka*, 493, 533.
28. See a memo from the mayor's office (Gradsko Poglavarstvo) to every municipal department in IAS, Gradsko Poglavarstvo, box 818 (April 24, 1941); and a request that the mayor's office made to the German command in IAS, Gradsko Poglavarstvo, box 825 (April 29, 1941).

in Zagreb was to abide by Sarajevo's customary response to foreign rulers: ignoring them. Disregarding new labor laws, Sarajevo's Office of Labor and Employment staffed local factories, some of which resumed production by May 9.[29] After delaying trials on the grounds that a transitional justice system should not be making decisions, city courts began hearing cases in early May and ruled according to a synthesis of the old legal system and new German laws.[30] When state officials failed to develop a plan for the distribution of food, Mayor Hadžikadić worked directly with the Italian army in Mostar to secure transports of fruit and vegetables.[31] The city government even developed a temporary budget when it realized that it could not count on the regime to maintain Sarajevo's normal social services. In early May the city limited its monetary handouts to the poor, and in June it organized public housing for those it considered the neediest: abandoned and orphaned children, the elderly, and displaced workers.[32] Although Sarajevo's leaders were doing the Ustasha regime a favor, the local Ustasha authorities felt that the leaders were undermining their power. Deputy Bralo repeatedly requested a transfer from Sarajevo, arguing to Pavelić and other state ministers that his position lacked substance and authority.[33] His complaints were not unfounded. By late May, city leaders began to view the Ustasha deputies as completely useless.

Early on, Sarajevans became suspicious of the Ustashas stationed in their city because they perceived them as outsiders. And indeed the majority were. When Marshal Kvaternik arrived on April 24, he brought with him an entourage that included roughly eight hundred members of the Ustasha militia, three hundred newly recruited Ustasha police officers, and a small group of Ustasha politicians.[34] The core of the Ustasha police and militia was made up of peasants. These men, many of whom came from the lower-class, rural, and Catholic areas of the country, were unfamiliar with the local codes of conduct in a complex multiconfessional city. The Ustasha Party expanded its ranks to include some Sarajevans, such as a small group of Muslims who donned the Ustasha uniform and participated in the party's activities.[35] But the regime continued to favor outsiders. Like Jure Francetić, the highest-ranking political authority in the city, Sarajevo's chief of police,

29. ABiH, Javni Ured Rada Sarajevo, box 1, document 465 (May 22, 1941).
30. ABiH, Sudbeni Stol, PL 261/41–1 (April 24, 1941).
31. *Sarajevski Novi List*, May 27, 1941, 4.
32. IAS, Gradsko Poglavarstvo, box 829 (May 2, 1941). For follow up reports on the city's social welfare program, see *Sarajevski Novi List* for May 5, 1941, 4; June 8, 1941, 5; and June 12, 1941, 5.
33. HDA, Ministarstvo pravosuđa i bogoštovlja NDH, Odjel bogoštovlja, box 5, document 565 (May 15, 1941).
34. Brčić, "Okupacioni sistem," 259–262.
35. Nametak, *Sarajevski Nekrologij*, 218.

Petar Petković, was an outsider. Petković hailed from Imotski, a hard-line Croat nationalist center on the border of Herzegovina and Dalmatia.[36]

The Ustasha authorities running Sarajevo never viewed their mission as one of winning local support. They acted crudely toward Sarajevo's civilians, raiding their stores and homes. Anyone who had fled the city, even if seeking temporary shelter from the bombing, was considered suspicious and faced persecution if he returned.[37] Local Home Guard officers expressed outrage at the violent tactics employed by Ustasha police and soldiers, especially protesting the mistreatment of Sarajevo's Serbs—a subject I will explore in chapter 3. The Ustasha leaders forced these officers into an early retirement.[38]

In addition to attacks on Serbs and Jews, local Ustasha officials harassed Muslims and Catholics regardless of whether they had papers from the Germans or the mayor's office. A shoemaker complained that Ustasha soldiers had taken his entire supply of leather with hardly any compensation, viewing the confiscation as theft.[39] A Muslim woman sent a distraught letter to the local Ustasha command asking it to find alternative accommodations for the eleven soldiers quartered in her home. She and another Muslim woman lived there alone, and they found it inappropriate and uncomfortable to live with so many soldiers.[40] In a society where many Muslim women refused to leave the house unless they were veiled and where non-Muslim men rarely interacted with Muslim women, such a situation was unprecedented and offensive.

Sarajevo's Muslim and Catholic political leaders felt similar harassment at the hands of Ustasha deputies Bralo and Hadžić, who tried to make up for their lack of real authority by intervening in local affairs. In May 1941, for example, Deputy Bralo flexed his muscles by packing Napredak, the local Croat cultural society, with priests and proregime Croats.[41] When members of Sarajevo's Croat Peasant Party refused to join the Ustasha Party, Bralo and Hadžić jailed or banned them from participating in public life. The Ustasha authorities thus alienated many of Sarajevo's Croats, a group that they could have profitably incorporated as a core constituency in order to build legitimacy. As I discuss shortly, Deputy Hadžić even dared to undermine the authority of Sarajevo's two highest religious leaders, Reis-ul-ulema Fehim Spaho and Archbishop Ivan Šarić, for apparently no reason

36. ABiH, Zemaljska komisija za utvrđivanje ratnih zločina okupatora i njihovih pomagača za BiH, box 3, Srećko Bujas, "Zločini nad Jevreijama u gradu Sarajevo," in fascicle "Gradska komisija za utvrđivanje zločina okupatora i njihovih pomagača za grad Sarajevo," 15. Hereafter "Bujas Report."
37. See the testimony of one returnee in IAS, Gradsko Poglavarstvo, box 818 (April 28, 1941).
38. Tomasevich, *War and Occupation in Yugoslavia*, 434.
39. HM, Ustaška građa, document 1732 (May 20, 1941).
40. Ibid., document 2335 (October 29, 1941).
41. Ibid., document 1135 (May 20, 1941).

other than to demonstrate his own power. Bralo and Hadžić each tried to foster a local cult of personality around himself. They monopolized the city's propaganda and separately published self-congratulatory articles that glorified the Ustasha regime and their personal roles in the state.[42] Several Sarajevo officials begged Pavelić to replace the Ustasha officials assigned to run the city, complaining of cronyism and bad governance, but the deputies remained in their posts until the end of August.[43]

Contempt for the Ustashas also emerged in the government-owned industries. Sarajevo's factory bosses openly criticized Ustasha-appointed managers as "incompetent." They complained that the new managers had fired loyal Muslim and Catholic workers—rescinding their benefits and pensions—and hired friends and relatives from Zagreb and northern Croatia at higher salaries. One factory official called on the ministers in Zagreb to protect the citizens of Sarajevo, claiming that they had never been treated this poorly, even by the Serb and Jewish bosses "in the darkest days of Yugoslavia."[44] Local factories also appealed to the Germans to intervene, hoping that pressure from the German army would force local Ustasha officials to improve their behavior. For example, one factory manager was upset that Zagreb had failed to provide comfortable transportation, bread, and other basic amenities to laborers from Sarajevo being sent to work in Germany. The Germans applied the appropriate pressure, forcing Zagreb to be more conscientious with Sarajevo's workers. Eventually Sarajevo's Labor and Employment Office set up new local laws, but these took several months to come into effect.[45]

By June 1941, two months after the creation of the NDH, none of Sarajevo's communities showed much enthusiasm for the Ustasha movement.[46] Vasilije Vojnović, a special attaché for the Kingdom of Yugoslavia, traveled secretly through the country to document its wartime situation and spent eight days in Sarajevo. In a report to the Yugoslav government-in-exile, he painted a picture of hostility and hatred toward the Ustasha regime from all sides of the city. He wrote that Sarajevo's Catholics were particularly angry with and wary of the local Ustasha authorities, who treated them no differently than the rest of the population. Some Catholics who had been active in Yugoslav politics had fled the country alongside their Orthodox Serb and Jewish colleagues; some who stayed found themselves imprisoned. Muslims, Vojnović claimed, were increasingly looking to the

42. *Sarajevski Novi List,* May 11, 1941, 3; *Novi Behar,* May 15, 1941, 2. Also see the pamphlets in HM, Ustaška Nadzorna Služba, document 15 (August 12, 1941).

43. ABiH, Javni Ured Rada Sarajevo, box 1, document 465 (May 22, 1941).

44. ABiH, Povjerenstvo za Radnje Drž. Hrv.—Sarajevo, box 2, document 165 (August 6, 1941).

45. See reports from the local Office of Labor and Employment from July to September 1941 in ABiH, Javni Ured Rada Sarajevo, box 1 and box 2. The factory manager's complaint is in box 1, document 723 (July 12, 1941).

46. Tomasevich, *War and Revolution in Yugoslavia,* 351f.

Germans for protection from the local regime.[47] Internal Ustasha reports suggest that he was not off the mark. Anti-Ustasha sentiments were rising in Sarajevo.[48]

A central point of conflict between Sarajevo's city government and the regime in the first month was that the Ustasha authorities focused on their own narrow ideological agenda. City leaders, by contrast, had more pragmatic concerns: currency and inflation, personnel, political transition, and widespread unemployment. They wanted concrete transitional laws and financial assistance.[49] Even town leaders who supported aspects of the regime's long-term agenda wanted to stabilize the city first. Ignoring these local concerns, the regime in Zagreb forged ahead with plans to Croatianize the state.

At the top of the Ustasha agenda was purging the country of non-Croats, purifying the Croatian language, and building a system of propaganda. The state's earliest laws included the Decree for the Defense of the People and the State, which called for the death penalty for anyone who acted against the interests of the state and for a version of the Nuremberg laws, which defined Aryan status and legalized discrimination against non-Aryans and non-Croats—Jews, Serbs, and Roma.[50] These alleged outsiders, who made up more than a third of Sarajevo's residents, faced strict curfews, random street checks, mandatory police registration, job dismissals, and property confiscation. By law Jews had to wear a yellow Jewish Star of David inscribed with the Croatian and German words for Jew (*Židov*, Croatian; *Juden*, German). They were forbidden to leave the city or to marry or socialize with Aryans. Attacks against Serbs focused on the Serbian Orthodox Church, which was outlawed alongside the Cyrillic alphabet and Serbian books and culture. From April to August 1941, local Ustasha police jailed, deported, or executed all of Sarajevo's Orthodox Serb priests and their families.[51] Other local laws forbade Jews and Serbs from going to the movies or wearing Croatian symbols, particularly Muslim attire like the fez (a type of hat). Zagreb added new laws throughout the summer and fall of 1941 to restrict and monitor all aspects of Jewish property, work, and lifestyles.[52] The local Ustashas worked closely with the Germans to establish

47. Report from Dr. Vasilije Vojnović, filed with the archives of the Federal Secretariat for Foreign Affairs (SSIP), Belgrade, Ministarstvo Unutrašnjih Poslova Kraljevine Jugoslavije London-Kairo (1941–45), F-1, pov. Br. 496.

48. HM, Ustaška građa, document 1263 (June 26, 1941).

49. ABiH, Javni Ured Rada Sarajevo, box 1, document 467 (May 19, 1941).

50. *Zbornik zakona i naredaba Nezavisne Države Hrvatske* (Zagreb: Narodne novine, 1941), 1:40 and 109–115; Tomasevich, *War and Revolution in Yugoslavia*, 383–384.

51. HM, Ustaška građa, document 1849 (August 12, 1941). For descriptions and background on the priests targeted, see *Spomenica pravoslavnih sveštenika—žrtava fašističkog terora i palih u narodnooslobodilačkoj borbi* (Belgrade: Savez udruženja pravoslavnog sveštenstva FNRJ, 1960), 50, 92–93, 148.

52. Specific laws and provisions for Sarajevo can be found in *Sarajevski Novi List*, May 14, 1941, 5; May 24, 1941, 5; May 25, 1941, 4; and July 4, 1941, 5.

Jewish labor battalions as well. The Roma escaped some of this early persecution, only to have similar property and social laws introduced against them later in the war.[53]

The Ustasha authorities in Zagreb were so busy with their ideological program that it took them months to create the basic laws Sarajevo's leaders needed in order to govern. They ignored multiple requests from local bureaucrats seeking advice on state policy. Instead, they reprimanded Sarajevo's civil servants for failing to speak "proper" Croatian, to replace Cyrillic signs on city buildings, and to enforce the strict Aryan employment laws.[54] City leaders wanted to introduce new laws slowly and systematically in order to minimize disruptions. They were not bothered by lower-level officials who corresponded using the Cyrillic alphabet, though it was a national offense. In a show of deference to the Sarajevo approach, the Germans initially published citywide edicts in the Latin and Cyrillic alphabets because residents used both.[55]

Pavelić's regime refused to postpone or soften its ideological and racial laws to appease the city's local elite. These laws were at the center of the Ustasha social revolution and the ideology of the rebirth of the Croat nation. The regime failed to recognize the inevitable, serious administrative complications that would occur in a city as diverse as Sarajevo. Knowing that the city needed expertise and manpower, Sarajevo's officials were reluctant to remove non-Aryans and non-Croats from the government and state-owned industries.[56] Two-thirds of all Sarajevo's schoolteachers were Serbs, 40 percent of the city's lawyers were Jews, and many—perhaps half—of its judges, doctors, and civil servants were Jews or Serbs.[57] Zagreb proceeded anyway. As the widespread dismissals commenced, the city began to suffer serious shortages in every profession, from veterinary to janitorial work.

In addition to being ignorant of—or, more precisely, indifferent to—the effects of national policy on Sarajevo, the Ustasha bureaucracy was disorganized. Officials made demands on the town without creating an infrastructure to support their policies. For example, authorities in Zagreb were frustrated that Sarajevo's officials had failed to complete the registration of the Serb population in a timely manner. In a letter to the minister of justice and religion, the head of the regional government in Sarajevo wrote that registering Serbs was a difficult task, since the new government had hastily

53. On new laws against Roma, see ABiH, Ured za kolonizaciju—Sarajevo, box 19, document 9988 (September 15, 1943).

54. IAS, Gradsko Poglavarstvo, box 842 (May 24, 1941); ABiH, Javni Ured Rada Sarajevo, box 1, document 765 (July 22, 1941).

55. City offices continued to use Cyrillic in some reports and on local receipts. See examples from IAS, Gradsko Poglavarstvo, boxes 821 and 822. For the German case, see *Narodno Jedinstvo*, April 19, 1941.

56. *Sarajevski Novi List*, May 13, 1941, 5.

57. HM, Ustaška građa, document 1263 (June 26, 1941). See also Haim Kamhi, "Jevreji u privredi Bosne i Hercegovine," in Kamhi, *Spomenica*, 67–70.

shut down the region's Orthodox parishes without delegating to another institution the responsibility for tracking Serbs.[58] Since births, deaths, marriages, and migrations were traditionally recorded by religious institutions, local officials were at a loss as to how to comply with the order. Furthermore, the purges had left the city administration short-staffed. Sarajevo was not the only city affected. Local governments from nearby towns, such as Vlasenica, warned officials in Sarajevo that the removal of Serbs would destabilize the entire region.[59]

The Ustasha regime also issued blanket laws that affected a broad constituency, leaving local officials to clean up the mess. On May 1, 1941, the Ministry of National Economy in Zagreb (Ministarstvo narodnog gospodarstva) ordered Sarajevo's treasury to cease payments for pensions, disability, and social welfare until it was determined that the recipient was a "citizen" and not a Jew, Serb, Montenegrin, Slovene, or someone aiding the Serb cause.[60] But because citizenship had not yet been clearly defined, the mayor's office was immediately inundated with petitions from civilians trying to prove their eligibility. There was also a mad rush to track down birth and marriage certificates from state institutions that had been done away with by the Ustashas only months before. Many city officials tried to comply with the regime's laws, but gradually they grew disillusioned with the futility of some laws and the absence of others.

Similarly, Ustasha authorities in Sarajevo carried out property confiscation in a frenzied manner. In one instance, they tried to take over Sarajevo's Volta Cinema on the grounds that the owner was a Jew. The owner wrote a scathing letter criticizing them for this injustice: "You justified your act by stating that [I] am a Jew from Zagreb. . . . I am not, nor have I ever been, a Jew. . . . I am a German citizen, and of course, an Aryan." He insisted on immediate restitution of his property and a full apology.[61] The Ustashas also ignored the sensitive issue of joint businesses and homes, often trampling on the rights of a Muslim or Catholic co-owner when confiscating a Serb's or Jew's business. One Muslim man, who had co-owned a building with a Jewish man since 1908, appealed to the city to evict the Ustasha tenants and force them to pay him back rent. A Catholic woman who had divorced her Jewish spouse a decade before fought for the return of her business, which had been taken. Another Catholic man complained that his café had been seized because it was situated in a building owned by a Jew, even though

---

58. HDA, Ministarstvo pravosuđa i bogoštovlja NDH, Odjel bogoštovlja, box 5, document 521 (July 1941).

59. Tomislav Dulić, *Utopias of Nation: Local Mass Killing in Bosnia and Herzegovina, 1941–1942* (Stockholm: Elanders Gotab, 2005), 184.

60. ABiH, Poglavnikovo Povjereništvo Sarajevo, Odjel za socialnu skrb i narodne zdravlje, box 1, document 482 (May 1, 1941).

61. ABiH, Povjerenstvo za radnje Drž. Hrv.—Sarajevo, box 3, document 552 (July 1, 1942).

the café owner himself was a "pure Croat."[62] Sarajevans from various corners of the town became annoyed by the ridiculousness of the new legal system, which made everyday activities challenging to accomplish. Curfew laws, for example, required people to be off the streets from 10:00 p.m. until 5:00 a.m. But the daily train to Mostar, the major city in Herzegovina, left each night at midnight. One man, Atif, noted that after dropping off his sister-in-law and her two small children at the train station to catch their train, he had to walk home, whereupon three Ustasha policemen accosted him for violating curfew laws. How, he wondered, was he supposed to get home from the train station?[63]

When the mayor's office recognized that its strategy of ignoring the Ustasha authorities was not working, it tried to minimize the damage to city residents. Some city departments undermined local Ustasha offices and sought advice directly from their superiors in Zagreb; others bypassed state decrees by creating their own regulations.[64] Such acts provoked the Ustasha authorities. In early June, the Ministry of National Economy in Zagreb accused Sarajevo's mayor's office of a laundry list of infractions: failing to organize local bureaus in accordance with state law, interfering in state processes, withholding mandatory reports and time-sensitive information, hindering the process of property confiscation, and allowing Jews and Serbs to retain "economic power."[65] The head of one city department admitted in June that he had ignored many of Zagreb's requests simply because his office could not handle the extra work.[66]

Rather than resolving Sarajevo's bureaucratic inefficiency and addressing the city's detachment from the Ustasha regime, Ante Pavelić in June 1941 added another layer to the government. He formed a system of regional governments, each under the direction of a Zagreb-appointed official called the *veliki župan*. The position is usually translated as "grand governor," but "county executive" seems more accurate since "governor" implies a degree of autonomy that was inconsistent with the responsibilities of the *veliki župan*. Sarajevo became the seat of the major county in Bosnia, called Velika župa Vrhbosna. The first county executive was Derviš Omerović, a member of Sarajevo's Muslim Croat elite. At first, Omerović aligned himself closely with the Ustasha deputies in Sarajevo; however, by the fall of 1941, he had joined other local Muslim leaders in trying to work around the Ustashas. This became easier in August because Pavelić finally

62. These examples can be found in ABiH, Povjerenstvo za Radnje Drž. Hrv.—Sarajevo, box 2, document 6 (August 1, 1941) and document 26 (no date), and box 3, document 606 (July 7, 1941).

63. Ibid., box 3, document 479 (June 23, 1941).

64. For example, ABiH, Javni Ured Rada Sarajevo, box 1, document 465 (May 22, 1941); HM, Ustaška građa, document 1163 (June 6, 1941).

65. ABiH, Povjerenstvo za Radnje Drž. Hrv.—Sarajevo, box 3, document 381 (June 3, 1941).

66. ABiH, Javni Ured Rada Sarajevo, box 1, document 609 (June 11, 1941).

heeded local pleas, transferring Bralo and Hadžić to other positions and eliminating their position altogether. Even so, local leaders could influence only certain aspects of Ustasha policy. They could mitigate the city's burdens but could not remove them. Law enforcement always fell outside their sphere of influence.

The city's powerlessness on matters related to policing became more apparent as the regime expanded its discriminatory agenda. While not yet murderous on a mass scale, this campaign included arrests and targeted executions. Local leaders complained about the erratic nature of the arrests and their inability to intervene.[67] This was one area, however, where the regime was simply not willing to compromise. The Ustasha regime faced an expanding Serb resistance force in the countryside, known as the Chetniks, which threatened to spread to cities with large populations of Serbs. The Chetniks were led by former Yugoslav army officers who maintained close ties to the Yugoslav king and espoused a Serb nationalist platform.[68] Although their presence in Sarajevo was minimal (in large part because sympathizers tended to flee), the Ustasha authorities justified their persecution of any Serb on the grounds of national security. Men were particularly susceptible to being singled out for persecution. From April to June, the Ustasha police arrested about a thousand Serb men from Sarajevo. They questioned and then released the majority, although they tortured and killed a few, notably the Serbian Orthodox metropolitan of Dabro-Bosna, Petar Zimonjić.[69]

On June 23, a day after the Nazis broke the Nazi-Soviet nonaggression pact by invading the Soviet Union, a new organized resistance emerged in the NDH: the Communist Partisans.[70] On Stalin's instructions, the Communists had remained on the sidelines in the early months of the war. Once given the go-ahead by Moscow, however, they quickly organized an insurgency. The Ustasha police in Sarajevo reacted by arresting well-known Communists, a group that included sixteen Serbs, five Jews, four Muslims, and

67. See, for example, the correspondence between Fehim Spaho and Marshal Kvaternik, IAS, Ostavština Fehima Spaha, box 3, document 696 (May 7, 1941).

68. The best historical accounts on this subject are Jozo Tomasevich, *The Chetniks* (Stanford: Stanford University Press, 1975); and Simon Trew, *Britain, Mihailović, and the Chetniks, 1941–1942* (New York: St Martin's, 1998).

69. For information on Serb arrests in Sarajevo in the spring of 1941, see IAS, Ostavština Borivoja Jevtića, box 4, document 460 (July 6, 1941). See also Mihajlo Lukić's testimony in Vladimir Dedijer and Antun Miletić, eds., *Proterivanje Srba sa ognjišta 1941–1944, Svedočanstva* (Belgrade: Prosveta, 1990), 382–384, and Branko Vašić's testimony in the same book, 499–502.

70. There are many scholarly studies on the Partisan leader, Josip Broz Tito, as well as studies on the relations between the Partisans and other forces. See the chapter on this subject in Redžić, *Bosnia and Herzegovina in the Second World War*. See also the biographies of Tito: Stevan Pavlowitch, *Tito—Yugoslavia's Great Dictator: A Reassessment* (London: C. Hurst, 1992); Milovan Djilas, *Tito: The Story from Inside* (New York: Harcourt Brace Jovanovich, 1980); and Phyllis Auty, *Tito: A Biography* (Harmondsworth, UK: Penguin, 1974).

two Croats.[71] Again, the local government simply stood by, partly because it was helpless in police matters, but also because it, too, viewed the Communists as a security threat. Throughout July, as news of military resistance in the countryside mixed with rumors of possible resistance cells in the city, the Ustasha police arrested more people, deporting many of them to newly constructed labor and concentration camps.

By August, Pavelić's regime realized that it was not fighting isolated pockets of resistance but was engaged in a full-fledged civil war. In Sarajevo, the situation became more explosive, quite literally, on July 30 when members of the resistance blew up the boiler room of the city's railroad. The Ustasha police promptly arrested twenty-six Serbs and Jews for the alleged sabotage. They believed that the Communists and the Chetniks—whom they viewed at the time as a single united enemy—had infiltrated the city under their noses. Rather than holding the detainees for interrogation, however, they publicly executed the men as a warning to the rest of the city. Leon Finci, the Sephardic Jew who had hoped to foster reconciliation with his Muslim neighbors in the days before the war, was among the dead bodies left rotting on a Sarajevo street for the next few days.[72] Though it is possible that he had become involved with the small underground resistance, his execution most likely resulted from his position as a Jewish community leader and his brother's pro-Communist activities before the war. Most of the Sarajevans executed by the Ustasha authorities over the summer of 1941 were considered political—not racial or religious—enemies. Thus, because the regime was not yet claiming exclusively racial motivations, local leaders were willing to accept the arrests.

Cultural Sphere: Toward a Linguistic Purity

Part of the tension between Pavelić's regime and Sarajevo's Muslim and Catholic leaders stemmed from their contradictory perceptions of what Sarajevo's role should be in the new state. When Sarajevo was plucked from its marginal position in the Yugoslav state to take on the prestigious role of the second-largest city of the NDH, members of the local elite believed it would finally be recognized as a cosmopolitan Balkan center. They were nostalgic for Sarajevo's grandeur and prominence during the age of empires. The Germans—ever a thorn in the side of the Ustashas—catered to this idea, particularly as they sought to strengthen their alliance with Sarajevo's

---

71. Moni Finci, "O hapšenju komunista i otkrivanju tehnike pokrajinskog komiteta u Sarajevu, krajem Juna 1941. godine," *Prilozi institut za Istoriju* 19(1982): 316.

72. On the executions, see Josip Albahari Čučo, "KPJ i pogrom nad Jevrejima," in Albahari et al., *Sarajevo u Revoluciji*, 2:684–685; HM, Ustaška građa, document 67 (August 11, 1941); Donia, *Sarajevo*, 193. On Leon Finci, see Josip Bilik Pepo, "Prva strijeljanja na vracama," in Albahari et al., *Sarajevo u Revoluciji*, 2:169.

Muslims. In May 1941, a German journalist complimented Sarajevo's culture and architecture by calling it a "Muslim Innsbruck."[73] This was not Zagreb's vision for Sarajevo's future.[74]

A clash began immediately as Zagreb tried to superimpose a homogenous Croat national culture on the city. In the realm of high culture, the Ustasha leaders planned to co-opt for its own cultural agenda Sarajevo's National Theater and the Land Museum, which had been transformed overnight into the Croatian State Theater and the Croatian State Museum in Sarajevo, respectively.[75] But Mihovil Mandić, the Ustasha-appointed trustee for the museum, and Alija Nametak, the trustee for the theater, had their own visions for shaping Sarajevo's culture. Although both men supported the NDH, they were dedicated to their hometown and wanted its cultural institutions to be first-rate. Moreover, they wanted to make Sarajevo a national center that could serve as a model for other parts of the state. In May and June 1941, Mandić sent a series of letters to Ustasha ministers in Zagreb requesting that they transfer intellectuals with academic expertise from Zagreb to Sarajevo to strengthen the museum's credentials. He also demanded that Pavelić issue the museum a *štatut*, a formal clarification of its official status. Museums in other cities all had one. Mandić felt slighted that the reputation of Sarajevo's museum was not considered on par with that of other cultural institutions in the NDH, even though it was the largest museum in the state.[76]

Meanwhile, at the Croatian State Theater, Alija Nametak, Fehim Spaho's son-in-law, warned Ustasha deputies Bralo and Hadžić in his first days on the job that for reasons of artistic integrity, he would not dismiss the Serbs and Jews in his ensemble until he found good actors of Muslim and Catholic backgrounds to take their places.[77] Like Mandić, Nametak appealed for more funding. He wanted to build a new National Theater. Sarajevo, he argued, should have a theater to reflect its standing as the "cultural center of Bosnia and Herzegovina" and "the second largest city in the Independent State of Croatia"—such a theater was a "state and national necessity."[78] In June, Nametak was joined at the theater by a new artistic director (*atendant*), Ahmed Muradbegović, a distinguished Muslim intellectual with long ties to the Croat national project. Muradbegović followed Nametak's line of reasoning and announced that the "theater's repertoire will consist primarily of national dramas, religious and popular folk pieces ... in which the Islamic culture of the East will be merged with the Catholic

73. *Sarajevski Novi List*, May 16, 1941, 2.
74. Ibid., August 30, 1941, 7.
75. ABiH, Zemaljski Muzej Sarajeva, box 37, document 2 (May 2, 1941).
76. Ibid., document 61 (May 23, 1941), and document 6 in the secret document collection (June 7, 1941).
77. ABiH, Narodno pozorište Sarajevo, box 2, document 735 (May 12, 1941).
78. Ibid., document 769 (May 29, 1941).

culture of the West." He also underscored a general perception among Sarajevo's intellectuals about their role in upholding the city's traditional codes, noting that "in order for the theater to serve the ethical and religious needs of the community, it needs to pay particular attention to religious content."[79] Regardless of their support for the state, Sarajevo's Croat intellectuals remained dedicated to Sarajevo and its confessional legacies. Like their political counterparts, they often ignored the regime's demands and continued to run their cultural institutions as they saw fit.

This did not deter Zagreb from implementing its cultural agenda in other ways. Language became a contentious issue. Just as the Croatianizing campaign sought to purge non-Croats from the state, so it sought to purge foreign influences from the Croatian language and culture. This move was problematic in Sarajevo, where Croatian, Serbian, and Turkish words mixed with a distinct local slang to form the Sarajevan dialect. In Sarajevo, not even the Croats spoke "proper" Croatian. Pavelić's regime demanded that Sarajevans change their vocabulary. An entire ministry in Zagreb was dedicated to overseeing language reforms to ensure that the country spoke what they determined to be a homogenous and pure Croatian. For example, in place of *kancelarija* (office), the language bureau wanted everyone to use *ured;* in place of *šef* (boss) it instituted *ravnatelj,* and then days later it replaced *ravnatelj* with *upravitelj.* Local offices that ignored the laws were censured.[80] Others got around them. In a subtle rebuke of the language laws, Muradbegović announced that the National Theater would use both classical and popular language in order to make its repertoire truly local (*domaći*).[81]

The word *domaći* would take on special significance in Sarajevo throughout the war, alternately referring to culture and people. The word can be translated as "domestic," "homemade," "indigenous," "internal," "local," "native," or "vernacular." When used to describe people, it often indicated that someone belonged to the community, or was *naši,* "one of us." Such a distinction in Sarajevo, as in many Balkan communities, not only meant that an individual belonged, fit in, or came from a particular place but also implied that the community had a certain obligation to look out for him. *Domaći* culture encompassed the dialect, customs, and shared experiences of the local culture, thus undergirding the entire concept of *naši.*

79. *Sarajevski Novi List,* July 4, 1941, 4.
80. On the language laws and subsequent tensions between Sarajevo's officials and the Zagreb regime, see reports from the local Office of Labor and Employment (ABiH, Javni Ured Rada Sarajevo). In box 1, see document 467 (May 19, 1941) and document 765 (July 22, 1941). In box 2, see document 1003 (August 1941). See also a warning from Jure Francetić on the importance of using the Ustasha greeting and language in all state offices: Hoover Institute Archives, Tomasevich Papers, memo, box 11 (July 16, 1941).
81. *Sarajvski Novi List,* July 4, 1941, 4.

Given the population's strong loyalty to its city, the most insulting linguistic reform that Zagreb imposed concerned the city's name itself. On June 23, 1941, the regime quietly changed it from "Sarajevo" to "Sarajvo," which it considered linguistically purer Croatian. The rationale, based on a Habsburg study from 1889, was that "Sarajevo" was a foreign word. Apparently anticipating a storm of protest, local Ustasha officials did not formally announce the change to the public until June 28, at which time it appeared on page three of *Sarajvski Novi List* (note the change in spelling from *Sarajevski*).[82] As expected, the city resisted. Two weeks later, Zagreb reversed the name change, cunningly blaming overzealous local officials who had acted without the regime's consent.[83] However, various Zagreb ministries had started using "Sarajvo" as early as June 7, which suggests that the initiative had begun in Zagreb long before it reached Sarajevo. For the next few months, officials in Sarajevo did not know whether they were supposed to embrace or reject "Sarajvo," so many used the two words interchangeably in hopes of appeasing their superiors.[84] By 1942, "Sarajvo" was dead.

Renaming institutions became another tactic that the regime used to reduce Sarajevo's sense of civic identity and put its own national stamp on the city. When Sarajevo's Yugoslav Club applied to change its name to Sarajevo's Civic Club, Députy Bralo rejected the request and unilaterally announced that it would be called the Croat Club.[85] Likewise, authorities in Zagreb refused to compromise with the staff at the Land Museum, who fought vehemently to keep the Habsburg name *Zemaljski*—a name they preferred because it implied "worldly." Attempting to remove all local distinctions, the Ministry of Culture even rejected the museum's suggestion of prefacing "Land Museum" with "The Independent State of Croatia." It was to be the Croatian State Museum and nothing else.[86] There was no room for a city identity in the regime's vision of the nation-state.

Nevertheless, Sarajevo's leading intellectuals were optimistic that they could transform the city into a reputable cultural center within the confines of the regime. They pressured Zagreb to open a college campus, arguing that Sarajevo should have a higher-education system to support its status as the center of culture and education in Bosnia.[87] When it came to working

---

82. Ibid., June 28, 1941, 3. The official name of the periodical is *Sarajevski Novi List*; it was spelled without the "e" for only about two weeks.

83. Ibid., July 4, 1941, 3.

84. For an example of a Zagreb ministry's use of "Sarajvo," see HDA, Ministarstvo pravosuđa i bogoštovlja NDH, Odjel bogoštovlja, box 1, document 9721-B-1941 (June 7, 1941). For an example of inconsistent use of the two terms by local officials, see ABiH, Poglavnikovo Povjereništvo Sarajevo/Odjel za socialnu skrb i narodne zdravlje, box 4, document 4877 (July 16, 1941).

85. HM, Ustaška građa, document 1130 (May 5, 1941).

86. ABiH, Zemaljski Muzej Sarajeva, box 38, document 1194 (October 2, 1942), and box 39, document 7 (January 13, 1943).

87. HM, Ustaška građa, document 2353 (May 15, 1941).

with the regime, the intellectuals had an advantage over their political counterparts because they were crucial to the local Ustasha propaganda network. They wrote articles, plays, and poems glorifying the regime and the state, which helped create a culture of loyalty in Sarajevo. In exchange, the Ustasha authorities limited their intrusions into cultural activities, allowing seemingly harmless plays to slip beneath the radar and nourishing the intellectuals' illusions that Sarajevo would become a leading city in the cultural and political life of the NDH.

Religious Sphere: A Marriage of the Secular and the Observant

While Sarajevo's political leaders wrestled with issues of jurisdiction and the city's intelligentsia grappled with shaping a localized national culture, its religious leaders faced off with the Ustasha regime over what "religious autonomy" really meant. The Independent State of Croatia had two official religions: Catholicism and Islam. The Lutheran (Evangelical) Church, as part of the German sphere, also functioned legally within the state and received state funding. The regime's discriminatory laws of April 1941 had dissolved the Serbian Orthodox Church and placed the Jewish communities under supervision.

The Ustasha regime hoped to use religious institutions to expand its influence and legitimize its message. In Sarajevo, as elsewhere, politicians delivered proclamations in the largest houses of worship and began state celebrations with formal blessings from every faith, giving events an air of ecumenical legitimacy.[88] At the same time, the regime courted religious leaders with promises of autonomy and a return to a more traditional society. It needed the clergy's assistance to deliver its message, especially in places like Sarajevo where civilians held their religious leaders in high regard. The way that the regime began to infiltrate religion was subtle. Religion had always been a state affair in Bosnia. Under the Habsburgs, clergy and religious judges were on the state payroll; under the Yugoslavs, they swore mandatory oaths to the king. Pavelić's regime followed suit. Clerics received state salaries and faced dismissal if they refused to take oaths of loyalty to the poglavnik.[89] Yet the private affairs of the religious communities had been left alone, which allowed for the maintenance of separate confessional structures. The Ustasha regime gradually crossed the line of acceptable government involvement and soon threatened the foundational premises of the very religious institutions whose support it hoped to secure.

88. ABiH, Poglavnikovo Povjereništvo Sarajevo, box 1, document 344 (May 7, 1941).
89. HM, Ustaška građa, document 1611 (May 8, 1941).

Figure 4. Baščaršija, circa 1941. Courtesy of the Historical Museum of Bosnia and Herzegovina.

Co-opting Islam

When the Germans confirmed rumors of Croatia's independence to Sarajevo's leaders on April 17, many Muslims had grave concerns. Although some supported the German occupation, they felt blindsided by the creation of a state without their consent. On April 19, 1941, Reis-ul-ulema Spaho received an anonymous letter from forty Muslim intellectuals begging him to intervene with the German command to fight for Bosnian autonomy with a Muslim government. These Muslims feared, correctly, that Catholic Croats would dominate the NDH. They wrote, "We must not allow ourselves to look on peacefully with disappointment and resignation while in front of our noses, our homeland, a land in which Muslims are a majority, is taken from us and given to the new Croat state."[90] They were too late. Spaho informed his advisers on April 26 that he had already met with Marshal Kvaternik and had received Ante Pavelić's personal guarantee that the Ustasha regime would respect the Islamic faith and secure "freedom, equality, and happiness" for Muslims in the Croat state.[91]

90. IAS, Ostavština Fehima Spaha, box 3, document 701 (April 19, 1941).
91. *Glasnik Islamske Vjerske Zajednice,* April–May 1941, 147.

From day one, however, the Ustasha leaders disagreed with Muslims over what this "freedom" entailed. For many Muslims, Islam was a way of life that privileged aspects of its own law, the Sharia, over civil law. In previous eras, a difficult process of negotiation had occurred wherein the Islamic Religious Community had maintained autonomy over socioreligious matters, such as marriage, conversion, custody, and inheritance, while relinquishing control of commercial and criminal matters. At the very least, Muslim leaders expected to retain this control; many Islamists hoped to expand and institutionalize it. The Ustasha regime made broad, ambiguous promises. For example, the minister of religion, Mile Budak, announced in May 1941 that the Islamic Religious Community would have "the same kind of religious educational autonomy as the Catholic Church has in the Independent State of Croatia."[92] It did not become clear until the following autumn, when Budak's office drafted a new statute for the community, exactly what this meant—that the community's autonomy over socioreligious issues would be subordinate to state laws.[93]

In the early months of the transitional period, however, Sarajevo's Muslim religious leaders still believed they could appropriate the regime's policies in Islam's favor. In late April, when the Ustashas arrived in the city, Reis-ul-ulema Spaho asked them to enforce laws that he deemed important for the community's ethics. His first request: Ustasha police must crack down on Muslim prostitutes. He informed the new local authorities that "the head scarf and veil are obligatory to Muslim women and serve as a sign of chastity and honesty" and asked that "in order to protect that significance and the reputation of such clothes . . . the police authorities prevent the misuse and abuse of such clothes by those persons who are not worthy to wear them."[94] This was hardly the kind of religious-political alliance the Ustasha party chiefs were seeking. Much to Spaho's dismay, they ignored his pleas, and some even frequented the bordellos.

From this point, Fehim Spaho's relationship with the Ustasha regime rapidly deteriorated. After the wrongful imprisonment of several Muslims in May, Spaho demanded that Marshal Kvaternik intervene. Kvaternik refused on the grounds that the police investigations were a necessary part of national security.[95] Less than two weeks after promising to work with Spaho, Kvaternik abandoned him. At the same time, Deputy Hakija Hadžić, the highest-ranking Muslim Ustasha in Sarajevo, began to exclude Spaho from meetings concerning the future of Islam in the new state. In early May 1941, Hadžić alluded to bad blood between Spaho and himself but hoped they could put their personal differences aside and work together as

92. *Novi Behar,* May 15, 1941, 3.
93. ABiH, Vrhovni Šerijatski Sud, box 7, document 491 (October 30, 1941).
94. ARIZBiH, Ulema Medžlis, document 2000 (May 13, 1941).
95. IAS, Ostavština Fehima Spaha, box 3, document 696 (May 7, 1941).

state servants. Hadžić needed Spaho to sanction the Ustasha agenda, but rather than trying to win him over, Hadžić demanded his cooperation. On May 11, without ever asking him directly, Hadžić announced that Spaho would preside over a special prayer for the NDH at the largest mosque in Sarajevo. A few weeks later, Hadžić informed Spaho that he had organized a meeting to discuss the religious-educational autonomy of Muslim Croats. He wanted Spaho to preside over the meeting, but he, Hadžić, would set the agenda. Hadžić invited the Muslim Croats he liked, ignoring Spaho's request to invite specific representatives from the imams. Spaho responded by ignoring the invitation and the meeting.[96]

Miffed, Deputy Hadžić turned to the leaders of El-Hidaje. Since its foundation in 1936, El-Hidaje had sought to return power to the Muslim ulema. Its leader, Mehmed Handžić, recognized that the regime change created a new opportunity for his career and his movement. How else could one explain his transformation from a religious leader who preached that Islam was incompatible with nationalism to one who asserted that the NDH offered the best possible protection for Islam?[97] Handžić and other leaders of El-Hidaje were pleased at the chance to help develop a statute for the Islamic Religious Community and deliberately went against Spaho's wishes that such an endeavor be handled privately through the official organs of the Islamic Religious Community.[98]

On June 6, 1941, Spaho issued a public statement in response to both El-Hidaje and Deputy Hadžić. Without naming names, he chastised El-Hidaje for breaking Muslim discipline and criticized Hadžić and other Muslim Ustashas for exploiting the Islamic Religious Community for their personal political objectives. He requested that the regime allow the administration to solve its internal divisions privately and leave questions of Islam alone.[99]

By the end of that week, however, Spaho had abandoned any fleeting illusions that Pavelić's regime had ever planned to work with him. First, he found out that Deputy Hadžić had gone behind his back to transfer and replace several religious judges in the Sharia courts. Next, the Ministry of Justice began revamping the entire Sharia court system. Soon afterward, the local Ustasha base infiltrated Muslim religious schools and private organizations. It also tightened its control over the Islamic Religious Community's purse strings, giving Spaho the runaround when he requested state subsidies to pay bills and salaries. For most of the summer of 1941,

96. Evidence of the ongoing exchange between Spaho and Hadžić can be found in IAS, Ostavština Fehima Spaha, box 3, document 697 (May 1941), document 707 (May 30–31, 1941), and document 709 (June 4, 1941).

97. On Mehmed Handžić's position in 1940, see lecture notes found in Hadžijahić, *Od tradicije do identiteta*, 75. On his wartime stance, see *El-Hidaje*, July 14, 1941, 221–223.

98. Zlatko Hasanbegović, "O pokušajima donošenja Ustava Islamske vjerske zajednice u Nezavisnoj Državi Hrvatskoj," *Časpois za suvremenu povijesti* 27, no. 3 (1995): 77–78.

99. IAS, Ostavština Fehima Spaha, box 3, document 710 (June 6, 1941).

Spaho unsuccessfully appealed to the city treasury, the state treasury, and the ministries of Religion, Education, and Justice to track down his missing funds. Time and again, the ministries either ignored his letters or advised him to contact another department.[100]

Meanwhile, the regime continued its incessant assault on Muslim religious autonomy. On June 19 Spaho was shocked to learn from the local newspaper that every mosque in Sarajevo would be holding special celebratory services for the birthdays of two important Catholic Croats: Ante Starčević, the nineteenth-century founder of a right-wing Croat nationalist movement, and the poglavnik, Ante Pavelić. Spaho shot a letter back to the minister of justice, asserting that such a service was unprecedented and, moreover, violated Islamic law. He argued that "these kinds of prayers are unknown to Islam; Muslims do not participate in them." Instead of explaining his refusal in terms of Islam alone, however, Spaho deliberately antagonized the regime by equating its request to the Yugoslav government's efforts to hold prayers in the mosques on Vidovdan, the Serb holiday commemorating the fall of Kosovo.[101] Comparing the Ustasha leaders to their archenemy, the Serbs, would not have endeared Spaho to his national leaders.

Failing to come to a consensus with Hadžić, Spaho appealed to Zagreb. He hoped to resolve their misunderstandings over state funding, religious courts, and the content of Muslim services by appointing his own representative to work directly with the Ministry of Religion. He selected an expert on Islamic culture and law who had excellent credentials, including time served in a Yugoslav prison for his Croat attitudes. Spaho sent a dossier filled with glowing recommendations to the Ministry of Religion in early June and waited. Failing to get any response, he contacted the ministry again in early July, only to discover that his letters had been set aside during an internal reorganization. A week later, the ministry sent him a one-line note rejecting the appointment on the grounds of "bad information," never bothering to clarify what that meant.[102]

Then, Deputy Hadžić and County Executive Omerović inflicted on Spaho a grave insult: they appointed a trustee, like those appointed for the Jewish and Serb organizations, to oversee the Islamic Religious Community

100. On the friction between Spaho and the Ministry of Religion, see correspondence in HDA, Ministarstvo pravosuđa i bogoštovlja NDH, Odjel bogoštovlja, box 3, document 34,443/41 (June 14, 1941). For the specific legal codes on the Sharia court system, see *Zbornik zakona i naredaba NDH,* 3:25 and 73–74.

101. HDA, Ministarstvo pravosuđa i bogoštovlja NDH, Odjel bogoštovlja, box 1, document 14,974/41 (June 19, 1941).

102. The exchange between Spaho and the Ministry of Religion can be found in HDA, Ministarstvo pravosuđa i bogoštovlja NDH, Odjel bogoštovlja. In box 1, see the series of documents labeled 12,118/41 (June 12—July 9, 1941) and document 16,405/41 (June 27, 1941). In box 2 see document 20,297/41 (July 6, 1941).

and its publications.[103] The appointment infringed on every aspect of Spaho's authority and autonomy. Hadžić justified his decision to Zagreb with claims that Spaho harbored secret loyalties to the old regime and had failed to incorporate the symbols and ideology of the NDH into his work. The central problem, it seems, was that although Spaho had removed the title "Kingdom of Yugoslavia" from the cover page of the official journal of the Islamic Religious Community, *Glasnik Islamske Vjerske Zajednice,* he had replaced it with a religious subtitle in Arabic rather than with "The Independent State of Croatia." To Hadžić, this was proof that Spaho was antiregime and needed supervision. Livid, Spaho warned Hadžić to stay out of his affairs. He demanded that the Islamic Religious Community be treated with the same respect as the Catholic hierarchy.[104] His appeal fell on deaf ears.

Four days later, Deputy Hadžić informed Spaho that Sarajevo's Ustasha headquarters (or rather Hadžić himself) had withheld state subsidies from his office. He cited two reasons: Spaho's failure to adopt an "official seal" that conformed to the laws of the NDH and his continued usage of "Kingdom of Yugoslavia" stationery. Shocked and dismayed at having his loyalty questioned, Spaho bypassed Hadžić and responded directly to the Ministry of Justice and Religion in Zagreb. He complained that Sarajevo's chief–of police and the local Ustasha deputies were putting enormous and unnecessary pressure on him, making it difficult to run the Islamic Religious Community.[105] Spaho then contacted the Ministry of the Interior with a more personal complaint. He wrote that in his forty-six years as a public servant, from the Austro-Hungarian period to the present, he had never been treated so poorly and disrespectfully. He was not upset only about the content of the complaints but about their derogatory tone, an insult to someone of his stature. Spaho acknowledged that yes, he still used Yugoslav stamps and stationery, but so did everybody else in Sarajevo because they had never received new ones. He noted that he might have expected this disrespectful behavior from Hakija Hadžić but not from other government officials, who should be more sensitive and reverent toward religious servants.[106] At the end of his letter he warned the ministries that this treatment must stop and the Islamic Religious Community must be left in peace, or else he would resign. However, he also made several discernible concessions to reaffirm his loyalty to the state. That month, a large picture of Pavelić graced the cover of the journal of the Islamic Religious

103. On the appointment and Spaho's reaction, see IAS, Ostavština Fehima Spaha, box 3, document 726 (July 25, 1941) and document 733 (August 1, 1941). See also the records in the Ustasha secret police: HM, Ustaška građa, document 1769 (August 2, 1941).

104. HM, Ustaška građa, document 1711 (July 25, 1941).

105. For Hadžić's accusation and Spaho's response, see HDA, Ministarstvo pravosuđa i bogoštovlja NDH, Odjel bogoštovlja, box 4, document 258 (August 4, 1941).

106. IAS, Ostavština Fehima Spaha, box 3, document 733 (August 4, 1941).

Community, which featured a lengthy article on the importance of Muslims in the NDH.[107]

Perhaps one of the most telling examples of Spaho's tense relationship with the local Ustasha leadership was a 1941 court dispute between Spaho and Deputy Božidar Bralo. In July, Bralo had borrowed two car tires from Spaho because he needed to go to Zagreb. He promised to return them but never did. After exchanging several letters on the matter, Spaho did what any self-respecting Sarajevan would have done: he brought the matter to court. Spaho sued Bralo for return of the tires or for their value, arguing that they were new and the property of the Islamic Religious Community. Bralo responded that the tires were old, and moreover that a ministry had requisitioned them and refused payment. According to Spaho, this was not his problem. He had lent the tires to Bralo personally, not to any ministry, and it was therefore Bralo's duty to return them or provide compensation. The case dragged on for two years with witness testimony offered by a range of top Ustasha leaders, including Kvaternik himself. The courts eventually ruled in favor of Spaho's ownership and right to compensation in 1943, nearly two years after Spaho's death.[108]

The fact that the local Ustasha authorities could not resolve such a simple matter illustrates the deep tensions between the regime and the Islamic Religious Community, as well as the deeply flawed structures of the transitional government. The court's decision in Spaho's favor, however, suggests that Sarajevo's judges respected local legal precedents and would not kowtow to unrealistic demands. Indeed, Spaho and other Muslim leaders consistently found an ally in Sarajevo's courts, which tried to soften the effects of the regime's policies on local institutions. In a land dispute involving a Muslim cemetery, for example, the local courts ruled in favor of the Muslims against the state treasury. Although neither side had proof of ownership, the courts sided with a local precedent for awarding land with religious graves to the communities buried there.[109]

The Church between Church and State

Ecstatic over Croatia's independence, Sarajevo's Catholic leaders welcomed the Ustasha leadership to the city. The archdiocese in Sarajevo had few complaints in the early months. It approved of the way that the Pavelić regime had initially separated the religious and political spheres and dismissed the notion that the NDH would or should become a clerical Fascist state.[110] Unlike the Islamic Religious Community, Catholic religious

---

107. *Glasnik Islamske Vjerske Zajednice*, August 1941.
108. See the various reports listed in the case file ABiH, Sudbeni Stol, PO 234/41.
109. ABiH, Sudbeni Stol, PO 164/1941, September 14, 1942. The case started in 1941 and was completed in 1942.
110. *Katolički Tjednik*, June 29, 1941, 3, and July 20, 1941, 1.

Figure 5. Archbishop Ivan Šarić and German soldiers, downtown Sarajevo. Courtesy of the Historical Museum of Bosnia and Herzegovina.

orders and priests promptly received salaries and grants for their humanitarian work.[111] Moreover, Catholic clergy had no problem offering mass for leading Catholic Croats or praying for the state. Such acts did not go against the church's religious tradition and were not uncommon in Catholic services. Archbishop Šarić was highly respected, and his appointments and concerns were addressed in a timely and efficient manner (see figure 5 for an image of the Archbishop). He enjoyed great flexibility in expanding and solidifying the Catholic Church in Bosnia. Sarajevo was not the administrative and religious center of Catholicism in Croatia—a distinction that fell to Zagreb's archdiocese—which meant that Archbishop Šarić did not have to deal with the kinds of theological and administrative issues that Spaho faced.[112] He could focus exclusively on his religious mission.

111. See, for example, HDA, Ministarstvo pravosuđa i bogoštovlja NDH, Odjel za bogoštovlja, box 3, document 45384 (July 22, 1941).

112. There is a substantial historiography on the relationship of the Catholic Church and the Ustasha regime, which ranges from the scholarly view that the Independent State of Croatia was a clerical Fascist state that participated enthusiastically in the Ustasha genocidal campaigns to the view that the Catholic Church was another victim of the state. Historian Mark Biondich succinctly reviews the Western historiography on the subject in "Religion and Nation in Wartime Croatia: Reflections on the Ustaša Policy of Forced Religious Conversions, 1941–1942," *Slavonic and East European Review* 83, no. 1 (1995): 71–116.

It is a testament to the incompetence of Sarajevo's Ustasha chiefs that they managed to offend the archbishop. In June 1941, Šarić locked horns with Deputy Hadžić over which appointments fell within the religious domain and which within the civil. All appointments, from pastors to teachers, had to be approved by the Ministry of Religion. To Šarić, this seemed to be a simple bureaucratic procedure. In June he appointed a priest to serve as a religious instructor at a local children's home. Deputy Hadžić, a Muslim, informed him that the candidate had been rejected because he lacked "moral qualifications."[113] The suggestion that a Muslim official had the right to determine who was morally qualified to teach Catholic education seemed to infuriate Šarić, who published an article the following week on the necessity of the Catholic Church's complete autonomy in matters of school, religion, and marriage.[114]

The Franciscan order had a more complicated relationship with the regime. The Franciscans' private monastic customs and independent pastoral work make it difficult to generalize about their role in the new state. Moreover, the order in Herzegovina formed a separate administrative organization from that in Bosnia, a fact often blurred in discussions of the Franciscans' wartime legacy. Among Bosnia's Franciscans, there were priests who joined the Ustasha movement and participated in attacks on Jews and Serbs (for which some were expelled from the order by the Franciscan provincial in Sarajevo) and others who joined the Communist Partisans (also frowned upon by the order).[115] Most of Bosnia's Franciscans adopted the rather Ottoman stance of avoiding politics and finding ways to continue with their pastoral and educational duties privately. Even when the order did support the political regime in the Independent State of Croatia, the Vatican forbade it from participating in the Ustasha Party or engaging in or benefiting from discriminatory policies.[116]

Archbishop Šarić apparently hoped to use the changing of the guard to take over the monastic order. He actively sought to limit the Franciscans' influence and reduce their state subsidies.[117] At the same time, he deliberately excluded local Franciscan societies from participating in larger Catholic movements, such as Catholic Action, a European religious movement designed to revitalize and mobilize Catholic youths.[118] For its part, the Franciscan provincial in Sarajevo appealed to local private organizations

113. ABiH, Poglavnikovo Povjereništvo Sarajevo/Odjel za socialnu skrb i narodne zdravlje, box 2, document 3451 (June 28, 1941) and box 3, document 3855 (July 15, 1941).
114. *Katolički Tjednik*, July 6, 1941, 4.
115. Ćiril Petešić, *Katoličko svećenstvo u NOB-u 1941–1945* (Zagreb: Vjesnikova Press agencija, 1982), 204.
116. Jure Krišto, *Katolička Crkva i Nezavisna Država Hrvatska, Dokumenti* (Zagreb: Hrvatski Institut za Povijest), 2:81–82; Novak, *Magnum Krimen*, 534.
117. Barun, *Svjedoci i učitelji*, 343.
118. Gavran, *Lucerna Lucens?* 119. A good article on the role of Catholic Action in interwar Croatia is Sandra Prlenda's "Young, Religious, and Radical: The Croat Catholic Youth

for donations and made its own compromises with the Ustashas to secure funding and continue its work.[119] The clash between the two Catholic institutions would take many forms during the war, revealing an ongoing power struggle to be the dominant voice in the Catholic community.

By comparison with the Islamic Religious Community, the Catholic Church fared extremely well under the new regime. Culturally, Catholicism was the dominant religion of the NDH; the church had more autonomy than any other private institution in the state. Thus the majority of Catholic leaders tended to overlook minor conflicts with local political leaders as side effects of the war and transitional era. Over the coming year, however, the archdiocese and the Franciscan order would find themselves struggling for a voice in defining what role Catholicism would play in the Croat national concept, a struggle that would lead to rifts among Sarajevo's Muslims and Catholics.

The Religious-Civil Legal Conundrum

Although the state was secular, the NDH had won broader support because the Ustashas had promised autonomy and influence to Catholic and Muslim religious leaders. While the regime placed restrictions on religious autonomy, it nevertheless kept some of its promises by allowing religious courts to have jurisdiction in cases involving divorce, custody, and inheritance. A separate religious legal system functioned parallel to the civil courts. Judges in the two court systems respected this division. If a Sarajevo Muslim brought a religious issue to the civil courts because he disliked the previous verdict of the Sharia courts, civil judges refused to hear the case.[120] Although the Catholic Church did not have the same elaborate court system as the Islamic Religious Community, Catholic leaders expected the same degree of autonomy. Napredak, a progressive Croat cultural society, reminded members to respect and uphold both "the state and church governments."[121]

In the institutionally and religiously heterogeneous society that existed in Sarajevo, it is not difficult to imagine the manifold problems produced by such a system. First, the Sharia courts did not have jurisdiction over Muslims from parts of the former Yugoslavia that fell outside the borders of the NDH. Since two Muslims could not marry in civil court, refugees and residents who lacked proper papers were often left without a legal

Organizations, 1922–1945," in *Ideologies and National Identities*, ed. John Lampe and Mark Mazower (Budapest: Central European University Press, 2004).

119. Such an appeal can be found in ABiH, Hrvatsko kulturno društvo Napredak, box 143, document 2116 (August 14, 1941).

120. For example, see ABiH, Banski Stol, Pl: 309/41–42 (March 12, 1942).

121. ABiH, Hrvatsko kulturno društvo Napredak, box 144, document 2835 (January 17, 1942).

means of marrying. Consequently, some of these Muslims lived together and had children out of wedlock, a threat to conservative Islamic notions of a moral society.[122] Mixed marriages presented other problems because the state could not force an individual of one faith to uphold the laws of a different faith. This was not a new issue. In 1938, Fehim Spaho had written an important article on the subject, underscoring that both Christian and Muslim leaders worried about the cultural implications of interfaith marriage because the offspring of such marriages were more prone to secular lifestyles.[123] In 1941 and early 1942, both the archdiocese and the Islamic Religious Community forbade their faithful from entering mixed marriages except in special cases, usually requiring the religious conversion of one's future spouse.[124] The Sharia courts ruled very conservatively on mixed marriages, refusing to recognize them even in cases where a couple had been married for years. At the same time, however, every judge had his own reaction to the challenges of the war and the pleas of individuals. For example, one judge allowed a marriage between a Muslim man and a non-Muslim woman whose papers were missing.[125]

Another problem with the parallel legal systems was that not everyone living in Sarajevo was Muslim or Catholic. The Ministry of Justice and Religion never worked out how other religious communities would fit into the system, forcing local judges and city leaders to sort out complex cases. Sarajevo's civil courts heard divorce and custody cases for Russian Orthodox residents, as they had in the interwar era. Yet when members of the now-defunct Serbian Orthodox Church took claims to the civil courts, local judges were wary of ruling because there were no precedents. In one custody battle between two Orthodox Serbs, a local judge ruled according to what he vaguely described as "German family law." However, the court of appeals overturned the verdict on grounds that the judge had ignored an earlier Orthodox Church ruling on the matter. The new verdict also emphasized that civil courts did not have the authority to retry a case that had been decided previously by a religious court.[126] In a case involving a divorce between a Catholic and an Orthodox Serb, the judges determined that the divorce was invalid in the "civil context," most likely because the marriage had originated in the Orthodox Church.[127] Yet that church was now obsolete, so what was the couple to do? While the judges and the

122. ABiH, Vrhovni Šerijatski Sud, box 7, document 401 (August 8–9, 1941).
123. Fehim Spaho, "Mješoviti Brakovi," *Glasnik Islamske Vjerske Zajednice,* January 1938, 1–9.
124. *Katolički Tjednik,* July 13, 1941, 1; ARIZBiH, Ulema Medžlis, document 387/42 (January 22, 1942).
125. In ABiH, Vrhovni Šerijatski Sud, box 195, see document 454 (February 22, 1942).
126. All the court transcripts are available in ABiH, Sudbeni Stol. For the case involving Russian Orthodox residents, see PL: 66/42 (February 20, 1942); on the lack of precedents in judging Serbian Orthodox cases, see PL: 688/41–2 (December 31, 1941) and PL: 340/41 (March 18, 1942).
127. HM, Ustaška građa, document 2324 (October 28, 1941).

government attempted to work out these questions of legal jurisdiction, Orthodox residents were left in the lurch.

The tiny Protestant communities faced different kinds of legal hurdles. Excluded from the state's earliest laws and policies, Protestants, as well as members of other small religious denominations such as the Old Catholic Church, a splinter Catholic Church in Yugoslavia, often found themselves on the margins of society.[128] In November 1941, Bosnia's Calvinists (Reformirana kršćanska filijana crkva) filed a claim in Sarajevo's courts for property erroneously awarded to the Lutherans (Evangelička crkva). Ignoring the fact that there were several Protestant denominations in the country, state law treated them as a single church. The Calvinists dissented and wanted their property returned. The case was complicated further by a division between the large German Lutheran Church and a small Slovak Lutheran Church, each with its own property and administration. When the Calvinists appeared in Sarajevo's courts, the judges refused to hear their case, stating that they could not interfere with the Protestant religious courts. It was irrelevant to the judges that no such Protestant court system existed in the NDH. They handed the case over to the minister of justice, who apparently ignored the issue.[129] Gradually, however, the Ministry of Justice realized that the separation of religious and civil courts impeded the functioning of a centralized nation-state. Much to the dismay of religious leaders, in 1944, the ministry would make overtures to legalize civil marriage and restrict the jurisdiction of all religious courts.[130] For the time being, however, Muslim and Catholic leaders continued to assert their moral authority and socioreligious autonomy.

• • •

With the backing of Nazi Germany, the Ustasha regime ascended to power in April 1941 and immediately began to encroach on all aspects of Sarajevo's government, cultural life, and religious institutions. By the end of the summer, the regime's influence in municipal affairs was entrenched and pervasive. Sarajevo's Muslim and Catholic leaders were unimpressed by Ustasha governance and resented the regime's attempts to usurp their authority. They were bothered not by the notion of Fascism or the new world order but rather by the Ustasha authorities' ineptitude, the regime's blatant contempt for Sarajevo's culture and traditional values, and the limitations

128. On Bosnia's Protestants, see the court case in ABiH, Sudbeni Stol, 62/42 (November 10, 1941). On the problems facing members of the Old Catholic Church, see HDA, Ministarstvo pravosuđa i bogoštovlja NDH, Odjel za bogoštovlja, report from the Stara Katolička Crkva, box 3, document 48527 (August 1, 1941).

129. ABiH, Sudbeni Stol, 62/42.

130. HDA, Ministarstvo pravosuđa i bogoštovlja NDH, Odjel za Pravosuđe, box 1, no document number (July 7, 1944).

placed on municipal authority. Thus many people came to dislike the foreign Ustashas even more than the Germans, who did not attempt to remake the city's image or oust local leaders. Instead, the German army welcomed a relationship with Sarajevo's leaders that left local decision making to the city government in exchange for obedience. In the years to come, these first impressions would lead some city leaders, particularly in the Muslim community, to view direct German occupation as preferable to the Independent State of Croatia. Distrust for the new regime soon changed to outrage as the number of Sarajevans excluded from participating in the new state began to outnumber those welcomed into the folds of citizenship. As the regime's genocidal agenda became more transparent over the summer of 1941, local leaders recognized that the regime was not only destabilizing the city but beginning to erode its social fabric.

3

CONVERSION AND COMPLICITY

Ethnically Cleansing the Nation

The complexity of Sarajevo's legal, cultural, and historical dynamics made it difficult, and at times impossible, for local authorities to lump city residents into the Ustasha regime's prescribed categories of Aryan and non-Aryan, Croat and foreigner. Instead of accepting the terms of identity set out by the Ustasha and German programs—or even the kinds of identities promoted by modern ideologies in general—Sarajevo's elite continued to conceive of their citizenry as belonging to a cultural community, which they defined by religion, and a civic community, which they defined in terms of the city. While bonds could form along one of these two lines, individuals had the strongest ties when they shared both faith and a Sarajevo identity.

At the forefront of the Ustasha regime's ideological agenda was purifying the nation, an idea that translated into a notoriously brutal genocidal campaign against Serbs, Jews, and Roma.[1] This campaign was hardly top-down or monolithic, as it was depicted in early histories. The regime implemented its policies at different tempos and to varying degrees across the state, often leaving the tasks of identifying and removing the so-called pariah groups to local officials. Consequently, the character of violence and the experience of victim groups differed from town to town.[2] In Sarajevo,

---

1. In addition to studies of the Ustasha regime and the NDH cited thus far (those by Tomasevich, Jelić-Butić, and Krizman), standard reference works on the Holocaust in the NDH include Yeshayahu Jelinek, "Nationalities and Minorities in the Independent State of Croatia," *Nationalities Papers*. 8, no. 2 (Fall 1980): 195–206; Zdenko Levntal, ed., *Zločini fašističkih okupatora i njihovih pomogača protiv Jevreja u Jugoslaviji* (Belgrade: Savez jevrejskih opština Jugoslavije, 1952); Jaša Romano, *Jevreji Jugoslavije 1941–1945. Žrtve genocida i učesnici Narodnooslobodilačkom Ratu* (Belgrade: Savez jevrejskih opština Jugoslavije, 1980); and Jonathan Steinberg, *All or Nothing: The Axis and the Holocaust, 1941–43* (London: Routledge, 1990).

2. This argument is made with broad empirical evidence from across Bosnia in Dulić, *Utopias of Nation*, and Marko Attila Hoare, *Genocide and Resistance in Hitler's Bosnia: The Partisans and the Chetniks, 1941–1943* (Oxford: Oxford University Press, 2007).

everything from the process of confiscating property to the deportations of Jews had a distinctly local quality. When city leaders realized that the state would not respect their criteria for determining who belonged to the national community, they began to question and, at times, challenge aspects of the regime's genocidal agenda.

Confronting the Fiction of Race and Nation

Citizenship laws in the Independent State of Croatia, like those in many parts of Hitler's Europe, were ambiguous and subjective, which left room for local interpretation.[3] Legally, the Ustasha regime defined a citizen as "a national member of the Aryan race, who exemplifies through his attitude that he is not against the goal of the independence of the Croat nation and who is prepared to serve the Croat nation and the Independent State of Croatia."[4] To clarify the racial component, the Ustasha regime adopted a version of the Nuremberg laws, which established elaborate blood requirements for Jews and Roma that required evidence of several generations of racial purity. The regime also restricted marriage and social interactions between Aryans and non-Aryans and forbade non-Aryans to participate in public life.[5] But determining who was an Aryan and implementing the racial laws were processes that took months. As the Ustashas navigated their way through the murky world of identity politics, slowly clarifying laws to establish a more uniform and biologically based standard for identity, Sarajevo's leaders attempted to protect their own standards for determining who belonged to the community. A large chunk of the Sarajevo citizenry eluded ready classification in the newly manufactured categories. In June alone, the city government was inundated with requests from people trying to determine whether they qualified for citizenship, a status that entitled them to jobs, property, and social welfare. Town officials repeatedly asked Zagreb to clarify citizenship requirements. But as late as July 1941, three months after the Ustasha regime came to power, the ministry of the interior still had no definitive answers. It asked Sarajevo's officials to delay responding to local petitions until the state passed legislation on the matter. It would

---

3. For comparative purposes, see Chad Bryant, "Either German or Czech: Fixing Nationality in Bohemia and Moravia, 1939–1946," *Slavic Review* 61, no. 4 (Winter 2002): 702.

4. "O državljanstvu" (April 30, 1941), in *Zbornik zakona i naredaba Nezavisne Države Hrvatske* (Zagreb: Narodne novine, 1941), 1:107–108.

5. "O rasnoj pripadnosti," *Zbornik zakona i naredaba Nezavisne Drzave Hrvatske*, 1:109–111; "O državljanstvu," *Zbornik zakona i naredaba Nezavisne Države Hrvatske*, 1:107–108; "O zaštiti arjeske krvi i časti Hrvatskog naroda," *Zbornik zakona i naredaba Nezavisne Države Hrvatske*, 1:113–115; and "O zaštiti narodne i arijske culture hrvatskog naroda," *Zbornik zakona i naredaba Nezavisne Države Hrvatske*, 2:40.

take months for Zagreb to offer any advice on how to resolve the petitions, leaving local officials to draw their own conclusions.[6]

Fueling the city's confusion was the regime's failure to articulate a hierarchy of racial, religious, and national identities, giving the entire process of discrimination an arbitrary feel. The regime established a subjective exemption process for each of the target groups, at times favoring race, at times religion. Local officials interpreted such laws in their own ways. For example, national laws allowed Jews to apply for a special "honorary Aryan" status. Top Ustasha leaders like Pavelić and Kvaternik intended such a provision to protect family members (according to the German embassy, both men had wives of Jewish descent).[7] But the ambiguity of the category meant that local officials often had power in ascribing identities. Much to the surprise of Ustasha leaders, officials in Sarajevo liberally used the provision of "honorary Aryan" to help local Jews.[8] Another subjective provision allowed imams in rural Muslim villages to use witness testimony instead of documentary evidence to prove a Muslim's racial background.[9] Such subjective approaches to determining race set the stage for great variation in how individuals were identified in the racial spectrum; it also granted significant power to local leaders.

In the Sarajevo mind-set, religion trumped race. If a Jew converted to Islam or Catholicism, most city leaders believed he had in essence solidified his right to be a Sarajevan and thus warranted exemption from racial laws and protection from discrimination. If a Roma was a Muslim, the Islamic Religious Community believed he fell under its jurisdiction and should be spared imprisonment. This is not to say that Sarajevo's Muslims and Catholics dismissed all notions of race. In chapters 4 and 5 I elaborate on the ways that certain groups invoked racial language to fit their agendas. But at this early point in the war, the vast majority of the city's political and religious leaders believed that being Catholic or Muslim de facto meant being an Aryan Croat.

One of the earliest controversies between Sarajevo and the Ustasha regime concerned the racial status of Muslim Roma. In April 1941, Pavelić's regime declared all Roma to be non-Aryan, making no legal distinction between Muslim, Catholic, and Orthodox Roma.[10] This law fit the paradigms of German racial theories, which suggested that the Balkan Roma

6. ABiH, Poglavnikovo Povjereništvo Sarajevo, Upravni Odjel, box 1, document 318 (July 17, 1941).

7. See a report from Nachbass Kasche in Hoover Institute Archives, Tomasevich Papers, records from the captured German documents held at the U.S. National Archives, box 3, T:120, roll 5782 (May 3, 1941).

8. Examples of these appeals can be found throughout ABiH, Povjerenstvo za Radnje Drž. Hrv.—Sarajevo, box 3.

9. "O rasnoj pripadnosti" (April 30, 1941), in *Zbornik zakona i naredaba Nezavisne Države Hrvatske*, 1:109.

10. Ibid., 109–111.

were nomadic "parasites" who threatened the new social order and should be cleansed from the nation.[11] In Sarajevo, however, the small Roma community was considered not a nomadic group or a recent arrival but an imbedded part of the town. Although the exact date of their arrival in Sarajevo is unclear, Roma are mentioned in regional documents as early as the sixteenth century and in town reports in the nineteenth century. As a community, Sarajevo's Roma spoke the local Slavic language in addition to a Romani dialect; they lived predominantly on the peripheries of the city in a neighborhood called Alipašina. Most were Muslim, although they generally lived, worshipped, and were buried separately from other Muslims. Still, they shared cultural customs with the town's other Muslims, such as holiday celebrations, food, and elements of attire (e.g., Muslim Roma women frequently wore the veil and head scarf).[12] Whereas the racial debate focused primarily on Muslim Roma, tensions also surrounded policies concerning Sarajevo's Orthodox Roma, a community that played an important role entertaining in Sarajevo's cafés, restaurants, and streets. Many restaurants refused to fire their "Serb Gypsies," despite orders from the Ministry of the Interior that the town had to to adhere to national employment laws that forbade Orthodox Roma from working in public venues.[13]

As the local Ustasha authorities began firing and interning Sarajevo Roma in the spring and summer of 1941, Muslim leaders spoke out against the discrimination against fellow Muslims.[14] The Ministry of the Interior in Zagreb did not want to risk losing Muslim supporters over the legal classification of one tiny group, so it opened an investigation into the racial background of Roma. In doing so, it recognized that this was "not only a question of theoretical value, but of practical importance, since there have already been several instances where Croats of the Muslim faith, particularly Gypsies with Aryan background, have been fired from state employment." The ministry formed a commission of Sarajevo's leading Muslim intellectuals, including Hamdija Kreševljaković, a prominent member of the Croatian Academy of Arts and Sciences; Šačir Sikirić, the rector of the central Islamic theological school; and Derviš Korkut, a curator at the Croatian State Museum. The commission thoroughly researched the history

11. Sevasti Trubeta, "'Gypsiness,' Racial Discourse and Persecution: Balkan Roma during the Second World War," *Nationalities Papers* 31, no. 4 (December 2003): 503.

12. Muhamed Hadžijahić, "Bosanski Romi 1941–1942," *Časopis Naše teme* 7–8 (1984): 1313–1323. On Roma in the earlier period, see Muhamed A. Mujić, "Položaj cigana u jugoslovenskim zemljama pod osmanskom vlašću," *Prilozi za orijentalnu filogiju* 3–4 (1952–53): 157, 164.

13. HM, Ustaška građa, document 2163 (September 19, 1941) and document 134 (October 13, 1941).

14. Statistical information on the Roma community is incomplete. Roma were not included in the Kingdom of Yugoslavia's formal census date. An 1871 Ottoman census estimated that Roma formed about 1 percent of Sarajevo's population, but thereafter they were defined according to their religion (predominately Muslim). Jozo Tomasevich estimates that twenty-five thousand Roma lived in the Independent State of Croatia, of which twenty thousand were killed by the Ustasha. See Tomasevich, *War and Revolution in Yugoslavia*, 608–610.

of Bosnia's Roma, using German, Austrian, and Bosnian sources. It concluded that two types of Gypsies existed in Bosnia: "White Gypsies," pure Muslim Croats who were integrated into Bosnia's major cities, and "Black Gypsies," who lived nomadic criminal existences and communicated mostly in the Gypsy language. However, much to the dismay of the Ustasha regime (and probably of the Germans as well), the commission concluded that "according to scientific evidence, both of these aforementioned classes of Gypsies are considered Aryan, particularly of the Indo-European/Indo-German races."[15]

Sarajevo's Muslims recognized that the racial classification of Roma had broader implications for Muslims in Croatia. In a state where racial status determined one's right to live, Muslims were justifiably wary of any ideology that defined a portion of their religious community as an inferior group. They realized that if the new rulers could label some Muslims non-Aryan, nothing prevented them from reclassifying other Muslims in the future. By August 1941, this concern, which had been limited to a small circle of intellectuals, began to interest the general reading public. *Sarajevski Novi List* published a lengthy article on the subject, noting that the "Gypsy question" was central to Croatia's goals and ideology and that it needed to be decided upon from religious, cultural, educational, and political perspectives. The author warned readers that the issue had immediate ramifications because Ustasha officials had forced many Muslims to register as non-Aryans, and this resulted in their termination from state jobs and factories.[16] Although everyone knew that the author was referring to Muslim Roma, the use of just "Muslim" reveals the community's intent to unite along religious lines.

Local Ustasha authorities responded shrewdly. They tacitly accepted the commission's conclusions and then adopted a new policy for persecuting Roma in Sarajevo: an antibegging campaign. Who could complain about a citywide effort to reduce street-side begging and poverty? The new program especially targeted poor Muslim refugees and Roma. After a protest from Muslim humanitarian groups, which believed that the Ustasha regime should provide services to people displaced by the war, the Ustashas started to distinguish between different kinds of beggars. Beggars deemed "genuinely needy" (refugees and city poor) became eligible for social welfare, while beggars deemed "criminal" were arrested and sentenced to hard labor. The police defined "criminal" as anyone from a group with a history of begging and a "proclivity for laziness," hardly a subtle reference to the popular perception of Gypsies. This new discourse allowed the police to continue their campaign against Muslim Roma by labeling them a social rather than a racial threat. The police established registries of beggars similar to those for non-Aryans and made failure to register punishable

15. HM, Ustaška građa, document 1742 (July 30, 1941).
16. *Sarajevski Novi List*, August 3, 1941, 5.

by forced labor or imprisonment.[17] By the fall, private Ustasha documents noted that the plan to remove Roma from areas around the city of Sarajevo had been successful.[18] Publicly, the city's daily newspaper avoided any mention of race, instead announcing, "Believe it or not, there are only 93 beggars in Sarajevo!"[19] From that point, the term "beggar" assumed an almost racial connotation in the Ustasha documents related to Sarajevo.

The city government did not seriously object to the removal of the beggars, whom it, too, found to be a strain on local resources. The Islamic Religious Community, however, grew outraged at the deliberate targeting of Muslims. The Ulema Medžlis complained to Zagreb that the Ustasha police frequently arrested and deported "White Gypsy Muslims" of "pure Aryan heritage" who had fulfilled all their religious and state duties.[20] Zagreb responded that any prisoner had the power to release himself by providing proof of religion from an imam and the police. Since the Roma were already held behind barbed wire, acquiring this documentation was impossible. The local press encouraged Muslim Roma still living in Sarajevo to wear the fez to physically mark their religious—and by extension, racial—identity.[21] Suggesting that a piece of clothing was enough to denote an individual's racial status mocked racial ideology and set the dangerous precedent of allowing individuals to assert their identity rather than waiting for the government to assign one to them.

Separating race from religion became even more complicated with Sarajevo's Jews. From April to October 1941, as many as two thousand Jews—20 percent of the city's Jewish population—converted to Catholicism or Islam.[22] Because the regime monitored religious institutions, these conversions, like religious appointments, required governmental approval. Zagreb initially left the process in the hands of local officials. Surprisingly, Sarajevo's bureaucrats handled conversion as a standard practice, just as they had done before the war. A priest or imam performed the religious service and sent an affidavit to the mayor's office. The Jewish convert then paid a

17. Ibid., August 12, 1941, 6.
18. HM, Ustaška građa, document 1572 (July 23, 1941) and document 2064 (September 2, 1941).
19. Sarajevski Novi List, September 20, 1941, 7.
20. Glasnik Islamske Vjerske Zajednice, August 1942, 228–229.
21. Sarajevski Novi List, August 26, 1942, 4.
22. The exact number of converts is difficult to ascertain because records are incomplete and scattered among different archives, but the available evidence suggests that at least 500 Sarajevo Jews converted to Islam, and around 1,400 converted to Catholicism. General conversion requests can be found in the records of the mayor's office. See IAS, Gradsko Poglavarstvo, boxes 877–1005. Box 878 has dozens of conversion petitions filed through the Ashkenazi community in September 1941, and box 1005 has a report from the mayor's office on the conversions of Jews to Islam in 1941. Jewish conversions to Islam are recorded in the records of the Ulema Medžlis. See ARIZBiH, Ulema Medžlis, documents 1111/43 to 1125/43 and 1824/43 to 1836/43. The Italian consulate in Sarajevo reported on conversions to Catholicism. In HM, Ustaška građa, see document 2340 (October 31, 1941) and document 4005 (November 25, 1941).

conversion tax to the city, whereupon a local official (sometimes the mayor himself) signed off on the conversion. Some priests and imams helped Jews submit the necessary forms; the mayor's office occasionally waived the tax for Jews who could not pay. After receiving all the paperwork, a city clerk sent a notice to the former and new religious communities, requesting that they update their books to record the Jew's new religion and, in the case of a Muslim convert, his or her new name.[23]

It appears that all parties involved—the local officials, the religious clergy, and the Jewish convert—hoped the conversion would eventually exempt the Jew from the Ustasha regime's racial laws or at least buy him time to escape. The new Muslim or Catholic often appealed to be exempt from forced labor or asked for permission to remove his yellow Star of David, requests that some local officials granted.[24] But as requests for conversions (and by extension racial exemptions) multiplied over the summer, the Ustashas grew perturbed. Although the regime had not banned Jewish conversion, state law clearly defined Jew as a racial category. Religious conversion should have been moot when applying anti-Jewish laws, since a Muslim or Christian of Jewish background remained racially a Jew. The Ustasha authorities reminded Sarajevo that racial law trumped religious affiliation and introduced regulations aimed at limiting conversions.[25] Afraid of upsetting Muslim and Catholic religious leaders, however, they refrained from banning conversion outright until October 1941, when the conversions began to complicate the deportation process.

Political laws barring conversion posed a problem for Sarajevo's Muslim and Catholic leaders, who realized that secular Fascists and religious leaders made awkward bedfellows. Until October, neither the Catholic Church nor the Islamic Religious Community excluded Jews from the list of eligible converts.[26] While adopting elements of antisemitic language, Sarajevo's Catholic Church rejected notions of a Jewish race, believing that Jews who accepted Christ could, and should, be saved.[27] Allegedly, even the Ustasha deputy Father Božidar Bralo, known for being one of the most radical Croat nationalists and Ustasha supporters in the city, personally oversaw the conversion of more than a thousand Sarajevo Jews and actively sought to protect

23. This pattern is revealed in the conversion records at the Sarajevo mayor's office. Individual examples are referred to throughout the text and can be found in IAS, Gradsko Poglavarstvo, boxes 840–1005.

24. In ARIZBiH, Ulema Medžlis, see correspondence in document 1117/41 (August 1941–January 26, 1942), document 3789/42 (September 30, 1941), document 4561/41 (November 6, 1941, and November 19, 1941), and document 1117/41 (January 16, 1942).

25. On the conversion laws, see the reports in ARIZBiH, Ulema Medžlis, document 2659/41 (May—July 1941). See also a decree in *Sarajevski Novi List*, July 27, 1941, 3, wherein the local government specifically notes that all Jews must register, "even those Jews who have converted to another faith."

26. See *Vrhbosna*, July—August 1941, 167–170; ARIZBiH, Ulema Medžlis, document 2659/41 (July 19, 1941).

27. "Židovi," *Katolički Tjednik*, August 3, 1941, 3–4.

them from deportation. Evidence of Bralo's involvement in the conversions of Jews can be found on the conversion requests, which he signed. It can also be found in reports by his Muslim critics. In the fall of 1942, several local Muslim leaders informed the German command that Bralo and other Roman Catholic priests had allowed 3,800 Jews to convert to Catholicism and attempted to protect them from deportation.[28] Although this number appears to be an exaggeration, especially when looked at in conjunction with the conversion requests and reports from the Italian consulate, it is indicative of a citywide trend that the church made no attempt to deny. Although Sarajevo's Catholic clergy were proud supporters of the NDH, they nevertheless expected to retain autonomy over the sacraments of baptism, confirmation, and marriage—and by extension, conversion. Thus in the early part of the war, they found it possible to be at once advocates on behalf of their Jewish converts and staunch supporters of the NDH. According to the Italian consulate, "the government, the civilians, and the church authorities" understood these wartime conversions to be genuine religious acts.[29]

The Ustasha regime tried to mitigate tensions by pretending to listen to religious leaders but continuing with its own plans to categorize Jews along racial lines.[30] In the process, however, the regime sent mixed messages, which further confused and frustrated town leaders. For example, while discouraging Jewish conversions and maintaining that religion had no bearing on race, the regime simultaneously launched a zealous campaign in the fall of 1941 to convert Orthodox Serbs to Catholicism.[31] In the case of Orthodox Serbs, then, religion determined race. Similarly, as mentioned above, the regime allowed Muslim leaders to vouch for Aryan Roma, thus bypassing the entire system of genealogy and blood requirements. The Ustasha political authorities were also known for their flexibility in applying racial laws to Jews married to Catholics, for which they were harshly criticized by the Germans.[32] Why, then, was the racial status of Jewish converts to Islam and Catholicism a nonnegotiable?

28. Hoover Institution Archives, Jozo Tomasevich Papers, Muslim National Committee's letter to Adolf Hitler, box 4, T:120, roll 5793 (November 1, 1942).

29. HM, Ustaška Nadzorna Služba, document 4005 (September 18, 1941).

30. For example, in July 1941, Archbishop Alojzije Stepinac wrote to Pavelić that he was concerned about rumors he had heard about the deportations of Serbs and Jews. He asked Pavelić to rethink the plan and to take measures that were human, godly, gracious, and in the Christian spirit. He requested that if such deportations were necessary, inmates have time to prepare their belongings, and be transported comfortably with adequate food and medicine in both the transports and the camps. The Ministry of Religion sent him a one-sentence reply denying that the deportations were happening. For the complete correspondence, see HDA, Ministarstvo pravosuđa i bogoštovlja NDH, Odjel bogoštovlja, box 3, document 48061/41 (July 21, 1941, and response on July 29, 1941).

31. The best study of the conversions is Biondich, "Religion and Nation in Wartime Croatia."

32. Tomasevich, *War and Revolution in Yugoslavia*, 596. For an example of Ustasha lenience to a Sarajevo Jewish man married to a Catholic woman, see HM, Ustaška građa, document 2444 (November 19, 1941).

Before this question was answered, the Ustasha regime abruptly ended the debate in October 1941 by unilaterally outlawing Jewish conversions and requiring that any marriage between an Aryan and a non-Aryan—defined specifically here as a Jew or Roma—be approved directly by the minister of the interior.[33] In the weeks that followed, most of Sarajevo's political and religious leadership came to accept that if they hoped to maintain good relations with the regime, they could not continue to welcome Jewish converts into the community. Under pressure from Zagreb, Reis-ul-ulema Spaho publicly acknowledged in late November that "changing religion does not mean changing one's race; Jews who become Muslims remain, as always, non-Aryans."[34] By the beginning of 1942 the Catholic press often adopted the regime's racial rhetoric on the dangers of Jewish influence, whereas previously it had depicted the Jewish threat primarily in moral terms—i.e., as a group that spread corruption, Communism, and liberalism and that was responsible for the death of Christ. Catholic leaders' rhetoric and failure to protest suggest that they were willing to sacrifice their converts to the greater good of the Croat nation, even though they never explicitly acknowledged this. On the local level, then, the Roman Catholic Church's complicity with the Holocaust in Sarajevo should be regarded as a process, one that incorporated both theology and political circumstances and that changed gradually over the course of 1941.

While religious leaders thus appeared to accept defeat, many Sarajevo citizens refused to do so, bombarding their leaders with petitions on behalf of Jews. One moving protest came from a young Muslim man, Džemal, who begged Reis-ul-ulema Spaho for a last-minute conversion for his Jewish fiancée, Roza. Writing to Spaho in a tone that suggested an old friendship, Džemal provided intimate details of his union with Roza and her subsequent conversion to Islam. He described how Roza had applied for and received permission to convert to Islam a few days before the laws changed in late October. Džemal swore that Roza was a genuine convert and that she understood and respected all Muslim customs and prayers. Having heard nothing for two weeks, he sent another desperate letter in which he threatened suicide if Spaho did nothing. On November 19, 1941, the day after the city's largest deportation, Spaho handed the request to the Ulema Medžlis with instructions to "immediately" track the case.[35] The Ulema Medžlis gave it a number and sent it to their clerk, who added it to his pile of 1,500 urgent unresolved cases related to Muslim victims of the state's racial laws.[36]

Surprisingly, despite the anticonversion laws, the Islamic Religious Community continued to record more than a hundred new Jewish converts

33. *Zbornik zakona i naredaba NDH,* 7:237–238.
34. ARIZBiH, Ulema Medžlis, document 1650/41 (November 22, 1941).
35. Ibid., document 4561/41 (November 6, 1941, and November 19, 1941).
36. Ibid., document 1117/41 (January 16, 1942).

over the next year. The mayor's office was aware of and even approved of some of these new conversions. A few Jews claimed that they had converted in 1941 before the government passed laws forbidding them to do so; most were married to Muslims. It is not impossible that Sarajevo's imams shrewdly backdated the paperwork. Unfortunately, the documents do not fully reveal what conversion meant to these Jews or how Muslim religious leaders were able to evade the regime's laws.[37] They do confirm, however, that in the minds of Muslim religious leaders, membership in the Islamic faith trumped the regime's arbitrary racial laws.

• • •

Just as policies toward race and nationality stemmed from a gradual, complex, and contested process on the local and national levels, so the question of who was a "foreign national" became hotly contested in the early months of the war. Although the Ustasha regime's racial legislation was often vague and subjective, it did seek to define non-Aryans. No similar legislation spelled out exactly who constituted a "national member" or foreigner and who did not. Thus while the Ustasha Party's ideological program described the Croat nation as an "identifiable ethnic unit" (*samosvojnu etničku jedinicu*) with a historical right to a sovereign state, the nation was identifiable only insofar as it was not "other" nations. The regime stipulated that "foreign nations" should be excluded from public life and political decision making, defining a foreign national as any person who was not "by origin and by blood" (*po koljenima i po krvi*) a member of the nation.[38] Thus a foreigner was somebody who was not a Croat, and a Croat was somebody who was not a foreigner—at best a political tautology and at worst a stage for national crisis.

Defining foreigners, a group that fell in the non-Croat category alongside non-Aryans, proved as complicated as the race-based categories of "Jew" and "Gypsy," if not more so. The vague category at times included people who identified (or were identified by the regime) as Serbs, Slovenes, Russians, Montenegrins, Jews, Roma, and members of the Old Catholic Church (a small Catholic sect). Moreover, the meaning of the term shifted with Ustasha policies, best illustrated in the case of the Slovenes. When the Ustasha regime first took power, it considered Slovenes foreigners and established decrees that justified removing them from their jobs and denying

37. Examples of 1942 and 1943 conversions can be found in ARIZBiH, Ulema Medžlis, documents 1238 (1942) and 1111–1125 (March 28, 1943), 1217–1224 (April 1, 1943), 1824–1836 (May 25–26, 1943), 1869–1877 (May 27, 1943); and in IAS, Gradsko Poglavarstvo, box 1005 (July 16, 1942) and box 941 (March 2, 1942).

38. Jareb, *Ustaško-domobranski pokret*, 124–128.

them the rights of citizenship.[39] This policy became problematic in June 1941, when Germany and the NDH concluded an agreement that allowed the Germans to relocate 10,000 Slovenes from German-annexed Slovenia to Bosnia. More than 2,500 Slovene immigrants under the auspices of the Germans arrived in Sarajevo that summer. The regime categorized them as "colonists," which had a positive connotation. Colonists received priority for prime agricultural real estate in the Sarajevo vicinity. By October, Zagreb announced that Slovenes were of "vital interest" to the Croat nation and should be granted immediate residency and citizenship; these onetime foreigners thus became participating members of the nation-state.[40]

Although debates over foreignness took on different tones, what the Ustashas usually meant by foreign national was Serb. But who were these Serbs? Other than being the opposite of Croat, or a foreign national in Croat land, how did the regime define Serb? The state's racial laws defined non-Aryans as Jews, Roma, and others but never specified Serbs.[41] Although Ustasha propaganda used racist terms to describe Serbs, and the discourse on the "Serb question" mirrored that on the "Jewish question," exactly what made someone a Serb was not explicit in the legal code.[42] Pavelić's regime created various caveats and categories of Serb, distinguishing between *Srbi*—Serbs born in Croatia—and *Srbijanci*—Serbs born in Serbia proper. Zagreb also allowed for personal exemptions because Pavelić and other Ustasha leaders wanted to ensure that Serb friends did not become victims of the discriminatory laws.[43] The Germans offered little guidance. In contrast to their elaborate and explicit codes regarding the racial identity of Jews, German theories of race did not categorize Serbs explicitly as non-Aryan.[44]

Across the state, local communities, and even individual officials, interpreted the term "Serb" variously: some used it to refer to members of the Serbian Orthodox faith, while others used it to denote a political group that

39. Examples of the targeting of Slovenes in Sarajevo early in the war can be found in ABiH, Poglavnikovo Povjereništvo Sarajevo, Opći Odjel, box 1, document 1250 (May 24, 1941), and ABiH, Povjerenstvo za Radnje Drž. Hrv.—Sarajevo, box 2, document 228 (May 30, 1941).

40. An estimated 15,800 Slovenes were forced to relocate to Croatia and Bosnia in 1941. Most of the Slovene immigrants to Bosnia came from Brežice, part of Slovenia annexed by Germany. Volksdeutsche living in the Italian zones of Slovenia were then resettled into the Slovenes' homes. On the general relocation of Slovenes, see Davide Rodogno, *Fascism's European Empire, Italian Occupation during the Second World War* (Cambridge: Cambridge University Press, 2006), 270. For specific examples of Slovene relocation in Sarajevo, see HM, Ustaška građa, document 1472 (July 12, 1941) and document 1508 (July 9, 1941).

41. The exact word for "others" used in the laws was *ini*. See the racial laws listed in *Zakoni*, vol. 1.

42. Fikreta Jelić-Butić describes these parallel systems in *Ustaše i Nezavisna Država Hrvatska*, 163–164.

43. Tomasevich, *War and Revolution in Yugoslavia*, 380–381.

44. Some theorists did, however, label Serbs a racially inferior group that lacked "blood purity." See Trubeta, "'Gypsiness,' Racial Discourse and Persecution," 497–498.

remained loyal to the Belgrade government. Sarajevo's leaders were sensitive to the Serb question precisely because it was dually linked to religion and to the notion of being a foreigner—categories that the city's elite liked to define in their own way. Thus Sarajevans often ignored the Ustasha prescriptions of foreign and instead treated many Serbs foremost as Sarajevans. On April 29, Marshal Slavko Kvaternik, Croatia's minister of defense, issued a severe public warning to residents of Sarajevo who were hiding Serb soldiers, which indicates that the practice was not uncommon.[45] Around the same time, Reis-ul-ulema Spaho petitioned the Ustasha deputies on behalf of a fired Orthodox schoolteacher, arguing, "[N]obody has ever heard her insult a Muslim or Catholic Croat during her time in service. . . . I think that dismissing this old schoolteacher is unfair, even if it is based on some legal regulation." Adopting a tone befitting a religious leader, Spaho concluded, "[H]e who believes in God and His eternal justice should know that such injustices will be avenged." The authorities were not yet prepared for such a moral standing against their policies, so they allowed Radić to return to her post.[46]

The inclination to protect some Orthodox Serbs did not occur simply because the city had a culture of confessional tolerance. Many town leaders agreed with Zagreb that there were certain enemies in their midst who needed to be dealt with promptly for national security. They, too, feared extreme Serb nationalists and Communists and readily removed them from the city. These local leaders were committed to building a new social order. Politically motivated Serbs, the alleged interwar agents of secular, liberal, Great Serbia philosophy, hindered their efforts. Thus they had no qualms about participating in arrests or confiscating Serbs' property. But at the same time, the vast majority of Sarajevo's Muslim and Catholic elite did not view their ordinary Orthodox Serb townsmen as a threat to society or seek to torture and massacre them just because they fell under the Ustasha regime's category of Serbs. And they certainly did not understand—or agree with—the regime's attempt to label Serbs unilaterally as outsiders. On the contrary, Sarajevo's leaders believed there were many good Serbs who played important roles in their society, who belonged to Sarajevo and to the national collective.

Sensing the city's discomfort with the sweeping attack against Serbs, on May 7, 1941, deputies Bralo and Hadžić authorized exemptions for Serbs who were domaći, which is best translated in this context as "our local Serbs."[47] Domaći Serbs, or "Sarajevo Serbs," comprised a loosely defined category that generally applied to Sarajevans of Orthodox background who

45. See the command decision by Slavko Kvaternik, April 29, 1941, in *Zločini na jugoslovenskim prostorima u prvom i drugom svetskom ratu, Zbornik Dokumenata* (Belgrade: Vojnoistorijski Institut, 1993), 20–21.

46. IAS, Ostavština Fehima Spaha, box 3, document 694 (May 6, 1941).

47. ABiH, Poglavnikovo Povjereništvo Sarajevo, box 1, document 343 (May 6, 1941).

posed no discernible threat to the goals of the NDH. The group consisted primarily of lower-level bureaucrats, women, children, and the elderly.[48] There was no formal means of differentiating local Serbs from other Serbs whom Ustasha officials considered racially inferior and potentially criminal. Some Sarajevo Serbs tried to apply for the special status by emphasizing that their families had resided in Sarajevo since before 1918 and thus were not Yugoslav imports but genuine Sarajevans.[49] Others sent family histories to the mayor's office to prove they were "one hundred percent Aryan Serb."[50]

The Ustasha police and political bureau, under the leadership of the protagonists of the previous chapter—Jure Francetić, Petar Petković, Hakija Hadžić, Božidar Bralo—unilaterally excluded certain Serbs from being considered local Serbs in Sarajevo: those who had relocated to Sarajevo in the interwar years for government or military posts and Orthodox priests and their families. These foreign Serbs outnumbered local Serbs in the earliest mass arrests.[51] Nevertheless, on several occasions the regime in Zagreb had to remind Sarajevo to fire these Serbs from public positions, a fact suggesting that the city had its own way of determining who qualified as domaći.[52] Some town institutions had their own systems for ascribing identities. Sarajevo's National Theater followed Zagreb's orders to fire non-Aryan employees by removing a Jew and a Serb but keeping twenty Aryan Orthodox in its employ.[53] Such a distinction suggests that officials interpreted Serb as a racial category but applied the term subjectively.

What becomes clear in this legal vagueness is the centrality of the social as a means of achieving (or at times, evading) a political reality. The more latitude such laws permitted, the more it was possible to hand-select particular individuals for privilege, to help friends avoid persecution, and to leave room for one traditional form of politics—nepotism. Politics became, in effect, personal: a matter of how people interpreted racial categories, a process of cultural intuition rather than positive law.

48. Different interpretations of the term are best illustrated by the way that local institutions used it. The local Ustasha bureau referred to "domaći Serbs" in its reports but rarely specified exactly who these were. See ABiH, Poglavnikovo Povjereništvo Sarajevo, Upravni Odjel, box 1, document 83 (May 8, 1941). Sarajevo's National Theater classified domaći partly along political lines and drew distinctions between Serbs who swore an oath to Croatia and those who did not. See ABiH, Narodno pozorište Sarajevo, box 2, document 735 (May 12, 1941). The city's museum simply submitted a list that categorized more than a dozen of their employees as Aryan Orthodox. See ABiH, Zemaljski Muzej Bosne i Hercegovine, box 37, document 132 (June 11, 1941).

49. IAS, Gradsko Poglavarstvo, box 842 (May 29, 1941).

50. ABiH, Povjerenstvo za radnje Drž. Hrv.—Sarajevo, box 3, document 606 (May 1941).

51. Testimony of Mihaljo Lukić in Dedijer and Miletić, *Proterivanje Srba sa ognjišta 1941–1944 svedočanstva*, 382–384.

52. *Zločini na jugoslovenskim prostorima*, 46–48.

53. ABiH, Narodno pozorište Sarajevo, box 3, document 1249 (September 2, 1942). The report refers to events that occurred in June 1941.

While the category of domaći Serb was subjective and ambiguous, the advantages of the label were not. In the summer of 1941, as Serbs in the Bosnian countryside were falling to Ustasha machetes, Sarajevo's city government passed special laws to help domaći Serbs. City institutions like the Croatian State Museum, the Croatian National Theater, the school district, and even the mayor's office kept dozens of Serb employees. In July, Serb police officers who had served in the army were awarded their pensions.[54] In August, Sarajevo's Office of Labor and Employment announced that loyal Serbs were entitled to severance pay and retirement benefits if they had been fired without reason and were not considered "terrorists."[55] Although the city was suffering from rising unemployment, a problem that purging Serbs could partially have solved, city offices often refused to replace their Serb employees with unqualified Muslims and Catholics. Ironically, as late as August 1941, Sarajevo's police department—an agency in charge of monitoring Serbs—still employed four Serb chauffeurs despite orders from the Ustasha deputies to replace them with Croats.[56] Unlike a doctor or an engineer, a driver required little expertise. The police department's insistence on keeping these Serbs strongly suggests that even some Sarajevans who worked for the regime placed their personal relationships ahead of the regime's discriminatory laws.

While many of Sarajevo's leaders used the subjective definition of Serb to serve their own interests, the ambiguity occasionally worked against them. Because the rhetoric of the Ustasha regime used the term primarily to denote a national orientation, Muslims who had adopted a Serb identity in the interwar era got caught in the crossfire of the anti-Serb campaign. Although Islam was an official religion of the NDH, being Muslim did not automatically qualify one as Croat. In April and May 1941, the Ustasha police arrested dozens of Muslims who owned property in Belgrade, wrote in Cyrillic, or were "Serb-oriented."[57] The political authorities fired others for similar reasons. They also closed Muslim businesses and organizations that had advocated a Yugoslav platform or worked closely with Belgrade. In early May, Reis-ul-ulema Spaho implored Deputy Hakija Hadžić to protect their Muslim brothers instead of "throwing them and their families out on the streets during this difficult time."[58] But Hadžić did not step in. Instead, he personally identified and fired suspicious Muslims. The victims were furious about their demotion to the class of non-Croats and bitterly complained to Muslim leaders, who found that the Muslim Serb question, like the question of Jewish converts to Islam, was dividing their community. By the fall of 1941, it was clear that though the regime's legal codes implied

54. HM, Ustaška građa, document 1566 (July 17, 1941).
55. In ABiH, Javni Ured Rada Sarajevo, see box 1, document 992 (August 20, 1941).
56. HM, Ustaška građa, document 1854 (August 12, 1941).
57. Ibid., document 1264 (June 14, 1941) and document 1600 (April 30, 1941).
58. Ibid., document 1131 (May 8, 1941).

that Serbs were foreign nationals of an inferior race, political affiliation and loyalty, not religion or ethnic background, would determine how Orthodox Serbs in Sarajevo would be categorized and treated.

Neighborhood Dynamics of Ethnic Cleansing

The debates over national identity, while important for understanding how Sarajevans were thinking, did not lead to a deferral of the genocidal agenda. On the contrary, the Ustasha regime introduced progressively harsher discriminatory laws throughout 1941, eventually leading to the deportations of Sarajevo's Jews in the fall. Thus while still wrestling with the ideological issues at stake in the regime's identity politics, city leaders and ordinary residents also had to deal with practical issues. How would the municipal government interact with Sarajevans who had not yet qualified (and might never qualify) as citizens? Would these people get pensions, welfare, and unemployment benefits?[59] Would local officials adopt the regime's hostile tone or try to make the process easier? On a personal level, would neighbors take advantage of neighbors, or would they help them? And did the victim groups themselves have any recourses?

In their efforts to navigate this shifting legal world, Sarajevo's leaders insisted on maintaining the city's ethical code of neighborliness—that is, showing deference to groups slated for removal. This played out in different ways at different institutions. Faced with ill-advised and poorly articulated laws, local judges often ruled according to local custom and the city's own sense of justice. Although they swore oaths of loyalty to the NDH, many judges refused to use their positions as interpreters or mediators of the regime's policies. City courts continued to hear cases involving Jews and Serbs, ruling in their favor as frequently as not. When two Jewish landlords sued their former Croat tenant for unpaid rent in June 1941, a local court (*sudbeni stol*) sided with the Jews. In another case, the court reversed a decision against two Jews on procedural grounds: the courier had not delivered the subpoena to the defendants, and thus the decision was invalid. Similarly, the courts ruled in favor of Serb residents on a variety of property, business, and personal claims. Jews and Serbs continued to serve as lawyers and witnesses as well; in one case, two Serb women were represented by a Jewish lawyer, and they won.[60] In other areas of the municipal government,

59. ABiH, Poglavnikovo Povjereništvo Sarajevo, Odjel za socialnu skrb i narodno zdravlje, box 1, document 482 (May 1, 1941).

60. There are dozens of examples from the files of the city courts (ABiH, Sudbeni Stol). This collection is not numbered in the standard manner (box 1, 2, 3, etc.) but rather according to groupings of court cases (PL, RO, etc.). For the examples above, see cases PL 239/41–3 (June 21, 1941), PL 229/41–42 (July 17, 1941), PL 78/43 (December 16, 1942), PL 215/1941–3 (June 28, 1941), and PL 309/41 (June 27, 1941). Additional examples of interest include PO 2/42, PL 340/41, PL 350/41–42, PL 313/1941, and PL 126/43.

local officials often abided by the city's unspoken code that people who belonged to the Sarajevo community warranted civil treatment. This code revealed itself in the respectful tone and timeliness of replies to requests made by non-Croats, as well as in occasional efforts by town officials to set aside money to assist unemployed women.[61]

Lawyers and judges who worked closely with the city's Jews were among those who found the discriminatory legislation most disconcerting. In May 1941, deputies Bralo and Hadžić appointed trustees to administer Sarajevo's Sephardic and Ashkenazi Jewish Communities. Both men were well-respected Catholic Croat judges with deep ties to Sarajevo whom the regime trusted to carry out one of its most important tasks. Both found their positions distasteful.

Srećko Bujas, the trustee for the Sephardic community, wrote a lengthy report immediately after the war documenting the devastating effects of the Holocaust in the city, which he had witnessed more intimately than most because he was the contact person between Sephardic Jews and the state. In addition to this postwar statement, his compassion and advocacy on behalf of Sarajevo's Jews are revealed in dozens of letters and petitions found in the archives of Bralo and Hadžić's office and in the records of Sarajevo's Trustee of Stores (Povjerenstvo za radnje Drž. Hrv.—Sarajevo). When a Jewish single mother requested the return of her hair salon so that she could feed her child, Bujas sent his "heartfelt plea" to the city official in charge, asking him to consider the case "as a human being with sympathy for poverty."[62] Fielding requests for jobs and back pay from other Jews, Bujas begged the city's Office of Labor and Employment for "one act of social good toward these poor, unemployed fellow city men, who are threatened with hunger and homelessness."[63] In July, Bujas arranged for packages of food and clothing to be sent on behalf of the Sephardic Jewish community to Serb and Jewish female political prisoners held at a transit camp near Sarajevo.[64] That same month, Ante Pavelić appointed him to the county court (kotarski sud), and in September he became the court's president, a fact suggesting that his advocacy did not reflect poorly on his position or negatively affect his career.[65]

Branko Milaković, the Ashkenazi trustee, left less of a paper trail but enough to show that he at least occasionally advocated on behalf of Jews. By contrast to Bujas, Milaković seemed most concerned with figuring out the laws and ensuring that innocent victims did not get caught in the middle.

61. ABiH, Javni Ured Rada Sarajevo, box 2, document 1006 (August 21, 1941).
62. ABiH, Povjerenstvo za radnje Drž. Hrv.—Sarajevo, box 3, document 396 (June 16, 1941).
63. ABiH, Javni Ured Rada Sarajevo, box 2, document 1042 (August 28, 1941).
64. Dedijer and Miletić, Proterivanje Srba sa ognjišta 1941–1944, 66.
65. HDA, Ministarstvo pravosuđa i bogoštovlja NDH, Odjel bogoštovlja, personnel dossier, Srećko Bujas, box 296.

For example, he came to the defense of a female member of the Evan-gelical Church whom the Ustashas had labeled a Jew. Milaković argued that her racial status was a mistake and thus it was not right to confiscate her property.[66] Although he appeared to pity his Jewish constituency—who, having lost their jobs and property, faced destitution when non-Jewish ten-ants stopped paying rent—Milaković appeared more accommodating to the regime than Bujas. He expressed frequent irritation with the local Ustasha officials who disrupted his difficult work and with the absence of an orderly and objective system of discrimination laws, but he seemed less aggressive in reversing the fate of his charges.[67] Nevertheless, he made attempts to treat them humanely, joining with Bujas in sending packages to Sarajevo Jews in holding camps.

As further evidence of the city's discomfort with aspects of the regime's discriminatory agenda, the Ustasha authorities found it difficult to find anyone in Sarajevo who was willing to serve as the trustee for the largest Serb cultural society, Prosvjeta. After several people refused on the grounds that the decisions required by the position were "too sensitive," a local Catholic professor, Ilija B., agreed to oversee the society's liquidation. Since Prosvjeta was the wealthiest Serb organization in the city, we can assume that the authorities viewed the professor as a trustworthy partner. Perhaps he was. Nevertheless, he was outraged when Ustashas confiscated, stole, or destroyed the society's property. In fact, he closely followed Prosvjeta's investments and established a new line of savings and credit in order to expand its economic holdings, an odd undertaking for an organization being liquidated. Since the society no longer had any Serb members and since the professor had much to lose by defying Ustasha directives, one can assume that he was motivated by a desire to keep local wealth in Sarajevo, by a sense of civic responsibility toward his neighbors' investments, or by personal gain. Understandably vexed by his behavior, Sarajevo's Ustasha police—in a blatant attempt to manipulate national and racial identities—recommended that the professor be replaced by a pure Croat. Who was a pure Croat if not a Catholic intellectual who identified as a Croat and sup-ported the regime? Eventually the minister of the interior responded by appointing a Zagreb-based trustee, who summarily liquidated Prosvjeta and moved on to the next order of business.[68] To some, it appeared that a pure Croat was increasingly understood as a Catholic Croat from Zagreb.

---

66. ABiH, Povjerenstvo za radnje Drž. Hrv.—Sarajevo, box 3, document 392 (June 19, 1941).

67. Ibid., document 373 (June 10, 1941).

68. All these materials can be found in the wartime archives of Prosvjeta: ABiH, Prosvjeta kulturno društvo, boxes 31 and 32. In box 31, see document 11 (October 11, 1941), document 41 (November 5, 1941), document 89 (November 17, 1941), document 103 (November 22, 1941), and document 138 (December 11, 1941). In box 32, see document 217 (June 16, 1942) and document 687 (July 22, 1943).

Property became the source of many local power struggles. Officially, the process of property confiscation in Sarajevo had started on May 7, 1941, when the Ustasha deputies appointed local Aryan trustees (*povjerenici*)—Catholics, Muslims, and Volksdeutsche—to oversee almost two hundred Jewish and Serb businesses, factories, and organizations in Sarajevo. (Unofficially, local Ustasha officials had confiscated property illegally as early as April 19.) The trustees were considered temporary monitors until the state could nationalize or sell the property.[69] They were a mixed bag, ranging from opportunists and criminals to decent businessmen. Some Serbs and Jews resisted corrupt trustees by shutting down their businesses (what the regime called "deliberately sabotaging"); most were powerless to do anything. Occasionally Muslims and Catholics reacted to negligence and animosity by petitioning the town on a neighbor's behalf. City leaders fielded complaints from residents who disliked the "immoral" behavior of the trustees, apparently believing that there was a certain ethical standard to which they should adhere. The residents expected a degree of civility to persist despite the uncivilized processes of disenfranchising an entire community. In one complaint, for example, a resident listed the "irregular and illegal" acts of a trustee who had used factory accounts to pay his personal debts, had sat around drinking all day, and had previously been accused of fraud in a different part of the state. His behavior was unbefitting a Sarajevan: further evidence of his immorality included the facts that he had stolen all his mother's money and that he lived with a concubine who had miscarried because he beat her while she was pregnant.[70] Although the tales of trustees who were cruel and took advantage of their posts outnumber those of honorable trustees, there were a few of the latter: for example, at a factory, Lik, the trustee continued to employ Jewish and Serb women through the fall of 1941.[71]

At the institutional level, the notion of local civility did not mean that locals refused to participate in the looting of Serb and Jewish property but rather that they wanted to do it on their own terms and to ensure that their participation would not be frowned upon. In April 1941, the Ustasha deputies informed various Catholic and Muslim organizations that they had been assigned Serbs' and Jews' property. The Society of Croat Catholic Women felt uncomfortable and decided to seek advice from the archbishop on the matter. According to their weekly minutes, a representative met with Father Bralo, after which time it was determined that the women's group should

69. On the appointment of the trustees, see IAS, Državno Ravnateljstvo za Gospodarstvenu Ponovu, document 35429 (August 20, 1941). On the role of the trustees, see an example of an appointment letter: ABiH, Povjerenstvo za radnje Drž. Hrv.—Sarajevo, box 2, document 53 (May 30, 1941).
70. ABiH, Povjerenstvo za radnje Drž. Hrv.—Sarajevo, box 2, document 228 (May 30, 1941).
71. Ibid., box 4, document 165 (September 18, 1941).

take the property and use it for humanitarian work in the city.[72] After wrestling with the same issue, the leadership of the cultural societies Napredak and Narodna Uzdanica reluctantly agreed to take the property of their Serb counterparts, arguing that it would be better for the citizens of Sarajevo if soup kitchens, libraries, dormitories, and cultural centers remained open.[73] Other organizations—such as Hurijet, a society of Muslim craftsmen, and Merhamet, Bosnia's largest Muslim humanitarian organization—used the same rationale when they took over profitable Jewish factories that manufactured goods for the German army. Although criticized for aiding the Germans in the postwar era, Merhamet did use the income from two of the city's most lucrative textile factories, Šik and Ključ, to aid the tens of thousands of Muslim refugees and orphans that Zagreb abandoned in the city.[74] The rationale that it would be best for the citizens of Sarajevo or the community is used again and again in discussions of property confiscation. For many community leaders accepting the property, it appears that the end—continuing services for the poor—gradually came to be accepted as a justification of the means—accepting unjustly confiscated property. Their new moral act became appropriating property for humanitarian reasons. Their new community became the people still left under their charge.

For the most part, municipal officials appeared to accept that they could do nothing to avert the deportation process (whether they wanted to or not) and instead focused on maintaining civility in their own offices. A particularly interesting example is that of housekeepers employed by Jews. State law forbade Aryans from working in Jewish homes but stipulated that the former housekeepers of Jews would continue to be paid from the Jewish employer's estate for a set period of time. When the housekeepers requested payment, the office for Jewish property wanted consent from the estate owner. In one case, a local detective spent two months tracking down a Jewish man from a jail in Sarajevo to a holding cell in Kruščić to his final internment in Jasenovac. Once he found the man, the detective requested his permission to use monies from his estate to pay his former housekeeper. Although he probably had little choice in the matter, the man agreed, signing and dating the form. The Jasenovac camp commander signed as a witness. After several similar cases, officials in Zagreb—no doubt annoyed and confused at this waste in manpower—ordered Sarajevo's officials to pay the housekeepers without the employers' consent.[75] But until that

72. IAS, Društvo Hrvatskih Katoličkih Žena u Sarajevu, minutes, box 1 (April 28, 1941, and April 30, 1941).

73. ABiH, Hrvatsko kulturno društvo Napredak, box 145, document 471 (November 7, 1941); IAS, Narodna Uzdanica, minutes (July 17, 1941).

74. On the takeover of the Šik factory, see IAS, Merhamet, box 5, document 287 (May 15, 1943). Merhamet's work with orphans and refugees is discussed extensively in later chapters.

75. IAS, Ured za upravu židovskim nekretninama, document 4956 (September 16, 1941) with various follow-up documents through May 1942.

order was issued, town officials insisted on respecting the rights of fellow townsmen.

Serbs and Jews: Experiences of Genocide

Although they shared a fear of their fates in the new state, Sarajevo's community of Jews and Serbs experienced the war differently. Throughout the spring and summer, many Serbs fled the city.[76] When a Serb had strong connections to Sarajevo and left legally, usually for the Nazi protectorate in Serbia, some city leaders tried to help. Rather than confiscating the possessions of Jovan Tanić, onetime manager at the National Theater, local officials shipped his belongings to the border with Serbia.[77] The Ustasha deputies granted the request of Borivoje Jevtić, the theater's acting manager, for a transfer to Belgrade.[78] Working-class Serbs sometimes found help through the German occupation command, which organized paid labor battalions in southern Serbia. However, the German army abruptly ended this program on August 22 because masses of Serb refugees had congregated on the border—fleeing Ustasha violence in the Bosnian and Croatian countryside—and had begun to destabilize the region. It did not help that the Germans learned that some of these fleeing Serbs had joined the Chetnik resistance army to fight against them.[79]

Leaving Sarajevo illegally was risky. Any Serb who fled the country rescinded his citizenship and property rights. To get around this law, some Serb men left their wives in Sarajevo to watch over the family's property. One wealthy Serb business owner played the system by relocating from Sarajevo to Zemun, a city on the border between the NDH and Serbia, just a few kilometers away from Belgrade. Since the man had not fled the country, he had not officially abandoned his property, which—according to another legal loophole—meant that the police could not confiscate it without cause.[80] In these kinds of cases, Sarajevo's officials typically followed the law, even when doing so benefited Serbs.

Although better off than Jews and Roma because of the possibility of domaći status, Sarajevo's local Serbs hardly had it easy. In June 1941, a visitor to Sarajevo noted that they were living on the fringes of society in a perpetual state of fear.[81] Nobody knew who would be arrested during

76. HM, Ustaška građa, document 59 (August 2, 1941).

77. ABiH, Narodno pozorište Sarajevo, box 2, document 1039 (July 3, 1941).

78. IAS, Ostavština Borivoja Jevtića, box 4, document 52 (May 10, 1941).

79. Tomasevich offers an overview of this subject in *War and Revolution in Yugoslavia*, 392–397.

80. IAS, Riznično Upraviteljstvo Ured za podržavljeni Imetak, box 1, document 92 (September 14, 1942).

81. Report from Dr. Vasilije Vojnović, filed with the archives of the Federal Secretariat for Foreign Affairs (SSIP), Belgrade, Ministarstvo Unutrašnjih Poslova Kraljevine Jugoslavije London-Kairo (1941–1945), F-1, pov. Br. 496 (December 12, 1941).

night raids, an Ustasha tactic designed to prevent organized resistance. Serbs who failed to use the Latin alphabet risked imprisonment. Even when they retained their jobs and property, local Serbs still encountered discriminatory laws, such as being prohibited from going to the movies or from wearing certain kinds of clothing.[82] Most frightening yet, they had no idea whether their status would change abruptly, as it did for Serbs in other parts of the state. The mother of Borivoje Jevtić, the Serb intellectual introduced in chapter 1, remained in Sarajevo after her son moved to Belgrade, documenting the communities' fears in her letters to him. In one note she attested that she would be content just to know she would find bread the next day; in another, she described the day-to-day difficulties of trying to keep track of family members and property.[83]

In late August 1941, the position of Sarajevo's Serbs changed when the Ustasha police launched a wave of arrests against Serbs with politically questionable backgrounds. Since July, Serb insurgents had captured strips of the countryside near Sarajevo's foothills and had begun to infiltrate Sarajevo.[84] Afraid of losing their hold on the city, the Ustasha authorities decided to remove Serbs with suspected ties to the resistance armies, focusing especially on workers, church officials, and intelligentsia.[85] They publicly executed a dozen Serbs—a warning to everyone in the city—and arrested and deported a few hundred others to newly constructed concentration camps in central and northern Bosnia.[86] By late August, the police thus had removed the most politically active Serbs, men with the background and motivation to organize others.

In the aftermath of the mass arrests, life for the city's remaining Serbs markedly improved. When a Serb city inspector received an anonymous letter accusing him of working for the Chetniks in September 1941, he brought it to the attention of the local Ustasha authorities before anyone else could, divulging the contents in order to prove his loyalty and keep his job.[87] A month earlier, the man would surely have been arrested. At the same time, the city expanded the number of Serbs eligible for social welfare and unemployment benefits.

The campaign to rid Sarajevo of suspicious Serbs certainly did not end that August. In October, the police arrested a group of new suspects and confiscated thirty-two new properties.[88] But the arrests and confiscations

82. *Sarajevski Novi List*, May 25, 1941, 4.

83. IAS, Ostavština Borivoja Jevtića, letters from Jovanka Jeftić, box 4 (July 14, 1941, and August 25, 1941).

84. Donia, *Sarajevo*, 193.

85. HM, Ustaška građa, document 67 (August 11, 1941).

86. On the concentration camps generally, see Jelić-Butić, *Ustaše i Nezavisna Država Hrvatska*, 186.

87. HM, Ustaška građa, document 2192 (September 29, 1941).

88. IAS, Državno Ravnateljstvo za Gospodarstvenu Ponovu, document 322 (October 2, 1941).

allowed for some negotiation, unlike those involving Jews. In November 1941, for example, local officials confiscated the home shared by two Serb brothers on the grounds that they were supporting the enemy and had no right to citizenship; however, the officials allowed the wives of both men to remain in the house so that they could guard the property and live safely.[89] This was part of a broader trend. Since the Ustasha police was more keen to arrest Serb men than women (as men were considered a greater political threat), many Serb women found they were marginally freer. This did not mean that the Ustasha police did not harass and target women: there are a host of letters from Serb women recording harsh treatment at the hands of Ustasha soldiers and police.[90] But unlike Jewish women, Serb women were able to make these claims known. They could even assemble in small groups. In a remarkable show of solidarity, dozens of them joined in a public letter-writing campaign on behalf of family members arrested and deported in August. The standardized nature of the letters suggests that the women were organized in this endeavor, perhaps through a humanitarian group that the city had legalized to provide aid.[91]

Over the fall, Sarajevo's officials stretched the slackening of Ustasha reprisals against Serbs as far as they could. That November, an Ustasha official discovered that 37 out of 149 civil servants employed by the municipality of Sarajevo were Orthodox Serbs.[92] When pressed on the issue, Sarajevo's new mayor, Hasan Demirović—a quiet man known for his gentlemanly manners—coolly alluded to a problem in the local chain of command.[93] It was a fitting response that reflected myriad tensions and miscommunications between the city and state and within the city itself. Demirović epitomized Muslim-Catholic unity in the Croat nation: he was a Muslim man married to a Catholic woman and a member of Napredak.[94] He was loyal to the regime, but he was not as enthusiastically pro-Ustasha as the city's first occupation mayor, a fact that gave him more local credibility. He also appeared somewhat ill equipped to be mayor of a city Sarajevo's size, and the municipal government functioned poorly during his ten months in office. However, it would be naïve and inaccurate to explain the presence of these Serb clerks and schoolteachers as a simple bureaucratic oversight or a

89. HDA, Ministarstvo Unutrašnih Poslova NDH, box 32, document 889/41 (November 10, 1941).

90. For an example see HM, Ustaška građa, document 2350 (December 20, 1941).

91. These petitions are found in HM, Ustaška građa, starting around document 157 and continuing intermittently through the 2000s. Serb organizations are discussed in Borivoje Knežić, "Neuspjeli pokušaji Četnika da formiraju ravnogorsku organizaciju u Sarajevu," in Albahari et al., *Sarajevo u Revoluciji*, 3:620–626.

92. HM, Ustaška građa, document 2411 (November 8, 1941).

93. Ibid., document 2403 (March 7, 1942).

94. On Demirović's family life and national orientation, see Nametak, *Sarajevski Nekrologij*, 217–218. On his involvement in Napredak, see ABiH, Hrvatsko kulturno društvo Napredak, yearly report, box 153, document 512, (1943).

sign of Demirović's weak political position. The Serb presence in the city's public life spoke to an institutional and ideological disparity between the goals of the central government in Zagreb and those of its second largest city. The mayor's office would continue to interpret domaći according to the norms of the city, not those of the state.

Like the Serbs, most Jews who had the means and opportunity to leave Sarajevo during the summer did. There were few misconceptions about what life under Nazi occupation had in store for them. Their options, however, were more limited than those available to Serbs since the Nazis controlled the majority of the Balkan Peninsula. Fleeing to the Italian zone was costly and difficult, if still the safest and most commonly chosen path.[95] Several hundred Jews fled to the mountains to join the Partisan resistance. A handful of the most desperate adopted pseudonyms and pretended to be Serb refugees, taking their chances in Nazi-occupied Serbia.[96] Sephardic Jews had a larger regional network to fall back on than did the Ashkenazim, and many made their way to other Sephardic communities in Kosovo, Macedonia, and Albania (regions under Italian or Bulgarian occupation), where they lived clandestinely or eventually joined some resistance army.[97]

Those who remained in Sarajevo encountered the harsh laws examined in the preceding chapter—registration, property confiscation, unemployment, and social restrictions. Some tried to use their connections with friends and neighbors to continue working illegally. Berta, a Jewish hairdresser, complained to her customers that since a trustee had taken over her shop, she had to work for nothing. She suggested instead that she visit them at their homes, and many agreed. The trustee whined to the local employment office, "I caught her carrying the tools for private work. I stopped her and gave her a warning, but she ignored it and continued with this sabotage."[98] Obviously Berta was not the only one engaging in such sabotage: her clients were complicit by letting her cut their hair. Such acts speak to the ways that human relations were able to trump the emotional

95. Jozo Tomasevich does not discuss Sarajevo's Jews specifically, but he reviews the flight of Jews to the Italian zone in 1941 and estimates that four thousand Jews from Serbia, Croatia, and Bosnia survived there. See *War and Revolution in Yugoslavia*, 597–598. For a general study of Yugoslavia's Jewish refugees, see Milan Ristović, *U potrazi za Utočištem: Jugoslovenski Jevreji u Bekstvu od Holokausta 1941–1945* (Belgrade: Službeni list SRJ, 1998).

96. On Jewish mechanisms for survival, see the personal testimonies in Jaša Almirli, ed., *Živi i Mrtvi: Razgovori sa Jevrejima* (Belgrade: S. Mašić, 2002), 18–19, 65–66, 148–164; Aleksandar Gaon, ed. *Mi smo preživeli: Jevreji o Holokaustu* (Belgrade: Jevrejski Istorijski Muzej, 2001), 61–70, 117–120; and Dušan Sindik, ed., *Sećanja Jevreja na logor Jasenovac* (Belgrade: Savez Jevrejskih opština, 1972), 64–65, 74, 191–196.

97. The Sephardic network is referred to in some of the cases above and can also be read about further in works such as Pavle Dželetović Ivanov, *Jevreji Kosova i Metohije* (Belgrade: Panpublik, 1988); Jasmina Musabegović, *Kultura španskih Jevreja na Jugoslovenskom tlu* (Sarajevo: Svjetlost, 1990); and Ženi Lebl, *Jevreji u Pirotu* (Belgrade: Privredni pregled Biblioteka Svedočanstva, 1990).

98. ABiH, Povjerenstvo za Radnje Drž. Hrv.—Sarajevo, box 2, document 146 (July 3, 1941).

Figure 6. Jewish forced labor battalion working in Sarajevo, circa 1941. Courtesy of the Historical Museum of Bosnia and Herzegovina.

response of fear and manufactured state loyalty. Yet at the same time there was no mistaking the position that Jews held in the new state: forced labor battalions were set to work in downtown Sarajevo, where townsmen could witness the degradation and prisoner status of their neighbors on a daily basis.

Throughout the summer of 1941, most of Sarajevo's remaining Jews sought to keep a low profile. Those arrested by the Ustasha police were considered Communists and shot alongside their alleged political counterparts. This changed on September 3, 1941. In the middle of the night, the Gestapo and Ustasha police abruptly woke five hundred Sarajevo Jewish men, women, and children, gave them a few minutes to pack their belongings, herded them down to the train station, and deported them in cattle cars to the Krivica holding camp.[99] The Jews were selected by the Ustasha police and had little in common other than their "race." Among them was Isidor Levi, who described in his memoir how he and the others lived in the transit camp for about three weeks, starving because the Ustasha guards refused to deliver relief packages from Sarajevo's Red Cross and other local organizations. Levi noted that as more Jews arrived from Sarajevo, the

99. The most vivid account of the deportation is ABiH, Zemaljska komisija za utvrđivanje ratnih zločina okupatora i njihovih pomagača za BiH, Bujas report, box 3. Robert J Donia analyzes the report in *Sarajevo*, 176–179.

guards divided the men from the women and transported them to separate camps in northern Bosnia. Levi, like many of the men, ended up in the infamous camp Jasenovac, where he worked as a prisoner for the next few years. Luckier than most, he eventually escaped and survived the war.[100]

City leaders felt blindsided and frustrated by the deportations, which continued steadily until December. They resented the manner in which the authorities carried out the deportation business. Immediately after the first deportation, Volksdeutsche and Ustasha soldiers raided and looted Jewish apartments, as in the first days of the German occupation. The Ustasha police and the Gestapo carried out a second night raid days later. Jews became frantic, sending last-minute pleas to city and Ustasha officials, begging futilely for their lives.[101] Escape became increasingly difficult; Ustasha soldiers guarded the train station and closed off parts of the city. But many Jews still tried. Their strategies ranged from disguising themselves as religious Muslim women to fleeing on foot into the mountains.

In the aftermath of the deportations, city officials grew especially hostile toward the Volksdeutsche, who became known for cruelly evicting Jews, claiming the best apartments for themselves, and tattling to the Gestapo whenever local officials constrained their actions.[102] The Volksdeutsche had a sense of entitlement that grated on the officials' nerves. On October 18, the city's housing office complained to the county executive that it had hired two expert engineers and invested several million *kuna* (Croatian currency) to construct a new building, only to have the engineers "taken away" by members of the Kulturbund, the local Volkdeutsche organization.[103] The housing office asked the county executive to pressure the Germans into releasing the engineers and their families, who had also been imprisoned. Because entire families were taken, we can assume that they were Jews, although the correspondence never mentioned the engineers' background. To many Sarajevo officials, the racial or religious background of these Sarajevans was irrelevant. They resented the involvement of Volksdeutsche in determining who had the right to live and work in their city.

After the war ended, the longest-lasting legacy of the Ustasha regime's first year in power would be the deportation and murder of Sarajevo's Jews. At the time, however, the angriest battles between the city and the new authorities occurred over the regime's disregard for the autonomy of religion. Whereas many of Sarajevo's ruling elite looked the other way as the Jews were dragged out of the city, they voiced immediate opposition to the deportation of those who had converted to Islam or Catholicism. In September 1941, Fehim Spaho ordered the Ulema Medžlis to take Jewish

100. Gaon, *Mi smo preživjeli,* 64–65.
101. See an example in HM, Ustaška građa, document 2339 (October 31, 1941).
102. On the tensions between Sarajevans and the Volksdeutsche, see IAS, Gradsko Poglavarstvo, box 898 (September 10, 1941) and box 941 (November 10, 1941).
103. HM, Ustaška građa, document 2281 (October 18, 1941).

Muslims "into shelter"; he personally intervened in so many cases that the Bosnian historian Enver Redžić suggests he did more for his Sarajevo Jewish converts than for Muslims outside the city.[104] St. Joseph's Catholic Church, where Father Bralo served as pastor, sent documents in support of its parishioners.[105] Although conversion would not spare Jews from deportation, it occasionally bought them time to flee to the Italian zone or to the mountains, where the armed insurgency was gaining ground.

Protecting converts was not simply a matter of Muslims helping Muslims and Catholics helping Catholics. Many members of Sarajevo's political elite viewed these converts as a part of the city's collective. For example, the county executive, Ismet Gavran-Kapetanović, a highly respected Ustasha appointee, fought to have a Catholic couple of Jewish descent released from Jasenovac. He argued that the couple had been deported "illegally." A high-ranking Ustasha official responded that it did not matter whether the Jews "had converted to a recognized religion" because they were still Jews. Undeterred, Gavran-Kapetanović solicited the intervention of Ante Pavelić, to whom he insisted that the couple should be released from Jasenovac and "returned to the same apartment from which they were taken."[106] The request was denied.

Local actions on behalf of Jews were not necessarily done with the intent to undermine the regime or show solidarity with the Jews. Many officials were struggling to preserve the city's civic codes and prevent antigovernment backlash, as well as to appease religious leaders. Yet in a few cases they seem to have acted with no other purpose than to alleviate the unnecessary cruelty inflicted on their Jewish townsmen. Sarajevo's chapter of the Red Cross, for example, disobeyed instructions from its headquarters in Zagreb and sent packages of food and clothing to Jews being held in Gospić, a nearby camp.[107]

Again, the reaction of ordinary Muslims and Catholics varied. Some Sarajevans forged documents so that Jews could travel. Others hid Jewish friends or colleagues in their homes. Indeed, hiding Jews became so commonplace that in early November the city's Ustasha authorities reprimanded the entire city for hindering the deportations and made assisting Jews in any way a criminal offense. Censure did not deter many Sarajevans, nor did the possibility of stricter punishment.[108] Yet for every Sarajevan helping a Jew, there was another eagerly awaiting to claim the property of a

104. ARIZBiH, Ulema Medžlis, document 3789/41 (September 30, 1941); Redžić, *Bosnia and Herzegovina in the Second World War,* 172.

105. See, for example, IAS, Gradsko Poglavarstvo, box 924 (October 6, 1941).

106. HM, Ustaška građa, document 232 (January 2, 1942).

107. ABiH, Društvo Crveni križ, box 22, document 1823 (July 25, 1941) and document 1965 (August 29, 1941).

108. Bujas report, 18–19. See also the public reprimand in the city newspaper, *Sarajevski Novi List,* November 29, 1941, 4.

Jewish neighbor dragged off in the night. Working-class Muslims and Catholics, men and women caught in the throes of the economic turmoil of war, lined up for Jewish clothing, shoes, and furniture.[109] At the same time, the squabbles over Jewish property provoked a harsh response from some of the city's religious leaders, who reproached Sarajevans for their "immoral" and materialistic behavior. A columnist at *Katolički Tjednik*, Sarajevo's main Catholic paper, wrote several critiques of Catholics' "embarrassing behavior," reprimanding Sarajevans for pilfering Jewish clothing.[110] Likewise, the Islamic journal, *El-Hidaje*, criticized Muslims for being obsessed with material goods, which the paper linked to a decline in religious morality.[111] Religious leaders expected their communities to act according to the values of their faith. These critiques, however, had little to do with reactions to Jewish mistreatment and much to do with regulating the behavior of Muslims and Catholics. Antisemitic references continued to appear in both the Catholic and Muslim press over the next year, often printed side by side with columns on how to live a moral life. But the nature of this morality and its incompatibility with the Ustasha system gradually was becoming a preoccupation of religious thinkers.

Explaining Different Paths

Two trains left the Sarajevo depot within days of each other in mid-November 1941. On November 15, a string of cattle cars filled with more than a thousand Jews departed for a nearby holding camp. Because of logistical problems, the prisoners were held for days without food before being transferred elsewhere. A week later, on November 22, a passenger train carrying forty-nine Serb orphans departed for Belgrade, where the children were to be repatriated with extended family members. The local chapter of the Croatian Red Cross coordinated with police and Red Cross chapters throughout Bosnia to ensure that the children, ranging in age from two to eleven, received warm dinners and coffee with milk during their journey.[112]

It is hard to imagine a starker contrast between the fates of the two trains' passengers and the communities they left behind. At the start of the war Sarajevo had a flourishing Jewish community of ten thousand members; by the war's end it had been completely destroyed. All but a few hundred of Sarajevo's Jews would be gone by August 1942. Some would find shelter in the Italian zone or fighting with the insurgents. Most would perish in the camps. By contrast, Sarajevo's Serbs would gradually be welcomed back on

109. There are numerous requests for property from the fall of 1941 in IAS, Gradsko Poglavarstvo, boxes 918–929.
110. *Katolički Tjednik*, February 1, 1942, 7.
111. *El-Hidaje*, December 4, 1941, 42–49.
112. The Red Cross transport is described in ABiH, Društvo Crveni križ, box 22, document 2523 (November 21, 1941).

local sports teams and invited to participate in Ustasha youth groups. By the end of 1942, they would be granted citizenship rights and encouraged to participate in all aspects of Sarajevo's public life, from its government to its defense. Such a trend was hardly indicative of the general narrative in the NDH. Elsewhere in the state, the Ustashas arrested, deported, and killed Serbs with infamous viciousness throughout 1941. Even Jewish survivors in some parts of the country noted that the Ustasha soldiers treated Serbs more brutally than anyone else.[113] But in Sarajevo the experience and treatment of the two pariah groups took dramatically different turns.

How do we explain the Ustasha regime's exhaustive and methodical attack on Sarajevo's Jews when they had willingly negotiated with city leaders over the fate of Serbs and Roma? It is possible that the regime understood that Sarajevo's Serbs were a useful bargaining chip in their negotiations with local leaders. Because Serbs were *not* non-Aryan, according to German racial codes, the Ustashas had some flexibility in the way they handled Serb policies. This would explain why in June 1941, for example, Zagreb requested that Sarajevo's mayor compile a list of *all* properties belonging to Jews, as well as those owned by Serbs that the city thought should be placed under supervision.[114]

In the city itself, most local leaders blamed the Germans for the regime's inflexibility toward Jews. In early October, Fehim Spaho complained to a fellow Muslim, "[T]he Germans take every Jew, even those who have converted to Islam and Catholicism . . . that is the work of the Germans and our own government cannot intervene, it can do nothing about it."[115] Given the Ustasha regime's willingness to entertain discussions on exemptions for converts, Muslim Roma, and domaći Serbs, it appears that Spaho was on to something. German officers frequently collaborated with the Ustasha police to locate and arrest Jews, at times even acting independently.[116] Removing Sarajevo's Jews was part of Nazi Germany's plan to cleanse the Balkans of non-Aryans. The treatment of Jews in other German-occupied cities such as Belgrade, Novi Sad, and Niš was similar to that of the Jews in Sarajevo, while Jews in cities without an active German presence, like Novi Pazar, Mostar, and Priština, were initially left alone.[117] It is well documented that the Italians had influence over policies toward Jews in the territories they occupied, though historians debate whether the higher survival

113. Cadik I. Danon "Braco," *Sasečeno stablo Danonovih, sećanje na Jasenovac* (Belgrade: S. Masić, 2000), 30; Gaon, *Mi smo preživeli*, 35, 61.

114. ABiH, Povjerenstvo za Radnje Drž. Hrv.—Sarajevo, box 3, document 381 (June 3, 1941).

115. IAS, Ostavština Fehima Spaha, box 3, document 763 (October 14, 1941).

116. HM, Ustaška građa, document 190 (November 28, 1941) and document 191 (November 29, 1941).

117. For comparisons with other cities, see Ženi Lebl, *Do Konačnog Rešenja: Jevreji u Srbiji* (Belgrade: Čigoja štampa, 2002), and Ejub Mušović, "Nešto o novopazarskim Jevrejima i njihovoj sudbini u drugom svjetskom ratu," *Jevrejski Almanah*, 1965–1967, 149–156.

rates stemmed from the Italians' humanitarianism or from their efforts to assert their authority in the region.[118] Even if the Ustasha leaders had been willing to negotiate with Sarajevo's leaders on the fate of certain Jews, as they were over the fate of some local Serbs and Roma, they could not. Since Sarajevo fell squarely in the German occupation zone and was something of a regional headquarters, Jews were slated for removal. There was no point in discussing the possibility of some kind of domaći status for Jews.

This is certainly not to say that the Ustashas were friendly toward Jews or blameless in the Holocaust. In fact, quite the opposite was true: Pavelić's regime became more enthusiastically involved in the deportations and the persecution of Sarajevo's Jews in October and November 1941. It is unclear whether Pavelić hoped to strengthen his position vis-à-vis the Germans and Italians in the area or whether he believed that controlling the Jewish question would help him to consolidate power in a city now famous for pursuing its own agenda. One plausible explanation, offered by Alexander Korb, is that the Ustasha believed that the Holocaust could help integrate the nation, that killing Jews would become the rallying point for national revival and help the struggling nation-state strengthen from within.[119] Whatever the Ustasha reasoning might have been, the result was that on October 20, Pavelić assigned a Ustasha deportation "specialist," Ivan Tolj, to "resolve Sarajevo's Jewish question." Days after Tolj's arrival, he organized a transport of 1,400 Jews, the largest deportation from Sarajevo to that point.[120] Satisfied with the deportation's success, Tolj decided to organize an even larger transport on November 15. This time, however, overzealous Ustasha police rounded up too many Jews too quickly and created a chaotic situation because there was no place to intern the prisoners. The Germans resumed control, returning some Jews to Sarajevo and temporarily halting large-scale deportations. Incensed by this impingement on his authority, the Ustasha deputy of Bosnia, Jure Francetić, wrote to the minister of the interior, Andrije Artuković, that the anti-Jewish measures had been successful and even uplifting for the city. He demanded permission to continue straightaway.[121] The Germans, however, insisted on waiting a few weeks. The last large-scale transport from Sarajevo occurred on December 22, 1941, and included 500 Jewish women and children. All but 200 of the city's remaining Jews left in smaller transports during the following spring

118. Competing explanations of Italian behavior are offered by Steinberg in *All or Nothing*, 15–49, and throughout Rodogno, *Fascism's European Empire*.

119. Alexander Korb, "The Drina Border, Nationalizing Civil War, and the Holocaust in the Independent State of Croatia, 1941–43" (paper presented at the Institute for Global Studies, University of Minnesota, 2007).

120. Bujas report, 18.

121. HDA, Ministarstvo Unutarnjih Poslova-NDH, box 36, document 3801/41 (November 21, 1941).

and summer, converts included.[122] From that point forward, Jews, not Serbs, became the essential foreigners in Ustasha ideology, synonymous with the other foreign enemy threatening the NDH: the Communists.

• • •

As the Ustasha regime began its messy and indiscriminate campaign to cleanse the NDH of non-Croats and non-Aryans, Sarajevo's leaders felt compelled to articulate their own definitions of community. Although many local leaders supported the Axis cause, they disagreed with a central tenet of the new European order: that biology could determine an individual's identity. Consequently, Sarajevo's leaders fought for exemptions for individuals—and at times, entire groups—who they believed belonged to their community because of a shared religious, ethnic, or civic connection. This led to noticeably different local policies for Jewish converts to Islam and Catholicism, Muslim Roma, and Sarajevo Serbs than were called for by the national agenda. Certainly there were active participants in the genocidal campaign—police who raided apartments and rounded up non-Croats, corrupt trustees who stole property and abused their charges, citizens who turned in neighbors. There were also countless city officials who participated in the discriminatory campaign through the everyday activities of their bureaucratic posts and townsmen who moved into their neighbors' homes, finding advantage in their neighbors' victimization.

But the other theme that emerges from studying local processes of ethnic cleansing in Sarajevo is the persistence of a civic community spirit despite the overpowering ideology of Nazism and Ustashism. In small and often strange ways, the city's codes of civility and neighborliness carried on, revealing institutional and cultural defiance of the regime's ideological agenda. Widespread efforts to hide Jews during the deportations, despite threats of imprisonment, suggest that many Sarajevans refused to condone, let alone participate, in the attacks on their neighbors. Civilians who visited blacklisted hairdressers, helped forge papers, or wrote letters petitioning for better treatment of neighbors victimized by corrupt trustees all exemplified the tight bonds of a civic collective. These codes of neighborliness were observed even at the bureaucratic level, as in the cases where local officials refused to confiscate property unless they received permission from the rightful owner. It was not uncommon for judges and town administrators to use their positions to protect and serve, rather than for opportunistic personal gain. Every agency from the police department to the mayor's office insisted on keeping some Serbs in its employ. All these examples illustrate the viability of certain local codes and traditions that intrinsically sought

122. HM, Ustaška građa, document 211 (December 22, 1941). On the deportations in 1942, see Stajić and Papo, "Ubistva i drugi," 239–240.

to protect the politics, social life, and culture of the Sarajevo community. Complicity was often employed as a way to protect the local community and could lead to either beneficial or detrimental outcomes for the individuals targeted for discrimination. On the whole, it was the preservation of community that Sarajevans took as their primary moral mandate, often grudgingly accepting the unfortunate fates of individuals as the cost of maintaining this higher structure.

In protecting their local identities, many Sarajevans placed greater importance on preserving the ethical system behind categorizing people than on protecting all the individuals who fell into that category. Serbs could be arrested as political enemies, but classifying Serbs along racial lines made the townsmen uneasy. Similarly, Muslim leaders refused to condone targeting Muslim Roma on racial lines; yet many of them had no qualms about imprisoning beggars of Muslim Roma background whom they perceived as a threat to the city's social order. This process could even be seen in the town's reaction to the deportation of Jews. Some Muslim and Catholic town leaders began to view Jews as a necessary sacrifice for participating in the new order, whether for genuine ideological reasons or for practical ones. Others accepted the futility of protecting those slated for removal and instead invested energy and resources into saving and serving communities that remained behind. What is fascinating about the Sarajevo case is that even when they accepted that Jews fell outside their civic community, most local leaders still insisted that Jewishness was a confessional identity. Consequently, they believed that Jews who converted to Islam or Catholicism were in effect changed back into Sarajevans.

For this reason, the abrupt commencement of the Jewish deportations in September 1941 signaled to the local elite that the social transformation they had embarked upon was irreversible and irreconcilable with Sarajevo's society. The foundation of the city's traditional social order was crumbling. As community leaders grappled with the possible long-term consequences of Nazism and Ustashism, they grew distressed. Perhaps if the transition from job purges to cattle cars had occurred over a longer period of time, as it did in many parts of Europe, Sarajevans would have adjusted to it. Instead they felt it as a sharp strike on their entire way of life. Ultimately, the Ustasha regime's poorly articulated laws of citizenship and identity disclosed the myth of Aryan identity for what it was, while subjective and fluctuating laws defining foreigners exposed the ideological inconsistency of Hitler's "New Order" and of the Croat nation.

4

BETWEEN IDENTITIES

The Fragile Bonds of Community

As Pavelić's regime sought to tighten its biologically based notions of identity and reinforce categories of "them"—non-Aryans, foreigners, and other non-Croats—Sarajevo's leaders increasingly tried to modify state policies to reflect local agendas. Notions of belonging took on new meaning in the winter of 1941–42 as the armed insurgency advanced into the hills above the city, where it would remain lurking for the rest of the war. The civil conflict not only accentuated local tensions but also contributed to a growing sense among Sarajevo's leaders that their town was not safe. A Croat army officer captured local anxieties with a warning to Zagreb that winter: "Sarajevo is not even remotely prepared to defend itself."[1] Panic spread among members of the local elite, who realized that their society—indeed, their way of life—was under siege. Local leaders became consumed by the fear that anarchy would topple the city, Communism would destroy religious life, and the Ustasha regime's ideological and genocidal campaign had permanently destroyed the city's character. The German, Italian, and Ustasha armies were too consumed with fighting the resilient insurgency to offer guidance or assistance, leaving local leaders with a perpetual sense of abandonment. Seeking communal cohesion amid an expanding insurrection, many local leaders sought to isolate Sarajevo and root the town firmly in its local culture.

Throughout 1941 and 1942, Sarajevans were suspended between two dynamics that this chapter explores: competition among Muslim, Catholic, and Orthodox communities over the meaning of "Croatianness" and the strengthening of a civic consciousness through renewed civic, cultural, and political ties. The former threatened to tear the delicate seams of the town's social fabric by pitting members of different communities against one

---

1. HM, Ustaška Nadzorna Služba, document 262 (December 20, 1941).

another; the latter aggressively attempted to stitch the town back together amid a grave humanitarian, security, and political crisis. Famine, typhus, refugees, homelessness, and wood shortages dominated the local agenda, provoking debates among local leaders over the meaning of civic responsibility and the boundaries of the community. In particular, the influx of tens of thousands of poor, predominantly Muslim peasant refugees forced local leaders to reflect on how to judge membership in the city's collective.[2] The refugees threatened to corrupt Sarajevo's cosmopolitan character, unbalance traditional confessional dynamics, and impair the local government's ability to take care of Sarajevans. In the minds of many, the fate of the nation began to take second place to the survival of the local community—yet the question of who belonged to that community continued to be heavily debated.

Muslims on the Margins of a Catholic Nation

The subjectivity of the Ustasha regime's national and racial ideologies, examined in the last chapter, highlighted the complex process of defining non-Croats. The other side of this equation was classifying Croats, an equally thorny issue. The Ustasha regime's vague national rhetoric and its proclivity to periodically redefine the Croat nation created tremendous friction in Sarajevo, particularly concerning the relationship of religion to national identity. On the one hand, the regime had made clear through its treatment of Jewish converts to Islam and Catholicism that confession took second place to race. Yet at the same time, the regime's policies and propaganda continually emphasized a national concept anchored in religion. Even in categorizing groups within the nation, the regime distinguished among Muslim Croats and Catholic Croats. The concept of the Croat nation consistently failed to serve as a unifying mechanism.

Disunity on the national level created mass confusion on the local level, and in no community was this more apparent than the Muslim. From the state's foundations in April 1941, Muslims had been uncertain of exactly where they fit into the Croat nation. Although many of them had taken part in interwar Croat political life, and though the regime welcomed them as Croats and made overtures to the Islamic Religious Community, the place of Islam in the NDH was unclear. Part of the issue was that Sarajevo's Muslims—even those who supported Fascism and the regime—maintained a distinct sense of their identity as Muslims. Men like Deputy Hakija Hadžić, a Muslim Croat Ustasha who placed his loyalty to Croats ahead of Islam,

---

2. A survey of migration patterns and the wartime refugee question in Yugoslavia can be found in Slobodan D. Milošević, *Izbeglice i preseljenici na teritoriji okupirane Jugoslavije, 1941–1945* (Belgrade: Institut za savremenu istoriju, 1981).

were rare. Most Muslims who worked for the regime thought of themselves as Muslim Croats, not simply Croats, and they believed it was vital to incorporate their religious and cultural heritage into Croat national culture. In the early wartime period, the Ustasha leaders in Zagreb encouraged a link between Islam and the nation and contended that the "center of the moral power of the Croat people is found in the orderly and religious life of the family." This suggested to some Muslims that Croat national culture and Islamic culture were compatible.[3] Yet the link between the two remained unclear.

How would it be determined that a particular Muslim was a Croat? Would such an identity be claimed by the Muslim or would it be decided by someone else, and by whom? Many Muslims considered themselves Muslims first but simultaneously felt a Serb or Croat national affiliation. Whereas the Ustashas assumed all Catholics were Croats until proven otherwise, Muslims consistently had to prove their membership in the national community. The Ustashas used "Muslim" as an adjective to modify national categories rather than as an identity in its own right. While the regime viewed Muslim Croats as Aryan Croats, it excluded Muslim Serbs, Muslim Roma, and Muslim Jews from eligibility in the Croat nation, firing and arresting Muslims who fell into one of these latter categories.[4] The regime also dismantled Muslim societies deemed pro-Serb, like Gajret, the organization that had organized the anti-Jewish conference in March 1941. Being antisemitic was not enough to prove loyalty.

Muslims who aligned with the regime were often in the uncomfortable position of watching and even participating in the attack on fellow Muslims. Members of Narodna Uzdanica, the Muslim Croat cultural society, spent countless hours debating whether they should participate in the confiscation of Gajret's property, which the regime had strategically assigned to them in an effort to strengthen ties between Muslims and the Croat nation and sever ties among Muslims themselves. The two Muslim organizations shared similar missions, and members were often friends and family. Some members of Narodna Uzdanica suggested that the society invite Gajret Muslims into their ranks. Deputy Hadžić bluntly rejected the proposal and criticized the board for delaying the confiscation process. Eventually Narodna Uzdanica agreed to take over Gajret's property, justifying its decision on the grounds that the society would be able to continue Gajret's important work. Yet not a single member of Narodna Uzdanica volunteered to oversee Gajret's liquidation. In the closing remarks of one meeting, a board member tried to assuage the organization's sense of guilt. He argued that members of Narodna Uzdanica had not taken part in the liquidation;

3. Tomasevich, *War and Occupation in Yugoslavia*, 336–339. For examples from wartime literature, see *Novi Behar*, May 15, 1941; *Sarajevski Novi List*, May 13, 1941, 3.

4. IAS, Ostavština Fehima Spaha, box 3, document 696 (May 7, 1941).

rather, it was something that had happened to them, and they should therefore use the income to help other Muslims. Increasingly, Muslims working
with the regime framed themselves as helpless or unwilling participants
in the Ustasha program rather than as partners in the nation-building
project.[5]

Sarajevo's Catholic press fueled Muslim insecurities. Although the
church accepted the necessity of a political alliance between the two religious communities, it remained hostile to the inclusion of Muslims in the
Croat nation.[6] Clerical Croat nationalists, among whom Sarajevo's Archbishop Ivan Šarić could be counted, fervently believed that the Croat nation
was a Catholic one and that religious life—specifically Catholicism—should
be the ethical foundation of society. The Catholic Church in Sarajevo had
held this position steadfastly for decades, despite attempts of some Croat
political and cultural leaders to embrace a nonreligious notion of nationhood. With the integration of Muslims into the political body, the local
church went on the offensive to protect its own understanding of nation.
Nearly every issue of *Katolički Tjednik* included an article arguing that Christianity and the "Catholic people" (*Katolički narod*) formed the foundations
of Croatia. In April, the paper noted that "only Christian morals can cement
national life."[7] In May, the Archbishop wrote, "One cannot be Croat without
his church. The Croat works and suffers for her. . . . We will always link our
loyalty to our religious belief. Always Croats, always Catholics!"[8] A month
later, the paper continued,

> In front of our eyes, a new Croat state is forming. It is our desire that this
> Croat state be a Catholic state. . . . All major historical components of our
> national life come from Christian and Catholic sources. Nowadays, the vast
> majority of the Croat people profess the Catholic confession. *A non-Catholic or
> anti-Catholic Croatia would be neither the old nor the historical Croatia.*[9]

As the church intensified its propaganda, Sarajevo's Muslims worried that
Pavelić's regime might gradually make Catholicism a prerequisite for membership in the Croat nation and—in the worst-case scenario—force Muslims to convert to Catholicism.[10]

---

5. The controversy over Gajret is discussed in *Narodna Uzdanica Kalendar,* 1942, 221–224.
The minutes of the actual debate can be found in IAS, Narodna Uzdanica, zapisnik, box 50
(July 1941).
6. The church's official line on the importance of the political relationship can be read in
Vrhbosna, June 1941, 131.
7. "Mir i Slobode," *Katolički Tjednik,* April 27, 1941, 7.
8. "Bog i Hrvati," *Katolički Tjednik,* May 18, 1941, 6.
9. "Katolička Država," *Katolički Tjednik,* June 29, 1941, 3. Italics are in the original.
10. On additional local Catholic propaganda, see Jozo Horvat and Zdenko Štambuk, eds.,
Dokumenti o protunarodnom radu i zločinima jednog dijela katoličkog klera, (Zagreb: Stamparija
Rozankowski, 1946), 28.

Ustasha leaders in Zagreb faced a delicate balancing act. They needed to allay Muslims' fears and counter local hostilities while simultaneously catering to church leaders, who served as a pillar of support for the NDH. In July 1941, the minister of justice and religion, Mile Budak, wrote an article for the Islamic Religious Community's official paper, in which he noted that Muslim Croats had every reason to be angry and dissatisfied with the behavior of Catholic Croats, who, he acknowledged, wrongly believed that Muslims were historically their "sworn enemy."[11] He called on Catholics to appreciate and respect important Muslim historical figures and to cooperate with Muslim Croats. In August, Pavelić made overtures to Muslim religious leaders, approving the construction of a mosque in Zagreb and setting up a committee to draft new laws for the Islamic Religious Community. He also gave speeches on the sanctity of Islam and the importance of Muslim Croats in achieving the dreams of Croatia's independence.[12] Following the lead of the party bosses in Zagreb, Ustasha officials in Sarajevo circulated notices that outlined Muslim religious customs, explaining to people unfamiliar with Islam why Muslim employees left early on Fridays and exactly what it meant to fast during Ramadan.[13]

In further attempts to counterbalance Catholic nationalist rhetoric by showing deference to the Muslim community, Sarajevo's Ustasha officials introduced in September 1941 the Ramadan Decrees, a set of city laws that forbade gambling, prostitution, and late-night drinking during the month-long religious holiday. Some of the decrees affected non-Muslims as well as Muslims. Sarajevans were forbidden to stroll before and after *iftar*—the breaking of the fast that occurs at sundown. Moreover, only restaurants not serving alcohol were allowed to remain open late in the evening. The decrees even included special laws to monitor and "protect" women, such as prohibiting men from attending gatherings of veiled women and severely punishing Muslim women who "shamelessly" exposed themselves (a law designed to combat prostitution). Women caught in violation were to be punished with a night in jail and a mandatory gynecological exam.[14] Although I have found no evidence suggesting the Ustasha police strictly enforced these laws, they nevertheless reveal the regime's interest in currying favor with observant Muslims.

But such overtures were never institutionalized in Ustasha political culture. Of the 2,500 Ustasha officials based in Sarajevo in 1941, only 150 were Muslim—and they were expected to work on Fridays, the Muslim holy day.[15]

11. Mile Budak, "Dr. Mehmed ef. Spaho," *Glasnik Islamske Vjerske Zajednice*, June–July 1941, 165–170.
12. On Pavelić's support of Muslim programs and the Muslim agenda, see *El-Hidaje*, August 1941, 300–301, and September 1941, 24–29.
13. HM, Ustaška građa, document 1936 (August 22, 1941).
14. Ibid., document 2148 (September 16, 1941).
15. See an essay by Muhamed Hadžijahić written during the war, which can be found in IAS, Zbirka Varia, document 487 (date unknown; most likely written sometime in 1943 or 1944).

The regime showed favoritism toward the Catholic hierarchy by allowing Muslims to convert to Catholicism, breaking Islamic law and defying the Ulema Medžlis.[16] Moreover, Jewish and Orthodox converts to Islam found it harder to get exemptions from state discriminatory laws than did converts to Catholicism. When Fehim Spaho grilled the Ministry of the Interior about the discrepancy, it responded that Muslims were not singled out because they were Muslim, alleging instead that the ill-treated converts were suspicious individuals who had converted to escape punishment or to hide.[17] There is no evidence to suggest any truth to this rebuttal.

Muslim workers documented discrimination in the workplace as well. Employees at the Health Department (*Higijenski zavod*), for example, complained to the Ulema Medžlis that they were allowed to attend Friday services only if they arrived at work at 6:00 a.m. or stayed until 9:00 p.m. The Ulema Medžlis contacted the county executive's office to express its concern that Muslims were being obstructed from practicing their faith, to which the county replied that it was "completely respectful" in its dealings with the Islamic community and that only by knowing exactly which Muslims were complaining could it properly redress the situation.[18] The threat implicit in such a request would not have gone unnoticed.

NDH education policies stirred up more discontent. Muslims complained that the Ustashas appointed mostly Catholic Croats to oversee Sarajevo schools and often transferred Muslim teachers to rural Orthodox Serb villages. In a letter to Mile Budak, Fehim Spaho petitioned on behalf one Muslim teacher who had been thus exiled, arguing that "although he was at one time a representative of the Muslim Serb cultural society Gajret, [the teacher] viewed that position as a cultural one and never emphasized any Serbianness."[19] Muslim administrators at a local crafts school argued that since Muslim Croats formed a majority in Sarajevo and among the student body, they should be given more influence in the school system—their particular demand was for a Muslim principal.[20] A further problem was that education laws passed in Zagreb often had a Catholic slant. For example, the Ministry of Education passed a decree in early September 1941 that every school day would begin with a recitation of the Lord's Prayer and that students would be required to attend Holy Services. Sarajevo's Muslims protested, demanding that noon prayers be substituted for Holy Services and that Christian services take place in churches, not schools.[21] The regime responded by passing new measures in early October that

16. See, for example, the case of Džemal C. in IAS, Gradsko Poglavarstvo, box 881 (September 15, 1941).
17. HDA, Ministarstvo Unutrašnih Poslova NDH, box 32, document 921/41 (August 14, 1941–September 5, 1941).
18. ARIZBiH, Ulema Medžlis, document 3361 (December 17, 1941).
19. IAS, Ostavština Fehima Spaha, box 3, document 749 (September 20, 1941).
20. HM, Ustaška građa, document 2250 (September 29, 1941).
21. Ibid., document 2160 (September 18, 1941).

allowed Muslim schoolchildren a one-hour break from school for Friday prayers and guaranteed that the schools would respect Muslim religious holidays.[22] However, the regime's underlying educational policies continued to favor Catholics over Muslims. The Department of Education, for example, budgeted money for the teaching of catechism in Sarajevo's schools but not for the Muslim equivalent.[23]

The role of women in the public sphere became another point of contention between Muslims and the regime. As a Fascistic movement, the Ustashas envisioned women as the centerpiece of the nation and family. Imitating policies in Nazi Germany, they developed an elaborate structure of women's organizations in order to indoctrinate women into their ideology and forge a new generation of mothers of the nation.[24] But Muslim leaders, approaching the matter from a fundamentally different sociocultural framework, viewed such organizations as blatant attempts to pry Muslim women out of the private sphere.[25] Against the wishes of Muslim religious leaders, Ustasha Party leaders forced Muslim girls to join the Ustasha youth group and required that Muslim women volunteer at party offices and military bases, contradicting Islamic laws that mandated gender segregation.[26] For its part, the Ustasha regime believed that duty to the nation should take precedence over religious custom.

It is easy to see why Muslims were angry and confused. In April 1941, they had been courted as an integral part of the Croat nation and promised autonomy. By August, an Orthodox Serb without political ties to Serbia could be declared an Aryan and retain citizenship; a Jewish convert to Catholicism could be classified as an honorary Aryan and reinstated in his job; but a Muslim with ties to the former Yugoslav government could be seen as racially Serb, denied property, and imprisoned. The deportations of Muslim Roma and Jewish converts to Islam underscored the limitations placed on religious autonomy; the targeting of Muslim Serbs made it clear that Muslims had to earn Croat status. It is impossible to know how the Muslim elite would have responded to the racial and discriminatory laws, let alone the Holocaust, had members of their own community not come under attack. But seeing fellow Muslims suffer raised their awareness of the dangers of extreme nationalism, religious intolerance, and racial

22. Laws from October 1, 1941, *Zbornik zakona i naredaba Nezavisne Države Hrvatske*, 15:55–57.

23. HDA, Ministarstvo Narodne Prosvjete NDH, box 1416 (November 18, 1941).

24. For an overview of Nazi German policies, see Claudia Koonz, *Mothers in the Fatherland: Women, the Family, and Nazi Politics* (New York: St. Martin's, 1987). There were several organized Ustasha women's groups in Sarajevo, which are discussed in *Sarajevski Novi List*, November 11, 1941, 3.

25. For examples of Muslim discussions of the "woman question," see *Glasnik Islamske Vjerske Zajednice*, August 1941, 214, and February 1942, 53–56; and *Osvit*, February 22, 1942, 4.

26. ARIZBiH, Ulema Medžlis, document 19/43 (December 21, 1941).

persecution. It also raised questions about what it meant to belong to this nation in the first place.

Throughout the fall of 1941, many Muslim leaders decided to extricate themselves from the stranglehold of the regime. Reis-ul-ulema Spaho became so leery of the regime's deceptive attempt to co-opt Muslim support that he refused to write articles or give speeches on its behalf.[27] Mehmed Handžić, the leader of the Islamic organization El-Hidaje, took an even more radical approach. No longer a trusted ally of Zagreb, Handžić published an article arguing that nothing about Islam made it incompatible with the state; thus if the state's ideology seemed to be in conflict with Islam, it was either the ideology or the state that had to change.[28]

Exasperated with the regime, a group of 108 important Sarajevo Muslims—including imams and ulema, merchants, judges, bureaucrats, and students—met in early October to discuss their grievances. On October 12, they issued a strongly worded statement to Zagreb and city leaders. The statement had two parts. The first criticized the Ustasha army's tactic of deliberately dressing non-Muslim "criminals" (the militiamen) in the fez, a hat worn by Muslims, which gave the victims of Ustasha violence the false impression that Muslims were the primary perpetrators. The petitioners complained that the soldiers' dress presented a contradictory image to Muslims' historical reputation in the region as being "gentlemanly and tolerant of everyone, regardless of religion." The second part of the statement entreated Muslim public figures to aid and defend suffering citizens of *all* religions, to protect the world's "virgins" with "all the strength of the army," to prevent riots and religious intolerance, and to guarantee that every accused criminal receive a fair trial. Sarajevo's Muslims thus attempted to distance Islam from Pavelić's regime and to create an image of Muslims as the agents of peace.[29] Muslims wrote similar resolutions in towns across Bosnia, revealing that their leaders were in contact with one another as they began to take a public stand against the policies of the Ustasha regime.

While it is tempting to interpret the Sarajevo resolution (or any of the resolutions) as a moral stand, it cannot be overlooked that most of the signers had supported the German and Ustasha agenda in the preceding months.[30] Though they now preached against religious intolerance, twelve of the men had also signed the antisemitic petition to "stop the Jews" in

27. IAS, Ostavština Fehima Spaha, box 3, document 761 (October 13, 1941).

28. H. M. Handžić, "Patriotizam, narodnost i nacionalizam sa islamskog gledišta," *El-Hidaje*, September 1941, 7–16.

29. A copy of the Sarajevo resolution can be found in IAS, Ostavština Fehima Spaha, box 3, document 759 (October 12, 1941).

30. Many Bosniak historians view this decree as an example of Muslims' anti-Fascist credentials, an interpretation that ignores the larger context and background of the signers. For examples from the Bosniak historiography, see Šaćir Filandra, *Bošnjačka politika* (Sarajevo: IP Sejtarija, 1998), 183, and Mehmedalija Bojić, *Historija Bosne i Bošnjaka (VII–XX vijeka)* (Sarajevo: TKD Šahinpašić, 2001), 190.

March 1941. Countless others were involved with the same institutions represented at that prewar meeting. Almost all the ulema belonged to El-Hidaje, the organization that had initially worked closely with the Ustasha deputies. Most of the politicians held posts in the NDH courts or bureaucracy. Although few had supported the Ustasha Party, many had benefited from the regime's discriminatory program, particularly the expropriation of property. And only a handful had criticized, let alone protested, the discrimination and deportation of Jews. The resolution, then, needs to be understood as a product of the situation. It was a direct response to the radicalization of Ustasha policies, the backlash felt within the Muslim community throughout the region, and the subservient position of Muslims in the NDH. It *was* an attempt to challenge the Ustasha; it was not an attempt to stall genocide.

Revealing its political insecurity, Zagreb did not arrest or sanction the signers but instead tried to appease them by giving in to a demand of Muslim religious leaders: a new statute for the Islamic Religious Community. But the statute was a disastrous endeavor that infuriated Muslim leaders even more. In essence, it aimed to restructure the Islamic Religious Community so that it functioned more like the Catholic Church.[31] For example, it joined the Muslims' administrative body with the administration of its endowment (*Vakuf*), which traditionally functioned separately. It also erroneously conflated the functions of various Islamic positions with those of their Catholic counterparts, failing to take into account that unlike priests, imams were married and had families, or that the Reis-ul-ulema was an elected community leader without the powers one might attribute to an archbishop. In a carefully crafted six-page response, the High Sharia Court in Sarajevo dissected the new statute, criticizing everything from the authors' use of poor Croatian grammar (a jab at the regime's attempt to position itself as the more cultured party) to the content of the laws, which misrepresented Islam. The bewildered, indignant judges accused the Zagreb regime of sticking its nose into the community's internal affairs and of having a woefully poor understanding of Islam. At one point, they retorted, "Do you even know who a mufti is and what his main functions are?" The judges complained that the regime was trying to create an unnecessary and expensive bureaucracy to control and monitor Muslims. They suggested that if the government had so much money to spare, perhaps it should direct it toward underfunded humanitarian agencies and Islamic schools.[32]

Again, Zagreb tried to assuage Muslim leaders. The Ministry of Religion withdrew the proposed statute and simultaneously (though not

31. A version of the statute can be found in IAS, Zbirka Varia document 2 (1941). This version was written sometime in late October or November, but that is not stated on the document itself.

32. ABiH, Vrhovni Šerijatski Sud, box 7, document 491 (October 30, 1941).

explicitly because of the judges' letter) increased the salaries of Muslim religious officials and awarded more state subsidies to the Islamic Religious Community.[33] These consolations, however, hardly solved the underlying problem: how to integrate Muslims into the Croat nation without forcing them to abandon their religious identities or upsetting Catholic leaders. By New Year's 1942, such integration seemed more and more impossible. According to an Ustasha secret police report from January 1942, a member of the Ulema Medžlis, Hadži Alija Aganović, publicly rebuked a young Sarajevo Muslim soldier, telling him, "You fought for Croatia, but you did not fight for Islam. What good is it to help Croats when there is nobody to help us!"[34] The sentiment resonated throughout the community.

The Catholic Church meanwhile forged ahead with its campaign to strengthen ties between Catholicism and Croatia. Muslims were not the sole target of this campaign. The church also took on Ustasha secularism. In February 1942, *Katolički Tjednik* published an article entitled "The Problem of the Catholic Intelligentsia," which argued that Catholicism had been the centerpiece of the Bosnian intelligentsia for centuries, and any attempt to separate it from the Croat national movement was tantamount to denying the community's tradition and heritage. The article even went so far as to call secular European nationalism a foreign concept. It noted that some foreigners (a reference to Germans, Italians, and possibly even Croats from Croatia) "are puzzled by our religiosity and 'fanatic' beliefs, but this is our tradition."[35] In the minds of local church leaders, the nation was a community rooted in religious heritage, not in modern, secular political programs. To this end, the church also criticized Catholics who supported the Ustasha Party line more fervently than their Catholic faith, reminding Sarajevans to place God ahead of nation.[36]

Part of the church's effort to limit who belonged to the Croat nation involved segregating Sarajevo's Catholics from other communities in the city, an approach that would be adopted by Muslim leaders in the following year as well. Church leaders publicly criticized Sarajevo's Catholics for succumbing to the deplorable behavior of their Balkan neighbors.[37] To Catholic religious leaders, "Balkan" was a derogatory term that referred to the other people with whom they shared the peninsula (i.e., Muslims, Orthodox Serbs, and Jews).[38] *Katolički Tjednik* warned readers that they had no one to blame but themselves for "our cursing, our corruption, our coarse

33. IAS, Ostavština Fehima Spaha, box 3, document 780 (November 24, 1941).
34. HM, Ustaška Nadzorna Služba, document 247 (January 20, 1942).
35. *Katolički Tjednik*, February 22, 1942, 1.
36. "Ratna Moda," *Katolički Tjednik*, February 1, 1942, 5.
37. "Balkanizacija ili Demoralizacija," *Katolički Tjednik*, March 1, 1942, 3–4.
38. This is an example of the phenomenon described by Maria Todorova on the ways that communities in the Balkans adopted the rhetoric of backwardness used by the West in describing themselves. Todorova, *Imagining the Balkans* (New York: Oxford University Press, 1997).

manners" as well as "the flood of immorality in our sexual and marital relations" and the "rapid spread of Communism." For two decades, Sarajevo's Catholics had willingly mixed with the Orthodox and other Balkan people in schools, societies, the army, and even in marriage, which led to a "cultural-national symbiosis" and "religious indifference."[39] Essentially, the church wanted Sarajevo's Catholics to reject the central tenets of their Sarajevo civic identity and align more fervently with a Catholic-based nation. At times, the church's message resonated in local Croat mind-sets, such as when a theatrical group suggested that only groups with Catholic majorities should represent Sarajevo in national competitions because clubs with Muslim majorities were not representative of the larger Croat population.[40] But, as I elaborate below, many Sarajevo Croats questioned the premises of clerical nationalism and promoted a more secular agenda.

Fragmented Croatianness: The Secular Agenda

The relationship of faith to national identity represented just one part in the larger discussion over the meaning and basis of Croat identity. Equally disconcerting to Sarajevo's Croats was the regime's relegation of the town's culture to an inferior status. From Zagreb's underhanded campaign to change the city's name to Sarajvo to its ongoing battle to eradicate the local dialect, the Ustasha regime made it clear that there would be no room for a Sarajevo variation on the Croat theme.

Early in the war, the regime used the discriminatory campaign against Jews and Serbs as a pretense to assert its anti-Sarajevo agenda. In late August 1941, for example, the regime announced a new phase in the campaign to wipe out Sarajevo's "Greek-Eastern and Jewish" influences, which had steered the city from its earlier, truer Croat path. "The time has come," the local newspaper preached, "to return to [Sarajevo] everything that she has lost . . . so that she can embrace her own greatness as the second city in the state."[41] Exactly what the regime meant by these bad influences became clearer in 1942 when the press published a negative critique of Sarajevans' behavior. The piece argued that Croats from Zagreb found living in Sarajevo difficult because of a culture clash: people from Zagreb were honest and industrious, living their lives in a manner conducive to national prosperity, while Sarajevans were lazy and "leisure-oriented" people who risked becoming "parasites" on the nation. Even more offensive to city leaders, the newspaper equated Sarajevans to Jews. "In the place of Croat honesty," the paper noted, "part of Sarajevo's community adopted dishonorable Jewish

39. *Katolički Tjednik*, March 1, 1942, 3–4.
40. HM, Ustaška grada, document 2084 (September 23, 1941).
41. *Sarajevski Novi List*, August 30, 1941.

conduct, as if the old Jews created the entire tradition of Sarajevo's way of life." The article concluded by calling on Sarajevans to abandon their "Jewish tendencies" and adopt Croat ones.[42]

Essentially, the regime was ordering the city to renounce everything Sarajevan about it. A follow-up article in November 1942—again contrasting Sarajevo and Zagreb as two different centers of Croat culture—claimed that Sarajevo's culture was not wrong; it was just "different" because of the city's Turkish and Islamic influences. The article implied that the Ustasha regime hoped to eradicate these differences and "reunite" Sarajevo with its Croat roots.[43] The threat in each of these examples was explicit: Sarajevo's Croats needed to either embrace the Ustasha national program or have it imposed on them. The Ustashas intended to stamp out local culture, reduce the influence of Islam in Croat national ideology, and replace regional and city loyalties with a cult of the nation-state.

In addition to these verbal attacks, the regime also sought to undermine local organizations that might vitiate Zagreb's agenda for homogenizing national identity. For example, when compiling a comprehensive list of organizations to which soldiers legally could belong, it omitted Napredak, arguably the most important Croat cultural society in Bosnia and Herze-govina.[44] That the organization was predominantly Catholic is noteworthy. After the society's leaders in Sarajevo expressed their outrage, the army apologized and called the omission a "misunderstanding." But many members of the group were suspicious that the slight had been intentional. They felt even more slighted when the regime refused to back their efforts to take back property that the German military command had confiscated. Feeling abandoned to their own devices, in August 1942 Napredak bypassed the Ustasha and contacted German headquarters in Salonica directly. "We understand only too well the needs of the great German nation, with whom we share a common fate," they began. But they wanted the Germans to understand that Croat nation in Sarajevo also had needs—and these needs were not being met. When the Germans still failed to return the property, Napredak grudgingly closed several of its schools.[45]

Consequently, the society's leaders grew more protective of their position as defenders of local culture. In the fall of 1942, Napredak announced a new agenda to spread its cultural mission to the rest of the region. The society first planned a drive to expand its membership from twenty thousand to one hundred thousand, declaring that "there should be no

---

42. Ibid., August 8, 1942, 3.
43. Ibid., November 22, 1942, 9.
44. ABiH, Hrvatsko kulturno društvo Napredak, box 148, document 1734 (June 12, 1942).
45. On the correspondence with the Germans, see ibid., box 147, document 1119 (August 4, 1942). On shutting down Napredak schools, see document 1518 (August 21, 1942) and document 1492 (August 27, 1942).

reasonable Croat in any village or city who is not a member of Napredak."[46] It also increased its publishing activities to produce more works on Croats in Bosnia and even opened an exhibit promoting Croatia's Bosnian culture, which, incidentally, was publicized also in the local Muslim press.[47] Such moves were a subtle attack on the notion that there was a true image of Croat culture that would be determined by Zagreb.

Sarajevo's Croats, Muslims and Catholics alike, launched a two-front battle to strengthen aspects of their local heritage and to posit local Croat culture as an alternative to that of the Ustasha. Using money from their membership dues and extensive private donations, the cultural societies invested in new libraries and reading rooms, published literary journals, and worked to open a college campus in the city.[48] Simultaneously, they aimed to raise Sarajevo's prestige in the national eye. In early 1942 a group of Muslim Croats led by Alija Nametak embarked on a project to write and produce a film that would inform other parts of the NDH about Sarajevo's cultural legacy and emphasize the dual nature of Croat identity by reflecting the nation's Islamic and Catholic past as well as its Habsburg and Ottoman roots.[49]

Ahmed Muradbegović, the artistic director at the Croatian State Theater, became something of a spokesman for this cultural mission. He consistently strove to make Sarajevo's theater a leader in the cultural life of the NDH, not a mere satellite of Zagreb's cultural scene. He deliberately interspersed plays that highlighted the city's identity and Muslim heritage with German- and Croatian-language plays and operas.[50] He was proregime and would remain so throughout the war, but he nevertheless clashed with Zagreb over how Croatia should be reflected in the cultural sphere of Sarajevo and who should direct this process. For example, when Muradbegović asked the Ministry of Culture to relocate prominent directors and musicians to Sarajevo in order to enhance the caliber of the city's theater scene, Zagreb responded by cherry-picking ideologues and Ustasha extremists to oversee the institution. Infuriated, Muradbegović dismissed Zagreb's choice for a conductor outright on the grounds that she "simply did not have the necessary qualifications as a singer nor the experience as a director" to run a theater of Sarajevo's stature.[51] While loyal to the NDH, Muradbegović would always defer to local expectations, for which he was commended by the local press.[52] In 1943, for example, he denied the Ustasha political

46. ABiH, Hrvatsko kulturno društvo Napredak, box 148, document 1788 (October 28, 1942).

47. *Osvit*, October 23, 1943, 6..

48. These initiatives are discussed in *Narodna Uzdanica Kalendar*, 1942, 217–226, and *Napredak Kalendar*, 1942, 208–210.

49. IAS, Zbirka Varia, document 69 (January 12, 1942).

50. *Narodno Pozorište u Sarajevu*, 135–138.

51. ABiH, Narodno Pozorište Sarajevo, box 2, document 1881 (December 27, 1941).

52. *Hrvatska Misao*, November–December 1943, 43.

authorities access to the theater during Bajram, the Muslim holiday celebrating the end of Ramadan.[53]

The understated, often silent battle to keep Sarajevo's heritage alive would become a wartime obsession for many local intellectuals, who knew from experience that regimes were transient, while culture persisted. The most well-known examples of these efforts involved hiding important relics and artifacts. The curators at the Croatian State Museum, for example, risked their lives to hide the Sarajevo Haggadah, the Sephardic scripture book from the fourteenth century, which the Germans hoped to send to Germany.[54] Publicly the museum requested jurisdiction over important cultural sites occupied by the German and Ustasha commands—namely, the Serbian Orthodox Church, the Old and New Jewish Synagogues, and the Jewish Library. The museum eventually agreed to pay the regime to return parts of one Jewish synagogue that had been dismantled and stored in a warehouse in Jasenovac, the same town where most of Sarajevo's Jews were interned.[55] In a more direct act of noncompliance, the mayor's office refused to send valuable icons from the Serbian Orthodox Church to Zagreb, arguing that these icons belonged to Sarajevo.[56]

While it is easy to interpret such risky acts as selfless, I suggest that local leaders were not as concerned with stopping the exploitation of Jews and Serbs as with preventing the exploitation of the city's cultural heritage. Ultimately, these cultural disputes were limited to the domain of elites. The number of Sarajevans who understood (or cared about) the nature of the tension was relatively small; it does not appear that these discussions were ever embraced by ordinary people struggling to survive famine and cold. Yet the cultural conversation proved vital for the persistence of the Sarajevo identity because it helped prevent the idea of Sarajevo from being submerged in the national rhetoric.

Although members of the local intelligentsia did not articulate it as such, their brand of Croat identity in many ways mirrored traditional concepts of Sarajevo pluralism—but with a Croat slant. This could be seen and understood best in the reincorporation of Sarajevo Serbs into the city's public life, which occurred gradually over the course of 1942. To understand this process, some background on Ustasha national policy is in order. In the fall of 1941, the Ustasha regime shifted its national strategy for ridding Croatia of Serbs. In addition to deportations and internment, the regime introduced a policy of mass and forced conversions of Orthodox Serbs to

53. ABiH, Narodno pozorište Sarajevo, box 4, document 1685 (November 12, 1943).

54. On the Sarajevo Haggadah, see Muhamed Karamehedović, "Sarajevska Hagada," in Kamhi, *Spomenica,* 22.

55. ABiH, Zemaljski Muzej Bosne i Hercegovine, box 37, document 537 (October 15, 1941), and box 39, document 752 (October 6, 1942).

56. IAS, Riznično upraviteljstvo: Ured za podržavljeni imetak, box 1, document 11885 (September 5, 1941), and document 551 (October 27, 1941). For a later memo from Sarajevo to Zagreb that refers to property rights, see ibid., box 1, document 15848 (April 27, 1943).

Catholicism. The historian Mark Biondich has described the protracted shifts in Ustasha rhetoric over the summer and fall of 1941 that culminated in the new policy. The Ustashas ceased talking about Serbs as "aliens" in Croatia and instead referred to them as Catholic Croats who had converted to Orthodoxy during the Ottoman era and then assumed a Serb consciousness. Reasoning that it could shepherd these lost Orthodox souls back to the Catholic flock, the Ustasha regime converted roughly one hundred thousand Orthodox Serbs to Catholicism in late 1941.[57]

The forced conversions did not have a great impact on Sarajevo, partly because the regime had forbidden conversions of Serb intellectuals (who had developed too great a Serb consciousness) and partly because Sarajevo's leaders already treated Serb identity primarily in local terms. But the rhetorical shift from identifying Serbs as an ethnic and racial "other" to a political threat confirmed a long-standing belief in Sarajevo: that Serb was not a biological category. This confirmation would give city leaders new confidence in challenging parts of the discriminatory campaign with which they disagreed.

Outside Sarajevo, the coercive conversions had fueled the Serb insurgency. Infuriated by their Croat ally, Italian and German commanders had become so outraged with Ustasha violence and military incompetency that they actually started working with groups of Chetniks in their battles against the Communists, who posed the most serious threat to Axis economic and military interests in Bosnia. Some Axis officials in Sarajevo even discussed giving the town, along with most of eastern Bosnia, to the Chetniks in exchange for a ceasefire and help fighting the Communists.[58] The Ustashas had to improve their treatment of Serbs or risk losing some, if not all, of its territories.

Ante Pavelić faced a dilemma. His regime had repeatedly emphasized that the health of the NDH required removing Serbs. If he continued down that path, he risked losing his state. However, if he changed the party's rhetoric and welcomed Serbs as citizens of Croatia, he risked undermining his authority and the legitimacy of the NDH. He had to come up with an alternative plan. His solution: the creation of a Croatian Orthodox church.

According to the Ustasha regime's logic, Orthodox churches were invariably linked to national groups and thus political by nature. Russia, Greece, Bulgaria, and Serbia each had its own Orthodox church, whose hierarchy had formal ties or strong cultural relations with the state. Pavelić reasoned that the best way to foster loyalty among Serbs in Croatia would

---

57. Biondich, "Religion and Nation in Wartime Croatia," 71–116. In my research I have also found evidence of group conversions from Orthodoxy to Islam in the fall of 1941; however, there is no indication that this was state policy or that it was in any way forced.

58. Paul N. Hehn, *The German Struggle against Yugoslav Guerillas in World War II* (Boulder: East European Monographs, 1979), 125–126. On the rumors of turning Sarajevo over to the Chetniks, see Hoare, *Genocide and Resistance in Hitler's Bosnia*, 171.

be to establish a rival Orthodox church tying Serbs to Croatia. By co-opting the Orthodox faith, the Ustasha regime would turn Orthodox Serbs into Orthodox Croats. Consequently, it hoped to drain the Chetnik resistance and establish order in the countryside. The Germans supported the idea, hoping that the church would resolve Croat-Serb tensions and align the Chetniks and the Ustashas against the Communist Partisans. Thus, the Croatian Orthodox Church was founded on April 3, 1942.[59]

As an institution, the Croatian Orthodox Church is usually relegated to the margins of histories on the NDH, often portrayed as a propagandistic move by Ante Pavelić and his regime to appease the Germans and stem Chetnik-Ustasha violence. It is true that the church had no national influence and little domestic support. It was officially a branch of the Ministry of Religion, which appointed clergy and monitored church activities. The few Orthodox Serb clerics who had survived the regime's killing spree the previous summer refused to participate in it, forcing Zagreb to import exiled Russian clergy to fill the church's hierarchy. The church was critical for Sarajevo, however, because it functioned as the vehicle for the return of Sarajevo's Serbs to the public sphere. The Croatian Orthodox Church created room for them to congregate and forge cultural networks, as, for example, through a choir and women's committees. Moreover, the church offered Serbs a chance to take part in the national community. In joining the new church, a Sarajevo Serb declared his loyalty to the NDH. He left the class of outcasts with contingent racial and national identities and—on paper—became a Croat. Over the next year, more than six thousand Sarajevo Serbs took advantage of this opportunity.[60]

Many civic leaders appeared to embrace the incorporation of Orthodox Croats into the town's tapestry. They believed the new community might help to stabilize the city and improve intercommunity relations. In the two months after the establishment of the Croatian Orthodox Church, Serbs who had fled the city began to return home. Their arrival did not go unnoticed by the Ustasha police, who reported in late June that a large number of Orthodox Croats had returned to the city from their hiding places in the forests. The police noted with some surprise that most of the returnees were harmless civilians who hoped to resume normal lives and showed little interest in moving to Serbia or fighting for the Partisans or Chetniks. Around the same time, the Ustasha signed a temporary ceasefire with the

59. For an overview of the Ustasha position on the Croatian Orthodox Church, see "Spas Pravoslavlja," in *Sarajevski Novi List,* January 3, 1943, 3. See also Ante Pavelić, *Hrvatska Pravoslavna Crkva* (Madrid: Sva Prava Pridržana, 1984), and Petar Požar, *Hrvatska Pravoslavna Crkva u prošlosti i budućnosti* (Zagreb: Naklada Pavičić, 1996).

60. HDA, Ministarstvo Narodne Prosvjete NDH, Odjel za Bogoštovlje, box 79, document 5189 (June 16, 1943).

Chetniks in the area, which gave many local Orthodox a sense of security they had not previously had.[61]

Although the Croatian Orthodox Church was supposed to resolve some of the tensions between the Ustashas and the Serbs, on the local level it was not entirely successful. The Germans continued to pressure the Ustasha regime to improve its relations with the Orthodox population. For example, a local German commander in Sarajevo expressed outrage in June 1942 that the Ustasha police had jailed an unknown number of Serbs and Muslims without proper indictments or the benefit of a trial. The local Ustasha commander subsequently sent a letter to Zagreb asking state leaders to tell the Germans to quit interfering in local policing.[62] Local Ustashas remained suspicious of Sarajevo Serbs.

Clerical Catholic Croats and religious Muslims also greeted the influx of Serbs into the town with little enthusiasm. The former viewed Orthodox Croats as further diluting the purity of the Croat nation, while the latter feared that Catholic and Orthodox Croats might forge a broader-based Christian movement that targeted Muslims.[63] Orthodox Croats themselves recognized that they had landed at the bottom of the national hierarchy. They were well aware that they had become Croats out of necessity and that the regime might reverse its policies at any time if such a stance proved advantageous.

By the end of 1942, the Croat nation had become a convenient mechanism by which the Ustasha regime could enforce a social order. As an ideology, however, Croat nationalism had lost credibility. Instead of becoming a rallying point for Catholics, Muslims, and Orthodox, it had gradually become a means for local leaders to compete for power as they sought to strengthen their local traditions in the developing nation-state.

Finding Common Ground: Winter Crisis and Civic Responsibility

Where the Ustasha national program failed, Mother Nature succeeded: the miserable winter of 1941–42 brought townsmen together in search of effective solutions to sustain the city. From December to March 1942, a heavy blanket of snow and ice covered Sarajevo, with temperatures hovering around -25 degrees Celsius. Frozen pipes, collapsed roofs, and damaged roads and railways crippled the municipality. Without soap or coal (to boil water), the typhus problem in autumn exploded into a springtime epidemic. The Italian army prohibited soldiers from fraternizing with

61. HM, Ustaška Nadzorna Služba, document 390 (June 23, 1942) and document 406 (July 8, 1942).

62. HM, Ustaška Nadzorna Služba, reports, document 376 (June 15–24, 1942).

63. HM, Ustaška Nadzorna Služba, document 390 (June 23, 1942) and document 426 (July 27, 1942).

Figure 7. Refugees on the streets of Sarajevo, circa 1942. Courtesy of the Historical Museum of Bosnia and Herzegovina.

Sarajevans, claiming that the city had the worst sanitary conditions and the highest disease rates in the region.[64] Food became scarce. Basic supplies like flour, potatoes, and cornmeal, as well as Sarajevo's staple items of coffee, tea, and sugar, were in short supply for weeks at a time.[65] Morale sank as low as the mercury.

Large-scale humanitarian crises force local leaders to think about community in a pragmatic way: who gets what in the distribution of resources. In Sarajevo, the arrival of ten thousand peasant refugees and orphaned children from rural eastern Bosnia—the vast majority of whom were poor Muslims—colored these debates. At first, Sarajevo's civic leaders expected the refugees to be a transient group and thus treated them as a temporary subsection of the local poor. Religious organizations bore the brunt of their care, with women's committees often put in charge of the new arrivals.[66] By

64. Rodogno, *Fascism's European Empire*, 169.

65. For administrative purposes (such as determining when heat should be turned on and off), Sarajevo's government considered winter to be from October 15 to April 15. On the freezing temperatures, typhus epidemic, and food shortages, see IAS, Ostavština Fehima Spaha, box 3, document 783 (December 13, 1941); HDA, Ministarstvo Unutrašnih Poslova NDH, box 46, document 4680/42 (1942); and ABiH, Veliki Župan Vrhbosna, document 2128 (March 1, 1942). There are also hundreds of reports and complaints related to the inclement weather that winter in IAS, Gradsko Poglavarstvo, boxes 955–965.

66. In particular, the Catholic Croat Women's Society and the women's committee of Merhamet took on these functions. See *Katolički Tjednik,* June 22, 1941, 3–4; IAS, Merhamet, box 4, document 220 (September 2, 1941).

September 1941, however, it became clear that the refugees were there to stay, at least for the winter, and that goodwill alone would not sustain them.

Representatives from various Muslim organizations met with town authorities in mid-September to discuss the problem. Shortages of food, clothing, heat, and apartments meant that the refugees further strained an already struggling system. Some officials were annoyed that they were collecting welfare and unemployment benefits, rights that—according to local custom—should be extended only to residents of the town. Others were angry that the refugees did not contribute to the war effort. In early September, County Executive Omerović expressed his concern to Mayor Demirović that few of the refugees were working. He suggested that the mayor "invite" them to volunteer for the city if they wanted to continue receiving public aid.[67] Although this was never stated explicitly, it appears that the urban Muslim elite also worried that the refugees' poverty, illiteracy, and peasant character might reflect poorly upon the Muslim community at a time when they were trying to assert their position in the NDH.

Faced with a disjointed and compartmentalized social welfare system that was dependent on private aid and plagued with corruption, Mayor Demirović tried to consolidate refugee services by creating a "bureau for refugee assistance," a one-room office that became known as the Department of Refugees.[68] From its inception, the department suffered from inadequate staffing and funding. Its low position on the administrative totem pole partly reflected the city's irritation with the burden of refugee care and partly underscored the regime's growing disregard for the Muslim rural poor. The Ustashas did not want a devout and largely illiterate Muslim peasantry to form the majority in the second-largest city of the NDH. Moreover, they worried that allowing refugees to remain in safe zones like Sarajevo, rather than forcing them to return to eastern Bosnia to fight, would mean abandoning the country's cherished eastern border on the river Drina. Over the winter, the regime ruled that men in eastern Bosnia between the ages of eighteen and fifty-five would not be allowed to seek refugee status.[69] In the future, some male refugees would be considered deserters.

Thus the refugees began to constitute a new other in the eyes of the regime and town leaders, both of whom drew a line between citizens of the city and the new peasant outsiders. The distinction was institutionalized through the state's policies of dividing new arrivals into two categories: refugees and colonists.[70] The state-sponsored Office for Colonization handled

67. HM, Ustaška građa, document 2063 (September 2, 1941).
68. *Sarajevski Novi List,* September 20, 1941, 4.
69. ABiH, Veliki Župan Vrhbosna, document 2128 (March 1, 1942).
70. On the distinction made between refugees (*izbjeglici*) and colonists (*kolonisti*), see the records of the Office for Colonization in Sarajevo (ABiH, Ured za kolonizaciju-Sarajevo). In box 1 there is an overview of the collection that introduces this distinction. In box 2, document 615 (March 13, 1942), there are references to how the state expected city institutions to treat colonists, particularly Slovenes.

Slovene immigrants, Catholic Croat immigrants (including some who could technically have been labeled refugees), and civil servants transferring to Sarajevo. The office received healthy state subsidies and reported directly to Zagreb. Because the regime considered colonists of vital national interest, they were eligible for such benefits as extra food rations, agricultural supplies, fuel, money, furniture, comfortable homes, and Jewish property. Refugees, by contrast, received only the most rudimentary accommodations. Whereas the regime earmarked homes for colonists, it neither designated a central camp nor considered refugees in the reallocation of confiscated property, which meant that refugees were often homeless, living in makeshift shelters organized by women's societies, or taken into private homes.[71] Consequently, they were at times caught in street sweeps of Roma and beggars and sent to the camps. Many Muslim refugees came from territories on the other side of the Drina—now part of German-occupied Serbia—but sought refuge in Sarajevo, which put them in a difficult position because they did not qualify for refugee services.[72] As a rule, the Ustashas did not consider Muslim refugees eligible for city residency or colonization.

Unlike the Office for Colonization, the Department of Refugees fell into the municipal domain, which meant that it did not have access to the same national resources. Indeed, the local bureau practically had to beg local Ustasha officials for access to stockpiled clothing and shoes that had belonged to Jews and Serbs who had "emigrated," which it hoped to redistribute to the refugees.[73] Its pleas often fell on deaf ears. Confronted with a growing homeless population, the mayor's office occasionally assigned vacated Jewish apartments to refugees, an initiative that triggered a barrage of nasty complaints. In late November, a Catholic woman sent a bitter letter arguing that it was unfair for refugees to get priority in the assignment of Jewish property when locals needed it.[74] Defying the mayor's provisional allocations, some landlords threw out poor tenants and resorted to the courts in an effort to evict refugee squatters.[75] Some locals pitied the refugees and viewed them as less of an outside community than the detested Ustashas. One Muslim man complained that an Ustasha detective had received several apartments, while "a large number of refugees in Sarajevo live without apartments or any materials necessary to live."[76] The Ustasha police found the eviction process an undesirable and difficult business, and so in late November 1941, following a contentious case in which someone broke into the apartment of an evicted Orthodox Serb priest—claiming

71. HM, Ustaška građa, document 2063 (September 2, 1941).
72. On this issue, see IAS, Ostavština Fehima Spaha, box 3, document 730 (August 1, 1941), and HM, Ustaška građa, document 2238 (September 10, 1941).
73. HM, Ustaška građa, document 2262 (October 13, 1941).
74. IAS, Gradsko Poglavarstvo, box 911 (November 27, 1941).
75. See two such court cases in ABiH, Sudbeni Stol, Pl:106/42 (October 30, 1941), and P:104/42 (February 19, 1942).
76. HM, Ustaška građa, document 2563 (December 20, 1941).

that he had received oral permission to move in—the local police ordered city officials to cease assigning temporary accommodations.[77]

With more refugees arriving weekly and no place to house them, the department often relied on the goodwill of Merhamet, the Muslim humanitarian society, and the Islamic Religious Community, which lent the city space in several Muslim religious schools (*mektebi*) in December. Imams and religious teachers frequently welcomed refugees into their own homes and encouraged other Muslims to do the same.[78] Over the next two months, the city designated for the refugees a few abandoned buildings, mostly places unsuited for other uses and lacking heat, windows, insulation, water, and other basic amenities.[79] Faced with a choice between living in subhuman conditions in Sarajevo and returning to the front in eastern Bosnia, some refugees chose a third route and applied for work in Nazi Germany.[80]

Housing the refugees was only part of Sarajevo's problem. As city officials braced for massive food shortages and inflation, they could hardly guarantee food for residents, let alone for the burgeoning refugee community. It should be noted that initial shortages had less to do with the availability of food than with the regime's poorly organized system of acquisition and distribution. Almost all the food that arrived in the city ended up on the black market, which tended to be in the hands of corrupt commissioners and opportunistic merchants.[81] Town leaders were well aware of the need for more imports and tighter price controls, but they did not have the necessary authority to override the Ustasha authorities. (Eventually they would demand German intervention.) In November 1941, the county executive requested that Zagreb cover 50 percent of the refugees' food budget, noting that at least half of the refugees had come from territories outside the county lines.[82] In some cases, Ustasha officials gave the refugees food meant for city residents, which caused a minor uproar among locals. The Department of Refugees complained that it was hardly fair for the refugees to be fed at the expense of Sarajevo's population.[83] Although the department was responsible for the refugees, its principal loyalty was to the town.

In an effort to alleviate the humanitarian crisis plaguing the region, in December 1941 the Ustasha regime launched Action Help, a collaborative humanitarian effort that aimed to raise money and collect food for both Sarajevo's poor and the refugees. It was based on an initiative started in Zagreb, which was inspired by the German program Winter Help. The

77. Ibid., document 187 (November 25, 1941).

78. *El-Hidaje*, January 28, 1942, 124.

79. ABiH, Veliki Župan Vrhbosna, document 2128 (March 1, 1942).

80. See the lists of labor applications available in ABiH, Javni Ured Rada Sarajevo, box 4, document 501 (March 1942). In box 5, see document 804 (April 29, 1942).

81. On the developing food crisis, see notes from Sarajevo's branch of the Croatian Red Cross in ABiH, Društvo Crveni Križ, minutes, box 22, November 7, 1941.

82. HM, Ustaška građa, document 2436 (November 17, 1941).

83. ABiH, Veliki Župan Vrhbosna, document 2128 (March 1, 1942).

Ustashas appointed a committee to buy food and redistribute goods collected by organizations like Merhamet and the Croatian Red Cross. Some organizations sent members door-to-door to raise money; others mobilized in front of mosques and churches during the Muslim and Catholic religious holidays. The Ustasha authorities made it clear that they expected every public and private organization in Sarajevo to participate, warning residents that contributing should be considered "an obligation, not charity."[84]

Some Muslim leaders voiced concern that Action Help might not have Muslim interests in mind.[85] The Ulema Medžlis had had enough experience with the Ustashas and the uncertain place of Islam in the NDH to question the regime's intentions. Muslim humanitarian organizations had already assumed primary responsibility for the care of Muslim refugees. No doubt the Ulema Medžlis worried that food drives and fundraisers intended for the Muslim poor would be distributed unevenly to the non-Muslim poor. For months they had witnessed the regime's prejudice against Muslims in every aspect of Sarajevo's daily life, from residency applications to food allocation. The Ulema Medžlis politely requested more details about the goals and intentions of Action Help before it used its position to encourage donations. Ustasha officials responded with a vague description of the initiative's objectives and a warning that "it is the duty of every Muslim" to participate.[86]

Although Action Help was no cure for the food crisis, it nonetheless symbolized an important transition in the way that members of the local elite approached their civic responsibility. Without support from the national government, Sarajevo's municipal government increasingly relied on private organizations with their own income and resources to help run the city. Starting with the refugee crisis in the fall 1941, the leaders of these organizations assumed an expanding role in managing local affairs, until they became de facto partners with the town government in matters as diverse as refugees, food distribution, disease prevention, and education.[87] Pavelić's regime benefited from the new arrangement. It relieved the pressure that had been on Zagreb to resolve the city's practical problems and allowed the regime to focus on its favored occupations: ideology and policing. In fact, the regime then provided material incentives to private organizations to encourage them to become more involved in the city's social welfare. In December 1941, for example, Ante Pavelić recognized Merhamet as the state's most important ally in the refugee crisis and awarded the

84. *Sarajevski Novi List*, December 11, 1941, 4.
85. ARIZBiH, Ulema Medžlis, document 4762/41 (December 4, 1941).
86. Ibid. (January 7, 1942).
87. See, for example, ABiH, Hrvatsko kulturno društvo Napredak, yearly report, box 173, document 70 (1941–1942), and box 145, document 35 (January 13, 1942) and document 187 (March 26, 1942). There were also a number of women's organizations involved. See, for example, IAS, Hurijet, Zapisnik Ženski Odbor, box 1 (March 2, 1942); ABiH, Društvo Crveni Križ, box 21, document 1569 (February 18, 1942); and *Katolički Tjednik*, January 11, 1942, 4.

organization a profitable Jewish textile factory that held a large contract with the German army.[88] In this way the regime tied the local elite to the war effort while shirking responsibility for the city's social welfare.

Sarajevo's dependence on private organizations (and their leaders) grew as the humanitarian crisis worsened and city funds dwindled—a problem exacerbated by wartime inflation, the regime's prohibition of municipal sales taxes, and the city's responsibility for the maintenance of Jews' and Serbs' property.[89] Sarajevo's principal source of municipal income appears to have been from road tolls and firewood taxes, token fees that actually made it difficult for the bureau in charge of acquiring food (*Gradski aprovizacijioni ured*) to import food into the city.[90] As the municipal budget shrank and goods became scarcer, pleas for assistance piled up on the mayor's desk. Administrators at Sarajevo's schools deplored that "many of the students live in terrible and nauseating conditions and are poorly clothed and fed." Schools had a 50 percent dropout rate in the middle of the year due to illness, hunger, and "irregular" circumstances. When the city government did nothing, the schools asked wealthy students to bring in food to share with poorer students—thus relying on local codes of neighborliness to care for their charges.[91] Nuns running Catholic orphanages pleaded for food and for exemptions from paying tolls and firewood taxes, hoping that their religious status might garner sympathy.[92] The mayor had little choice but to deny the requests. The entire city was experiencing a terrible famine that month. Even the families of important city leaders suffered.[93] In February 1942, the office of County Executive Ismet Gavran-Kapetanović harshly reminded the city government that *it* was ultimately responsible for all the refugees who resided there. Mayor Demirović responded that his office was providing the refugees with everything it could in the realm of "food, accommodations, and health care."[94] Both men knew that this was hardly enough. Refugees were not a priority; the entire city was in dire straits.

On March 1, the Department of Refugees issued a comprehensive report on the refugee crisis, which it hoped would convince the Ustashas to ease the burden. The report stated that more than 11,000 registered refugees were living in Sarajevo and 3,000 more were en route. (Sarajevo's fire department viewed this as an underestimate, claiming that the city's

88. *Osvit*, March 8, 1942, 6.

89. On the economic situation generally, see ABiH, Javni Ured Rada Sarajevo, box 2, document 1070 (August 29, 1941). On the burden of managing property, see records from IAS, Ured za upravu židovskim nekretninama, document 2702 (March 2, 1942) and document 2676 (February 28, 1942).

90. IAS, Gradsko Poglavarstvo, box 975 (April 23, 1942).

91. ABiH, Poglavnikovo Povjereništvo Sarajevo, Odjel za bogoštovlje i nastavu, box 2, document 1246 (February 7, 1942).

92. IAS, Gradsko Poglavarstvo, box 941 (February 19, 1942).

93. Nametak, *Sarajevski Nekrologij*, 113.

94. IAS, Gradsko Poglavarstvo, box 941 (February 12, 1942).

population had expanded from 90,000 to 130,000 over the winter.)[95] Divided almost equally between male and female, the group consisted of 11,120 Muslims, 93 Catholics, and 53 Orthodox, most of whom came from eastern Bosnia. The refugees lived in sixteen public buildings, of which six were "new" school buildings (interwar constructions) and ten were "congested and unsanitary" but "usable" spaces. None of the buildings had hot water. Ninety percent of the refugees slept on bare stone floors without blankets. Their daily diet consisted of half a kilogram of cornbread, "a little" olive oil, and a small cup of soup made of beans or oatmeal. Lacking proper clothing or footwear, many refugees were spotted walking barefoot in the snowy streets. Lest anyone forget, the report reminded officials that Sarajevo's average daily temperature was -25 degrees Celsius.[96]

Local officials hoped to accomplish two things with this report. First, as noted above, they wanted relief. They believed that refugees were a national problem, regardless of where they resided, and that they should be the responsibility of Zagreb's budget rather than Sarajevo's. It seemed unfair that the city had to use its limited resources to support the victims of the war. But the authors of the report had another plan in mind: they wanted the Germans and Ustashas to encourage refugees to return home. Town leaders associated the refugees with disease, homelessness, and street-side begging. Many civilians viewed them as competition for food, housing, and wood. Even when people in the local community did not blame the refugees for their discomfort, they still showed bitterness toward the refugee problem. For example, in late 1941, the Department of Refugees had requisitioned a *mekteb* to house refugees. Although the Muslim administrators eventually got the refugees moved elsewhere, they could not resume classes because the refugees had brought typhus to the school, which needed to be disinfected (an expensive and difficult process, given the shortages of disinfectants). Thus, the school remained closed through most of 1942.[97]

Many town officials saw the refugees as not only a humanitarian problem but also a security threat, a symbol of the encroaching front lines and the blurring boundaries between rural anarchy and the city's stability. The refugees sometimes heckled Sarajevo students on the streets of the old town, encouraging them to flee into the mountains and join the fighters.[98] One senior town official became so fed up with the refugee crisis that in the summer 1942 he threatened to send three thousand of them "across the Sava River," meaning to Zagreb's jurisdiction in northern Croatia.[99] But

95. Ibid., box 1090 (April 8, 1942).
96. ABiH, Veliki Župan Vrhbosna, document 2128 (March 1, 1942).
97. ARIZBiH, Ulema Medžlis, document 215/42 (June 6, 1942).
98. HM, Ustaška građa, document 329 (March 12, 1942).
99. Ibid., document 426 (August 27, 1942). The reference to across the river Sava could alternatively mean sending the refugees to the concentration camp Jasenovac, which was located on the other side of the river.

Sarajevo's government had neither the resources to forcibly remove the refugees nor the clout to convince the Ustashas or the Germans to intervene. The vast majority of the refugees, meanwhile, had no interest in leaving Sarajevo, despite their discomfort, because their only real option was to return to war-torn eastern Bosnia, where bandits roamed the countryside burning villages and killing people. So they remained, adding further complexity to Sarajevo's wartime social fabric and the question of who belonged to the city and nation.

Political Transition: A Return to Autonomy and Pluralism

Whereas the refugees offered a negative rallying point for the town, the crisis itself served as a positive catalyst in reviving the city's traditional networks. In the absence of state assistance, private institutions that assumed responsibility for refugee services gradually acquired more and more power in determining how the city would function. This new dynamic became a critical means of developing and sustaining cross-cutting civic bonds that had long been the foundation of the community. The crisis also served as the impetus for reviving local political traditions that the Ustasha regime had attempted to destroy.

Under pressure from the German and Italian commands to get the country under control, Pavelić's regime decided to transfer more power to Muslims—particularly a subgroup of Sarajevo's Muslims who had supported the Axis but had been lukewarm to the Ustashas. In July 1942, the Ministry of the Interior appointed a new mayor, Mustafa Softić, a member of the wealthy, politically connected Muslim elite.[100] Born in fin-de-siècle Sarajevo, Softić had graduated from the local Islamic high school and served in the Austro-Hungarian army during the First World War. In the interwar period, he had worked for the Islamic Religious Community's vakuf and the city's savings bank, and he was a member of the Yugoslav Muslim Organization. At the start of the war, Softić was not a public figure, though his father-in-law, Uzeir-aga Hadžihasanović, was a prominent Sarajevo merchant and an important local actor (and no doubt had played a part in getting Softić the job). Hadžihasanović, a close friend of Mehmed Spaho in the interwar era, had been accused of nepotism in the past, having pushed his son-in-law into positions of power in order to manipulate the political dynamic behind the scenes.[101] Softić and Hadžihasanović had supported the German occupation of Yugoslavia but were among those Muslims who would have preferred that Bosnia become a German protectorate rather than a part of

100. For biographical information on Mustafa Softić, see Nametak, *Sarajevski Nekrologij,* 17 and 157; *Sarajevski Novi List,* July 17, 1942, 4; and the short biography in Milenko Pajić, *Sarajevski gradonačelnici.* Sarajevo: Večernje Novine, 1998.

101. Hasanbegović, *Jugoslavenska muslimanska organizacija,* 279.

the NDH.[102] Like so many members of the city's Muslim elite, they signed (and possibly were among the authors) of the famous Muslim resolution in October 1941. While the Ustasha police did not arrest or sanction the signers, they kept a close watch on them afterward. Softić's appointment as mayor can thus be seen as an Ustasha concession to form a more genuine coalition with Muslims.

When Softić assumed office in July 1942, Sarajevo's humanitarian crisis had been continuing unabated. Disease, especially typhus, was still rampant, forcing city health officials to shut down public buildings and quarantine the sick. By September, the city's hospital was in such a state of "unhygienic filth and disarray" that local Ustasha officials claimed it was contributing to rather than curing infections.[103] Moreover, the influx of refugees remained steady, aggravating the social, health, and housing problems.[104] Exacerbating the already tense political and military situation was the rivalry among the Italians, Germans, and Ustashas for control over the region. The Germans and Italians frequently intervened in local affairs, pressuring the mayor's office to defer to their interests. Always a nuisance, the Volksdeutsche demanded money and donations from city offices in exchange for their services, which they vaguely described as "protecting the city and citizens from irresponsible and destructive elements."[105] Although Sarajevo was in the German occupation zone of the NDH, the Italians demanded equal treatment as the other senior Axis partner (and hoped eventually to move Sarajevo into their zone of occupation).[106] Feeling slighted by their minimal influence in the city, in August 1942 the Italians demanded that the city provide a suitably grand seat for the Italian Fascist Party and the Institute for Italian Culture. Such a request was impossible to fulfill, largely because the German army had seized the choicest buildings in the city. Mayor Softić found himself in the unenviable position of trying to navigate these political tensions within the Axis camp while simultaneously fixing the city's manifold problems. He soon determined that the best approach was a closer alliance with the German command. Although his immediate aim was to encourage the Germans to provide food, Softić envisioned a future relationship based on political and military ties.

102. A copy of the April 1941 Muslim letter to Spaho requesting that Bosnia become a German protectorate can be found in IAS, Oštavina Fehim Spaho, box 3, document 701 (April 19, 1941). Although the original is unsigned, most historians in the region agree that the authors were people with whom Softić was friendly. See Redžić, *Bosnia and Herzegovina in the Second World War,* 168.

103. HM, Ustaška građa, document 428 (September 3, 1942).

104. On the ongoing refugee crisis, see ibid., document 431 (September 11, 1942).

105. ABiH, Javni Ured Rada Sarajevo, box 5, document 1035 (May 22, 1942).

106. Tomasevich dedicates an entire chapter to the rifts and tensions between the Germans and Italians. See *War and Revolution in Yugoslavia,* 233–302. For specific references to Sarajevo, see 246–249 and 264. On the Chetnik-Italian collaboration, see Redžić, *Bosnia and Herzegovina in the Second World War,* 126–129. On the German-Ustasha meetings held in Sarajevo, see Hehn, *The German Struggle against Yugoslav Guerillas in World War II,* 125–126.

In early September 1942, going over the heads of the Ustasha authorities, Softić sent a letter to SS headquarters in Sarajevo warning the German officers that the Ustasha regime had lost all credibility and authority in the city because of the dire food situation:

> It seems ironic to introduce different coupons for flour, butter, oil, lard, shoes, etc. when we don't have any of those goods, or if we do, they are not in a sufficient quantity. . . . What kind of authority can the government have when it issues food coupons but has no food to redeem? Such a system is justifiably criticized by the citizens, and it compromises the authority of the entire government.

Softić suggested that the Germans had an interest in preventing a famine, as this would further their goal of maintaining stability. "It is obvious," he noted, "that Sarajevo . . . cannot change the system by itself." Softić concluded by asking for tangible assistance and especially for more mayoral powers.[107] He hoped to use the food situation as a means of securing more control over the town's political affairs. The Germans responded positively, becoming more involved in the acquisition and distribution of food in Sarajevo.[108]

Seeking German aid was only one part of the Softić solution for Sarajevo. As the mayor jockeyed for power with the Ustashas, he also decided that Sarajevo's loyal Serbs could be an important local ally. After eighteen months of Ustasha mismanagement in every domain from food to cultural policies, the city's political leaders turned to the legacy that they knew best: plurality in the local government. Over the summer and fall of 1942, the Softić administration oversaw the return of Serbs to many aspects of Sarajevo's public sphere. The decision of some Serbs to return to the city and assume identities as Orthodox Croats, despite the strong anti-Serb bias of the regime, reflects the town's openness. Certainly some of Sarajevo's Serbs still faced imprisonment and persecution, but their position in society gradually normalized. Some felt comfortable petitioning the local government for food and clothing; others even began writing in Cyrillic again. The climax to these incremental changes occurred in December 1942 with Mayor Softić's announcement that an Orthodox Croat, Milivoje Simić, had been selected as his deputy mayor. Simić had been president of Sarajevo's local courts and was, according to the local press, "well known in our city" as a "hard-working man and public servant, as well as a worthy intellectual and jurist."[109] He was also a registered member of the Croatian Orthodox Church, as were the other five Serbs appointed to the city council that

---

107. IAS, Zbirka Varia, document 368 (September 1942).
108. Redžić, *Bosnia and Herzegovina in the Second World War,* 179.
109. HM, Ustaška Nadzorna Služba, document 4035 (December 15, 1942), and *Sarajevski Novi List,* December 29, 1942, 5.

month. In the future, Orthodox Croats would govern Sarajevo alongside their Muslim and Catholic counterparts.

The incorporation of Orthodox Croats into the town government was a ceremonial recognition by Muslims and Catholics that the city's Orthodox community had been restored to a position on a par with that of other Croats. It also set out a framework of expectations: if Orthodox citizens wanted to participate in society, they had to be willing to accept certain political responsibilities. It is unclear whether Mayor Softić and other town leaders believed that incorporating Serbs was vital to protecting their own power, a slap in the face at the regime, or the best tactic to stabilize Sarajevo and heal rifts among the city's communities. In any case, the city reacted positively to the change. The Italian consulate reported in December that most Sarajevans thought Mayor Softić was doing a good job and on the whole were optimistic that the next winter would be less devastating and less chaotic than the last.[110] At the most basic level, Sarajevans now had more to unite them than a shared humanitarian nightmare: they had a local government that they trusted.

• • •

Two trends characterized Sarajevo over the course of 1941 and 1942: the fragmentation of the Croat national idea and a growing consciousness among local leaders of the need to reestablish civic ties. Despite the complexity of these processes, they were both part of a growing recognition that the Ustasha regime and its vision of the nation-state did not offer a viable future for the city. Feeling wholly abandoned by the state, city leaders slowly began to take control of the town by finding local solutions to humanitarian problems, developing independent relations with the Germans, and stabilizing the municipal government by bringing Serbs back into the fold of society. In the course of seeking local solutions, Sarajevo's leaders found themselves trying to define more narrowly who belonged to the community. This process became easier with the solidification of two distinct groups as outsiders: the Ustashas and the refugees. Whereas mutual disdain for the Ustashas was rooted in a positive notion that the city's cosmopolitan values distinguished good Sarajevans from the rural thugs who ruled them, local responses to the refugees revealed that the civic consciousness shared by Sarajevans could be used to justify targeting groups that the city could not or did not want to take care of. Sarajevans were not willing to sacrifice their security, comfort, and culture for the sake of the nation-state.

Ideologically, the ineffectiveness of the concept of the Croat nation to bind the city stemmed partly from the regime's efforts to ethnically cleanse the city of non-Croats, as discussed in chapter 3, and partly from the failure

110. HM, Ustaška Nadzorna Služba, document 4035 (December 5, 1942).

of Ustashism to anchor Croatianness to a political and cultural program that resonated with the diverse communities living in the country. Ruling a fledgling state embroiled in a multisided civil war, the regime periodically calculated that the quest for national homogenization needed to take second place to the struggle for political survival. Consequently, it adapted its national rhetoric to fit the shifting political climate. Belonging to the Croat nation became a test of loyalty—both an individual's expression of loyalty and the regime's acceptance of it. Because the regime regularly revised who would be included in the nation, the national idea lacked cultural or political capital on the ground. Furthermore, the regime's insistence on classifying Croats by faith—i.e., as Muslim Croats, Orthodox Croats, and Catholic Croats—gave the entire national program a fractured feeling. The religious descriptors also had two other consequences: they allowed for a hierarchy to develop within the Croat nation, one that left Muslims feeling particularly apprehensive, and they illuminated the conflict between secular and religious identities in the region. In this respect, 1942 marked a critical turning point away from the city's traditional model of society. Although secularism had made deep inroads into Sarajevo's society before the war, religious networks had continued to function as an essential bond fusing Sarajevo's civil society. Town councils still designated their seats on the basis of religion, schools and clubs were affiliated with religious institutions, and most people felt a stronger connection to their mahala and čaršija than to some abstract nation or state. Like sandpaper wearing down a piece of wood, the policies of the Ustasha regime and the German occupation slowly wore down these local networks and reduced the saliency of faith.

DILEMMAS OF THE NEW EUROPEAN ORDER

The Muslim Question and the Yugoslav Civil War

In the spring of 1943, members of Sarajevo's Muslim elite reached out to Nazi Germany and—under the direct authorization of Adolf Hitler and Heinrich Himmler—created a Bosnian Muslim Waffen SS unit.[1] This act would cast a long shadow on the history of Bosnian Muslims, branding them as collaborators and linking their demands for political and religious autonomy to the Fascist project. With the birth of the Waffen SS Division Handžar, as it became known, Muslim leaders went from serving under the occupation to serving the occupation directly. This was by no means an easy decision. But why did they choose to pursue this alliance? What did they hope to gain? And why in 1943, at a time when the Axis hold on the Balkans was tenuous?

This chapter will explore Muslim efforts to craft an autonomous and future-oriented policy in the midst of civil and world wars. It begins with an overview of Sarajevo's experience with the largest armed resistance movements—the Partisans and Chetniks—analyzing how these movements developed early in the war, what they stood for, and how the Ustashas and the Germans responded to them. Although Sarajevans showed very little support for the armed insurgents, the Ustashas and Germans feared that mass discontent over food, housing, health care, and refugee policies indicated that the city might be preparing for an uprising. These fears led to

---

1. The Waffen SS was a front-line armed combat division of the Schutzstaffel (SS), the Nazi Party's military and security organization. Instead of reporting to the Wehrmacht, the Waffen SS units reported directly to Heinrich Himmler, the commander of the SS. The most important study of the Waffen SS unit, as it pertains to local Muslim dynamics, is Redžić, *Muslimansko Autonomaštvo i 13. SS Divizija.*

a spike in police brutality, which in turn contributed to a surge in efforts among the local Muslim elite to break from the NDH.

But the new Muslim movements were hardly what one might think of as resistance. On the contrary, they eventually developed into the purest example of collaboration that wartime Bosnia had to offer: the Handžar Division. By examining the internal rifts within the Muslim leadership and the diverse factions that eventually came to support a Muslim-German alliance, I suggest that Muslims aligned with the Germans because they desired a political stake in the new order and an army that could compete against the Partisans, Chetniks, and Ustashas. In 1943, the only group in the region *not* killing Muslims, or at least not outright, was the Germans. When it became clear that the Germans had no intention of awarding Muslims political autonomy in addition to the Waffen SS unit, Muslim leaders sought other solutions.

It has long been the tendency of historians to describe the civil conflict in Yugoslavia as one between Fascists and non-Fascists, or between the pro-Axis and pro-Allied camps, or between groups fighting for the rehabilitation of Yugoslavia or a permanent death to the post-WWI construction of Yugoslavia. Yet when examining how civil war evolved in Sarajevo, one is struck by the ambiguity of allegiance and the shifting nature of local alliances. At times, various local groups were simultaneously anti-Axis *and* against the resistance armies; they could be simultaneously anti-Ustasha, anti-Partisan, and anti-Chetnik. As the war progressed, there were an increasing number of individuals and groups that were first and foremost anti-Ustasha—they would just as soon align with the Germans as with the Partisans in opposition to the status quo. Instead of joining existing groups, some of Sarajevo's leaders proposed new platforms. By emphasizing local perspectives on the civil conflicts, particularly the Muslim story, this chapter suggests that the paradigm of a three-sided civil war is insufficient: there were at least four sides, perhaps more, in this quest to redefine the political and social order of the central Balkans.

Resistance and Its Illusion

Anyone familiar with Yugoslavia's wartime history is no doubt surprised to find the first detailed discussion of the civil conflict in the fifth chapter of a book on the war. The victory of the Partisan armed resistance was Yugoslavia's most enduring wartime legacy, one that was cemented through postwar Communist historiography and pop culture. But the armed resistance did not dramatically shape Sarajevo's early wartime years. Again, this may be surprising to readers because in the postwar era, Sarajevo became a symbol of the Partisan victory. Its symbolism was forged in part through one of Yugoslavia's most famous films, *Valter Defends Sarajevo,* which depicted the valiant struggle of Sarajevo's Partisans against the Germans at the end of the war.[2] By referring to characters with identifiable Muslim, Croat, and Serb names, the film helped to cement the country's foundational myth of the multiethnic, united "Yugoslav" Partisan army that single-handedly drove evil from the region. To this end, it emphasized the Yugoslavs' common— and foreign—enemy, the Germans, while ignoring the vicious sectarian war and ruthless collaboration that was another reality of the Yugoslav wartime experience. It also painted Sarajevo as a center of anti-German resistance by promoting an idealized brand of the town's civic spirit and linking that spirit to the Communist resistance movement. In the last scene of the film, a Nazi spy is leaving Sarajevo after having failed to capture the elusive resistance leader known as Valter. The spy looks down on the city from a hillside vista and reflectively tells another German officer, "Ever since I came to Sarajevo, I've been searching for Valter, but could not find him. Yet now, when I must leave, I have finally found him." "You know who Valter is? Then tell me right away!"—the other officer demands. Gesturing toward the city below, which the camera captures in panoramic view, the spy utters one of the most famous lines in Yugoslav cinema: "Do you see this city? *Das ist Valter.*"[3] The film, like so many powerful dramas about the past, strongly shaped both the history and the memory of the war.

By all credible accounts, the Partisans did not have much luck in Sarajevo early in the war. Although the Partisan movement had expanded rapidly in the countryside, cities like Sarajevo tended to be resistant to the rural and violent character of the insurgencies. Sarajevo was growing progressively more anti-Ustasha, but it had not yet made a mass turn to one of the organized resistance movements.

At the start of the war, the city had an estimated 279 Communist Party members, but most had either fled the city or been imprisoned by the Ustasha police and the Gestapo in the summer of 1941.[4] Sarajevo's party organization had become so small by 1942 that the secretary, Olga Marasović—who was memorably known by her comrades as "the round one" (*okrugla*)—found it difficult to articulate its dynamics when asked to write a testimonial decades later.[5] Marasović was one of a few dozen

---

2. *Valter brani Sarajevo* (directed by Hajrudin Krvavac, 1971). An excellent analysis of the film can be found in Pavle Levi, *Disintegration in Frames, Aesthetics and Ideology in the Yugoslav and Post-Yugoslav Cinema* (Stanford: Stanford University Press, 2007), 65–66.

3. As translated and quoted in Levi, *Disintegration in Frames,* 65–66.

4. The exact number of Communists living in the city that winter is difficult to ascertain and varies in accounts from 32 to 360. According to Budimir Miličić, a Bosnian historian, there were 218 Communists living in the city that summer, a group that included 93 Serbs, 63 Muslims, 54 Croats, 61 Jews, and 8 "other." See Miličić, *Radnička klasa Sarajeva 1919–1941* (Sarajevo: Institut za Istoriju, 1985), 335. Other estimates can be found in *Zbornik dokumenata i podataka o narodnooslobodilačkom ratu jugoslovenskih naroda* (Belgrade: Vojnoistorijski Institut, 1949–72) vol. 4, bk. 2, 157 and Hoare, *Genocide and Resistance in Hitler's Bosnia,* 39.

5. Olga Marasović, "Narodnooslobodilački pokret u gradu u prvoj godini ustanka," in Albahari et al., *Sarajevo u Revoluciji,* 2:472.

Communist Party members living and working in Sarajevo during that first wartime winter. Those who remained organized into cells of three to five members, in which they wrote and distributed pamphlets, couriered news to Partisan battalions and party headquarters, and occasionally sabotaged the city's infrastructure (by, for example, severing telephone wires).[6] The group suffered both from external police raids and from internal rivalries, brought on to some extent by the appointment in July 1941 of a Monte-negrin, Svetozar Vukmanović-Tempo, as the locally based commander of the Partisan military headquarters in Sarajevo. Vukmanović-Tempo, an outsider, allegedly provoked a feud within the city's party organization by mocking Bosnian culture and criticizing local party members for bungling terrorist acts (even after the regime had executed some of the city's Com-munists for these attempts in late July 1941).[7] Ironically, the Ustasha leader-ship in Sarajevo and its most prominent organized enemy in the city shared a central trait: both were considered insolent outsiders and found it diffi-cult to win support among Sarajevans.

Although Sarajevans from every community eventually participated in Partisan battalions, initial recruitment was slow. Moreover, individual Partisan units had fallen victim to the region's civil strife. In one famous episode in June 1941, a Serb Partisan commander operating in the hills around Sarajevo turned away several hundred Jewish prospective recruits for no apparent reason other than antisemitism.[8] In another episode, the Partisans transferred a Muslim official from military duties in the field to an administrative post in Sarajevo out of concern that the Serb rank and file might try to kill him.[9] Eventually the Partisans began to cleverly tailor their recruitment propaganda to win over members of every group living in Bosnia, building a powerful multiethnic guerrilla army that fought under the banner of "brotherhood and unity."[10]

But in Sarajevo the movement remained small and isolated. Members of Sarajevo's small Communist Party expressed frustration with the slow pace of expansion. Cut off from the central party organization for weeks at a time, they were often confused about their purpose in the city. One member wrote to headquarters in the fall of 1941 that he felt as if he was stationed in Sarajevo "for no reason at all" (*bez veze*) and wondered if he should be doing something more productive in the field.[11] But the Partisan troops depended on the "urban-rural lifeline," as Robert Donia terms it,

6. Donia, *Sarajevo*, 193.
7. Hoare, *Genocide and Resistance in Hitler's Bosnia*, 30, 67–70.
8. Donia, *Sarajevo*, 179.
9. Hoare, *Genocide and Resistance in Hitler's Bosnia*, 101–102.
10. For a breakdown of the national and regional composition of the Partisans, see Marko Attila Hoare, "Whose Is the Partisan Movement? Serbs, Croats, and the Legacy of a Shared Resistance," *Journal of Slavic Military Studies* 15, no. 4 (December 2002): 24–41.
11. *Zbornik Dokumenata*, vol. 4, bk. 2, 158.

for information, weapons, and supplies.[12] Sarajevo was considered a critical node of this lifeline. Moreover, as peasants filled the ranks of the Partisan troops, top Communists needed Sarajevo's small party network to hold its ground if they hoped to retain the movement's political character. So Marašović and her comrades remained in the occupied city. Fearful of jeopardizing their clandestine operations, they kept their inner circle small, recruiting at most a few hundred volunteers for the nearby Partisan army.[13]

Meanwhile, the Chetniks, the other major resistance army battling for control over the former Yugoslavia, had no infrastructure in Sarajevo. Founded in April 1941 by Yugoslav army generals who refused to capitulate to the Axis forces, the Chetniks initially presented themselves as a spin-off of the Yugoslav army. Consequently, a few of the city's pro-Yugoslav Muslims and Catholics joined.[14] But over the summer and fall 1941, the character of the Chetnik movement changed. After a series of Serb peasant uprisings, rural Serb nationalists began to dominate the Chetniks' Bosnian forces. Chetnik commanders lost control over these rogue factions, which changed from battalions in the quasi-official resistance army into bands of violent Serb guerrillas ransacking the countryside and driving tens of thousands of Muslim peasants from their homes. Whatever public support the Chetniks might have mustered among pro-Yugoslav circles in Sarajevo—even among Sarajevo's Serbs—evaporated when Sarajevans learned of these atrocities.[15]

Thus in the first year of the war, less than 1 percent of Sarajevo's population belonged to the organized resistance. Nevertheless, support for the opposition—or more precisely, for political change and humanitarian relief—dramatically increased over the miserable winter of 1941–42. The prevalence of this sympathy was unclear, but the Germans, the local Ustasha leaders, and the city government all sensed that public opinion was changing. Whereas postwar Yugoslav historiography paints this trend as a collective movement of Sarajevans toward Communism and Yugoslavism, available evidence clearly suggests that Sarajevans felt no particular affinity to Communism, the Partisans, or the armed insurgence. They were bitter toward the Ustasha government and the occupation system, and they felt insecure about their position in a city overwhelmed with refugees, food shortages, disease, unemployment, and uncertain citizenship and residency laws. The bazaars buzzed with talk of food riots; piles of complaints mounted ever higher on the mayor's desk.

12. Donia, *Sarajevo*, 189–192.
13. Uglješa Danilović, "Sarajevo i sarajevska oblast," in Albahari et al., *Sarajevo u Revoluciji*, 3:14.
14. *Zbornik Dokumenata*, vol. 4, bk. 1, 634 and 718.
15. For an overview of the factions in Bosnia, see the pamphlet *The Četniks, a Survey of Četnik Activity in Yugoslavia, April 1941-July 1944* (Allied Forces Headquarters, September 1944), 38–36. For a history of the Chetnik divisions, see Hoare, *Hitler's Bosnia*.

Much to the dismay of city residents, public expressions of anger and frustration had an effect opposite to the one they had anticipated: instead of alleviating hardship, they contributed to a growing paranoia among Ustasha and German officials that insurgents lurked in every corner of the city. When the Partisans conquered dozens of villages and towns in the mountains around Sarajevo, the Ustashas cracked down with stricter police searches. As town leaders pleaded with the regime for humanitarian relief over the winter of 1941–42, Zagreb consolidated and expanded local military and police agencies, as well as training and recruitment camps.[16] The regime also tightened its hold over the local branch of the Home Guard, fearing that some Muslim soldiers might defect to the armed resistance or form independent militias, as they had started to do in other parts of Bosnia.[17] A high-ranking Croat officer visiting Sarajevo warned his superiors in December 1941 that a panic had developed among Muslims, who believed that the regime "was not seriously defending Bosnia."[18]

When the armed insurgents won a series of minor victories in January 1942, the Ustashas began a new wave of arrests. Their targets were often people who appeared to be passively resisting, such as schoolteachers who strayed from the curriculum or young men caught taking a coffee break instead of working for the war effort. The street sweep was a popular Ustasha tactic: police would patrol Sarajevo's streets in search of the smallest sign of suspicious activity, picking up men regardless of their religion, their citizenship, or the importance of their employment. Calling the men new "recruits," the police immediately transferred them to the Home Guard, to Ustasha labor battalions, or to factory work in Germany.[19] Women were not spared from interrogation, in part because the Ustasha police knew that women like Olga Marasović comprised a central base of Communist support in the city.[20] By February, the mood on the streets became so menacing that Vukmanović-Tempo wrote to his commander, Josip Broz Tito, that the Ustasha police's "dreadful" reaction was making it "impossible for us to move around the city." But he also noted that the local police seemed too inexperienced to actually find the insurgents. Apparently the central government in Zagreb felt the same way because it began to send its own agents

16. Rafel Brčić, "Okupacioni sistem i ustaška Nezavisna Država Hrvatska u Sarajevu (1941–1943)," in Albahari et al., *Sarajevo u Revoluciji*, 2:272–273.

17. On the defections of Muslim Home Guard soldiers and new militias formed in Bosnia, see Hoare, *History of Bosnia and Hercegovina*, 267–273.

18. HM, Ustaška Nadzorna Služba, document 262 (December 20, 1941).

19. Svetozar Vukmanović-Tempo, *Revolucija koja teče, Memoari* (Zagreb: Globus, 1982), 2:63.

20. On the network of female couriers and their activities, see testimonials by Dragica Tošić-Stanić, Ankica Albahari, Vukosava Vukica Šain, Feriha Bostandžić, Olga Nakić, and Olga Marasović in Albahari et al., *Sarajevo u Revoluciji*, vol. 2, and accounts of Olga Marasović in *Pokrajinsko savjetovanje KPJ za Bosnu i Hercegovinu*, ed. Zdravko Antonić et al. (Sarajevo: Institut za Istoriju, 1983), 151.

to oversee local investigations.[21] Working under the radar, the Communists continued their clandestine operations.

Ordinary civilians, especially Muslims, felt under attack. By late February, the police searches, coupled with the humanitarian crisis, had made life in the city unbearable. On February 25, a Croat army colonel informed Marshal Kvaternik that Sarajevo's "entire population is anxious, particularly Muslims." He warned that the city had lost faith in the regime. "Everybody is talking about the [Ustasha army's] unsuccessful actions" in eastern Bosnia. "Discontent toward the army and the Ustashas has grown" as Sarajevo was "more or less surrounded" by battle on all sides. For the sake of regaining Muslims' trust and stabilizing Sarajevo, he begged Kvaternik to "establish responsibility for the catastrophe of eastern Bosnia, for tens of thousands of slaughtered Muslims, for the massacres of women and children, and for the Muslim villages that were torched" by admitting that the "shoddy leadership" of the local Ustasha authorities was largely to blame.[22] The colonel warned the authorities that their behavior was driving a deeper wedge between the regime and its citizens, and he hoped that some small act of humility might help to heal local animosities. But the Ustasha bosses in Sarajevo, most of whom came from other parts of the NDH, had no interest in being lectured to by a Sarajevan army officer. Instead of responding to the colonel's entreaty, they accused him of collaborating with Serbs and Muslims who identified as Serbs.[23] Such a rebuke underscored the widening rift between the interests of town leaders and the regime's agenda. Anyone critical of the regime's official policies could be labeled a political enemy, a label that could have deadly consequences.

On March 12, 1942, the Ustashas received a report that added fuel to the fire: two days earlier, eight Muslim students from the Islamic religious high school and the Muslim Croat cultural society Narodna Uzdanica had left Sarajevo to join the Partisan resistance. Panic-stricken, the Ustasha police arrested seventy Muslim students and teachers for interrogation. They had no clue how wide a net the resistance had cast, so they feared the worst, reporting that the Communist Party had infiltrated every part of Sarajevo and armed three thousand people.[24] Not even the Communists claimed such success.[25] But the Ustashas grew frantic. In a report titled "The Difficult Political Situation in Sarajevo and the Threat of Communism to the City," one local Ustasha official advised Ante Pavelić to dispatch immediately five thousand of the best Ustasha soldiers with truckloads of

21. These reports are reprinted in *Zbornik Dokumenata*, vol. 4, bk. 3, 85–87, 142, 181, and 510–514.
22. HM, Ustaška Nadzorna Služba, document 262, (February 25, 1942). For parts of this quote, I have used the translation by Aida Vidan as published in Redžić, *Bosnia and Herzegovina in the Second World War*, 83.
23. Redžić, *Bosnia and Herzegovina in the Second World War*, 83.
24. HM, Ustaška građa, document 329 (March 12, 1942).
25. See, for example, Danilović, "Sarajevo i sarajevska oblast," 3:14.

clothing, food, and ammunition to secure Sarajevo. Anything less might mean losing the city for good, a frightening prospect and a realistic one, since the Home Guard and Ustasha militias had already lost control of most of the surrounding countryside. He warned Zagreb, "[E]very day there are new groups of young people who escape the city to join the Communist ranks."[26]

A witch hunt ensued. Several of the prisoners were eighth-grade boys, perhaps thirteen or fourteen years old. Their youth reveals itself in the interrogation transcripts: one boy notes that the Partisans do "bad things" and another tells the police that he knows "we're supposed to study, not go into the forest." The boys swore that they had no idea the other students had planned to join the Partisans.[27] The arrests seemed to be a deliberate attempt by the Ustasha police to remind Sarajevans, particularly Muslims, who was in charge.

Sarajevo's Muslims reacted angrily. On March 18, one father wrote an impassioned letter to County Executive Gavran-Kapetanović describing how the night before, two Ustasha secret agents had stormed unannounced into his house and arrested his daughter, Hajrija, who taught fourth grade at a Sarajevo school. The father wrote that his family was pure Croat without any questionable ties to Yugoslavia. The father even worked for the state as an inspector at the Croatian Railway in Sarajevo. Horrified at this intrusion into his home and family life, he begged Gavran-Kapetanović to find and return his daughter. The county executive tried to intervene with the Ustasha police, who only confirmed that they had indeed taken the woman.[28] In an attempt to quell the growing panic in the city, later that month Zagreb appointed a new police chief, Gregorović, who—according to the Germans—was known for working closely with Muslims and Germans.[29] Meanwhile, the German Occupation Command trusted neither city nor Ustasha authorities and began patrolling Sarajevo independently. The Germans also enforced a long-ignored ban on public gatherings, allowing only events officially sanctioned by the regime.[30] Their renewed presence signaled to local leaders that the Germans might be losing faith in the Ustashas.

Given the famine, arrests, and general sense of panic brewing in the city, why weren't more people joining the armed resistance? This is a question that the Partisans would ask themselves repeatedly during the war. Part of the problem was that many Sarajevans viewed the armed insurgents as

26. IAS, Zbirka Varia, document 233 (March 14, 1942).

27. HM, Ustaška grada, document 329 (March 12, 1942).

28. Ibid., document 328 (March 18, 1942).

29. Hoover Institute Archives, Tomasevich Papers, records from the captured German documents held at the U.S. National Archives, box 4, T:120, roll 5785 (date illegible, likely from early 1943).

30. HM, Ustaška grada, order from the Stadortkommandtur Sarajevo, document 339 (April 11, 1942).

little different from the Ustashas: both were deemed unsophisticated, violent, peasant-based movements that threatened to undermine their way of life. Indeed, the Communists stood in direct opposition to Sarajevo's religious-based culture and social norms. Even the Communists later admitted that Sarajevans were apprehensive over their plans to overhaul society.[31] Furthermore, Sarajevans who did join the Partisans often misunderstood the movement's objectives. Local Ustasha officials suggested in a report to Zagreb that many of the Muslim youths who joined the Partisans had little comprehension of Communism—they fought out of religious solidarity and believed that the Partisans represented their side.[32] Such an explanation is not implausible, especially since it was true that once out in the field, some Muslim Partisans defected to the Ustasha paramilitaries upon realizing that the Partisans often worked closely with Chetnik units known to be anti-Muslim. Sarajevans were trying to make sense of a war replete with complexity; they did not understand that chaos and ambiguity defined the civil conflict in which they desperately sought to find the "right" side.

Town leaders knew that Sarajevo was not a beacon of resistance activity, but they could not deny that it was a city filled with starving, disgruntled people who would not remain peaceful for long. Although sympathetic to the petitions of innocent citizens, Mayor Demirović and County Executive Gavran-Kapetanović were genuinely concerned that antigovernment attitudes had spread in their city. In the minds of many town leaders, resistance was any threat to authority. Individual leaders could thus be personally against the Germans and the Ustashas yet find themselves doing their dirty work on the ground in order to prevent insurrection. Civil war had completely devastated most of the surrounding county by the spring, and bandits roamed the hills around the city.[33] Fear of sabotage in Sarajevo had encouraged the Croatian State Theater and other public institutions to request extra police patrols over the winter.[34] The city remained relatively secure because of the Ustasha and German military presence, but there was persistent uncertainty about whether the Ustasha army could hold it if the Germans had to redirect resources elsewhere. As the war on the eastern front worsened, such concerns became ubiquitous.

Throughout April and May, the Ustasha police brought more than two hundred Sarajevans into custody on charges of working for the resistance. The prisoners included men and women, Muslims, Catholics, and Orthodox.[35] Without an investigation or a trial—and in spite of heated protests by the Muslim elite against the arrests of Muslim youths—the police quietly

31. ABiH, Zbirka NOR-a Okružni Komitet KPJ Sarajevo, box 1, document 13 (November 4, 1944).
32. IAS, Zbirka Varia, document 233 (March 14, 1942).
33. *Zbornik Dokumenata*, vol. 4, bk. 3, 481–484.
34. ABiH, Narodno pozorište Sarajevo, box 3, document 150 (January 17, 1942).
35. On the arrests, see HM, Ustaška Nadzorna Služba, document 304 (April 24, 1942).

deported many of the prisoners to Jasenovac. There they lived in barracks adjacent to their old Jewish neighbors, with whom they shared a dismal life of hunger and hard labor. A number of innocents got caught in the police raids, including a group of Muslims who had donated money to Communists impersonating humanitarian fund-raisers.[36] But the Ustasha police also successfully apprehended important local Communists, including Olga Marašović. They discovered the identities of other spies for the resistance in the course of interrogations and house searches, forcing dozens more to flee. By the time summer arrived, the official resistance had been almost completely decimated. Periodic raids by the Gestapo and Ustasha police ensured that any nascent insurgency within the city's boundaries was promptly crushed.[37] The local Partisan movement would not be revived until September 1943. In the meantime, however, a new local movement had started to gain momentum: the Muslim Autonomists.

Muslim Autonomists: The Fourth Side

In the wake of the arrests in the spring of 1942, rumors spread around the Muslim community that the Ustasha police had tortured Muslim prisoners with such excessive force that one died. Consequently, Muslim family members began to rally their townsmen to fight for children who had "disappeared into the darkness of the notorious camps."[38] Even the German command stepped in, criticizing local Ustasha officials for imprisoning people without an investigation or proper evidence (which prompted a complaint from local Ustashas to Zagreb that the Germans were interfering in domestic police activity).[39] Internal Ustasha police memos from late June described how "rumors were spreading wildly across the [Muslim] bazaars" that the Ustashas were out to get Muslims.[40] The appointment of Mayor Softić was part of the regime's attempt at a solution, and indeed, Softić worked overtime to regain citizens' trust. But, as I described in the previous chapter, the feeling of crisis raged on for months after he took office. Only gradually, particularly with the stabilization of the municipal government and the reincorporation of Serbs into the city council, would the city's morale improve.

36. ARIZBiH, Ulema Medžlis, document 1671/42 (June 4, 1942).
37. Džemal Muminagić, "Hapšenja brojnih aktivista partije i SKOJ-a u proljeće 1942. godine," in Albahari et al., *Sarajevo u Revoluciji*, 2:664–665; Mehmed Džinić, "Velika hapšenja komunista i drugih pripadnika NOP-a od proljeća 1942. do ljeta 1943. godine," in Albahari et al., *Sarajevo u Revoluciji*, 3:547–569. On the imprisonment of Olga Marašović, see Vukmanović-Tempo, *Revolucija koja teče, Memoari*, 2:199.
38. ARIZBiH, Ulema Medžlis, document 1671 (June 4, 1942).
39. HM, Ustaška Nadzorna Služba, document 376 (June 15, 1942).
40. Ibid. (June 24, 1942).

While the mayor and other Muslim leaders worked to resolve humanitarian issues like the food and refugee crises, they were also dealing with the bigger Muslim question. Across Bosnia, Muslim leaders recognized that their position in the NDH had deteriorated beyond the point of repair. They understood that sustaining the social structures of their community was impossible in a state run by the Ustashas. But what was the alternative? Their perceptions of the anti-Muslim Chetniks and the atheist Communists made an alliance with either unsavory. Some local leaders believed in Bosnian autonomy, but this raised more questions than it answered: would an autonomous Bosnia be governed primarily by Muslims or would representatives from every community have an equal voice? Would it be linked to the Independent State of Croatia or to Nazi Germany? What role would Islam play in the state? And most critical, would such a political entity be sustainable after the war?

Over the course of 1942 and 1943, different Muslim factions developed platforms to address these questions. Many looked to the independent Muslim militias forming in the countryside as inspiration. Although these militias had military objectives—namely, the protection and defense of Muslim communities—they did not yet have the strength or savvy for mass political mobilization. Thus some of Sarajevo's leaders began to ponder whether they might develop a political base that coordinated them. Gradually the various Muslim movements seeking political, religious, or military power metamorphosed into what has become known more broadly as the Muslim Autonomy Movement. This term inaccurately presents the factions as a single movement rather than a collection of discrete Muslim organizations and militias across Bosnia with often conflicting long- and short-term goals.[41] In Sarajevo, Muslims overwhelmingly agreed that the system was intolerable. But they disagreed over the role that Islam should play in the new European order, the value of their experiences under the region's three past governments (Ottoman, Austro-Hungarian, and Yugoslav), and where Bosnia's Muslims fit in the taxonomy of European nations. The challenge facing Muslim leaders was to determine, or to guess, who among the Ustashas, Partisans, Chetniks, Germans, or Italians would offer the path of least destruction and maximum opportunity for Muslims. Each faction would make its own choices, responding to the politics of war and the moves of its local competitors.

Muslim Croats, a small group of progressive Muslims, believed that the NDH still offered the best path for Muslims to participate in modern European society. Politically, members of this group held positions in the Ustasha

41. Most scholars who address this topic refer to a Muslim Autonomy Movement in the singular. See Donia, *Sarajevo*, 188, and Enver Redžić, *Muslimansko autonomaštvo i 13. SS divizija: Autonomija Bosne i Hercegovine i Hitlerov Treći Rajh* (Sarajevo: Svjetlost, 1987). I prefer to use the plural "movements" because, as I show throughout this work, several competing Muslim factions existed in the city, and each conceived of autonomy differently.

administration. A small minority were considered by their townsmen to be "ultra Croats," such as Hakija Hadžić, the onetime deputy for Sarajevo who now held a post in Vienna.[42] The majority adopted a more mainstream Muslim Croat identity most commonly associated with the society Narodna Uzdanica. They maintained that "Bosnian Muslims are a part of the Croat nation and they have the purest Croat blood,"[43] yet they also acknowledged that the Muslim half of the Croat nation was deeply fragmented on the issue.[44]

The Softić circle, a group of Muslims working closely with Mayor Softić, shared many characteristics with the Muslim Croats: members of both groups had supported the Yugoslav Muslim Organization in the interwar era and thought of themselves as proponents of modernity.[45] Culturally, they adopted a more progressive attitude than religious Muslims associated with groups like El-Hidaje. Softić's wife, for example, participated in fund-raising and refugee assistance with the women's committee of Narodna Uzdanica, suggesting that she, like her husband, supported elements of women's emancipation and secular culture.[46] Unlike the die-hard Muslim Croats (or even the lukewarm ones), the Softić circle did not think it beneficial, or possible, for Muslims to remain a part of a Croat nation-state.[47] Softić; his father-in-law, Uzeir Hadžihasanović; and their clique of merchants, intellectuals, and businessmen knew that an independent Bosnian state would be unsustainable in the European system, and thus they hoped it would become a protectorate or an autonomous province of another state. They viewed Nazi Germany as the most viable option at this point in the war. In their quest to secure a political solution for Muslims, the group appeared ideologically inconsistent, particularly when it came to Jewish policy. For example, when the Ustashas opened an exhibit about the evils of Jewry in September 1942, Softić and other prominent Muslims boycotted it out of contempt for the regime. Yet months later, the group adopted passionate antisemitic rhetoric in an effort to secure a closer collaborative relationship with the Germans.[48] Such ideological inconsistency underscores

42. Alija Nametak uses the term "ultra-Hrvat" as a way of distinguishing the extreme Croats, like Hakija Hadžić and Asim Drljević, from individuals whose Croat identity was less emphatic. See Nametak, *Sarajevski Nekrologij*, 201. Other members of the group included Muhamed Alajbegović and the important Zagreb politician Ademaga Mešić.

43. HM, Ustaška Nadzorna Služba, document 426 (July 27, 1942).

44. IAS, Narodna Uzdanica, Mjesni odbor, box 49 (September 4, 1942).

45. Details on this circle can be found in Alija Nametak, "Merhum Uzeir-aga Hadžihasanović," *Kalendar Napredak*, 1944, 71–74.

46. IAS, Narodna Uzdanica, Ženski Odbor, zapisnik (December 3, 1942).

47. HM, Ustaška Nadzorna Služba, document 426 (July 27, 1942).

48. On the Muslim boycott, see Yeshayahu A. Jelinek, "Bosnia-Herzegovina at War: Relations between Moslems and non-Moslems," *Holocaust and Genocide Studies* 5, no. 3 (1990): 288. Examples from the exhibit are held in Zbirka Plakata at the Historical Museum of Bosnia and Herzegovina and the Historical Archive of Sarajevo, which were coordinated at an exhibit in Sarajevo entitled, "Izložba Antisemitiski plakat u vrijeme NDH i Nedićeve Srbije" (Bosnian Cultural Center, October 26–29, 2006). For a discussion of the 1942 exhibit, see the "Bujas

the ways in which a local group could integrate or reject parts of rightist ideology depending on whether it was being espoused by an enemy or an ally.

A third faction of Muslims emerged in the spring of 1942 around a new Sarajevo daily called *Osvit*. According to the Croat historian Nada Kisić-Kolanović, the Osvit circle hoped "to find a balance between tradition and progress" and to ease Bosnia into the modern era without inciting "a spiritual and moral earthquake."[49] Many of the twenty men involved with the paper had joined the Ustasha Party in the early months of the war. The paper's founder, Hasan Hadžiosmanović, was an Ustasha official with close ties to Hakija Hadžić; Sarajevo's first wartime mayor, Atif Hadžikadić, was an active member of the group.[50] While openly supporting the regime and its policies, Osvit disagreed with the way that the majority of progressive Muslim political leaders treated the religious establishment.[51] These men did not believe that Muslims should abandon the religious legacies of five centuries in order to become a part of Europe. Unlike those Muslims who were nostalgic for the Habsburg days, Osvit criticized the Austro-Hungarian leaders for making a "great mistake" by building a modern city directly next to the old town, thus "destroying the charm of the traditional city."[52] Architecture was not the paper's only gripe. Instead of supporting the Islamic Religious Community, a by-product of the Habsburg era, Osvit publicly and enthusiastically supported El-Hidaje, the association of traditionalist ulema, congratulating the society for protecting and defending Islamic culture and heritage at a time when other Muslim organizations had abandoned the tenets of the faith.[53]

For its part, El-Hidaje tried to guard Islam from the onslaught of the secularizing state and promote Islamic values within the community. Members viewed contemporary Muslim rulers like Softić and Hadžić as sellouts, akin to the nineteenth-century Muslim Austrophiles who compromised core Islamic traditions in order to join Europe.[54] With more than two thousand male members across Bosnia and a small but important committee of women in Sarajevo, by the spring of 1942 El-Hidaje had developed a large social network in the city and countryside; it also had connections

---

report" in ABiH, Zemaljska komisija za utvrđivanje ratnih zločina okupatora i njihovih pomagača za BiH, box 3.

49. Kišić-Kolanović, "Muslimanska inteligencija i islam u Nezavisnoj Državi Hrvatskoj," 916–917.

50. Other men in this circle included Kasim Nadžić, the main editor of *Osvit*, Alija Kopčić, Husein Muradbegović, Mustafa Mehić, Enver Čolaković, Ubejd Mehić, and Alija Kopičić.

51. See, for example, an article from March 8, 1942, "Naša Društva: Merhamet," in which the paper blames Jews for the difficulties facing Muslim in modern times.

52. *Osvit*, April 10, 1942, 5. For the opposing view of Muslims who believed the Austrian era was a better model for the city's future, see IAS, Narodna Uzdanica, zapisnik, box 50 (January 13, 1943).

53. See Smail Balić, "El-Hidaje u našoj budućnosti," *Osvit*, October 11, 1942, 2.

54. See an article by one of the leading members of the organization: Kasim Dobrača, "Uređenje naše vjerske uprave," *El-Hidaje*, June 22, 1942, 206–207.

with Muslim militias in the countryside—connections that would be useful later in the war. For all intents and purposes, El-Hidaje viewed itself as the voice of Islam. But exactly what this would mean in the larger context of war was not yet clear.

Over the summer of 1942, the Young Muslims (Mladi muslimani), the small fringe student group, began to represent the intellectual wing of Sarajevo's younger Islamists. Most of the men studied at the University of Zagreb in 1941–42, returning to Sarajevo during summer and winter breaks. Consequently, their ideas were often newer than those of their more traditionally observant elders. The Young Muslims publicly embraced Islamic life, law, and culture but in a modern way. They advocated creating an Islamic movement that incorporated Arabic and Islamic symbols (like the crescent and star). Although the group had formed in March 1941, the Ustasha authorities had rejected its application to organize legally because the regime did not want any student group competing with the official Ustasha youth group. In 1942, El-Hidaje sought to resolve this problem by making the Young Muslims its youth sector, bringing the movement under its wing and providing it with resources and press. The relationship between the Western-educated students and the Sarajevo ulema was often tense and antagonistic.[55] They agreed, however, on the necessity of strengthening Islamic culture.

Further confounding this complex picture of Muslim political factions, religious movements, and cultural organizations was the reality that these groups were not mutually exclusive. They coexisted and shared members, agreeing on some points and disagreeing on others. At times progressive members of competing political camps despised each other and worked instead with Islamists. The Islamists occasionally chose tactics that seemingly aligned them with the Communist Partisans. Personal animosities stemming from interwar rivalries also shaped wartime alliances.

There existed several organizations that bridged these factions, such as the humanitarian group Merhamet, trade organizations, and sports teams like Đerzelez, a Sarajevo Muslim soccer team. Moreover, all Muslims were part of the Islamic Religious Community, which remained the legal voice of Muslims and a liaison between the community and the state. But the Muslims' administrative body was not always a source of unity. On the contrary, it occasionally fueled factionalism, particularly during a leadership struggle after the death of Reis-ul-ulema Fehim Spaho on February 14, 1942. Spaho had anticipated a fallout after his death and thus months before, he had named a temporary successor, Salih Bašić, a judge who had served as Reis-ul-ulema from 1936 to 1938 and shared Spaho's vision of the

---

55. On El-Hidaje and Mladi Muslimani in the spring of 1942, see Behmen, *Mladi Muslimani 1939–1999*, 28–29 and Kisić-Kolanović, "Muslimanska inteligencija i islam u NDH," 927–929.

religious bureaucracy.[56] A small group of ulema associated with El-Hidaje tried to circumvent the appointment by going directly to Zagreb, but Ante Pavelić did not want to meddle in internal Islamic business or be the arbiter of different Muslim factions. So Bašić assumed his post and remained there for the duration of the war.[57] He understood that the war was temporary and complicated and considered it his mission to guide Muslims through trying times and to maintain stability between the community and the state until the war ended. Thus on the occasion of the state's first anniversary, he proposed honoring it by building and restoring small mosques, each with a plaque that noted its foundation under the NDH. This gesture served to expand Islamic institutions and demonstrate loyalty to the state.[58] Although Islamists considered Bašić far too secular (and had vehemently protested his earlier appointment as Reis in 1936), it cannot be argued that he was not devoted to the preservation of Islamic culture. During his tenure he tried to combat corruptive social trends, such as coed youth groups and mixed marriages.

Because the Muslim political crisis was linked to the humanitarian and refugee crises, Merhamet assumed a role as a central meeting place for Muslims of all political convictions to express their mutual grievances.[59] As an organization, Merhamet's mission was to protect and assist the Muslim poor and victims of the war, which its leaders appeared to do without much thought for the social or political implications of their decisions. A classic example of what Jacque Burrin has called "structural accommodation," the organization worked with the Ustashas, the Germans, and various city institutions to maintain soup kitchens, refugee camps, and other essential humanitarian services.[60] Its members included high-ranking representatives from El-Hidaje, Narodna Uzdanica, and the Ulema Medžlis, as well as members of the city's intellectual and merchant communities.[61] Supporters of National Socialism mixed with men who had risked their lives to save Jews; war hawks worked side by side with Islamic pacifists. In August 1942, the group held several meetings in an effort to address the refugee and orphan crises. Although one can presume that these meetings were not without their share of friction, the minutes reveal limited tensions and a joint effort to resolve the humanitarian nightmare plaguing Sarajevo and

56. For an overview of the life and career of Salih Bašić, see Šeta, *Reis-ul-uleme u Bosni i Hercegovini i Jugoslaviji*, 47–48.

57. Kisić-Kolanović, "Muslimanska inteligencija i islam u NDH," 936.

58. ARIZBiH, Ulema Medžlis, document 1228/42 (April 7, 1942).

59. This was not new to the wartime era. In the late 1930s, Merhamet had also offered its space for meetings of Muslims during particularly tense political times. See Hasanbegović, *Jugoslavenska muslimanska organizacija*, 307.

60. Phillipe Burrin, *France under the Germans: Collaboration and Compromise*, trans. Janet Lloyd (New York: New Press, 1993), 461–462.

61. See lists of major donors in Bavčić, *Merhamet (1913–2003)*, 251.

the larger region.[62] While disagreeing on key political and religious questions, Muslim leaders shared a common concern: they had no voice in the war among the Chetniks, Ustashas, and Partisans, and they felt that the war threatened to wipe out their community. Something needed to change to ensure its survival.

Although Muslim leaders would meet several more times over the fall of 1942 in an effort to develop a collective plan, their meetings actually brought their differences into stark relief and thus sparked another layer of internal competition.[63] They never agreed on a unilateral approach to solve their political issues. In September, El-Hidaje criticized Muslim intellectuals who eagerly embraced Western culture, treated their wives as equals, and gave their children non-Muslim names.[64] Feeling threatened, the intellectuals running Narodna Uzdanica lashed back with a new campaign to expand their organization by welcoming more youths from Gajret, the defunct Muslim Serb society, and expanding activities for students and women.[65] Ignoring their religious differences with the NDH, various groups of Muslim Croats tried to negotiate with the regime, while some local intellectuals began to view the Partisans as the lesser evil. The Softić circle, meanwhile, reached out to the Germans.

The "Muslim Autonomy Movement" was thus defined by political infighting and heated debates over whether Islamic or civic culture should be the glue uniting the Muslim community. The inability of Muslim leaders in Sarajevo, Bosnia's political center, to find common ground in either political or religious-cultural matters ultimately prevented them from developing a united front that could pose a legitimate challenge to the powerful movements fighting for control of the region.

False Promises of the Waffen SS

On November 1, 1942, the German base in Sarajevo received an anonymous eighteen-page letter addressed to Adolf Hitler, begging him to establish a Nazi German protectorate in Bosnia and designate Sarajevo as its new capital city.[66] The Germans later attributed the secret letter to Mayor

62. A report of the meeting on August 10, 1942 can be found in Hoover Institution Archives, Tomasevich Papers, records from the captured German documents held at the U.S. National Archives, box 4, T:120, roll 5787 (August 10, 1942). For an overview of the more famous conference in late August, see Redžić, *Bosnia and Herzegovina in the Second World War*, 174–175.

63. Hoover Institute Archives, Tomasevich Papers, records from the captured German documents held at the U.S. National Archives, report from the German embassy, box 4, T:120, roll 5793 (May 12, 1943).

64. *El-Hidaje*, September 11, 1942, 19–20.

65. IAS, Narodna Uzdanica, zapisnik, box 50 (January 13, 1943); ibid., Ženski odbor (July 16, 1942).

66. Copies of this letter can be found in various archives. I use the one found in the captured German documents at the U.S. National Archives, which I accessed through the

Softić, Uzeir Hadžihasanović, and Suljaga Salihagić, a prominent Banja Luka Muslim. Though the men never publicly confirmed or denied such reports, the local German consul, Erich Gördes—and subsequent historians working with these documents—seemed confident that the Softić circle was responsible.[67] This would make sense, given the men's history of supporting Bosnian autonomy and Softić's previous missive to the German command in which he begged for intervention in the food crisis and hinted that he had a political plan in the works.[68] In the letter to Hitler, the authors professed Muslims' deep loyalty to Germany and underscored the historical and political ties between Muslims and Germans. They claimed to have "genuine sympathies for National Socialism" and to be the only ethnic group in Bosnia to support the Germans' efforts to resolve the Jewish question. Indeed, they warned Hitler that many leading Ustasha Catholics, such as Father Božidar Bralo, had allowed Jews to convert to Catholicism in order to escape persecution. The Muslim authors even adopted the Germans' racializing language, arguing that Bosnian Muslims were descended from the Goths, not the Slavs, making them "by blood and by race" kin of the Germans, not the Croats.

While the authors tried to legitimize their claims to power from every angle, a single goal was clear: breaking away from the Ustasha regime. They emphasized to Hitler that Pavelić's "insane regime" had failed and that his "hellish plan"—especially the "slaughter" of the Serbs—was having disastrous consequences for the entire region. After listing their grievances, the authors appealed to Hitler to remove every Ustasha from Bosnia and allow Muslims to formally establish a military guard. In effect, they wanted to consolidate the self-regulating Muslim militias into a real army that worked in conjunction with politicians in Sarajevo.[69] Noting that Bosnia had always existed as a part of some outside entity and might not succeed independently, they argued that direct German rule was essential for peace and stability in the region. However, they also indicated that they expected to enjoy a degree of autonomy once the war ended. They included a map of the region with the letter, outlining areas that they believed should be included in postwar Bosnia. They even suggested that the Germans should consider transferring the population of some (but not all) Bosnian Croat

Hoover Institution Archives, Tomasevich Papers, Muslim National Committee's letter to Adolf Hitler, box 4, T:120, roll 5793 (November 1, 1942).

67. Hoover Institute Archives, Tomasevich Papers, records from the captured German documents held at the U.S. National Archives, report from the German consul in Sarajevo, box 4, T:120, roll 5794 (January 20, 1943).

68. IAS, Zbirka Varia, document 368 (September 1942).

69. The authors specifically requested that Muslim major Muhamed Hadžiefendić be made commander of the new guard. Hadžiefendić had organized the most powerful and most successful Muslim militia in the Tuzla region. On Muslim militias in Bosnia, see Redžić, *Bosnia and Herzegovina in the Second World War*, 173–174.

and Bosnian Serb communities in order to give Muslims an absolute majority in the postwar state.

There are many ways of interpreting the letter to Hitler. It has all the standard ingredients of a political national movement and can be seen as an early moment in the formation of the Bosnian Muslim national identity—or the Bosniak nation, as it became known officially after 1993. It attempts to separate a Muslim national body from other people living in the region, it provides a historical and cultural rationale for the legitimacy of the nation, and it pleads for political sovereignty. Yet, unlike contemporaneous national programs in eastern Europe and the Balkans that emphasized peasant culture and tradition, the letter adopts a more sophisticated, Sarajevo-centric focus. There is an element of city pride, or cosmopolitan elitism, in the Muslims' hope of revitalizing Sarajevo's position as a political capital for the region. At the same time, the letter can be interpreted cynically as a quest for power or as a pragmatic effort by Muslim leaders to prevent further destruction in the region. Although the letter suggested reorganizing Bosnia's population in order to give Muslims a majority, it seems likely by Mayor Softić's other actions that fall—especially the reincorporation of Serbs into the city's public life and the appointment of a Serb as deputy mayor—that the group ultimately hoped to secure a political order where Muslims would assume a dominant role in conjunction with the city's other religious communities. Many Muslims realized that the only chance their community had to ward off the Communists and overthrow the Ustasha regime would be to build a strong network of support with like-minded leaders. This approach had proven successful in previous political and wartime crises.

There is also an element of realism in the plea, an admission that collaboration was the best path for Muslims. Most of Sarajevo's Muslim elite knew that their own position in the region was in jeopardy; an alliance with Hitler's Germany offered a remedy. The idea of a Yugoslav state had become entwined with the Great Serbia project espoused by the Chetniks—a group with an explicitly anti-Muslim agenda in many parts of the region—while Communism threatened to destroy both the political and religious legacies of the region.[70] The Allies were too far away to offer any realistic support. Working with the Italians was out of the question. Italian-Muslim relations had soured when the local Italian forces refused to disarm Chetnik units attacking Muslim civilians.[71] Even worse, rumors had surfaced in Sarajevo throughout the fall of 1942 that Italian soldiers had raped Muslim women in nearby villages.[72] If Sarajevo's Muslims wanted to end their union with

70. In the letter, the authors specifically noted that they detested the Yugoslav state and Yugoslav national ideology, which they believed was an ideology created by Serbs and Croats in order to suppress Muslims.

71. HM, Ustaška Nadzorna Služba, document 454 (September 1, 1942).

72. Ibid., document 4065 (November 7, 1942).

the Ustasha regime and the NDH—and the vast majority did—they needed to find a different strongman. Did they really think that becoming a protectorate of Nazi Germany would fulfill their future goals? It is hard to tell. Clearly, however, many did not think they had a better alternative.

Upon receiving the letter, a German SS officer stationed in Sarajevo, Rudolf Treu, met privately with some of the authors as well as with other Muslims in the city, recording their grievances in a series of reports to his commanders in Zagreb. Treu described Muslims' disappointment with Germany's failure to offer them a political stake, as well as their leaders' concern that the Ustasha regime's governing techniques were driving Muslims to the Partisans. Moreover, thinking about the broader relationship between Nazi Germany and the Muslim world, Treu suggested that if Turkey joined the Allies, Bosnia's Muslims might follow their example. German consul Erich Gördes also forwarded reports on Muslim discontent to Zagreb and Berlin. The consulate had been documenting Muslim dissatisfaction since 1941.[73] In the winter of 1942–43, Gördes noted in several reports that different Muslim leaders had promised to rally forty to fifty thousand volunteer recruits in exchange for a promise of autonomy, a proposal supported by the local Wehrmacht officers, who needed extra hands to fight the Partisans.[74]

Although the Germans had no intention of allowing Bosnia's Muslims to secede from the NDH, a state that Germany had created, they nevertheless understood that appeasing Muslims was critical to the region's stability. The war was not going well in Bosnia. Once considered a mere nuisance, the Communist insurgents by 1943 had coalesced into a powerful army that threatened Germany's economic and military goals in the region. In January 1943, the Wehrmacht launched a major three-month offensive against the guerrillas. Much to the Germans' irritation, the Partisans retreated but did not surrender. Moreover, despite signing cooperative agreements with the Germans, the Chetniks continued to provoke a rebellion in the hills around Sarajevo. Infuriated, the Germans dropped leaflets over Serb villages that warned, "If you will not be responsible for peace and order in your territories and for upholding the contractual agreement, the German command will have to undertake the appropriate measures."[75] Between the anarchy in the countryside and the crisis in the city, the Germans desperately needed a stable command center, which depended on cooperation with Sarajevo's Muslim leadership.

73. It had, for example, kept a copy of a detailed letter from Fehim Spaho that outlined atrocities committed against Muslims. See Hoover Institution Archives, Tomasevich Papers, records from the captured German documents held at the U.S. National Archives, box 4, T:120, roll 5797 (December 6, 1941).

74. Hoover Institute Archives, Tomasevich Papers, records from the captured German documents held at the U.S. National Archives, box 4, T:120, roll 5793 (January 29, 1943).

75. HM, Ustaška Nadzorna Služba, document 1448 (May 8, 1943).

Over the winter, high-ranking Nazi officials in Germany mulled over the various letters and reports regarding Sarajevo's Muslims and in February 1943 decided to make two tactical changes. They strengthened their direct authority in parts of the NDH, including Sarajevo, and they awarded Muslims more autonomy in the parts of the NDH where they dominated.[76] Paolo Rossi, the Italian consul in Sarajevo, reported that "the Germans are expanding their influence in Bosnia because they have to concede that the Croat regime resolves very little." He continued, "The Muslim element in Sarajevo is the focus of the most German attention, since the [Germans] know that if they successfully win over [Muslims] to a new German-Croat regime that they are introducing in Bosnia, then the political order would be secure."[77] Rather than bringing in more troops, the German command focused on organizing its existing forces in Sarajevo—the Gestapo, the SS division Prinz Eugen (a volunteer division composed of Volksdeutsche from Serbia and Croatia), the consulate, the police bureau (Polizeigebietsfuehrer), and a collection of Field Gendarmerie—into a more cohesive occupation force. Until now, these different bodies had worked mainly in an advisory and policing capacity without a common agenda.[78] Starting in the fall and continuing over the winter, the Germans also oversaw the creation of the Department of Regional Security for the Protection of the Nation (Kotarsko nadzorničtvo narodne zaštite), which merged Sarajevo's bureau for public protection, the fire department, and committees responsible for building shelters and planning air-raid drills under a joint German-Ustasha supervisory board.[79] Both Chetnik and Ustasha reports in early 1943 pointed out that the Germans controlled much of the city, noting that the Gestapo dominated the local police and that Muslims worked primarily with the German authorities and not with the Ustashas.[80] The Chetnik report also observed that the Communists had started to have success with

76. On Sarajevo's ongoing military importance, see Džemal Bijedić, "Razvoj NOP-a u Sarajevu od ljeta 1942. Do drugog zasjedanja AVNOJ-a," in Albahari et al., *Sarajevo u Revoluciji*, 3:407.
77. HM, Ustaška Nadzorna Služba, document 4035 (February 15, 1943).
78. Jonathan Gumz, "German Counterinsurgency Policy in Independent Croatia, 1941–1944," *Historian*, September 22, 1998, 5–6, http://www.highbeam.com/doc/1G1-53461482.html (accessed November 10, 2006). Gumz describes the relationship between the different German military, diplomatic, and police officials working in Croatia as "byzantine" and "internecine," calling communication between them "haphazard." Specifically, the local German included SS captain Frank Abromeit and the chief of police, Verner From. At different points in 1943, General Paul Bader, Lieutenant-General Aleksander Lohr, and General Von Oberkampf were stationed in the city.
79. On the creation of the supervisory board, see IAS, Kotarsko Nadzorničtvo Narodne Zaštite u Sarajevu, box 1 (October 6, 1942). Subsequent reports in the same collection detail the board's organization and responsibilities vis-à-vis air raids and measures to protect the city's security.
80. HM, Četnička građa, document 76 (February 5, 1943); HM, Ustaška Nadzorna Služba, document 1275 (April 21, 1943).

Muslims in Sarajevo, using the food situation in their efforts to spark a riot. This did not go unnoticed by the Germans.

Then, responding to Muslim leaders' desire for a recognized military force, in late February Adolf Hitler gave the go-ahead for the creation of a Bosnian Muslim Waffen SS unit. German officials in Zagreb worked out the details of the unit with high-ranking Ustasha representatives and Muslim leaders. Pavelić and his top advisers opposed the move, as they opposed any measure that granted Muslims autonomy, but realizing they could not prevent the division's formation, they tried to shape its public image as proof of the close relationship among the Third Reich, the poglavnik, and all the Croats of Bosnia-Herzegovina.[81] In late March, the Waffen SS Handžar Division was born. The Germans appointed Yugoslav Volksdeutsche as the officers and planned to fill the rank and file with Bosnian Muslims, although to appease the Ustashas and stem local Catholic backlash, they made a provision allowing "other Croats" to join.[82] The German commanding office, SS Gruppenführer Arthur Phleps, deliberately avoided working with certain Muslims in Pavelić's inner circle on the grounds that they were against the Muslim autonomists and vehemently anti-Serb.[83] Everyone in the town knew that the Waffen SS unit symbolized Muslims' favorable position in the German order. Given Muslim demands for political autonomy, the unit was perceived by many Catholics and Ustashas as a direct threat to their nation-state.

It did not take long for both the Germans and the Muslims to realize that they viewed their collaborative arrangement from vastly different perspectives. The Germans hoped that the unit would help to reinvigorate the Axis forces in their fight against the Partisans; Muslims wanted the unit to undermine Ustasha authority and provide military support for a new political arrangement (though they still disagreed on the best form for the future political order). It was in the Germans' interest to strengthen the NDH and encourage Muslims, Catholics, and Orthodox Serbs to work with them to stabilize the region and defeat the Partisans. Thus while attempting to cater to the local Muslim elite, the Germans continued to allow the Ustashas to keep important policing and judicial functions. With such powers, the local Ustasha police arrested several hundred people in early February and then set up a temporary court-martial, which arrested, tried, and deported eighty-seven people; the police also retained the authority to interrogate anyone they deemed suspicious, periodically deporting such

81. *Osvit,* April 25, 1943, 2.
82. On the order for the new command structure, see Hoover Institute Archives, Heinrich Himmler Papers, box 5, folder 281 (March 31, 1943). See also Redžić, *Muslimansko Autonomaštvo i 13. SS Divizija,* 81–89.
83. Hoover Institution Archives, Heinrich Himmler Papers, box 5, folder 281 (April 19, 1943).

Figure 8. Soldiers in the Handžar Division (Bosnian Muslim Waffen SS unit). Courtesy of the Historical Museum of Bosnia and Herzegovina.

people to Jasenovac during the spring.[84] Moreover, much to the dismay of the local Muslim politicos, Zagreb tried to tighten its control over the city by appointing insiders to key positions. Most significant, in January 1943, Pavelić replaced County Executive Ismet Gavran-Kapetanović with Muhamed Kulenović. Although Gavran-Kapetanović did not always see eye to eye with Mustafa Softić and other local leaders, they shared friends, colleagues, and a mutual respect for the city. By contrast, Muhamed Kulenović, a member of the famous Kulenović family, whose members were active in Ante Pavelić's administration, had closer ties to Zagreb, where he had attended law school and lived for many years, than to Sarajevo, where he had spent only his high school years.[85] Sarajevans, including Mayor Softić, viewed him as an outsider who toed the unpopular Ustasha party line. But the Germans did not protest. They needed to keep the Ustashas happy too. Indeed, they tried to keep them in the loop of the city's activities, even when it was the Germans calling the shots.[86]

84. On Ustasha police activity, see HM, Ustaška Nadzorna Služba, document 4035 (February 15, 1943) and document 1264 (April 20, 1943). See also Džinić, "Velika hapšenja komunista," 560–561.

85. *Sarajevski Novi List*, November 13, 1943, 5.

86. See, for example, a report that shows General Von Oberkamp consulting with Petar Petković, the local Ustasha security chief in IAS, Kotarsko Nadzorničtvo Narodne Zaštite u

Despite the Germans' support of the Ustashas, most of Sarajevo's Muslim leaders clung to hopes that the tables would turn. They were thus enthusiastic about having their own military force, even at the cost of deferring to the German command. Phleps, who had previously commanded the Prinz Eugen Division, had no trouble recruiting volunteers for the Handžar Division.[87] Starting in early April, the local press issued daily calls for recruits, promising the prospective soldiers food, insurance, and monthly salaries, as well as rent and basic sustenance for their families—material promises that were critical for recruitment in the war-weary city.[88] By April 25, Phleps wrote to Berlin that he had recruited about twenty thousand men from across Bosnia and Herzegovina.

Certainly not everyone was enthusiastic about the new unit. Some religious Muslims were wary about the Germans' intentions toward Islam. Heinrich Himmler, the head of the SS, tried to allay their concerns by appointing several imams to minister to the new division and by ordering his German commanders to withhold pork and alcohol from Muslim soldiers.[89] He also carefully spelled out the ideology behind the unit, noting that "it is not our intention to synthesize Islam with National Socialism" but instead to build a "union" of Muslims and Nazis against their common enemies.[90] Consequently, the Handžar Division acquired an element of authenticity among some circles as a Muslim army.

To boost recruitment for the Handžar Division, the Germans arranged for the grand mufti of Palestine, Emin El-Husseini, to visit Sarajevo in early April 1943.[91] El-Husseini had been a spokesman for Muslim-Axis relations since the 1930s. He lived in Berlin and traveled to Muslim areas in order to assuage concerns about German intentions and to convince Muslim leaders to work with the Nazis.[92] Himmler gave him a symbolic leadership role in the Handžar Division in an effort to strengthen the unit's Muslim credentials. In El-Husseini's speeches in Sarajevo, he linked the plight of Muslims in Palestine, who suffered from the "British-Jewish tyranny," to Muslims in Bosnia, who now had a Waffen SS unit through which they could fight that tyranny. The Germans hoped to use the visit as a way of healing internal Muslim divisions. They thus arranged for the grand mufti to have private audiences with Muslim political, cultural, and religious leaders, as well as

Sarajevu, box 1 (July 21–23, 1943).

87. Recruitment numbers are listed in a report from Phleps to the chief of the German police. Hoover Institute Archives, Heinrich Himmler Papers, box 5, folder 281 (April 29, 1943).

88. See, for example, *Sarajevski Novi List*, May 21, 1943, 5, and May 23, 1943, 3.

89. Hoover Institute Archives, Heinrich Himmler Papers, box 5, folder 281 (August 6, 1943).

90. See Himmler's report to the Waffen SS commanders, ibid. (April 19, 1943).

91. Historians refer to El-Husseini as the grand mufti, which was a title bestowed on him by the British, but in official documents he is sometimes called simply the mufti of Palestine.

92. Redžić, *Muslimansko Autonomaštvo i 13. SS Divizija*, 92–93.

with the German and Italian consuls. They also coordinated meetings in Sarajevo between El-Husseini and Muslim representatives from Mostar, Sandžak, and Albania, demonstrating an increasing awareness that Muslims in all areas needed to be consulted.[93] Phleps wrote home that Sarajevo Muslims had responded positively to the visit.[94]

Recognizing that non-Muslims might feel threatened by the new unit, the Germans presumably encouraged El-Husseini to help heal local divides. While he focused on the fact that Muslims had fallen on hard times and needed to cling to Islam and their Muslim brothers, he also spoke of the Ottoman legacy of pluralism.[95] He emphasized that Palestine had also been a tolerant, multireligious society before England and the Jews took it over.[96] According to the Ustasha secret police, El-Husseini encouraged one audience of around a thousand Sarajevo Muslims to work closely with the city's Catholics:

> Islam as a religion teaches us to love our neighbors. You Muslims need to love and get along with Catholic Croats because in this critical collision of worlds, together you can find satisfaction for all of your aspirations and desires, as well as protect your faith and your civilization. Keep in mind always that in the world, the only enemy of Islam and of us Muslims is England and America, who are united with the Jews.[97]

Such lip service did not convince local Ustasha authorities that Muslims would cooperate with the NDH. The local Ustasha intelligence bureau reported to Zagreb that El-Husseini had met secretly with Sarajevo Muslims it considered enemies of the state, and—the bureau emphasized—he did not meet with Archbishop Šarić (although it appears that Šarić had no interest in meeting with El-Husseini).[98]

Various segments of the Catholic Croat community responded defensively to the Muslim-German alliance and the possibility that Muslims might break from the NDH and take Sarajevo with them. In January 1943, Napredak, the local Croat cultural society, emphasized that it hoped to have its important work recognized by "all the layers of the Croat nation, and by all state and church authorities."[99] In referring to "all" Croats, the society emphasized its position that Muslims, too, were Croats. In Napredak's minutes from February 1943, the group mentioned the need to establish itself as the true protector of the "patriots of the city of Sarajevo."[100]

93. *Osvit*, April 25, 1943, 3; *El-Hidaje*, May 5, 1943, 250–252.
94. Hoover Institute Archives, Heinrich Himmler Papers, box 5, folder 281 (April 29, 1943).
95. *El-Hidaje*, May 5, 1943, 250–252.
96. *Glasnik Islamske Vjerske Zajednice*, May–June 1943, 105–108, 489.
97. HM, Ustaška Nadzorna Služba, document 4089 (April 19, 1943).
98. Ibid., document 1377 (April 29, 1943).
99. ABiH, Hrvatsko kulturno društvo Napredak, box 170, document 12003 (January 27, 1943).
100. Ibid. (February 5, 1943).

The Catholic Church's position in the city meanwhile grew increasingly precarious. In late April 1943, just a few weeks after El-Husseini's visit, the papal emissary to the NDH, Giuseppe Marcone, paid an important visit to Sarajevo in an effort to improve the church's position in the public eye. The German consul reported that the Vatican appeared to be distancing itself from Archbishop Šarić and his pro-Ustasha circle, which had fallen out of favor, and that Marcone's primary goal seemed to be the removal of Father Božidar Bralo from his position in the city. Bralo was subsequently transferred to a less political role of ministering to the troops. Marcone deliberately avoided meeting with civil authorities during the visit, a fact suggesting that the Vatican aimed to distance itself from the political leadership of the town.[101] There is no doubt that the archbishop and his inner circle recognized that they were losing their once privileged position in Bosnia. Whether they blamed the Germans or their Muslim neighbors for this changing tide is not readily apparent in the documents.

Nobody in Sarajevo knew precisely what the new German-Muslim collaboration meant for their community or for the future political and social order in the city. Religious Muslims who had supported the Waffen SS unit had expected it to lead to reforms in the position of Islam in the state: that the jurisdiction of the Sharia courts would be resolved once and for all, that Muslim religious personnel would be exempt from conscription in the army, and that a formal legal statute would finally be approved for the Islamic Religious Community.[102] But these issues remained in the jurisdiction of Zagreb, not Berlin, and pleas for resolution continued to invoke the same stony response from the Ustasha regime. Progressive Muslims who supported the Handžar Division expected it to be a military force that would eventually be combined with real political power, but such power still remained beyond their grasp. The Softić circle—which, incidentally, the Ustasha police had begun to refer to in their reports as pro-Serb—fully anticipated a shift in power in their favor after El-Husseini's visit.[103] In fact, during the visit, someone from Softić's office wrote a hostile opinion piece in *Sarajevski Novi List* that criticized state intrusions into the city's autonomy. The piece maintained that legally the municipal government was supposed to be a self-governing administration (*samoupravna vlast*). It demanded the return of its traditional powers.[104] In late April, Mayor Softić also connived to reduce the power of County Executive Kulenović—Zagreb's eyes and

101. Hoover Institute Archives, Tomasevich Papers, records from the captured German documents held at the U.S. National Archives, report from the German consulate in Sarajevo, box 4, T:120, roll 5788 (April 26, 1943).

102. ABiH, Vrhovni Šerijatski Sud, box 198, document 89 (March 3, 1943); ARIZBiH, Ulema Medžlis, document 1328 (March 1, 1943).

103. HM, Ustaška Nadzorna Služba, document 4089 (April 19, 1943).

104. Editorial, *Sarajevski Novi List,* April 10, 1943.

ears on the ground—filing a formal complaint with the regime that hinted at irreconcilable differences between the two men.[105]

Ultimately, German police patrols, the Handžar Division, and El-Husseini's visit made for compelling propaganda, but these initiatives failed to resolve the two fundamental questions that had haunted Muslims since 1941: what would the new European order look like when the war ended, and what role would Islam play in Bosnia's future? Infuriating Muslims across the spectrum, the Germans avoided addressing any of their major concerns, leaving religious, political, and legal issues to the Ustasha domain. The Germans were concerned with defeating the Partisans, fixing Italy's catastrophic military operations, and transferring their forces to fight the Red Army on the eastern front. They had no intention of cultivating an entirely new Bosnian government or figuring out how Islamic legal traditions would fit into a Fascist legal system. Gradually Muslims realized that the Germans were indifferent to the cultural clash tearing their community apart. Take, for example, the role of women. Many Muslim religious leaders expected the Germans to protect (and revive) traditional gender roles. They wanted tighter restrictions on mixed-sex events and Islamic marriage laws; they wanted Muslim women to rebuff European fashion trends in favor of conservative religious garb. The Germans did not seem to understand the depth of their concerns. Imagine the surprise among local religious leaders when a German-produced paper on the Handžar Division featured two pictures on the same page: one of a Muslim woman wearing a head scarf and modest attire and the other of a modern woman in a two-piece bathing suit standing under the Mostar Bridge.[106]

By the summer of 1943, many religious Muslims—of various political persuasions—abandoned hope that the Germans could resolve their problems. Under the leadership of Hafiz ef. Muhamed Pandža, a wealthy Sarajevo Muslim who served as a member of the Ulema Medžlis and belonged to El-Hidaje, Merhamet began to more aggressively combine its charity work with political activism.[107] Allegedly an enthusiastic supporter of the Handžar Division, Pandža recognized earlier than most that Muslims had changed nothing by aligning with the Nazis.[108] In June he established a new Merhamet committee known as the Propaganda Section, which was assigned the task of collecting information on missing and murdered Muslims, examining the "dangerous intentions" of the Christian churches toward

105. ABiH, Veliki Župan Vrhbosna, 1945, box 1, document 792 (April 29, 1943).

106. *Handžar*, vol. 1, no. 1 (July 15, 1943) as found in IAS, Zbirka Varia, document 535.

107. "Hafiz" is a title awarded to a Muslim who has memorized the Qur'an. In his necrology of Bosnian Muslims, Alija Nametak wrote an anecdotal obituary of Pandža that discussed his relations with various Muslims in the prewar and wartime period. See Nametak, *Sarajevski Nekrologij*, 84–85.

108. Tomasevich, *War and Revolution in Yugoslavia*, pp 496–501. Tomasevich also claims that Pandža was one of the anonymous writers behind the letter to Hitler, but I think this claim is inaccurate.

Muslims, and publishing a book on crimes committed against Muslims. At the same time, he established new chapters across Bosnian towns and villages, encouraging Muslims to take responsibility for their own affairs.[109] Merhamet developed clout among ordinary Muslims through its work with refugees, orphanages, and food kitchens, a position that the society used to aggressively defend the community from the encroachment of outside forces. For example, upon discovering that an orphaned Muslim girl had been adopted by a German Catholic couple and that she had converted to Catholicism and was now living in Germany, Merhamet successfully intervened. The Germans returned the girl to a Muslim family in Sarajevo.[110] While grassroots activism became the organization's mainstay, Merhamet also continued to apply pressure on the regime in the realm of Islamic ethics, demanding that the Sharia courts be given an active legal role in the administration of Muslim orphans and refugees and that the state increase funding to the Sharia legal system.[111] Whereas Merhamet had previously served as an umbrella organization and meeting place for diverse Muslim political agendas, now it was developing an overtly political agenda.

The timing of Merhamet's new campaign was not coincidental. Pandža, like many members of the Muslim elite, recognized by summer 1943 that the Axis partners were having a run of bad luck. In June, the Germans assembled a force of 127,000 German, Croat, and Italian troops in order to engage and defeat the Communist Partisans. Although the armies successfully surrounded and attacked a mere 16,000-strong Partisan force in the mountains of Herzegovina, in a humiliating setback for the Germans, the small Partisan force slipped the German net with only minor losses.[112] By early August, the Partisans had conquered enough territory in Bosnia to disrupt service on two of the region's main railway lines. Later that month they attacked Sarajevo's airport as well, temporarily preventing German aircraft from taking off.[113]

In the larger picture of the war, the Allies, meanwhile, scored a series of formidable victories in the Mediterranean, overpowering the Axis in North Africa in May and invading Sicily in July. They also sneaked into the NDH. In May 1943, British secret service agents began parachuting behind German lines to advise Partisan and Chetnik commanders in Bosnia; American agents followed in August.[114] Throughout the summer, rumors spread in Sarajevo that the Allies were dropping weapons and supplies to Serb

109. IAS, Merhamet, box 5, document 489 (June 26, 1943) and document 493 (June 28, 1943).
110. Ibid., document 314 (May 15, 1943).
111. ABiH, Vrhovni Šerijatski Sud, box 7, document 435 (July 12, 1943).
112. Redžić, *Bosnia and Herzegovina in the Second World War*, 36–40.
113. Vladimir Dedijer, *The War Diaries of Vladimir Dedijer* (Ann Arbor: University of Michigan Press, 1990), 2:362, 396.
114. Kirk Ford, *OSS and the Yugoslav Resistance, 1943–1945* (College Station: Texas A&M University Press, 1992), 3–4, 15.

insurgents hiding out in nearby villages.[115] As British and American troops tightened their hold in the Mediterranean that August, the Italian king unseated Mussolini, whose replacement immediately began negotiating Italy's defection to the Allies.

Anticipating Italy's collapse, the Germans sent advisers and fresh troops to the NDH. Although the Italians had been an unreliable ally, they had nonetheless helped the German army contain the Partisan resistance and secure vital railways, roadways, and ports. The weak and ineffectual Pavelić regime would be unable to circumvent the encroaching Allied forces. German officials stationed in Zagreb voiced this concern to Hitler and German foreign minister Joachim von Ribbentrop at a meeting in mid-August 1943, suggesting that Germany use Italy's collapse as an opportunity to establish direct military rule over the NDH or to replace it with several protectorates (of which an autonomous Muslim Bosnia was one possibility). Rejecting this advice, Hitler concluded that the best course for Germany would be to continue supporting the Ustasha regime. Accordingly, he bolstered Ante Pavelić's power and permitted a major expansion of the Home Guard, which was tasked with occupying the Italian territories and disarming the Italian troops.[116]

As the situation worsened, Sarajevo's Muslims grew shocked and angry. By late August the Germans had officially taken Muslim autonomy off the table. Civil war continued to spiral out of control, and new waves of refugees poured into the city. The Chetniks forged ahead in their campaign to cleanse eastern Bosnia of Muslims, while the Ustasha militias began killing as many Muslims as Serbs.[117] Fear of Communism spread, particularly among religious Muslims, who panicked at the thought that some of their brethren might view the Partisans as the best viable political alternative.

Responding to these threats, a group of Islamists took a stand in late August to show that they would not back down to intimidation and pressure. At a meeting held in Merhamet's offices on August 15, the leaders of the powerful trio of Merhamet, El-Hidaje, and the Ulema Medžlis swore to uphold their religious mission under any circumstances.[118] Again, women's issues proved a critical test of how far the Germans and Ustashas would bend to maintain a coalition. After the meeting, the Ulema Medžlis sent

115. HM, Ustaška Nadzorna Služba, document 1968 (July 22, 1943).

116. See Gumz, "German Counterinsurgency Policy." When the German general Lothar Rendulic arrived in Croatia in August 1943, he believed the best solution for the region would be to create a German administration under his own command. Likewise, General Glaise-Horstenau, based in Zagreb, was committed to creating a "Reich Plenipotentiary for Croatia." Field Marshal von Weichs reported in October 1943 that he believed the greatest danger facing the Germans in southeastern Europe came from the NDH. Other Germans stationed in the region believed that Muslims would be their greatest ally. They continued to propose dividing the Croat state into several occupied parts.

117. On the escalating crisis in the Muslim community in the summer and fall of 1943, see Redžić, *Bosnia and Herzegovina in the Second World War*, 41–42 and 187–188.

118. *El-Hidaje*, September 1, 1943, 41–56.

a notice to every Muslim organization in the city with a list of demands. These seemed simple enough: women should be guaranteed bread so they did not resort to prostitution, women should stay at home instead of unnecessarily mixing with men in public venues, women's organizations should not meet during Ramadan, and Muslim leaders should cease sponsoring mixed-gender social events. The tone of this letter, however, differed markedly from that of earlier requests. Now the Ulema Medžlis made it clear that any organization that failed to meet these standards would relinquish its right to identify formally as a Muslim or Islamic group.[119] It also underscored its power by again securing from the local Ustasha headquarters special Ramadan police decrees, which were published in both of the city's main newspapers.[120] It is notable that such decrees were issued only in Sarajevo. When other towns made similar requests, the Ustashas refused, claiming that it was the duty of an individual to obey the laws of his faith, but it was not the state's responsibility to enforce religious laws.[121] In Sarajevo, however, the regime seemed to hope that appeasing Muslim leaders would quiet campaigns to break away from the state.

The August meeting reveals that for one segment of Sarajevo's Muslim community, identities hardened along religious lines during the course of 1943. Indeed, many Muslims had started to adopt a more parochial, isolated identity for Muslims that could compete with the Croat and Serb projects. Some feared that Sarajevo's customs of "common life" and "neighborliness" were actually contributing to the declining status of Muslims in the social hierarchy and that only in emphasizing a distinct Muslim identity could they protect themselves. In February 1943, for example, the well-known Muslim teacher and scholar Mustafa Busuladžić told Muslims to stop imitating European culture, advising instead that they embrace their own Islamic heritage. Busuladžić described a host of non-Muslim customs that Bosnian Muslims had erroneously adopted over the past decades that they needed to drop, from the seemingly innocuous acts of lighting candles on graves and wearing black as a color of mourning to the more serious affronts of allowing women to go uncovered in public and consuming alcohol and pork. He also warned Muslims to cease celebrating the holidays of other faiths and—in an even more extreme step—to stop fraternizing with people of other faiths.[122] In many minds, the Nazi "New Order" was undermining Islamic values and threatening the Muslim community, whose protection had been the main reason for the alliance with the Germans in the first place.

Though glowing propaganda for the Handžar Division appeared in the Muslim press well into 1944, the hype surrounding the division died down

119. ARIZBiH, Ulema Medžlis, document 1291 (August 29, 1943).
120. See *Osvit*, August 29, 1943, 5; *Sarajevski Novi List*, September 1, 1943, 5.
121. ARIZBiH, Ulema Medžlis, document 3522 (September 15, 1943; October 20, 1943).
122. *Novi Behar*, February 15, 1943, 1.

quickly as Muslims grew disillusioned with the realities of service in the unit. Soldiers deserted in protest of their assignment to the French front rather than Bosnia, as they had been promised. In one instance, Muslim soldiers shot their German commanding officers.[123] Back at home, the mayor's office received dozens of petitions for back pay, food, and assistance from Muslim women, who had never seen a mark, let alone a loaf of bread, since their husbands and sons had left with the German unit.[124] At the end of the day, the Handžar Division had accomplished very little. Muslims remained as divided as ever over essential questions of faith, politics, and Bosnia's future, but now their divisions were laced with the bitter aftertaste left by the false promise of the Waffen SS.

• • •

Although many scholars have discussed the appearance of the Muslim militias, the Muslim autonomy movements are rarely examined in the context from which they emerged. I suggest that these movements, together with the Waffen SS unit, should be analyzed as another side of the multifaceted civil war rather than as a cut-and-dried case of ideological collaboration with the Nazis. By 1942, Bosnia's Muslims overwhelmingly thought that alignment with Germany would produce a more favorable outcome for their community than alignment with the NDH. While acknowledging that the German vision of society did not conform to their own vision of the future, Muslims hoped to use the Germans to gain power, just as the Germans hoped to use the Muslims to achieve order. But the Germans' concessions—the Handžar Division, a greater German military presence, and a visit by the grand mufti—failed to resolve the underlying crisis confronting Muslim leaders: how to develop a modern society of Muslims that complemented the new Europe without abandoning the community's religious and cultural customs.

The complexities of the Muslim-German relationship also shed light on the local dynamics of Nazi administration. Instead of espousing a uniform ideological platform, the German administration determined that its interest was best served by courting ideologically diverse local allies that could combine forces to defeat the Communists. In what could be called an uncharacteristic move for Nazi Europe, the German command encouraged Sarajevans to embrace pluralism and work together as political partners. In so doing, the Germans ignored the discord between the long-term goals of each side. This approach would hold things together temporarily, but it soon exacerbated the rift between the Sarajevans and the Germans and directly contributed to the spread of even more resistance activities.

123. Donia, *Sarajevo*, 188–189.
124. For example, see the appeal of B. Sarić to Mayor Softić in IAS, Gradsko Poglavarstvo, box 1131 (June 21, 1943).

While Sarajevo's Muslims were among the first of the townsmen to grasp the incompatibility between the city's culture, traditions, and goals and those of the warring parties, national and international alike, it would not take long for diverse groups of local Catholics and Orthodox Serbs to recognize the implications of being caught in a war in which they, too, had no discernible side. Over the next year, leaders from every community began to share similar concerns: that the war was out of their hands, that local political institutions were no longer effective, that Sarajevo's masses were disaffected, and that the war was transforming Sarajevo into an unrecognizable shadow of its former self. But what they did not yet realize was that the moment for them to demand a voice in the region's affairs had passed. The Ustasha, Partisan, and Chetnik forces—backed by their various Axis or Allied partners—would decide on the battlefield whether Sarajevo's fate would lie in the hands of the Ustasha ideologues in Zagreb or the guerrilla commanders hiding out in the woods.

6

AN UPRISING IN THE MAKING

The war took a turn in the fall of 1943 with Italy's capitulation. The Italian withdrawal created a vacuum of power in the Balkans that invigorated the Communist rebels. Partisan units rushed to the front lines, disarming surrendering Italian divisions and emptying Italian warehouses of food and supplies.[1] Within a few weeks, they had occupied large parts of Croatia's coast, western Bosnia, and Herzegovina, as well as several important Adriatic islands that soon became gateways to the British and American bases across the sea. Though German troops swiftly reconquered much of the region, securing a tight hold on Sarajevo, they never recovered an iron grip on the rest of Bosnia.

Sarajevo increasingly felt like a besieged city. It suffered relatively heavy Allied bombardment that November as the Allies sought to cripple the smaller Axis partners and persuade them to switch sides.[2] The bombing killed hundreds of civilians and left countless more homeless. Furthermore, the escalating civil war severely hampered city supply lines. Of fifty wagons of potatoes en route to Sarajevo from Slavonia in October, only two made it. Shipments of flour, meat, and butter never reached their destination. A desperate Mayor Softić warned Zagreb in November that civil servants and factory workers were starving and thus had lost all incentive to work for the state. Municipal receipts from early 1944 suggest that the entire city subsisted for months on little more than beans. German soldiers passed around a collection to aid the starving city. But serious help never arrived. The burgeoning population, meanwhile, grew too large for the available resources. As sectarian violence escalated in the countryside, twenty

1. Tomasevich, *War and Revolution in Yugoslavia*, 298–299.
2. Information on the bombing can be found in IAS, Kotarsko Nadzorničtvo Narodne Zaštite u Sarajevu, monthly reports, box 1, (September 1943; November 29, 1943), and in *Sarajevski Novi List*, December 3, 1943, 1.

Figure 9. Devastation from the Allied bombing of Sarajevo, fall 1943. Courtesy of the Historical Museum of Bosnia and Herzegovina.

thousand new Muslim refugees flowed into Sarajevo, nearly doubling the size of the city's community of displaced persons. Typhus and tuberculosis spread like wildfire. Humanitarian groups realized that they could barely take care of Sarajevo; to compensate, some cut support to the provinces.[3]

Fearful that the expanding insurgency would reach Sarajevo, the Germans and Ustashas cracked down on the town through enhanced police surveillance, censorship, and direct control. Likewise, religious reactionaries and rightist politicians tightened their grip on their communities in hopes of fending off leftist resistance ideas. Sarajevans felt besieged from all sides. Resistance to the ideas of the Nazi "New Order" and the Ustasha regime took root in the city, in organized and unorganized forums, among members of the elite as well as the general population. Religious organizations, cultural societies, humanitarian groups, unions, factories, and youth groups soon became new sites of political activity and agitation, though as late as the fall of 1944, it was not entirely clear who or what they were resisting.

3. Comprehensive reports on the humanitarian crisis can be found in the weekly records of Merhamet, IAS, Merhamet, box 6 (zapisnik) and box 9 (1944 folder). For the German perspective on the crisis, see the SS reports in Hoover Institute Archives, Heinrich Himmler Papers, box 5, folder 281 (January 12, 1944), and German consulate reports in Hoover Institute Archives, Tomasevich Papers, records from the captured German documents held at the U.S. National Archives, box 4, T:120, roll 5796 (October 23, 1943).

A City Besieged

The political, military, and psychological occupation of Sarajevo entered a new phase in the fall of 1943 as a direct result of the strengthening armed resistance movement. By November 1943, the Communists had gained enough confidence—and enough control—to include in the maneuvers of their growing armed insurgency the first steps of state building. In two important meetings held in Bosnia that month, Communist leaders formed the National Committee of Yugoslav Liberation (AVNOJ)—which became their transitional wartime government—and formally mapped out a government for the postwar Yugoslav state.[4] Faced with this expanding, solidifying, and multiethnic guerrilla enemy across the Bosnian countryside, the Germans and Ustashas grew nervous that they could lose their firm grip on Sarajevo. The city was vital to their economic, transportation, and communication lines in Bosnia; its security could not be compromised. Consequently, the Ustasha authorities expanded the local police force and passed stricter curfews and public safety laws, including those that sanctioned imprisonment for defeatist speech.[5] In late December, the regime mandated that males between the ages of fifteen and sixty and females between seventeen and fifty, regardless of religion, had to register for manual labor or face a jail sentence. The local press emphasized that young women should sign up as soon as they finished high school, ignoring the contentious issue of gender segregation that Muslim leaders had raised continuously during the war.[6]

Meanwhile, German regional security took precedence over fostering good relations with local allies, which meant that the Germans targeted potentially hostile communities that they thought might join the resistance. This provocation in turn led to greater resentment and hostility on the part of civilians who had once supported the Germans. In November 1943, a Muslim SS officer serving with the Germans warned his commanding officers that the Muslim community was quickly losing faith in the German cause.[7] But the German command grew progressively more exasperated by its inability to control Bosnia, where rebels familiar with the mountainous terrain bested the larger, better-equipped, and formally trained German force.[8] Humiliated by their losses, German soldiers occasionally took out their frustration on civilians, which created a backlash in Sarajevo. News of such incidents in other parts of the region had reached Sarajevo by word

---

4. Redžić, *Bosnia and Herzegovina in the Second World War*, 226.
5. Šarac, "Uslovi i pravci razvoja narodnooslobodilačkog pokreta u Sarajevu od Novembra 1943. do Aprila 1945. godine," in Albahari et al., *Sarajevo u Revoluciji*, 4:21.
6. IAS, Kotarsko Nadzorničtvo Narodne Zaštite u Sarajevu, box 1 (December 28, 1943).
7. Hoover Archives, Heinrich Himmler Collection, box 5, folder 281 (November 15, 1943).
8. On the escalating violence in the hills surrounding Sarajevo, see Walter R. Roberts, *Tito, Mihailović, and the Allies, 1941–1945* (Durham, NC: Duke University Press, 1987), 153.

of mouth, but in the winter of 1943–44 Sarajevans increasingly witnessed German brutality in their own city.

Many townsmen were shocked, for example, when the German army forcibly relocated several thousand Catholic men, women, and children from Partisan strongholds in Dalmatia (coastal Croatia) and the Adriatic islands to Sarajevo. Although they officially referred to this as an "evacuation" of a war-torn area, the Germans treated the Dalmatians like enemy combatants. They rounded up their prisoners in the middle of the night and herded them into cattle cars, leaving them no time to pack money, food, shoes, or other basic material goods. Ill-informed about their final destination, the coastal refugees—many of whom were fishermen accustomed to the mild Adriatic climate—arrived in Sarajevo without winter clothing or boots. According to local Red Cross reports, the German army handled the situation "without a touch of humanity." The evacuees "did not know where they were going or what awaited them. They were looked upon as prisoners. It was not until the Dalmatians reached Sarajevo that local officials could allay their fears that they were still free Croat citizens." While officially "free," many of the Dalmatians found themselves confined to barracks at the Alipašin Most refugee camp along with scores of hungry and sick Muslim peasants. Others remained in the cattle cars to be dropped off in the north of Croatia. Lest the evacuees get too comfortable, the Ustasha security forces required anyone arriving from Dalmatia to sign up for work with the Home Guard in Sarajevo.[9]

There were also cases of harassment in Sarajevo. In February 1944, a Catholic woman visiting from Zagreb described a growing "bitterness of our people toward the Germans" because of their inappropriate behavior toward Catholic women.[10] In a more serious grievance, in March 1944 the families of twenty-two Muslim boys from Travnik, a city in central Bosnia, claimed that the German army had abducted their sons, ranging in age from ten to fifteen, and deported them to work assignments in Germany. Officially, the boys had left as volunteers under German escort, but Muslim leaders charged foul play. Representing their Travnik brethren, Sarajevo's Muslims pressured local and national Ustasha authorities to intervene, and eventually Ante Pavelić himself became involved. The poglavnik allegedly asked the Germans to intercept the train carrying the boys and reroute them to Sarajevo. If the request was made, the intervention had no effect, for the boys never arrived. Weeks later, amid growing Muslim hostility, Sarajevo's Ustasha chief of security stepped in. He wrote to the Ministry of

9. On the evacuations, see reports from Sarajevo's Red Cross in ABiH, Društvo Crveni Križ, box 24, document 911 (March 26—April 6, 1944). Jozo Tomasevich estimates the number of evacuees was close to twenty thousand. This number seems high, however, and likely includes Dalmatians who fled the hinterland on their own, as well as some who joined the Partisans. See Tomasevich, *War and Revolution in Yugoslavia*, 320.

10. HM, Ustaška Nadzorna Služba, document 2933 (February 2, 1944).

the Interior demanding information on the whereabouts of the children. Although an investigation ensued, its paper trail ran out during my investigation in both the city and state archives.[11] Around the same time, Sarajevo's Ustasha headquarters reported that German soldiers around Sarajevo had participated in "purposeless violence and destruction" that greatly upset Muslims. Most offensive was their destruction of a mosque.[12] The German leadership in Sarajevo, which continued working with town officials and the Ustasha police on matters of security, seemed oblivious to the tremendous psychological impact of the army's transgressions.

While occasionally intervening on behalf of the city when the Germans misbehaved, the Ustasha regime also placed its security objectives first. Over the winter the regime ordered city institutions to appoint members of their own staffs to serve on local labor brigades. Though the Ustashas probably thought such a system would be easier than sorting through massive registries, it drove a deeper wedge between the regime and the city's officials, who resented being made into middlemen between the Ustasha authorities and the general population.[13] Local resentment grew steadily over the course of 1943 and 1944 as a result of the regime's tightening of its propaganda, an increase in police harassment, and, most serious, its inability to provide adequate material provisions. Mayor Softić repeatedly warned the authorities that the regime would lose the city if it failed to deliver food.[14] He was replaced that spring.[15] His prediction was realized in April 1944, when employees at the Department of Appropriations, an agency with the most access to food supplies, stopped coming to work because even they had nothing to eat. Teachers and legal clerks followed suit over the following months.[16]

Local political leaders attempted to maintain order and convince Sarajevans that they had the city's best interests in mind while simultaneously maintaining good relations with the occupying forces. It was a tricky balancing act. To this end, the city tried to present an image of fair representation. As of December 31, 1943, the composition of the city council was six Muslims, four Orthodox, two Catholics, and one Volksdeutsche.[17] The tradition continued even as pressures from the Ustashas and the Germans

11. HDA, Ministarstvo Unutrašnih Poslova NDH, box 20, document 1709 (March 31, 1944) and document 2014 (April 18, 1944).

12. Ibid., Document 2130 (April 19, 1944).

13. *Sarajevski Novi List,* December 16, 1943, 5; and January 12, 1944, 5. There are hundreds of these requests from the Regional Security Forces to various city agencies in 1944 in IAS, Kotarsko Nadzorničtvo Narodne Zaštite u Sarajevu, box 1.

14. IAS, Gradsko Poglavarstvo, box 1264 (March 20, 1944).

15. *Sarajevski Novi List,* May 24, 1944, 5.

16. On the effects of the food shortages on city institutions, see ABiH, Državno zastupništvo u Sarajevu, box 10, document 73 (April 29, 1944); HDA, Ministarstvo Narodne Prosvjete NDH, box 1107, document 1257 (June 5, 1944); and IAS, Gradsko Poglavarstvo, box 1238 (August 28, 1944).

17. IAS, Gradsko Poglavarstvo, box 1121 (December 31, 1943).

tightened. Mayor Nasih Repovac, who replaced Mustafa Softić in spring 1944, brought on two deputy mayors—one Catholic and one Orthodox—and promised Sarajevans that the people running things were still "those who love this city."[18] But the Ustasha authorities steadily usurped the municipality's power until it became little more than an agency for drafting Sarajevans into labor battalions or, worse, one of the Axis armies.

Local Resistance

It is not surprising that the seeds of a popular uprising germinated in Sarajevo over the course of 1943 and 1944. Political unrest and empty cupboards are the perfect ingredients for generating a rebellion. And twelve-hour winter blackouts ensured that Sarajevans had ample time to mull over their despair in the discomfort of their unheated homes.[19] Life had grown intolerable. Whether standing up for personal convictions or scraping by for survival, Sarajevans began to behave in ways that threatened the political order. Town employees helped friends who had been working with the insurgents to return to the city, children stole soldiers' shoes to sell on the black market, local peasants defiantly smuggled meat into the city, and saboteurs diverted electricity from military bases to their homes.[20] These were not the acts of ideological extremists or militant insurgents but those of ordinary people making do under extraordinary conditions. The Italian general Mario Roatta, who spent time in Bosnia and Croatia from 1941 to 1943, described it well in his memoir when he noted that there was "a great quantity of people [in the region] entirely indifferent to the state structure of the zone, and perhaps also to whoever might eventually assume power; they asked nothing more than to be left in peace to attend to their daily chores, take care of their property and practice their customs."[21] These simple tasks had become impossible, and Sarajevans sought to take control over some aspects of their lives.

One of the first to act was Muhamed Pandža, the head of Merhamet, a member of El-Hidaje, and a well-known Muslim community leader. On October 20, 1943, Pandža fled to the nearby mountains with twenty Young

---

18. *Sarajevski Novi List,* May 24, 1944, 5.

19. On the blackouts, see a monthly report in IAS, Kotarsko Nadzorničtvo Narodne Zaštite u Sarajevu, box 1, (January 1944).

20. On Sarajevans returning from the woods, see ABiH, Ured za kolonizaciju—Sarajevo, box 17, document 8027 (September 12, 1943). On the children, see HM, Ustaška Nadzorna Služba, document 3172 (April 26, 1944). On the peasant smugglers, see IAS, Gradsko Poglavarstvo, box 1179, (December 22, 1943). On "stealing" electricity, see *Sarajevski Novi List,* January 3, 1944, 5.

21. As quoted in Rodogno, *Fascism's European Empire,* 300.

Muslims in tow and formed a militia.[22] His force joined the crowded battle-field in eastern Bosnia, hoping to succeed where the Handžar Division had failed. Pandža's goal, according to a letter he left behind for his supporters, was to free Bosnia from the "Ustasha monsters, who hoisted the flag of criminal chauvinism in our regions of proud Bosnia, and wanted to impose the Croat stamp on a land in which barely one-fifth are Croats." Admitting that some Muslims had joined the Ustasha cause, he noted, "To be sure, here and there was a Bosniak,[23] an insurgent, who had signed away his body and soul to the Ustasha." But Pandža called on them to right the wrongs: "Muslims!" he pleaded. "Those of you who are in the ranks of the Home Guard and other branches of military service, enter into the ranks of the Muslim Bosnian freedom movement, and battle for the well-being of your hard-tested congregation and for the fatherland."[24]

Days after the Muslim leader departed, the minister of the interior of the NDH, Mladen Lorković, traveled to Sarajevo to address the vexed city and try to scare Muslims into cooperating with the regime. "Croatia is big enough for all of its sons," he began, and "our Muslims know well that there is no other homeland for them except Croatia." Warning Sarajevans that there was no middle ground between "complete defeat and complete victory," Lorković echoed the fears of some Muslim leaders: "It would be very naive and reckless to believe that if the Croat nation loses this great and decisive struggle, one confession might come out better than another. The enemy wants to eradicate us all equally."[25] Minister Lorković, a passionate Croat nationalist who would soon seek to cooperate with the Allies to protect his country's independence, hoped to touch a nerve among Sarajevo's Muslims. As disgusted as Muslims might be with the NDH, what was their alternative? A Communist regime supported by the much-feared Red Army? A Chetnik victory and a Great Serb state?

For Pandža, none of these options was attractive, so he had tried to form his own force. But his militia had a short life. Within days of his departure from Sarajevo, Muslim officers in the Handžar Division sent frantic memos to the German command claiming that Pandža had disappeared.[26] Their intelligence suggested that he might have even gone to work for the Partisans, a fear confirmed by some Partisan field officers who claimed that

22. For a discussion of meetings Pandža allegedly attended regarding his plans to flee the city, see Hasan Ljubunčić, "Dani nevolja i previranja," in Albahari et al., *Sarajevo u Revoluciji,* 3:615.

23. The term "Bosniak" here refers to a Muslim Bosnian. Although this term was not adopted universally until 1993, it was used by some locals to refer to Muslims in Bosnia prior to that time.

24. I work with a wartime German translation of the original document, which can be found in the Hoover Institution Archives, Heinrich Himmler Papers, letter from Muhamed Pandža to the people of Bosnia, box 5, folder 281 (November 4, 1943).

25. *Sarajevski Novi List,* October 27, 1943, 2.

26. Hoover Archives, Heinrich Himmler Collection, box 5, folder 281 (November 15, 1943).

the reactionary had agreed to cooperate with them, though they did not necessarily want him.[27] Whether true or not, the rumor added to the tensions among the city's Muslim elite. Whichever group Pandža last served was soon irrelevant: the Germans captured him in a raid on eastern Bosnia in December.[28] His troops dispersed themselves among other Muslim militias, the Ustasha paramilitaries, and Partisan bands, a fact that indicates the ideological indifference of the soldiers. Allegedly, the Germans handed Pandža over to Ustasha commanders, who interrogated and imprisoned him for the rest of the war.[29] But a few witnesses claimed—not without a hint of bitterness—that Ustasha leaders released Pandža to the custody of top Muslims in Zagreb, where he lived out the war as a free man, even attending mosque with Muslims in the Pavelić regime.[30] Pandža did not become a hero, a martyr, or a spokesman for Muslims. If anything, his main accomplishment was to reveal that Muslims would not be able to sustain a fourth front of armed resistance in this multisided civil war.

Because the city was largely disconnected from the military conflict in the countryside, resistance activities within the town took on a different, less militant character than is suggested by the narrative of armed insurgency that pervades histories of resistance in the Balkans. For many groups, Sarajevo became a meeting ground, a place to share and spread ideas and information. The town's position as a German and Ustasha hub meant that it was a central crossroad for people and goods moving across the region, from Volksdeutsche and Croat troops deploying to the front to refugees arriving en masse. Local officials estimated that in addition to the thousands of people moving in and out of the city legally, around twenty thousand people "visited" Sarajevo over the winter of 1943–44 to trade (or smuggle) goods and to meet with friends and family (or rebels). County officials grew so concerned that by March 1944 they felt compelled to restrict movement and travel into Sarajevo.[31] The government was too debilitated to keep track of who came and went, an oversight that enabled guerrillas to take hold of the surrounding hills and make contact with people in the city. Local sabotage increased as Sarajevans grew more sympathetic to the cause of resistance.

Though the Ustasha authorities were convinced that an uprising was being organized under their noses, they were unable to identify the people involved. The difficulty of their task stemmed from the character of the resistance developing in the city. Sarajevans were forming oppositional groups within governmental institutions, social clubs, factories, and religious organizations. These groups were neither tied to any specific ideology

27. Redžić, *Bosnia and Herzegovina in the Second World War,* 224.
28. Šarac, "Uslovi i pravci razvoja narodnooslobodilačkog pokreta," 4:27.
29. Traljić, *Istaknuti Bošnjaci,* 271.
30. Nametak, *Sarajevski Nekrologij,* 85.
31. ABiH, Veliki Župan Vrhbosna, 1945, box 2, document 2076 (March 10, 1944).

nor under central leadership. Whenever the German or Ustasha police destroyed one, dozens of others sprouted up elsewhere. With their paranoia mounting, the Ustasha police pounded the streets in search of insurgents, interrogating, arresting, and incarcerating people at will but failing to root out the main culprits. As secret police are inclined to do, they often exaggerated the presence of local enemies in order to justify their own activities and their inability to maintain order in the town.

More often than targeting individuals, the Ustasha Surveillance Service (Ustaška Nadzorna Služba) investigated institutions. Among the first groups it placed under surveillance, in the fall of 1943, was Sarajevo's branch of the Home Guard. Faced with the crisis in the Italian zone, the Home Guard had conscripted tens of thousands more men across the state, bringing their total troop level to a wartime high of around one hundred seventy thousand.[32] With every new conscript, the regular army—which still functioned separately from (and in competition with) the ideologically driven Ustasha Party army—grew more unstable and disloyal. By the end of 1943, thousands of soldiers had deserted their units to join bands of Partisans or the independent militias.[33]

The Home Guard Institute (*Domobranski oružno-tehnički zavod*), a large weapons' warehouse and factory in Sarajevo, allegedly became a center of antistate activities. For months, Ustasha police investigated soldiers at the warehouse, reporting in March 1944 that about two thousand had shirked their official duties. The police blamed their failure to capture the culprits on the culture of the soldier-workers, who dutifully looked out for one another.[34] By the end of April 1944, the Ustasha police reported that "all of the Home Guardsmen working in the institute had lost the will to work" for the state.[35] The secret police also investigated hundreds of men working for the military who they believed were involved with illegal activities, from the seemingly benign cases of workers who stole wood to the more egregious instances of soldiers caught running military supplies to the insurgents.[36]

In their investigations into the army, the secret police correctly ascertained that insubordination had no particular ethnoconfessional source. In October 1943, for example, the police reported that the Orthodox employees at the Home Guard Institute had developed contact with the Partisans. When a large sum of money disappeared from the institute

32. Tomasevich, *War and Revolution in Yugoslavia*, 423. The size and strength of the Croat army at any given time is difficult to ascertain. In 1941 it had about 45,000 soldiers, and the Ustasha army had 6,000; by the end of 1942 the Croat army had 110,000 soldiers and the Ustasha army had 40,000. See Jelić-Butić, *Ustaše i Nezavisna Država Hrvatska*, 122–123.

33. On the dynamics of Bosnia's various militias, see Tomasevich, *War and Revolution in Yugoslavia*, 428–430; Redžić, *Bosnia and Herzegovina in the Second World War*, 227.

34. HM, Ustaška Nadzorna Služba, document 3045 (March 15, 1944).

35. Ibid., document 3180 (April 28, 1944).

36. For example, see HM, Ustaška Nadzorna Služba, document 2406 (November 2, 1943) and document 2534 (December 2, 1943).

the next month, however, the police accused the factory's treasurer, Josef Walha, possibly a Volksdeutsche, and promptly arrested him.[37] There were also noncompliant Muslims and Catholics: in May 1944 the Catholic Croat lieutenant Ivan Vidović refused to wear his military uniform with a "U" on it; two Muslim soldiers helped an Orthodox Serb Communist escape from a Gestapo jail in June. Orthodox townsmen suffered disproportionately, especially following a temporary pact between some Chetnik forces and the Germans. The impetus behind the alliance was mutual concern about the Partisans' growing strength. At the Tehran Conference in December 1943, Churchill, Roosevelt, and Stalin had agreed to recognize the Partisans as the legitimate Yugoslav resistance and to end support for the Chetniks. The Allies believed that the Chetniks viewed the Communists, rather than the Germans, as their principal enemy, and that this had led Chetnik leaders to compromise the Allies' central mission in Yugoslavia by collaborating with the enemy.[38] The Allied decision to end support for the Chetniks cost them vital material aid and their status as an official Allied partner in Yugoslavia, while the Communists gained international support and a fresh cache of weapons and supplies. In response, some Chetniks made overtures to the German command, which was eager to recruit assistance in its struggling campaign against the Partisans, and representatives of the two armies met in Sarajevo in early 1944.[39] The alliance brought trouble to both sides. The Allies viewed it as confirmation that the Chetniks had joined the German cause, which eventually led to a complete break in Chetnik-Allied relations. The meeting similarly damaged German relations with Sarajevo's Muslim and Catholic leaders, both of whom feared that—in the event of an Axis victory—the Germans would pay back the Chetniks by awarding them all of Bosnia, including Sarajevo.[40] The German alliance also hurt Orthodox civilians in Sarajevo because it invoked fears of conspiracy among Ustasha officials, who lashed out against family members of important Serbs, particularly those with connections to the Orthodox Church.[41]

37. Ibid., document 2390 (October 30, 1943) and document 2465 (November 14, 1943). My assumption that Josef Walha was possibly a German is based on two factors: the letter "W" does not exist in the South Slavic languages, and Walha is an old Germanic word meaning foreigner.

38. The British, who held the greatest stake in the former Yugoslav government in exile, hoped to convince the Communist leader to work with the Yugoslav king in the re-creation of a postwar Yugoslav state. Tito had no intention on reviving the monarch and instead concentrated on expanding his rebel force and solidifying his own political power in anticipation of the Red Army's advance. See Ford, OSS and the Yugoslav Resistance, 34–35.

39. Tomasevich, The Chetniks, 315–388; Sarac, "Uslovi i pravci razvoja narodnooslobodilačkog pokreta," 4:24–25.

40. HM, Ustaška Nadzorna Služba, document 2861 (January 17, 1944). This became quite a pervasive fear among the Ustasha secret police in Sarajevo. In February 1944, for example, an agent anxiously reported that a shop had started selling maps that physically linked Serbia and Croatia. See ibid., document 2878 (February 18, 1944).

41. See, for example, police investigations described in ibid., document 2980 (March 3, 1944) and document 3045 (March 15, 1944).

In the months after the Italian capitulation, the Ustasha secret police attempted to infiltrate every segment of Sarajevo society, from social clubs to humanitarian groups. They even placed Sarajevo's chapter of the Croatian Red Cross under surveillance. Prior to 1944, the 122-member Red Cross chapter rarely acted outside its state and international mandates, which included gathering information on POWs and missing persons, aiding wounded soldiers, and raising money to provide services for refugees.[42] The organization functioned respectfully within the constraints of the occupation and actively fostered a public facade of loyalty. For example, it invited the Ustasha choir and Wehrmacht orchestra to perform at its annual fundraiser.[43] Gradually, however, Red Cross administrators crossed the line of what Ustasha headquarters thought to be appropriate behavior by placing their humanitarian objectives ahead of the regime's wishes. The Sisters of the Croatian Red Cross of Sarajevo handed out biscuits and cigarettes to Jewish prisoners passing through Sarajevo's train station that fall; they also aided wounded Chetnik soldiers who required amputations. In December, the chapter published a pamphlet entitled "A List of Those Who Died and Were Executed in Fascist Camps," which included the names of 139 men from Sarajevo—many of them Orthodox Serbs—who had been killed in German camps in 1942 and 1943.[44]

Ustasha political authorities disliked the attitude of Sarajevo's Red Cross and began to question the organization's policies. In a dispute in January 1944, the local headquarters for the Ustasha women's youth organization (*Stožer ženske ustaške mladeži*) demanded that the city's Red Cross chapter fire several women volunteers who had failed to fulfill mandatory service requirements for the regime. The letter concluded, "I hope that you will execute your duty to Croatia and take the high ground, so that it will not be necessary to cause you any embarrassment."[45] The Red Cross refused to fire the women, complaining that the regime had never appointed adequate staff to help them. Moreover, the organization argued, the women were volunteers, not paid employees, so Ustasha officials could not demand their termination. Using the regime's own rhetoric, the Red Cross asked the Ustashas to refrain from intervening in its important work "for the benefit of Croatia and all Croat people."[46] The request was not heeded. In March 1944, Ustasha soldiers harassed and threatened Red Cross employees of Slovene descent whom they suspected of aiding the resistance.[47] In April, the secret police added Ivan Pavičić, the president of Sarajevo's Red Cross,

42. ABiH, Društvo Crveni Križ, box 23, document 1934 (December 30, 1943).

43. IAS, Hrvatski Crveni Križ, box 1, invitation for fund-raising concert,(October 4, 1943).

44. ABiH, Društvo Crveni Križ, box 23, document 1934 (December 30, 1943). Additional information on the sisters' springtime activities can be found in ibid., box 24, document 949 (April 23, 1944).

45. Ibid., box 24, document 54 (January 19, 1944).

46. Ibid. (January 21, 1944).

47. Ibid., document 635 (March 20, 1944).

to its dossier of suspected "Jews and freemasons"; the next winter they appointed two party commissioners to oversee the organization.[48]

Ivan Pavičić, like many of the people under investigation, was a Catholic Croat. Indeed, a major development in 1943–44 was the spread of resistance activities among Catholics in Sarajevo and throughout the NDH. In part, Sarajevo's Croats were responding to their growing resentment toward the foreign Croats who were trying to impose their own definition of Croat on them. In the fall 1943, the Ustasha regime renewed its campaign to crush Sarajevo's persistent local culture and align the city more firmly with the regime's concept of Croat national culture. Although this had been an aim of the regime since 1941, the Ustashas used the Italian capitulation as an excuse to increase censorship and direct control over Sarajevo publications and institutions. One part of this new campaign was the foundation of a literary journal, *Hrvatska Misao* (*Croatian Thoughts*), with which the regime intended to revive earlier nationalist propaganda.[49] The first edition hit the stands in November 1943. Instead of steering Sarajevo back on the path of the Ustasha ideological plan, however, the magazine illustrated the extent of the deep rift between Zagreb and Sarajevo Croats. It upbraided the regime and revealed the hostility local intellectuals felt toward their foreign bosses. Whether the censors trusted the editors' judgment and therefore skipped the standard reviews, or the editors themselves rushed the journal to press without carefully reading all of the content, the innocuously titled piece "Curators and Museums in the Croat Territories" surely escaped someone's eye. Written by Jozo Petrović, a Sarajevo Catholic Croat who had been recently sacked by the regime from his position as director of the Croatian State Museum, the article criticized the regime's mismanagement of Sarajevo's museums and claimed that Zagreb was using Sarajevo as a dumping ground for civil servants who had misbehaved or failed in more prestigious positions. In addition to having "a poor work ethic," Petrović complained that the Ustasha employees behaved in an uncivilized manner that contradicted Sarajevo's traditions.[50]

While Petrović never directly singled out his successor at the museum, Vejsil Ćurčić, readers familiar with the museum's internal politics would not have mistaken his target. When Ćurčić read Petrović's article, he sent an angry letter to the magazine, calling the article "dishonest and discourteous." He warned the editors of their legal obligation to "protect the image of state institutions in the public eye." To parry the attack, Ćurčić pointed

48. HM, Ustaška Nadzorna Služba, document 3139 (April 19, 1944). On the commissioners appointed to oversee the Red Cross, see *Sarajevski Novi List*, February 3, 1945, 5.

49. For background on the journal, see Jelić-Butić, *Ustaše i Nezavisna Država Hrvatska*, 206. Fikreta Jelić-Butić describes how this magazine was viewed by many Croats as the first Croat literary journal in Sarajevo. There is also information on the journal in the introduction of its first edition, *Hrvatska Misao*, November–December 1943.

50. *Hrvatska Misao*, November–December 1943, 34–35.

the finger back at his predecessor, accusing Petrović of stealing from the museum; Ćurčić also requested a police investigation into the previous director's affairs.[51] In a letter of response, Petrović denied taking anything, sardonically suggesting that things might have gotten lost in the shuffle of his departure because he had been fired by a special emissary and given just a few minutes to pack up his lifetime of work. Such a response again underscored how the regime had started to take a more hostile and abrupt attitude toward local Croats. Petrović warned Ćurčić that he planned to save the latter's private letters in his personal archive so that future generations of Sarajevans could see the "illiteracy and meanness" that characterized local Ustasha officials.[52]

The fight between the two directors was emblematic of the escalating tensions between Sarajevo's local Croat elite and the regime. The regime's efforts to centralize left city leaders feeling stripped of their remaining control. With the approval of the city's high Ustasha officials, Ćurčić sought to move the museum squarely into the Ustasha sphere of influence. He rescinded privileges to museum employees, strictly enforced Ustasha language laws (which had been a bone of contention between Zagreb and the museum since 1941), and threatened to transfer Sarajevo's monuments and historical relics to the protection of the state, a prospect that the local cultural elite had found terribly offensive earlier in the war. He even suggested it would be best to fire all the Sarajevo employees so that he could run things alone.[53] There is little doubt that other Ustasha officials in the city felt the same way.

By the spring of 1944, several Catholic Croats who had belonged to the Croat Peasant Party, the most influential Croat political party during the interwar era, began to meet secretly to discuss political alternatives. The Ustasha police suspected they were in secret talks with Orthodox Serbs.[54] In June police reports noted that local Catholic and Orthodox citizens were jointly running a radio; by July it was becoming clearer that some Sarajevans had developed contacts with a national group of Croats who were thinking about joining the Allied side.[55] This switch of allegiance had been in the works since the spring of 1943, but it gained momentum in the months following the Italian capitulation. In Zagreb, top members of the Croat Peasant Party worked with a handful of regime insiders, including the minister of the interior, Mladen Lorković, and a high official in the Ministry of the Armed Forces, Ante Vokić, to secure Croatia's independence in the event of an Allied victory. The men planned to co-opt the Home Guard

51. ABiH, Zemaljski Muzej Bosne i Hercegovine, box 40, document 6 (January 1, 1944).
52. Ibid., box 40, document 20 (January 5, 1944) and document 376 (April 20, 1944).
53. Ibid., document 518 (May 16, 1944), document 813 (July 27, 1944), document 876 (August 14, 1944), and document 1010 (October 12, 1944.)
54. See HM, Ustaška Nadzorna Služba, document 2982 (March 3, 1944).
55. Ibid., document 3372 (June 11, 1944).

as their army, thus playing off the wartime tensions between the official army and the Ustasha regime's political army.[56] Throwing ideology out the window, these Croats were prepared to make whatever alliances were necessary to save the NDH—a compromise that many Axis allies made as German defeat became more likely.

In early July 1944, the German embassy in Zagreb got wind of a top secret meeting in Sarajevo in which a high-ranking Ustasha minister had warned his audience not to let Germany dictate their future and suggested that Croats develop a plan to disarm the Germans in the event of an Allied invasion.[57] On August 8, six Sarajevans, all former Croat Peasant Party members, held another meeting at a local restaurant, which the Ustasha police perceived as further proof that a plan was in the works.[58] After the war the German police chief in Sarajevo noted that he had been worried that August that local officials might attack the German forces.[59] A division had occurred within the Ustasha ranks between those who believed that the regime had to be overthrown in order to maintain the possibility of a postwar Croat nation-state and those who continued to show loyalty to the regime. By the end of the month, Ante Pavelić and the top Germans in Zagreb—all of whom were now familiar with the plot—swiftly crushed the movement by executing and imprisoning its Zagreb leaders.[60] There would be no breakaway Croat movement in the NDH.

Political resistance within the Muslim community was more difficult for the Ustasha police to define, largely because Muslim advocates of resistance preached a similar version of the Ustasha regime's anti-Communist and anti-Serb message. The Ustashas knew that Sarajevo's Muslims desperately wanted out of the NDH; however, they also knew that Muslim leaders did not feel they had any realistic political alternatives. The lesson of Pandža's failed flight lingered among Muslims in the city, who regularly pushed for greater autonomy but did not develop concrete plans for how to implement this autonomy in the context of the war.

While adopting an openly anti-Muslim attitude, the regime occasionally threw a bone to important Muslim leaders, such as when it released several Muslim political prisoners from the camps and granted a few military deferrals.[61] But such gestures failed to persuade most Muslims to abandon their dreams of autonomy and secession. In February 1944, an Ustasha police

---

56. For an overview of the plan, see Tomasevich, *War and Revolution in Yugoslavia*, 442–448.

57. Ibid., 450; Jelić-Butić, *Ustaše i Nezavisna Država Hrvatska*, 289.

58. HM, Ustaška Nadzorna Služba, document 3570 (August 8, 1944).

59. United States Holocaust Memorial Museum Archive, statement from Antun Fest, Freising, RG-49.005M, reel 4a (August 8, 1945).

60. Tomasevich, *War and Revolution in Yugoslavia*, 452–456.

61. See the case of Mustafa Kurto in Nametak, *Sarajevski Nekrologij*, 187–188, and the correspondence between the Ministry of Defense and the state theater about deferrals in ABiH, Narodno pozorište Sarajevo, box 4, document 1785 (December 7, 1943), and box 5, document 521 (February 16, 1944).

agent complained that few Muslim peasants in the city knew they were not Croats or took pride in their citizenship in the NDH: "[A] peasant knows that he is a Muslim. . . . Among our Muslim peasants, there has never been any discussion about belonging to Croatia."[62] The local Muslim press did not help matters by publishing articles like "The Question of Muslim Life in a Non-Muslim State," which called on Muslims to strengthen their religious values and laws and maintain their separateness as a community.[63] Muslim leaders increasingly understood that in order to preserve their community on their own terms—as opposed to the terms being set by other groups who ruled them—they needed to anchor their religious ideology to a national-political program that could compete with the other national groups.

Nevertheless, a political alliance between Muslims and the Ustashas still made sense on many levels: the two groups shared concerns about the spreading insurgency and its potential to annihilate the world they knew. Thus in a final effort to find common ground as the Communists became more powerful, Sarajevo's Muslim leaders sat down with Ustasha authorities on April 28, 1944. The president of Croatia, Nikola Mandić, came to Sarajevo to preside over a joint meeting; his presence underscored the seriousness and priority that the regime granted to the dialogue, which covered topics ranging from Muslim underrepresentation in the government to strategies against Communism.[64] Instead of leading to a compromise or a renewed alliance, however, the meeting created more friction because neither side was willing to give the other what it wanted; Muslims still wanted autonomy and the Ustashas still wanted unconditional loyalty. After the talks, Muslims feared that Pavelić's regime had a hidden agenda for their community, while the regime became even less assured of Muslim loyalty.

Matters were not helped by an article published that month. A Catholic priest, Dragutin Kamber, wrote an essay titled "The Refugee Question," in which he analyzed the grave threat that refugee guerrillas posed to Sarajevo's moral and cultural order. Instead of discussing the question as a shared humanitarian crisis affecting every community, Kamber described the refugees as uneducated and uncivilized foreigners, "who had emerged from the lowest depths of cultural and moral standards." He believed they threatened the city's moral order and must be removed.[65] Kamber was an advocate of an exclusive Catholic Croat national identity, and his language mirrored antisemitic discourse, now applied to the mostly Muslim refugees. The Ustasha police reported that the essay frightened Muslims in Sarajevo and stirred up the community's fears of the regime's long-term intentions.[66]

62. HM, Ustaška Nadzorna Služba, document 2878 (February 18, 1944).
63. Novi Behar, March 1, 1944, 77.
64. Redžić, Bosnia and Herzegovina in the Second World War, 187–188.
65. Hrvatska Misao, May 1944, 126–127.
66. HM, Ustaška Nadzorna Služba, document 3334 (June 3, 1944).

Throughout May, Sarajevo's downtown bazaars buzzed with rumors that Zagreb planned to send three infamous Ustasha police agents to the city to assassinate several important Muslims, including (possibly) the former county executive.[67] Soon afterward, a group of Muslim leaders, including those who had met with Mandić, sent the Ustasha leaders a signed memorandum, attesting to the persistent fear within the Muslim community that Catholics had no intention of ever including Muslims as equal partners in the Croat nation. Muslims living in Sarajevo, it stated, suffered from unlawful and brutal police searches and interrogations; thousands had been sent to concentration camps. The authors dramatically concluded that the position of Muslims, which had once deteriorated day by day, was now growing worse by the hour.[68]

Although the local Muslim elite hoped the letter would scare the regime into treating them better, in fact it had the opposite effect. The Ustasha authorities interpreted it as an attack.[69] Outraged, they began to look upon the city's Muslims as a fifth column. Some intelligence reports blamed Muslims for provoking a conflict with the city's Catholic population and with the state. Others described how "Muslim hostility against Croats was strikingly obvious" at public events, like a famous soccer match between local Muslim and Catholic teams.[70]

In the late spring of 1944, Zagreb announced that it had authorized the University of Croatia to open a small campus in Sarajevo with two faculties. Although Sarajevo's intellectuals had long dreamed of building a university in the city—an indication that Sarajevo was an intellectual center—the regime's propaganda spoiled their enthusiasm. When announcing the opening of the medical school, the city's paper emphasized that the faculty was not intended to "decorate Sarajevo's bazaars" or give her a "big-city appearance." Rather, the regime hoped it would train a new generation of doctors who could end the chronic poverty and illness embedded in Bosnia. The article claimed that Bosnia's situation mirrored that of an African colony and that the regime hoped the new doctors would aid in the difficult task of moving Bosnia into the "civilized" and "Western world."[71] Six weeks later, the paper announced that a faculty of theology would soon open in Sarajevo. Its goals were to spread "peace and goodwill" in Bosnia and strengthen the region's Catholic life.[72] The day after the announcement, another article commemorated the fiftieth anniversary of Archbishop

67. Ibid., document 3265 (May 22, 1944).
68. Ibid., document 3293 (May 28, 1944).
69. Redžić, *Bosnia and Herzegovina in the Second World War,* 187.
70. On the soccer match, see HM, Ustaška Nadzorna Služba, document 3292 (June 21, 1944); *Sarajevski Novi List,* June 18, 1944, 4; ibid., June 20, 1944, 6. On police concerns about Muslim-Catholic hostility more generally, see HM, Ustaška Nadzorna Služba, document 3404 (June 29, 1944).
71. *Sarajevski Novi List,* May 30, 1944, 5.
72. Ibid., July 18, 1944, 3.

Šarić's first mass, highlighting his lifelong dedication to the Croat nation.[73] The emphasis on Western civilization and Catholic education seemed to leave little room for local Islamic culture. The flower of the Croat nation, as Pavelić's regime had called Muslims in the early days of the war, had now become a noxious weed.

Then in July 1944, a legal decision in Zagreb stunned Muslims: the NDH would not uphold Sharia law in questions of mixed marriages, and Christian conversion to Islam would be outlawed in northern Croatia.[74] Muslims felt that every aspect of their community and tradition was under attack. In just a few short weeks, the Ustasha authorities had managed to annul Islamic legal traditions and remove Muslims from important political positions while strengthening Catholic institutions, authorizing courts to place Muslim children with Catholic relatives, and outlawing Catholic conversion to Islam. By late August 1944, the Ustasha police were jailing and executing Muslims with such frequency that a local German officer wondered in a letter whether the Ustashas viewed Muslims as a greater enemy than the Partisans.[75] Furthermore, the comparisons of Muslims to Africans and Jews sent a frightening message to Muslims about their place in the social order of the NDH.

Despite the tremendous surge in anti-Ustasha and anti-German sentiment, the Communist Party still complained that it was having trouble recruiting Sarajevans. Indeed, as late as 1944, neither the Chetniks nor the Partisans were having much success in the city because they did not speak to the overarching needs or values of Sarajevans. The townsmen might have become anti-state and might have engaged in illegal behavior, but they remained skeptical of the two rebel groups and their visions of the postwar order.

Sarajevo's Communist Party had been severely debilitated by police raids on several occasions since 1941.[76] In September 1943, after another sweep of the city by the Ustasha police, party leadership changed hands again, and a regional party commissar, Vladimir Perić (known as Valter) took over. Though Valter would become in popular mythology one of the most famous Sarajevo Partisan heroes, he struggled to develop an underground movement in the city, although he did have a strong base among villagers living nearby.[77] Throughout 1944, local party officials complained that Sarajevans were frightened of Communism, held false conceptions about the Partisan hierarchy and army, and supported other kinds of opposition

73. Ibid., July 19, 1944, 3.
74. HDA, Ministarstvo pravosuđa i bogoštovlja NDH, Odjel za Pravosuđe, reports, box 1, Vrlo tajno, bez broja (top secret, no number) (July 28–August 7, 1944).
75. Redžić, *Bosnia and Herzegovina in the Second World War,* 188.
76. Donia, 192–196.
77. Danilo Štaka, "Aktivnost okružnog komiteta KPJ za Sarajevo," in Albahari et al., *Sarajevo u Revoluciji,* 4:240.

groups. Muslims and Catholic Croats supported their own militias, while Orthodox Serbs leaned toward the Chetniks. Regional party leaders reprimanded the city's Communist organizers for their pessimism and encouraged them to nurture networks among the refugee community, which was politically and morally disgusted with the regime. Local party members thus tried to galvanize the movement by familiarizing themselves with the concerns of Sarajevans (namely, food, health care, and education); publicizing the work of the city's Communist student organization, which had garnered some support among educated youths; and combating misconceptions of the Partisan aims for a postwar Yugoslavia—such as a widespread fear that they would bring back the Yugoslav king. Despite these efforts, no substantial local Partisan movement materialized in the city.[78]

Like the Communists, the Chetniks also found it difficult to build a Sarajevo movement. Several Chetnik organizers arrived in the city during the chaos following the Italian surrender—some dressed in Italian uniforms—and began to network with wealthy Orthodox Serbs.[79] Over the winter, as the Chetnik-German alliance solidified, regional Chetnik officers visited Sarajevo as well. One of them, Todor Perović, reported that most of Sarajevo's Serbs disagreed with the Chetnik agenda.[80] Historians who have studied the Chetniks appear to agree with this assessment, since they rarely mention Sarajevo in their research on the movement.[81] Yet both the Partisan and the Ustasha leaders believed that the Chetniks were a genuine threat. In May 1944, the Ustasha police blamed local Chetniks—not Communists—for an explosion at Sarajevo's railway station that killed two Ustasha soldiers. Later that month, the police claimed that the Chetniks had successfully rallied some local Muslims, and in July, agents reported that a civil servant in the mayor's office was in cahoots with the movement.[82] The German consulate corroborated many of the claims. In March 1944, it issued a lengthy report on the military and political demands of the Sarajevo Chetnik Brigade, which was fighting in the nearby hills. The consulate also reported on prevalent Chetnik propaganda and espionage in Sarajevo itself.[83]

78. ABiH, Zbirka NOR-a Okružni Komitet KPJ Sarajevo, box 1, document 6 (March 13, 1944), document 8 (June 25, 1944), and document 13 (November 4, 1944). In September 1944 the Ustasha police agreed that the Partisans were not a major threat within the city. See HM, Ustaška Nadzorna Služba, document 3668 (September 9, 1944).

79. HM, Ustaška Nadzorna Služba, document 2371 (October 23, 1943).

80. Donia, *Sarajevo,* 184.

81. For example, Jozo Tomasevich's book *The Chetniks* does not discuss Sarajevo in terms of Chetnik activity in 1944. Likewise, recent Serbian literature on the movement ignores the city. See Miloslav Samardžić, *General Draža Mihailović i opšta istorija četničkog pokreta* (Kragujevac: Novi pogledi, 2005).

82. In HM, Ustaška Nadzorna Služba, see document 3272 (May 16, 1944), document 3301 (May 31, 1944), and document 3557 (August 3, 1944).

83. See reports from the German consulate in Sarajevo to the embassy in Zagreb in Hoover Institute Archives, Tomasevich Papers, records from the captured German documents held at the U.S. National Archives, box 4, T:120, roll 5788 (March 15, 1944, and July 11, 1944).

Given the lack of historical confirmation of the strength of the Chet-niks in Sarajevo, it is possible that these attributions were fabricated, with the Ustasha police and German officials finding it better to blame Serb nationalists than to admit their inability to identify and destroy Sarajevo's resistance. I also find it plausible that in 1944 support for the Chetniks grew in Sarajevo as members of the local elite wrestled with the real likelihood of a Communist victory. Although I discovered no evidence for this possi-bility, it seems to be a reasonable, if controversial, conclusion in light of the extensive German and Ustasha reports on local Chetnik activity. Moreover, given the city's well-documented fear of Communism, it is not implausible that facing a choice of Communist dictatorship or a renewed Great Serbia, some Muslims and Catholics chose the latter.

Because the Partisans won the war and shaped the postwar memory of the resistance, Sarajevo's various underground resistance groups were later either falsely incorporated into the Partisan narrative of a unified libera-tion struggle or else left out of the story altogether. In reality, resistance in Sarajevo—like collaboration and every other significant current in the city—had a distinct local character. There were underground groups stem-ming from prewar political parties that hoped to reassert their influence before the next changing of the guard. There were religious, humanitarian, and social groups that wanted to protect their communities and continue with their work. And there were civilians trying to take control of their lives, secure food and heat for their families, and practice their customs. Though many groups and individuals eventually joined the victorious Partisan cam-paign, they did not start out as supporters.

Confessional Fragmentation

In this period of political oppression and fomenting resistance, religious and civic leaders struggled with how best to serve their communities. Many detested the existing system but feared the insurgents more. As different groups within their communities began acting independently, they often treated them like children in need of special attention. They combined constructive praise with reprimands and warnings, and they developed pro-grams to bring people together under the umbrella of the community. This proved to be problematic, as it had been for years, because of the conflicting understandings of what community meant. Confessional communities had fragmented on the institutional and neighborhood level. Competition for moral hegemony and political power created deep internal struggles within institutions: the Roman Catholic archdiocese, the Franciscans, and Napredak each struggled to be the primary voice heard by Catholic Croats; the Islamic Religious Community, El-Hidaje, and Narodna Uzdanica simi-larly competed for authority among Muslims. As they struggled to use their positions effectively, community leaders regularly faced a choice between the often conflicting goals of influence over the local community and a political stake in the postwar order. None of the confessional communities reached consensus on the best path forward.

The Catholic community was fragmented, not only along the lines of different approaches of religious and political leaders but also as a result of the shifting character of the city's Catholic Croat community. The community had been flooded during the war with two very different kinds of outsiders, poor peasant refugees and Ustasha militiamen; neither of these groups operated with the social conventions or civic consciousness on which Sarajevo's Croat intelligentsia had long relied for cohesion. Napredak complained in early 1944 that its membership in Sarajevo had declined drastically, with only 1,464 members left in the entire city. The society noted that elite Catholics had left the city and the "new" Catholic population was out of touch with the society's goals and unaware of its importance.[84] There also continued to be tension between civic and religious understandings of what belonging to the Croat community entailed. For many townsmen, being Croat offered a cultural complement to their religious identity, but it did not define their political views. This became evident in the spring of 1944 as Catholics in the Croat Peasant Party, the Home Guard, and private institutions like Napredak increasingly organized against the regime. They viewed themselves as Croats and Catholics, but they opted for a different political path than the one presented by the Ustashas. Borrowing models from their central European counterparts, they also aimed to limit the influence held by conservative religious organizations in shaping collective identity, seeking instead to root the Catholic Croat community firmly in a secular mind-set.

Sarajevo's Roman Catholic leadership—including such well-known figures as Archbishop Ivan Šarić, Father Božidar Bralo, and Dragutin Kamber—continued to support the Ustasha regime and promote a staunchly Catholic Croat national agenda. Church leaders worried that Bosnia might be excluded from a postwar Croat nation-state, a possibility contemplated by the Yugoslav government in exile and by German leaders.[85] They therefore emphasized Catholics' duty to preserve the Croat nation in Bosnia, regardless of what happened to the Ustasha regime. In an article in the archdiocese's monthly journal, Monsignor Ivan Jablanović noted, "Now that we have political freedom, in control of our own destinies and forging our own paths, it is not sufficient for us to rely solely on the state's national program; instead we must forge a complete cultural program, a comprehensive and

84. ABiH, Hrvatsko kulturno društvo Napredak, box 170, document 12004 (January 28, 1944).

85. On the idea of a Croat state composed of just the "Danube provinces," see Tomasevich, *War and Revolution in Yugoslavia,* 578–579.

universal one."[86] For many clerics, the Croat nation was a community that would integrate cultural, familial, religious, and social values. Croatia had become to some church leaders in Sarajevo what Islam was to some observant Muslims: an all-encompassing community, society, and way of life that should integrate religious ethics with the political order.

The archdiocese continued to bicker with the Franciscan order. The institutional rift had developed a new twist in 1942 when Zagreb approved the final construction of a Franciscan high school and seminary in Sarajevo's town center. The Franciscans aimed to use the school to expand religious education and foster a new "cadre."[87] The school had been under construction since 1938, but the Franciscans lacked the funds and administration necessary to complete their plans. Upon hearing of the renewed construction plans, the archbishop wrote a long personal letter to the Ustasha minister of religion, Mile Budak, complaining that funds allocated for Catholic education had been unfairly dispensed to Sarajevo's Franciscan provincial for constructing the seminary. Šarić argued that the Franciscans, as a monastic order, were not entitled to state funding. Moreover, he criticized them for wasting resources on a new seminary in the middle of war. Because the regime had earmarked funds for the Franciscans, the archbishop claimed, he no longer had enough money for the archdiocese's educational programs. He complained that he would probably have to close down a number of Catholic schools, including the high school in Travnik that the poglavnik, Ante Pavelić, had attended. In case Minister Budak misunderstood this threat, Šarić noted that surely the "poglavnik would not be pleased to hear that."[88] In the larger scheme of Catholic affairs in Sarajevo, the establishment of a Franciscan seminary could hardly have threatened Šarić's entire educational program. Such flailing protests by the archbishop reveal that he remained insecure about his dominant role among Sarajevo's Catholics.

The Ustasha regime's sponsorship of the Croatian Orthodox Church added further insult to the archdiocese, but the regime believed that its ongoing co-option of the Serb community through the institution of the Croatian Orthodox Church would increase prospects for stability. Thus in August 1944, Ante Pavelić expanded the Croatian Orthodox hierarchy, appointing a bishop for Sarajevo. The prelate, Spiridon Mifka, happened to be an old schoolmate of Mile Budak. The local Ustasha authorities rang in his appointment with a formal ceremony and celebration, filling the city's press with visions of how Spiridon would help to heal the divided city.[89] The archdiocese resented the move, which conflicted with its mission to link

86. *Vrhbosna*, February 1944, 31–34.
87. Barun, *Svjedoci i učitelji povijest franjevaca Bosne Srebrene*, 386.
88. A copy of this letter is reprinted in Gavran, *Lucerna Lucens?* 208–211.
89. IAS, Gradsko Poglavarstvo, box 1238 (August 30—September 3, 1944). See also *Sarajevski Novi List*, September 29, 1944, 3.

Catholicism to the Croat national idea and to rid Bosnia of Orthodoxy. It did not help that the Franciscans welcomed the new bishop to the town and even invited him to appoint clerics to teach Orthodoxy at a nearby Franciscan school in Visoko.[90] In late 1944, Archbishop Šarić appealed to Rome to censure the Franciscans for maintaining "unhealthily" close relations with people of other confessions, citing particular Franciscan priests who had attended the consecration of the Croatian Orthodox bishop.[91]

Were these squabbles of power or identity? Was the archbishop using a disagreement about the Croatian Orthodox Church as the latest means in a decades-long attempt to assert control over the Franciscans, or was he seeking approval from Rome to legitimize his desire to exclude non-Catholics from the Croat nation? Were the Franciscans provoking the archbishop by reestablishing themselves as the custodians of Roman Catholicism in a time of crisis, or did they see an alignment with Orthodox Christians as a means of combating contemporary political trends that advocated turning Bosnia into a Muslim political entity?[92] This latter possibility is not far-fetched given the anti-Muslim public stance of the Croatian Orthodox Church. In his first published interview, Bishop Mifka designated Christians in Bosnia as the historical victims of the Turks; this suggested a break from the Ustasha rhetoric of the Muslim-Catholic alliance in the Croat nation and a return to the idea of a Christian front.[93] The Ustashas found it politically expedient to nurture such rhetoric, even though it meant dismissing the goals and objectives of Roman Catholic leaders.

Sarajevo's Muslims faced different obstacles to unity. Although there were continued efforts to work together to combat the humanitarian crises, particularly among Muslim women's groups, Muslim leaders remained deeply divided over the relationship among Islam, the national idea, and secular politics.[94] In 1943–44, Muslim youths became increasingly radicalized, with some joining the Communist resistance and others turning to Islamist organizations. Both the Young Muslims and its parent organization, El-Hidaje, reported gains in membership during that period. El-Hidaje attracted older and wealthier Muslims who strongly supported Muslim autonomy; Muslim students and teenagers gravitated toward Sarajevo's Young Muslims, whose local chapter grew to 640 members by the summer of 1944.[95] In September 1943, the Young Muslims founded their first women's committee, based

90. ABiH, Veliki Župan Vrhbosna, 1945, box 1, document 61 (December 25, 1944).

91. Gavran, *Lucerna Lucens?* 123–124.

92. On the Franciscans' anti-Muslim rhetoric, see their yearly almanac, *Kalendar Sv. Ante*, 1943, 59–62.

93. *Glas Pravoslavlja*, August 18, 1944, 3–5.

94. See a discussion of joint activities among different organizations in IAS, Narodna Uzdanica, Ženski Odbor, zapisnik (November 4, 1943) and memo to Narodna Uzdanica from the Women's Committee, October 1944; ABiH, Društvo Crveni Križ, box 23, document 1934 (December 30, 1943).

95. *El-Hidaje*, August 20, 1944, 25–28.

in Sarajevo, which evolved into an important center of the club's humanitarian work.[96] In their memoirs, a few of the women involved explained that they enjoyed having a sanctuary from the war and a place to meet, socialize, and fulfill their religious charity obligations with other girls from similar backgrounds.[97] Yet it cannot be denied that their charity work also took on a political character, one that did not conform to the ideological or political goals of the Ustasha state.

Some women's groups appear to have used faith as a facade while they were actually working in conjunction with overtly political movements. In March 1944, El-Hidaje discovered that several small factions had popped up in Sarajevo that claimed to be a part of the Young Muslim movement but were actually "against the spirit and ideology" of Islam. In other parts of Bosnia, similar groups had encouraged members to ignore draft notices and break away from Ustasha organizations. To combat emergent factionalism, El-Hidaje self-policed the organization and restricted Young Muslim activities, forbidding new women's chapters and outlawing mixed-gender committees.[98] The emphasis on shutting down women's groups suggests that many of the factions involved Muslim women, however, it can also be understood as an attempt by Muslim elders to blame women for the fragmentation of the community, a tactic frequently employed by reactionary thinkers who believe their community is in crisis.

Whereas different movements had different motivations, some of which were explicitly religious, there appear to be at least a few instances in which Muslim women's groups teamed up with underground Communist networks. During a debriefing in December 1944, a Communist activist, Nata Božić, told Partisan agents that the Anti-Fascist Front of Women (AFŽ), the Communist Party's women's committee, had slowly started infiltrating and organizing various local women's groups over the spring and summer of 1944 after a two-year hiatus when they had limited women's activities in the city.[99] The veracity of such reports is difficult to ascertain; however, the fact that official Muslim women's societies, such as Narodna Uzdanica, reported a decline in membership at the same time that the illegal groups claimed to be expanding supports the claim.[100]

From their discrete vantage points, different Muslim leaders recognized that their community was changing character and that the war

96. Ibid., October 1, 1943, 103–104. On the ongoing activities of the women's committee, see *El-Hidaje*, December 1, 1943, 167. For the women's perspective, see the short memoir of Ismeta Dalagija-Dobrača in Korkut-Spaho and Šiljak, *Mlade muslimanke*, 46.

97. See interviews with Muniba Korkut-Spaho and Safija Solak-Šiljak in Korkut-Spaho and Šiljak, *Mlade muslimanke*, 76–78 and 166.

98. *El-Hidaje*, March 7, 1944, 262–263. See also Redžić, *Bosnia and Herzegovina in the Second World War*, 105.

99. ABiH, Zbirka NOR-a Okružni Komitet KPJ Sarajevo, box 1, document 32 (December 20, 1944).

100. IAS, Narodna Uzdanica, Ženski Odbor, zapisnik (April 2, 1944).

would determine how Muslims would be integrated into the modernizing European state. The schism within the Muslim community was played out nightly on the stage of the Croatian State Theater. Although the theater catered to a Sarajevo audience and performed plays with local themes, the image it projected was not that of the multiconfessional city in which it operated but rather a vision of the pluralist modern society local intellectuals wanted it to be. Plays frequently included female Muslim characters, but these roles had to be played by Orthodox or Catholic women because not a single Muslim woman belonged to the 112-person company.[101] Such a public act of gender integration would have been too offensive to Muslim religious leaders. In fact, many Muslims found the entire concept of theatrical performance foreign. *Osvit*, the city's main Muslim newspaper, refused to publish play reviews on the grounds that few Muslims actually attended the theater. The head of the theater, Ahmed Muradbegović, a Muslim himself, denounced this as nonsense, arguing that on any given night half the audience was Muslim.[102] But *Osvit* claimed to know that its readership favored traditionalism over secularism.

Central to the debate over whether modern theater was compatible with Muslim culture was the idea of what comprised Bosnian culture and how Muslims should be represented in it. In a review of Alija Nametak's farce *Zabavni odbor* (*Entertainment Committee*), which painted a portrait of contemporary Muslim life in Bosnia, a drama critic writing for *Hrvatska Misao* dismissed the play as a "superficial" and "annoying" mockery of Bosnian culture that portrayed Muslims as backward. A scene that depicted young Muslims drinking and singing especially offended him. The critic called it shameful and disrespectful for the theater to stage such a scene at the height of the Muslim quest for political autonomy.[103] A different critic was equally unreceptive to the play *Džaferbegov jemin* (*Dzaferbeg's Pledge*), written by a young Sarajevo Muslim, Safvet Kafedžić.[104] The play, which centers on a Muslim girl who marries for love despite her father's disapproval, revealed the tensions between observant, old-fashioned parents and their more progressive offspring.[105] The reviewer's complaints ranged from the portrayal of what constituted a "modern emancipated Muslim girl" to the depiction of traditional Muslim life. He argued that Kafedžić missed the essence of Bosnian morality in the final scene, in which the father arrives at the

101. ABiH, Narodno pozorište Sarajevo, box 5, document 924 (August 8, 1944). As of August 1944, the state theater had 112 employees: 55 Catholics, 22 Muslims, 26 Orthodox Croats, 8 non-Croat Orthodox (Russian, Montenegrin, or Hungarian), and 1 Protestant. None of the women have Muslim names.

102. For both *Osvit* comments and the theater's response, see *Hrvatska Misao*, November–December 1943, 44.

103. *Hrvatska Misao*, May 1944, 137–138.

104. The word *jemin* is rarely used today. Though its official meaning is "pledge," it was used traditionally to refer to a Muslim's solemn oath.

105. *Sarajevski Novi List*, February 27, 1944, 5.

wedding to kill his daughter and her betrothed but instead begs for their forgiveness. The critics' observation: no observant Muslim would grovel thus before the repugnant youths.[106]

Sarajevo's theatrical life gave the Muslim elite a safe place to debate their different visions of society. But these debates did not actually resonate with the lower-class youths most prone to joining the Partisan resistance. Realizing this, some Muslim intelligentsia reached out to the younger generation by organizing supervised social outings and lectures for teenagers and young adults. They hoped that through these activities, Muslim youths would become more invested in their own community and resist outside influences. But religious leaders threw what can only be described as a fit. They wanted to shelter women and girls and ban social groups that allowed Muslims to drink, smoke, or sing. The Ulema Medžlis censured the societies that sponsored social activities, targeting especially the cultural society Narodna Uzdanica and the craftsmen society Hurijet. When Narodna Uzdanica received a complaint about activities that it held for women, the board tried to win over its religious leaders in a January 1944 note. Defending itself, the society argued that idle hands are the devil's playthings; that is, it was better for young women to meet in formal settings than to be left with free time, during which they might engage in illegal or immoral activities. Narodna Uzdanica requested that the religious council work with it to provide organized activities for Muslim youths, an offer the Ulema Medžlis rejected.[107] When Hurijet received a similar complaint in April 1944, the group reiterated the importance of providing Muslim youths—both men and women—with safe and supervised social settings. Though it refuted the religious leaders' claims that it allowed young people to dance, sing, and drink alcohol at its events, the group also defended such actions. Young people, the group warned, would always be attracted to forbidden activities. Religious leaders should thus opt for the lesser of two evils by allowing and encouraging young people to assemble in supervised Muslim settings.[108] The Ulema Medžlis rejected the ultimatum and continued to censor the activities of Muslim societies throughout the summer of 1944.[109] What many Muslim leaders failed to realize was that the only way to compete against the Ustasha, Chetnik, and Partisan movements was either by anchoring Islam to a political idea or by transforming it into a mobilizing factor. Either of these projects would have required unity. By the time the leaders came to terms with this fact, in November 1944, it was too late.[110]

By contrast with our understanding of the Catholic and Muslim communities, very little is known about the inner workings of Sarajevo's Orthodox

106. *Hrvatska Misao,* May 1944, 138–139.
107. ARIZBiH, Ulema Medžlis, document 1291 (January 21, 1944).
108. Ibid. (April 17, 1944).
109. IAS, Narodna Uzdanica, zapisnik (July 25, 1944).
110. *El-Hidaje,* November 26, 1944, 141–143.

community or its responses to the political changes late in the war. Though it no doubt faced internal conflicts similar to those of the Muslim and Catholic communities—particularly given the nature of the relationship between Orthodox Croats and the regime and the severe oppression that Orthodox civilians faced at the hands of the Ustashas—the dynamics of these divisions are unclear. The Croatian Orthodox Church in Sarajevo left few archival records, and most of them involved requests to the Ministry of Religion for money to repair its buildings and pay its employees.[111] *Glas Pravoslavlja* (*The Voice of the Orthodox*), the state-sponsored religious-political paper that constituted the local Orthodox press, alluded to an alliance with Sarajevo's Franciscans, but the exact nature of this friendship remains uncertain.[112] Notably, some local Orthodox leaders tried to work with the regime to combat the spread of resistance. In April 1944, the president of Sarajevo's Croatian Orthodox Community, Kosta Ćurčić, met with Ustasha leaders in Zagreb to discuss their mutual fears that the small Russian intelligentsia in Sarajevo was involved with the resistance, a fear reiterated by one of Sarajevo's Orthodox Croat priests, Bogdan Popović.[113] Yet other Orthodox groups eschewed any contact with the Ustashas and instead worked closely with the Germans.[114]

Regardless of how Sarajevo's Orthodox community felt individually about guerrillas, Communists, or Chetniks—feelings not revealed in the documents—they had a practical concern about the spread of local insurgency in any form, which gave the Ustasha police new ammunition to target Orthodox civilians. As an institution, the Orthodox Church was in a unique position to use its official status to help Sarajevo's Orthodox citizens. By working with the Ustasha regime in monitoring the sources of resistance and emphasizing the foreign roots of underground movements, the Orthodox leaders likely hoped to minimize backlash against their community as the Red Army advanced. These fears proved well founded, as the Ustasha police immediately tried to link the city's Orthodox population to the Soviets when the Red Army reached Serbia's borders in October 1944.[115]

In her work on nation building and national construction in the Balkans, the historian Theodora Dragostinova coined the term "emergency identity" to describe how socially marginalized individuals (or, more

111. Examples can be found in HDA, Ministarstvo pravosuđa i bogoštovlja NDH, Odjel za bogoštovlja, box 80, document 5574 (July 16, 1943) and document 277 (January 15, 1944).

112. *Glas Pravoslavlja*, August 18, 1944, 3–5.

113. HM, Ustaška Nadzorna Služba, document 3135 (April 17, 1944). According to the German embassy in Zagreb, there were eight hundred Russian émigrés living in Sarajevo at the start of the war. The German political authorities kept them under close supervision. Hoover Institute Archives, Tomasevich Papers, records from the captured German documents held at the U.S. National Archives, box 4, T:120, roll 5785 (July 29, 1941).

114. See, for example, HM, Ustaška Nadzorna Služba, document 3298 (May 31, 1944).

115. See ibid., document 3840 (October 14, 1944).

subtly, individuals excluded from the mainstream national body) become "active agents" who "shape policymaking while at the same time resourcefully adapting to the rules of the nation-state."[116] This model works well as applied to Sarajevo's Orthodox community. While Sarajevo's Serbs had limited options, they nevertheless had choices: many fled to Serbia, left for work in Germany, or joined the armed resistance. Playing by the rules of the regime offered some Orthodox Serbs the best hope for surviving the critical, emergency situation. By *not* joining the resistance, by keeping a low profile, and above all by converting to the Croatian Orthodox Church, they could make public declarations of their loyalty and their intent to remain bystanders in the civil war, thus offering tacit agreement to support—at least for the time being—the NDH. In so doing, they could also help to effect further change and protect their community from further attack.

After the war the Yugoslav government and the Serbian Orthodox Church viewed the Croatian Orthodox Church solely as a tool of the Ustasha genocidal agenda; participants were considered collaborators of the regime.[117] Certainly there were opportunities for and instances of wrongdoing among the Orthodox Croat clergy and laity. But I suspect that there were also local leaders who used the new church as a means to protect Sarajevo's Orthodox heritage and provide a comfortable home for the Orthodox community. Hints to this effect appear in various documents. In 1943, for example, Sarajevo's Orthodox leaders requested that the Ministry of Religion repair the bell on the New Orthodox Church.[118] This might be seen as a benign request for wartime repairs if not for the historical significance of the repair in question. The church bell was a source of great pride to Sarajevo's Orthodox Serbs, whose ancestors had fought with Ottoman officials and local Muslim leaders in the 1860s for the right to ring it from the steeple of the New Orthodox Church.[119] In the 1870s this right marked a major success and turning point for Christianity in Ottoman Bosnia. Fixing the bell in 1943 would have sent the subtle but deliberate message to the regime that Orthodoxy would endure this new crisis as it had endured earlier ones. Throughout 1944 Orthodox leaders in Sarajevo made similar attempts to protect church relics and property, usually by working with the city government. In September 1944, for example, the city agreed to turn over to the Croatian Orthodox bishopric a confiscated apartment that had belonged to an Orthodox Serb priest who had fled the city.[120] By ensuring the return and protection of some church property, local Orthodox Croat

116. Dragostinova, "Speaking National: Nationalizing the Greeks of Bulgaria, 1900–1939," 157.
117. Tomasevich, *War and Revolution in Yugoslavia*, 548.
118. HDA, Ministarstvo pravosuđa i bogoštovlja NDH, Odjel za bogoštovlja, box 80, document 5579 (July 23, 1943).
119. Donia, *Sarajevo*, 33–34.
120. IAS, Riznično upraviteljstvo: Ured za podržavljeni imetak, box 1, document 177 (September 1, 1944).

administrators attempted to serve as custodians of the Orthodox tradition in this moment of crisis.

Ultimately, religious leaders from all three confessional communities concluded that the best means of protecting the ethics of their community, regardless of the overarching political framework they supported, would be by strengthening conservative, religious ethics and isolating their communities from other groups in the city. Whereas many Muslims and Catholics had once viewed the war as an opportunity to expand their bases and even promote conversion, late in the war they hoped to segregate their communities from the dangerous influences of outsiders, whom they blamed for both the secularization of society and the growing guerrilla movement. The Islamic Religious Community, the Catholic Church, and the Croatian Orthodox Church issued or reiterated bans on interfaith marriage and made conversion increasingly difficult as the war dragged on.[121] Although forming a unified conservative front might have been the optimal solution in their efforts to ward off the leftist resistance, religious leaders grew concerned that such unity threatened to dilute the integrity of their own confessional communities.

As the war continued and religious leaders found themselves aligned against the victors, confessional entities lost the power even to mitigate, much less challenge or reframe, secularizing agendas. Religious decrees, public lectures, and severe warnings had little sway over their starved and anxious flocks, who needed more than moral nourishment to keep them going through the war. While conventional wisdom suggests that traditionalism became more pronounced in the face of the Communist threat, in Sarajevo religious networks were becoming increasingly unsustainable. Consequently, the confessional aspect of collective identity became less salient.

• • •

The capitulation of Italy ushered in an era marked by stricter occupation policies, a surge in resistance activities, and the polarization of Sarajevo's confessional communities. So many different sides were jostling for power that political and military alliances lost meaning. Sarajevo's leaders were facing two crises simultaneously: they had been invaded, and the invasion had brought with it a different kind of modern world from the one that even the progressives had anticipated. Muslims were caught between Scylla

---

121. HDA, Ministarstvo pravosuđa i bogoštovlja NDH, Odjel za bogoštovlja, box 80, document 5579 (July 23, 1943); ABiH, Vrhovni Šerijatski Sud, box 198, document 87 (1944); *Glas pravoslavlja*, September 1, 1944, 9. This trend may have also been partly in response to an announcement by the Ustasha regime that it planned to implement civil marriage laws. See HDA, Ministarstvo pravosuđa i bogoštovlja NDH, Odjel za Pravosuđe, Pravni Institut pododsjek za ženitbeno pravo, box 1, report from the Pravni Institut podosjek za ženitbeno pravo, (1944).

and Charybdis, facing one political group that swore to stamp out all religion and another that was actively working to eradicate Muslims. The Third Reich—the empire once imagined by many Muslims as a bulwark against the Ustashas and Communists—had proven itself ineffective in securing Muslim religious and political goals. Sarajevo's Catholic Croats were hardly in a better position: it became clearer now that the Ustasha regime had fastened Croatia's independence to the Axis cause, leaving no room for an alternative. And some of Sarajevo's Orthodox leaders found themselves sleeping with the enemy in order to protect their children. Ironically, attempts to resist fragmentation within confessional communities led to greater fragmentation among them.

By 1944, the majority of Sarajevo's masses had begun to identify any critical stand against resistance as a stand for the regime. One Sarajevan, Muhamed Hadžijahić, referred to the armed resistance vaguely in the fall of 1944 as "the new movement" (*novi pokret*), which captures its nebulous quality nicely.[122] An array of movements, some armed, some peaceful, had started to assemble in the shadows of the cobblestone streets, ready to emerge at the slightest hint of the German army's retreat. That there were thousands of townsmen involved with resistance activities after 1943 but only a handful working for the Partisans and Chetniks reveals the desire among many Sarajevans to evade ideological alliances and forge a postwar order rooted in the city's own legacies. Exactly which legacies would endure, however, was still undetermined.

122. IAS, Zbirka Varia, document 487 (1944).

7

THE FINAL MONTHS

From Total War to Communist Victory

An Ustasha police agent reported in September 1944 that Sarajevans expected the worst was yet to come.[1] He was right. As the Red Army advanced across central Europe, the survival of the NDH grew ever more unlikely, and Sarajevans panicked. One by one, Germany's allies in southeastern Europe surrendered or switched sides—Romania in August, Bulgaria in September, Hungary and Serbia's puppet regime in October. Only Croatia remained standing at the Third Reich's side, an especially ignominious distinction from the postwar perspective. Driven by their ideological fervor (and lacking any real alternative), the Ustasha leaders prepared for a fight to the death.

On September 18, 1944, Ante Pavelić and Adolf Hitler met for the last time. The two leaders decided—given the turmoil within the NDH, the disintegration of Croatia's armed forces, the Red Army's advance, and the Partisans' successes—that the Ustasha regime would take over the Home Guard (the equivalent of the Nazi Party's taking over the Wehrmacht, which it did at roughly the same time) and that the German army would increase shipments of arms and ammunition to assist the new Ustasha force.[2] The deal worked out well for both. Hitler secured an ally in a strategic zone, while Pavelić, who clung to false hopes that his regime could survive, welcomed the chance to militarize his country and pursue a more aggressive agenda.

Over the next two months, Pavelić mobilized for total war. He augmented the powers of the Ustasha police and appointed top military commanders to run the government. In November he launched a popular mobilization, drafting every able-bodied man and woman from age seventeen upward into special work battalions. In December he assumed personal control of

1. HM, Ustaška Nadzorna Služba, document 3667 (September 9, 1944).
2. Redžić, *Bosnia and Herzegovina in the Second World War,* 51–53.

the new Ustasha army, promoting close friends and trusted Ustasha officers to high-ranking posts.[3] Because most of Bosnia had fallen to the Partisans or descended into anarchy, Sarajevo became a key focus of the mobilization. The Ustasha police and party bosses seized control of local institutions and cracked down on petty criminals, jailing butchers for slaughtering too many cows and arresting merchants on charges of price gouging.[4] In late October they sentenced to death twenty-four Catholic and Orthodox men for various nonviolent crimes, including forgery. The methods they employed stunned civilians. In one case, the Ustasha police killed a suspected insurgent by hammering a nail into his forehead and then presented the body to the man's relatives as a warning against joining the resistance.[5]

Keeping Hitler's side of the bargain, the German army aided its ally in its final stand. Bosnia served as the only safe corridor between Germany and the southern Balkans, and the Reich needed to ensure that the roughly three hundred thousand German troops stuck on the peninsula had a way home. Earlier in the war, the German army had used two main rail lines to transport troops and equipment back to Germany: the Višegrad-Sarajevo-Brod railway through Bosnia, which had the distinct disadvantage of running through swaths of Partisan territory, and the Skopje-Belgrade railroad, which had been the faster and safer alternative. But in October 1944, the Red Army conquered Belgrade, which forced the Germans to reroute all traffic through Sarajevo. Despite a surge in Partisan attacks in November and frequent Allied bombings of passenger trains, the Germans steadily made their way through the central Balkans, arriving in Sarajevo over the winter.[6] The dejected Wehrmacht troops were joined by various pro-German groups, notably the Albanian wartime government, which sought

3. Tomasevich, *War and Revolution in Yugoslavia*, 457–458. For Sarajevo's local Office for National Mobilization, see ABiH, Veliki Župan Vrhbosna, 1945, box 2, document 1965 (January 17, 1945). On the draft and work battalions, see reports in IAS, Kotarsko Nadzorničtvo Narodne Zaštite u Sarajevu, box 2.

4. ABiH, Državno zastupništvo u Sarajevu, box 10, document 4 (November 10, 1944); *Sarajevski Novi List,* January 25, 1945, 3.

5. *Sarajevski Novi List,* October 28, 1944. See also the postwar testimonies from 1946 in ABiH, Zemaljska komisija za utvrđivanje ratnih zločina okupatora i njihovih pomagača za BiH, box 197, document 49365, and box 195, document 493.

6. On the German army's withdrawal via Sarajevo, see Karl Hnilicka, *Das Ende auf dem Balkan 1944/45* (Musterschmidt: Gottingen, 1970), 73 and 109–120, and Erich Schmidt-Richberg, *Der Endkampf auf dem Balkan, Die Operationen der Heeresgruppe E von Griechenland bis zu den Alpen* (Heidelberg: Kurt Vowinckel Verlag, 1955), 66–69. In Hnilicka's study, there is a series of maps at the end (no page numbers) showing the German routes for retreat over the course of 1944 and 1945. The path through Serbia is shown to have been officially cut off in mid-December 1944, after which point the maps indicate that all soldiers were sent through Sarajevo. The Ustasha police also discussed the German retreat in HM, Ustaška Nadzorna Služba, document 3875 (November 12, 1944). On the Allied bombing of German trains in the region, see Michael McConville, *A Small War in the Balkans: British Military Involvement in Wartime Yugoslavia, 1941–1945* (London: Macmillan, 1986), 268 and 299.

shelter in Sarajevo in January 1945 after being chased out of Tirana by the Albanian Partisans.[7]

As German troops swamped the city, Sarajevans felt the full effects of total war. The German and Ustasha armies co-opted the entire human and material resources of the city for the war effort. They took possession of every train, wagon, car, and set of skis, leaving town officials with no means of importing food, while trapping civilians who had hoped to flee.[8] Shortages proliferated. The city reported that "nearly every day civilians and soldiers submit complaints that there are simply no vegetables to buy in the market."[9] Food, medicine, milk, even shoes were nowhere to be found. A report from the city's health commission in February 1945 complained that the German army had commandeered hospital supplies for its wounded soldiers; the lack of supplies contributed to an outbreak of lice and typhoid fever. Without pesticides—which the German army also took—town officials found it impossible to exterminate germ-carrying rodents and insects in order to contain the typhus.[10]

The Allies knew that Sarajevo was a center of German operations and thus continued to target the city. Air-raid sirens screeched through the city from morning to night, drowning out church bells and the muezzin.[11] Early in the fall, a bomb struck the Alipašin Most refugee camp, killing several hundred refugee women and children (some estimates went as high as a thousand) and destroying the camp's basic infrastructure.[12] On October 14, 1944, an Ustasha intelligence officer reported, with surprising candor, that "in the soul of every [Sarajevan] there is an inexplicable conviction that the city would be better off if the German army left the state." But he also noted, "On the other hand, there is also a fear that the Germans' departure would leave the city defenseless against its internal enemies." His words suggest that Sarajevans remained as apprehensive about the future order as they did about the current one.[13]

From September 1944 to April 1945, Sarajevo experienced its most physically and psychologically devastating chapter of the war—one characterized by bombings, police occupation, total war, terror, and the introduction of a new revolutionary government. This chapter explores the town's response

7. *Sarajevski Novi List,* January 20, 1945, 5.
8. Not a single private car remained in civilian hands as of October 1944. See ABiH, Javni Ured Rada Sarajevo, box 13, document 95 (October 10, 1944). On the confiscation of skis, see *Sarajevski Novi List,* January 19, 1945, 5.
9. IAS, Gradsko Poglavarstvo, box 1260 (December 12, 1944).
10. ABiH, Veliki Župan Vrhbosna, 1945, box 2, document 1856 (February 15, 1945).
11. For example, on November 7, 1944, a typical day, the first of seven air raid drills screeched through the city at 11:10 in the morning; the last one rang at 9:00 p.m. See IAS, Kotarsko Nadzorničtvo Narodne Zaštite u Sarajevu, monthly report, box 1 (December 1944).
12. See the report from the German consul in Sarajevo to the German embassy in Zagreb in Hoover Institute Archives, Tomasevich Papers, records from the captured German documents held at the U.S. National Archives, box 4, T:120, roll 5789 (September 9, 1944).
13. HM, Ustaška Nadzorna Služba, document 3840 (October 14, 1944).

to the gradual collapse of the NDH and the birth of the next new order, Tito's socialist Yugoslavia. It suggests, first, that members of Sarajevo's local elite refused to abandon their posts or cave in to anarchy as the public sphere imploded. Using the social, cultural, and civic networks they had fostered for three years, they sought to chaperone Sarajevo safely through this final, devastating chapter of war. In their struggle to keep the city functioning, many local leaders abandoned their political and ideological alliances and made Sarajevo itself a priority. Such a focus became increasingly difficult to maintain as terror descended upon the city in February and March 1945. Reacting to its imminent demise, the Ustasha regime lashed out at Sarajevans in irrational, vengeful acts of cruelty that left the town reeling in a state of shock. Sarajevo was on the brink of a psychological collapse when the Partisans arrived in April 1945. The new occupiers took advantage of this mood to secure the town and fill the vacuum of leadership. While the complex process of socialist revolution would take years, the Partisans set it in motion within days of Sarajevo's liberation. Stunned from the barbaric viciousness of the Ustasha regime's final days, most Sarajevans simply accepted it.

The Collapsing Public Sphere

The onset of total war in the fall of 1944 contributed to the final implosion of Sarajevo's local government. Municipal authorities were expected to provide services that previously had been the responsibility of national authorities.[14] But they could handle little more than the city's basic safety and security needs. Few schools began fall classes in September 1944, and those that did closed soon after.[15] Coal shortages and electrical outages forced other public institutions to lock their doors for the winter. By November the city government was experiencing extensive labor shortages; by January 1945 the only department at the mayor's office still functioning regularly was the new Office for National Mobilization.[16] City employees refused to work for their salaries alone, demanding food in addition to money.[17] Sarajevo was shutting down.

The Ustasha regime exacerbated the situation by treating local officials suspiciously. After the untimely death of County Executive Muhamed

14. This is the opposite dynamic from the one that typically occurred in capital cities at war. See Jean-Louis Robert and Jay Winter, "Conclusions: Towards a Social History of Capital Cities at War," in Winter and Robert, *Capital Cities at War*, 1:547.

15. See a report on the status of Sarajevo schools in IAS, Narodna Uzdanica, box 49, folder 1928 (October 7, 1944).

16. For labor shortages resulting from the national mobilization, see ABiH, Veliki Župan Vrhbosna, 1945, box 2, document 1965 (January 17, 1945), and ABiH, Veliki Župan Vrhbosna, 1945, box 4, document 3113 (March 16, 1945).

17. ABiH, Javni Ured Rada Sarajevo, box 12, document 215 (April 4, 1945).

212 ~ CHAPTER 7

Kulenović in early November, Ante Pavelić appointed Ragib Ćapljić, an enthusiastic Muslim Croat, to fill the post. Ćapljić had served earlier in the war as the county executive of Tuzla, and in that capacity he had been instrumental in rallying Muslims against the Chetnik uprising.[18] Unlike many of the Muslim politicians in Sarajevo, who were now considered disloyal, Zagreb trusted Ćapljić to carry out orders. Indeed, Ćapljić placed the regime's concerns ahead of the city's needs, even when doing so irritated local politicians. He refused to allow Mayor Repovac to collect road taxes from county departments, and he denied military exemptions to town officials.[19] Then in December, around the same time that Ante Pavelić assumed command of the Ustasha army, Sarajevo's Catholic deputy mayor, Ante Glavina, was promoted to mayor. Glavina was an engineer, one of the most respected professions in the region.[20] He was also the first non-Muslim appointed to run the municipality during the war, and his appointment clearly signified the regime's complete mistrust of Sarajevo's Muslim elite.

Mayor Glavina was hardly in a better position than his predecessors. He, too, recognized the grave pressures of mismanagement and total war. Although the facade of city and county governance remained, by January 1945 local Ustasha officials were overseeing civilian matters in Sarajevo, focusing especially on local elements of national mobilization. A leading Ustasha officer, Ivica Frković, worked closely with the Ustasha police and security chief Ivo Bogdan, who announced in early January that nothing would stop the Ustasha regime from consolidating the Croat nation and purging Sarajevo of its "enemies"—a term that increasingly referred to ordinary Sarajevans trying to survive the war.[21] On January 17 Mayor Glavina complained to the county executive's office that between the draft and the budget crunch, he was left with only a handful of unqualified employees in the city. He noted that the city government "no longer has even one employee with a high school diploma, let alone any form of

18. Ćapljić ran the county from Sarajevo from November 5, 1944, to April 6, 1945. For background on him, see Sarajevski Novi List, November 2, 1944, 3, and Sajma Sarić, "Arhivski fond velika župe Vrhbosne," Glasnik Arhiva i društva arhivskih radnika Bosne i Hercegovine 14–15 (1974–75): 39. Ćapljić's role in Tuzla is discussed in Esad S. Tihić, "Jedinice domobranske dobrovoljačke pukovnije (Domdo) na teritoriji Trebave, Ratiša i Posavine (1942–1943)," Gračanički Glasnik 2 (November 1996).

19. ABiH, Veliki Župan Vrhbosna, 1945, box 1, document 791 (November 15, 1944).

20. A short biography of Glavina can be found in Sarajevski Novi List, May 23, 1944, 5. Unfortunately, not much has been written about him. Both he and Mayor Repovac are conspicuously missing from histories of the city's municipal government, even from the anthology of Sarajevo's mayors, Milenko Pajić, Sarajevski Gradonačelnici (Sarajevo: Večernje Novine, 1998). Moreover, the exact date of Glavina's appointment is unclear from the documents. Repovac was still mayor when County Executive Kulenović died in early November, as he served in an official capacity at the funeral. See Sarajevski Novi List, November 2, 1944, 3. By January 1945, however, his name disappears from local documents and from the city's press, and Glavina is listed as the mayor. See, for example, ABiH, Veliki Župan Vrhbosna, 1945, box 2, document 1965 (January 17, 1945).

21. Sarajevski Novi List, January 4, 1945, 2.

higher education."[22] The city could not compose a budget for 1945 because its entire financial staff had been called to national service.[23] The city courts reported similar problems. By March 1945 not a single court employee had finished high school.[24] Even county executive Ćapljić had to scale back his staff, handing over civil responsibilities to the Ustasha police and military commanders.[25]

If Sarajevo's civic institutions were going to survive the war, something had to change. Sarajevo's High Sharia Court argued as much in late 1944, suggesting that "state authorities are too occupied to assist us or to help individuals. It is therefore the duty of philanthropic and humanitarian groups to do whatever they can to alleviate these hard conditions."[26] And they did. It was not in the character of local leaders to watch helplessly as their city deteriorated and their communities suffered. Thus while the Ustasha regime mobilized for total war, a handful of Catholic and Muslim leaders running the well-known groups Merhamet, Napredak, and Narodna Uzdanica took up where the municipal government had left off and attempted to sustain Sarajevo's social services, educational system, and cultural life. The private societies generally worked independently, coordinating their efforts only to combat the city's gravest problems, like the famine in February 1945.[27]

They faced an uphill battle. Each of the private societies was run by a small core group of six to ten men, while their broader membership numbers rapidly declined over the winter.[28] The state's inefficiency made their work difficult, as did the corrupt Ustashas who hoarded money intended for social services.[29] The German command posed another problem. German officials capriciously confiscated whatever property or supplies they considered possibly useful, often in an offensive manner. In November 1944, for example, German soldiers ripped down the fence of a local Catholic boarding school and stole artwork from the school's offices.[30] On December 7 representatives from the German army arrived in the offices of Narodna Uzdanica and *Novi Behar,* the Muslim cultural society and its sister press, and announced that the army would requisition the building at 3:00 p.m. that day. This was the most recent in a series of

22. ABiH, Veliki Župan Vrhbosna, 1945, box 2, document 1965 (January 17, 1945).
23. Ibid., box 3, document 2177 (March 3, 1945).
24. Ibid., box 4, document 2796 (March 16, 1945).
25. Ibid., box 2, document 1993 (February 16, 1945).
26. Ibid., box 7, document 435 (1944).
27. In early February members of the societies gathered to discuss the food crisis and figure out ways to resolve it. See the meeting's report, ABiH, Hrvatsko kulturno društvo Napredak, box 155, document 160 (February 19, 1945).
28. For examples see ibid., box 155, document 26 (December 1944); IAS, Narodna Uzdanica, box 49, folder 1928 (January 20, 1945).
29. IAS, Merhamet, box 6, document 259 (February 9, 1945).
30. ABiH, Hrvatsko kulturno društvo Napredak, box 154, document 1290 (November 20, 1944).

such confiscations, and the organizations' leaders were irate. The president of Narodna Uzdanica stormed down to the mayor's office, claiming that the Germans had deliberately and systematically disrupted the important work of his society, seizing all its prime real estate but never using it.[31] In another example, a group of German policemen broke into the offices of El-Hidaje that December, searching for information about affiliates of the Young Muslims, who they believed were working against them.[32] The Germans were no doubt responding to the growing anti-German sentiment among Muslims after the death of the El-Hidaje leader Mehmed Handžić in August 1944, as well as the defection of more than two thousand Muslim soldiers from the Waffen SS Handžar Division to Tito's camp.[33]

Despite these obstacles, the private societies carried on with their work, focusing on three main issues: food acquisition, refugee care, and education. On the few occasions when food arrived in the city, the Ustasha authorities asked the societies to dole out provisions.[34] Most of the time, however, the groups could only resentfully distribute the regime's valueless food coupons. Napredak thus opened its own food kitchens and worked closely with the Red Cross to develop a system of "grain trains" for Sarajevo, mirroring a program developed in Zagreb to shuttle food into the city after the military confiscated all the trains.[35] In mid-February 1945, Napredak, Narodna Uzdanica, and Merhamet worked directly with local officials at the train station and in the Department of Agriculture to try to procure food, presenting plans to the local Ustasha authorities.[36]

Feeding civilians became more difficult as the refugee count climbed. Despite the Allied bombings, Sarajevo remained one of the only safe havens for peasants evacuating southern and eastern Bosnia. The Department of Refugees was defunct by 1945, so refugees often had to fend for themselves in finding food, firewood, and housing; many resorted to theft and prostitution. Although a few social programs still existed, new refugees were at a distinct disadvantage because city aid programs now had a six-month residency requirement.[37] The refugee count exceeded fifty thousand in January 1945 and continued to expand throughout February and March.[38]

With the government incapable of resolving the city's urgent social crises, Merhamet decided to take over refugee services. Since the middle of

31. See the lengthy letter from Narodna Uzdanica to the mayor's office in IAS, Gradsko Poglavarstvo, box 1260 (December 13, 1944).

32. IAS, Zbirka Varia, document 105 (December 1944).

33. Hoover Institute Archives, Tomasevich Papers, records from the captured German documents held at the U.S. National Archives, box 5, T: 120, roll 5784 (October 5, 1944). On Handžić's death, see *El-Hidaje*, September 19, 1944, 82–86.

34. HM, Ustaška Nadzorna Služba, document 3921 (January 2, 1945).

35. ABiH, Hrvatsko kulturno društvo Napredak, box 155, document 1 (January 2, 1945), document 37 (January 13, 1945), and document 139 (February 16, 1945).

36. Ibid., box 155, document 160 (February 19, 1945).

37. *Katolički Tjednik,* January 14, 1945, 2.

38. *Sarajevski Novi List,* March 2, 1945, 3.

1944, town officials had relied heavily on the Muslim humanitarian group to handle refugees—Muslim and Christian alike. At one point during the previous summer, Sarajevo's officials had even expected Merhamet to relocate the refugees and their shacks from the camp at the Alipašin Most into the city.[39] Although such acts went beyond Merhamet's charitable mission of aiding the Muslim poor, the society's leaders felt an obligation to help the city government and grudgingly took over many of its social services. After months of frustrating and inconclusive meetings on the city's refugee problem, in January 1945 Merhamet decided to develop a tracking system to process and monitor the thousands of refugee requests for food, shelter, and clothing. By the end of February the organization had streamlined the city's distribution services for refugees of all backgrounds.[40] While taking responsibility for the city's poorest, Merhamet made sure that local politicians knew that it was going above and beyond. "Having actively participated for many years in solving the numerous problems of our community," Merhamet complained to the mayor's office that February, "this society incidentally assumed responsibility for most public functions that should have fallen to state agencies."[41] Both sides were fully aware, however, that the state was incapable of handling even the most basic social services.

Just as community leaders shouldered the brunt of humanitarian work, so, too, did they assume responsibility for other civil services like education. When it became clear that many public schools would not open for the 1944–45 school year, Narodna Uzdanica opened its own. In October 1944 the society hired teachers to work after hours and improvised classroom space in its offices.[42] Classes commenced immediately with a curriculum that included German, Croatian, Latin, math, social studies, chemistry, and choir for both elementary and high school students. Though Narodna Uzdanica anticipated enrolling 350 students, by November 17, 463 pupils were attending classes.[43] Despite the society's Muslim majority and focus, the student body included Orthodox and Catholic children as well.

Napredak, the Catholic Croat cultural society, remained equally committed to preserving education in the city, earmarking money for stipends and education "whether schools were working or not." The society berated Zagreb for its failures in the city, sending a letter to the Ministry of Education in October that criticized the German army's disrespect for Sarajevo's education system, the scarcity of school books in the city, and the regime's apathy toward educating Sarajevo's youths. Napredak also fought with local

39. IAS, Merhamet, minutes, box 9, folder 1944 (August 7, 1944).

40. IAS, Merhamet, box 6, document 284 (February 2, 1945) and document 485 (February 22, 1945).

41. Ibid., document 259 (February 9, 1945).

42. See reports from Narodna Uzdanica's minute books in the fall of 1944, such as those in IAS, Narodna Uzdanica, zapisnik (October 26, 1944).

43. IAS, Narodna Uzdanica, reports, box 49, folder 1928 (October 7, 1944, and November 14, 1944).

officials for heating in classrooms. In addition to running classes, Napredak promoted education through its private library, which served 1,171 readers in 1944 and remained open well into 1945.[44]

When the last of Sarajevo's fourteen public schools closed in January 1945, responsibility for education fell entirely on community leaders. In February the local press congratulated Narodna Uzdanica for educating 563 high school students.[45] More than 100 high school students at Napredak passed their exams and completed the semester that February.[46] Hurijet, the Muslim craftsmen society, opened a small technical school that graduated about a hundred students in February 1945. They were the first craftsmen to complete formal training in two years.[47] Although it is remarkable that these societies managed to sustain some form of education in the city, it cannot be overlooked that thousands of students went without formal education throughout the last years of the war.

Though the local elite felt a duty to aid their city, charity was not their sole motivation in setting up schools and food kitchens. For many community leaders, social work became a means of garnering power. It gave them leverage in negotiations with the regime and a voice in shaping their community's ethics during a time of transition. For example, as Merhamet assumed control of the city's refugee population in January, the group pressured the regime to allow humanitarian work to count as military service, hoping to free volunteers from the regime's harsh labor requirements.[48] At the same time, the group continued its campaign to preserve and proliferate traditional Islamic values. This had been one of the organization's goals since 1943, but the Ustasha regime in effect promoted their cause by integrating negative rhetoric about Muslims into its national mobilization campaign. In one hostile article in *Sarajevski Novi List*, the regime warned Sarajevo's Muslims that they would have to accept the "modern way" (i.e., the Ustasha way) or be run over by it. The article accused Sarajevo's Muslims of backwardness, arguing that they hampered progress and cultural development in the city. In an especially cutting attack, the piece claimed that as a group, Sarajevo's Muslims lacked the sophistication and intelligence of their Muslim ancestors.[49] Such rhetoric was accompanied by new anti-Muslim legislation that fall. For example, Zagreb limited the parts of the country that could recognize Islamic holidays as state holidays and

44. ABiH, Hrvatsko kulturno društvo Napredak, box 154, document 1083 (October 21, 1944) and document 1172 (November 4, 1944); box 155, document 26 (December 13, 1944) and document 70 (January 1945).

45. *Sarajevski Novi List*, February 5, 1945, 3.

46. ABiH, Hrvatsko kulturno društvo Napredak, box 155, document 138 (February 14, 1945).

47. *Sarajevski Novi List*, February 7, 1945, 5.

48. This had been on Merhamet's agendas since late 1944. See IAS, Merhamet, zapisnik, box 6 (January 5, 1945).

49. *Sarajevski Novi List*, September 19, 1944, 10.

insisted that Muslim women working in Sarajevo's religious institutions be mobilized for the war effort. Muslim leaders argued that these women were the equivalent of Christian nuns, who were exempt from the general mobilization because of their religious position.[50] But their pleas went unheard. Islam was no longer on equal footing with Catholicism, not even in the Ustasha propaganda. To combat this negative press, Merhamet and other Muslim organizations sought to strengthen the idea and practices of Islam through lectures, meetings, and social work.

Communism and its growing appeal among Muslim peasants and youths further unsettled Sarajevo's Muslim elite, who feared that regardless of the war's outcome, Islam would be its greatest casualty. In November 1944 El-Hidaje published an article in its journal that acknowledged—for the first time—that the ulema were partly to blame for the divisions in the Muslim community because they had refused to reach out to secular Muslims. However, it also assigned blame to the intelligentsia, noting that they had sinned by ignoring Islamic law and culture. Both sides, the article continued, would need to accept their faults and work together if they hoped to save Islam in Bosnia.[51] Religious leaders tried to boost the influence of Islam in popular culture, publishing new school textbooks with lessons in Arabic and monographs that emphasized a stricter interpretation of Islam.[52] Mustafa Busuladžić, an important Muslim thinker, published widely in both the secular and religious presses, hoping to reach every corner of his community with a warning: as a minority in Christian Europe, Muslims needed to stand together and fight anyone who stood against "our religion, family values, and life views."[53]

The future of Muslim orphans living in state homes became a major source of concern. In December 1944 Reis-ul-ulema Bašić initiated a program of mandatory Islamic education in state orphanages.[54] But this would hardly safeguard the children if the regime changed hands. Thus in January Merhamet teamed up with local imams to remove Muslim orphans from institutions and find them private homes. Despite mass upheaval across Bosnia and the dangers of guerrilla warfare, volunteer social workers from Sarajevo organized by Merhamet traveled around Bosnia over the next two months, surveying children's homes and identifying good Muslim families to take the orphans.[55]

50. HDA, Ministarstvo pravosuđa i bogoštovlja NDH, Odjel za Pravosuđe, box 31, document I104 (October 23, 1944); ABiH, Veliki Župan Vrhbosna, 1945, box 2, document 1325 (January 27, 1945).
51. El-Hidaje, November 26, 1944, 141–143.
52. See the promotion of Kasim Handžić's book Muslimanske imovinske dužnosti, which was published in February 1945. Sarajevski Novi List, February 15, 1945, 5. On the reintroduction of Arabic, see ARIZBiH, Ulema Medžlis, document 502 (January 12, 1945).
53. Mustafa Busuladžić, "Naš životni put," El-Hidaje, February 25, 1945, 255–259.
54. ARIZBiH, Ulema Medžlis, document 222 (December 12, 1944).
55. IAS, Merhamet, box 6, document 685 (March 20, 1945).

In contrast to the Muslim community, which had found causes to unite it, Sarajevo's Catholics remained bitterly divided, particularly when it came to supporting the Ustasha regime. In January 1945 the Croats running Napredak confronted the Ustasha army regarding its policies of drafting Catholic youths. In late December Ustasha soldiers had allegedly rounded up a group of eleventh- and twelfth-grade Catholic students from the streets of Sarajevo and deployed them to Zagreb. Upon their arrival in the capital city, the boys discovered that they had been listed as "volunteers" rather than "draftees," so they left the army base and returned home. Hearing of the teenagers' audacious desertion, Sarajevo's Ustasha police organized a night raid of the students' homes, capturing all the deserters and sending them back to Zagreb.

Outraged, Napredak sent a letter to the local Ustasha official in charge, Ivan Frković, warning him that the draft and night raids were turning Sarajevo's Catholics against the state.[56] Napredak worried that the regime had failed to grasp the importance of cultivating an educated and nationally conscious generation that could help rebuild the city after the war. They advised Frković, "Napredak considers it an obligation to draw your most serious attention to the inconvenience of this order, which is damaging not only to the individuals involved but to the entire generation of Croat intellectuals." The leaders of Napredak had invested time and money in these students' education despite the severe hardships of war. In a way, they looked at the draft as a personal affront. Warning Frković that "our young country and its successful future" depends on these educated youths, Napredak demanded that the students be returned to Sarajevo and exempted from serving in the army, that the regime forbid local Ustasha police from carrying out street raids on high school students, and that Ustasha authorities desist in the cruel practice of night raids.[57] To Napredak, the survival of the Croat nation as a cultural and political project depended foremost on the survival of Croats. The NDH might be doomed, but the nation would survive. They were hopeful, as were many Croats once affiliated with the Croat Peasant Party, that despite their participation in the NDH, they could still play a role in building the postwar order, at least on a local level. Thus in the winter of 1945 they believed that the immediate needs of Sarajevo's Croats trumped the abstract national good of Croatia. The Ustashas could find their soldiers somewhere else.

By contrast, Archbishop Šarić and church leaders seemed to believe that there was no future for Sarajevo's Catholics except as a part of the NDH. The church encouraged local Catholics to leave the city to fight against the Communists.[58] *Katolički Tjednik* even hinted that the Ustashas had to

---

56. ABiH, Hrvatsko kulturno društvo Napredak, box 155, document 180 (March 1, 1945)
57. Ibid., document 180 (March 1, 1945).
58. *Katolički Tjednik*, March 18, 1945, 4.

lash out against Catholics because their disobedience to the state was tantamount to disobeying God.[59] The paper used the prospect of defeat as an opportunity to criticize the community for yielding to negative influences. For example, one article harangued against women in public life, calling them "freaks" who sadistically enjoyed men's misfortunes and connived to destroy traditional society.[60] It was becoming clear that if faced with the alternative of a Communist regime or one in exile, the archbishop and his circle would choose the latter.

By early 1945, Sarajevo had become little more than a cog in the Ustasha and German military machine. The city's infrastructure could not handle the strains of the war, and so it collapsed. Pavelić's regime had nothing left to offer. It could not secure food, medical supplies, or coal; it could not pay the salaries of soldiers, workers, or civil servants.[61]

Taking advantage of the deteriorating situation, the city's Communists, under the leadership of Secretary Vladimir Perić, spent the long winter months preparing for an uprising. Party members used the refugee traffic to smuggle books by Marxist thinkers into the city, hoping to win over some of Sarajevo's intellectuals.[62] They also developed propaganda that was tailored to the Sarajevo audience, broadcast news from underground radios, and recruited civil servants working for the Germans and the local government. The party had no central headquarters other than Perić's apartment; different cells, usually made up of five people, were organized in private homes, where they focused primarily on gathering intelligence.[63] As the city's public sphere continued to collapse in the early part of 1945, party reports began to discuss a surge in Partisan activities, especially among Muslims.[64] In the end, the local Ustasha regime seems to have served as the Communists' most effective propaganda tool, as their terrorizing methods slowly convinced most Sarajevans that any governmental option would be preferable to the one in front of them.

But this took time. Although most Sarajevans detested the regime, Communism as an ideology still failed to resonate with the majority, a fact suggesting that elite efforts to uphold particular social and cultural traditions had been somewhat successful. As late as November 1944, a local Communist correspondent wrote to Partisan headquarters that in Sarajevo,

59. Ibid., January 7, 1945, 1.
60. Ibid., January 28, 1945, 2.
61. This is apparent in numerous appeals found in the records of the city government and the humanitarian organizations. See, for example, IAS, Gradsko Poglavarstvo, petitions, box 1260 (December 1944).
62. ABiH, Zbirka NOR-a Okružni Komitet KPJ Sarajevo, box 1, document 32 (December 1944).
63. Mira Stanišić-Popović, "Posljednji sastanak mjesnog komiteta u okupiranom gradu," in Albahari et al., Sarajevo u Revoluciji, 4:176–177; Dušan Uzelac and Muharem Kreso, "Sarajevska Operacija," in Albahari et al., Sarajevo u Revoluciji, 4:682–683, and 699–700.
64. ABiH, Zbirka NOR-a Okružni Komitet KPJ Sarajevo, box 1, document 62 (February 26, 1945).

"the people are afraid of us." He described how Sarajevo Serbs feared that the Muslims would turn against them, while Muslims contended that the Partisans had fallen into Serb hands and might bring back the Serb king. He also claimed that Muslims overwhelmingly believed that the Home Guard would better protect them from the Chetniks, a perception that likely stemmed from Partisan-Chetnik collaboration earlier in the war. The correspondent requested that party officials infiltrate the city, a request echoed in late January by another local party member, who encouraged regional committee members to disguise themselves as refugees from eastern Bosnia.[65] While acknowledging their difficulty in rallying support, local party members simultaneously emphasized that most Sarajevans were—and always had been—against the Ustasha regime. In one debriefing, a Serb Communist sympathizer noted that few of the city's Muslims and Catholics had engaged in anti-Serb behavior during the war.[66] The problem was not that Sarajevans liked or agreed with the Ustasha agenda but that they feared the Communists.

At All Costs: The Carnage of *Die Festung*

In late January 1945, the German army moved its supreme command (*Oberkommando*) from Sarajevo north to Nova Gradiška, leaving about thirty-five thousand soldiers in Sarajevo.[67] Around the same time, tens of thousands of Partisan soldiers mobilized in Bosnia's mountains and countryside, capturing Mostar, Višegrad, and Travnik—major cities to Sarajevo's north, east, and west—over the next month.[68] In early February, the Partisan command met in Belgrade and mapped out Operation Sarajevo, a campaign to liberate Bosnia's capital. In light of the grave food shortages, German and Ustasha leaders knew it was only a matter of time before rebellion erupted in Sarajevo. But they refused to give up the city just yet. In mid-February, Hitler ordered his commander of southeastern Europe, air force marshal Alexander Löhr, and the highest-ranking German in Zagreb, Field Marshal Maximilian von Weichs, to keep a firm grip on Sarajevo and its surrounding railways at any cost.[69] He declared Sarajevo a *Festung*—a city to be defended forcefully—and assigned General Heinz Kathner as *Kampfkommandantur* of Sarajevo. Kathner's primary assignment was to prevent the Partisans from taking the city.[70]

---

65. Ibid., document 13 (November 14, 1944).
66. Ibid., document 61 (February 22, 1945).
67. Schmidt-Richberg, *Der Endkampf auf dem Balkan*, 96. See also Donia, *Sarajevo*, 198.
68. Uzelac and Kreso, "Sarajevska Operacija," 4:671–672.
69. Redžić, *Bosnia and Herzegovina in the Second World War*, 54.
70. Uzelac and Kreso, "Sarajevska Operacija," 4:673.

Ante Pavelić then appointed General Vjekoslav Max Luburić as his representative in Sarajevo, awarding him far-reaching powers to destroy the local insurgency. Luburić belonged to the inner circle of Ustasha extremists who had lived together in exile before 1941. A Catholic from Mostar, he had been good friends with top Ustasha officials in Bosnia, such as Jure Frančetić, the first Ustasha deputy of the region. Like many of the Ustasha commanders, Luburić had had no formal military training before 1941. He nevertheless had received the illustrious post as chief of the Ustasha concentration camps at the start of the war. He oversaw the deaths of an estimated two hundred thousand prisoners from 1941 to 1943 and was responsible for many of the atrocities associated with Jasenovac. Referred to in the histories of the period as a "sadistically creative specialist in police terror" and "a monstrous cutthroat sadist," Luburić arrived in Sarajevo on February 15 and put his brutal skills to work.[71] General Kathner held a dinner in his honor, informally giving German authorization for him to do whatever was needed to defend the city. Although the Germans would attempt to minimize their involvement with Luburić—prohibiting press coverage of his activities—they were aware of his past acts. In December 1943, for example, local German officers had written a report on Ustasha officials in the region, noting that Luburić was one of the most "blind followers" of Pavelic and would do whatever the Poglavnik asked of him.[72]

In the days that followed, terror descended upon Sarajevo. General Luburić appointed nine Ustasha officers to a special task force. The men worked closely with the Ustasha secret police, but ultimately Luburić laid down the law. He established headquarters at a villa in the center of town that became known as the "house of terror."[73] Mass arrests commenced immediately. In late February the Luburić crew detained two hundred of the workers at the Home Guard weapons' factory, whom they accused of treason. The police also arrested several hundred store owners on charges of price gouging.[74] According to Partisan reports, Luburić's agents contemplated broad arrests of Muslims, whether they aligned with the Ustashas or not.[75] They also hunted down the estimated two hundred Jews known to be

71. The quotes come from Donia, *Sarajevo*, 197, and from Slavko Dadić, "Posljednji dani okupatorske tiranije u Sarajevu," in Albahari et al., *Sarajevo u Revoluciji*, 4:182. For general background on Luburić, see also Tomasevich, *War and Revolution in Yugoslavia*, 458, 462, 571, 722.
72. Hoover Institute Archives, Tomasevich Papers, records from the captured German documents held at the U.S. National Archives, box 4, T:120, roll 5793 (December 17, 1943).
73. On Luburić's arrival and the house of terror, see Dadić, "Posljednji dani okupatorske tiranije u Sarajevu," 4:182–184.
74. ABiH, Zemaljska komisija za utvrđivanje ratnih zločina okupatora i njihovih pomagača za BiH, box 195, document 669 (1946); *Sarajevski Novi List*, March 15, 1945, 3.
75. ABiH, Zbirka NOR-a Okružni Komitet KPJ Sarajevo, box 1, document 62 (February 26, 1945).

Figure 10. Excavation of the house
of terror, April 1945. Courtesy of
the Historical Museum of Bosnia
and Herzegovina.

still living in the city.[76] The arrests and police raids terrified the city. People
regularly disappeared into the house of terror and were never heard from
again. Mutilated bodies were sometimes found later on the streets; others
were buried in the villa's yard, to be excavated in the weeks after the Ustashas left the city.[77] Adding to the panic, the Germans threatened to arrest
any civilians or soldiers who abandoned posts on German bases or in the
Waffen SS units.[78]

On March 1, in the midst of this new wave of terror, the Partisans officially began Operation Sarajevo.[79] The Partisan army burrowed into the
hillsides, and insurgent activities and sabotage attacks increased in the city.
Luburić responded by establishing the Criminal War Court of Commander
Luburić, which oversaw the interrogation and execution of several hundred

76. ABiH, Zemaljska komisija za utvrđivanje ratnih zločina okupatora i njihovih pomagača
za BiH, Bujas report, box 3, 23–25.
77. Photographs of the excavation and the bodies found throughout the neighborhood can
be seen in HM, Zbirke Fotografija, fond NOB. See, for example, images 2097, 2100, and 2104.
78. *Sarajevski Novi List*, February 10, 1945, 5.
79. Uzelac and Kreso, "Sarajevska Operacija," 4:671.

people accused of treason during that month.[80] The first group, tried on March 5, 1945, consisted of seventeen Muslim refugees from Mostar, the commander's hometown. Over the next two weeks, the court tried men and women from every ethnoreligious community in the city. Some of the prisoners had been incarcerated by the Ustasha police months earlier; others were picked up off the streets and accused of bogus offenses, such as an attempted assassination of Luburić. The Ustasha police even arrested a group of actors who refused to perform in a play. The arbitrariness of the process compounded the threat and thus the fear for Sarajevans. Anyone could be a victim. Because apartments had changed hands so many times during the war, the Luburić agents occasionally targeted the wrong person. Thus, for example, in an attempt to arrest a Sarajevo Serb man, they detained instead an innocent Muslim refugee woman from Trebinje who happened to be squatting in his former apartment.[81]

Survivors recalled that the Luburić agents had a favorite interrogation method. They tied a prisoner's hands behind his back, pulled his hands between his legs, placed a thick stick behind his knees, and then hung the prisoner upside down between two tables and beat him until near death. After interrogation, the agent would either execute the prisoner or deport him to a camp. Anyone caught escaping from the trains—and a few tried— was shot on sight. In some cases, General Luburić invited family members of prisoners into his office for a chat, seemingly enjoying their anguish as he informed them that their loved ones had been tortured and condemned to death. This kind of personal contact served as part of the terror, as did the public nature of the atrocities. One witness asserted that an execution in the Ciglane neighborhood on March 15 was the most horrific event he had witnessed during the war.[82]

As Luburić and his crew settled into the city, some Sarajevans hid in bunkers afraid for their lives, even though no bombs had fallen for weeks.[83] Fear permeated the city. Everyone knew about the house of terror, but no one knew until after the war what had occurred inside. Even the officials running the regime's local paper appeared to be nervous about it, publishing an article in mid-March that encouraged Luburić and his men to allow prisoners to spend time outside. While the authors couched

80. On the court and its first trials, see Dadić, "Posljednji dani okupatorske tiranije u Sarajevu," 4:185–191. See also Donia, *Sarajevo*, 197.

81. All these examples come from testimonies compiled immediately after the war. The testimonies are listed by the year they were taken and can be found in boxes 194–197 of ABiH, Zemaljska komisija za utvrđivanje ratnih zločina okupatora i njihovih pomagača za BiH. For those listed above, see box 195, document 5971/6 (1945) and document 485 (1946), and box 196, document 48235 (1945).

82. For testimonies that refer to torture, see ibid., box 195, document 5971/6 (1945). On executions, see ibid., box 197, document 49372 (1946), and box 194, document 239 (1946). On meetings with family members, see ibid., box 195, document 5971/6 (1945).

83. This is the theme of an article in *Katolički Tjednik*, March 4, 1945, 3.

their advice in practical terms—that the prisoners should be put to work cleaning the city rather than eating free food in their cells—the tone of the article, including a note that it was unhealthy for prisoners to remain locked indoors all the time, suggests that even regime insiders disliked the Luburić tactics.[84]

Meanwhile, Operation Sarajevo gained momentum. The Partisans closed in on the city, successfully isolating it from the rest of the NDH. On March 13 the Department of Labor and Employment issued its yearly report for 1944, noting that all of its branch offices in Bosnia now fell "outside the jurisdiction of the Croat government," except for those in Sarajevo and Banja Luka. Sarajevo's Red Cross received correspondence from regional chapters in Jajce and Prijedor on stationery bearing the agency's new name in that part of the region: the Red Cross of the Federation of Bosnia (which was the Communists' new name for Bosnia).[85] Such isolation fueled panic. Sarajevans wanted to organize their finances and secure their property before the next changing of the guard, not realizing that their efforts would be futile in the new system. Muslims and Catholics who had accumulated wealth during the war tried to purchase homes and businesses, while German émigrés fought for the proceeds from property that the Ustasha authorities had auctioned off in February and March.[86] People close to the regime began to flee the town.

On March 16, 1945, Luburić, Frković, and other top local Ustasha officials convened a well-publicized meeting that brought together a thousand representatives from the Ustasha Party and army, Sarajevo's government, the German consul, and Sarajevo's local organizations. They all renewed their vows to the NDH and denounced the Yalta Conference, Bolshevism, and Tito's regime in Belgrade.[87] Among those present were the well-respected and outspoken Muslim leaders Edhem Muladbić, the president of Narodna Uzdanica; Mustafa Softić, the former mayor of Sarajevo; and Kasim Dobrača, the president of El-Hidaje. Given the political climate of the city, many of these men were probably coerced into participating. Yet a handful of Muslims continued to support the NDH. Confronted by the depressing choice between an Ustasha or a Communist regime, they supported Pavelić's regime in its final hour, hoping that a new conservative government might take its place. A few Muslims even advocated forming a new guerrilla force to fight the Communists.[88] The prospect of allowing Sarajevo to fall to Tito and Communism was unbearable.

84. *Sarajevski Novi List*, March 15, 1945, 3.
85. ABiH, Društvo Crveni Križ, box 25, document 1754 (March 21, 1945).
86. See, for example, ABiH, Ured za kolonizaciju-Sarajevo, box 30, document 532 (February 9, 1945), and box 31, document 1190 (March 14, 1945) and document 1110 (February 22, 1945).
87. *Sarajevski Novi List*, March 16, 1945, 1.
88. Redžić, *Bosnia and Herzegovina in the Second World War*, 110 and 191.

Archbishop Šarić and the Catholics running *Katolički Tjednik* agreed, emphasizing to readers that Communism was dangerous and incompatible with Catholicism and that their only option would be to fight it.[89] On March 18, in what would be the final wartime edition of the paper, the editors published a scathing satire of Tito and the Communists. Set in the Kingdom of Mbobi, a fictional African kingdom, the story described a meeting of the anti-Fascist council where wild animals gathered around the table to listen to the King Lion preach. The Mbobi, beastly creatures lacking any basic humanity, pounded on their drums of war, while the King Lion—representing Tito—slapped his belly, which contained the entire leg of a hippopotamus—a symbol of Sarajevo, of Catholicism, and of Croatia. Stressing that the Communists were the antithesis of white European civilization, the church called on all the Catholics of Sarajevo to travel across the great water and search for "Moses." He would help them rebuild the community and return to the region to teach the white men how to be decent and civilized again.[90]

Sometime in the next week, Archbishop Šarić, along with his secretary and closest circle of clergy, took the lead and fled Sarajevo. Afraid for their lives at the hands of the Partisans, eighty Franciscan friars followed suit.[91] As the Partisan forces victoriously swept through Bosnia, the archbishop's circle made its way to a monastery in Klagenfurt, Austria, and later to Spain and Argentina, where it would support a nationalist émigré movement that continued for the next few decades to call on Croats to fight against the Communists.[92]

Despite the situation's hopelessness, the arrests and trials of friends and neighbors, and the exodus of people close to the regime, a handful of committed local leaders continued to impress upon their communities the importance of maintaining their institutions and keeping some semblance of Sarajevo's civic culture alive. Clubs petitioned to hold social events and lecturers at the faculties of medicine and theology held special talks. Intellectuals insisted that—despite the difficulties of war and severe paper shortages—it was imperative for the city's spirit that they maintain an active print and literary culture.[93] The few men left at Napredak and Narodna Uzdanica that March carried on with discussions of curriculum and school functions.[94] And the Croatian State Theater opened its doors each night to entertain soldiers and civilians seeking to escape from the reality around

89. *Katolički Tjednik*, March 11, 1945, 2.
90. Ibid., March 18, 1945, 4.
91. HDA, Ministarstvo pravosuđa i bogoštovlja NDH, Odjel za bogoštovlja, box 137, document 2065 (April 14, 1945).
92. Tomasevich, *War and Revolution in Yugoslavia*, 558.
93. *Sarajevski Novi List*, January 17, 1945, 5.
94. ABiH, Hrvatsko kulturno društvo Napredak, box 155, document 287 (March 20, 1945); IAS, Narodna Uzdanica, zapisnik (March 7, 1945); and *Sarajevski Novi List*, March 29, 1945, 3.

them.[95] One of the theater's final performances, *Čaršijska posla,* reveals that the local intelligentsia still hoped to revive their ideal of Sarajevo. The play tried to capture the spirit of the city's everyday life. Its title can be literally translated as *The Business of Town Folks* or *Bazaar Business,* but I prefer to think of it as indicating, in a local parlance untranslatable beyond the town's borders, the general goings-on about town. Explaining his decision to write such a local drama, the author, Safvet Kafedžić, told *Sarajevski Novi List,* "In these more than difficult times, people need some rest for their souls, but not in the form of banal and obsolete jokes. What they need is a piece of modern reality in an accessible form. Therefore, I have tried to produce a local Sarajevan play that captures our everyday lives. Through it, I hope to recognize those silent and unknown fighters, who live day by day, suffering through the war."[96] For a few hours a night, as terror descended around them, the Sarajevo audience was thus reminded of what bound them together as a community.

On March 20 Hitler gave the order for the Germans to leave Sarajevo. Local German officers noted that the departure had been "inevitable" for some time. They had no supplies and had several thousand wounded soldiers to evacuate.[97] Local skirmishes had increased steadily.[98] The Partisans now held all the territory within a few kilometers of the city and frequently attacked the Axis armies' vital infrastructure. Around the same time Communist Party operatives allegedly managed to steal the Germans' master plan for Sarajevo's defense, inciting a major panic in German and Ustasha headquarters.[99] The heist resulted in the arrests of nearly two hundred German and Croat soldiers.[100]

As the Germans began their final retreat, Luburić launched his most brutal round of terror, imprisoning dozens of town policemen alongside other alleged insurgents.[101] On March 27 his special court sentenced eighty-five people to death, including a number of these policemen. The Ustasha police carried out the sentences immediately. On the evening of March 28 they drove to Marijin Dvor, the residential neighborhood on the city's western edge, where—according to Gojko, a local factory worker who watched the events through his work window—they unloaded the bodies

95. The Croatian State Theater continued to perform about thirty plays per month. See ABiH, Narodno Pozorište Sarajevo, box 5, document 252 (February 14, 1945) and document 417 (March 10, 1945).

96. *Sarajevski Novi List,* March 23, 1945, 3.

97. Schmidt-Richberg, *Der Endkampf auf dem Balkan,* 107.

98. On the Partisan attacks near Sarajevo, see Uzelac and Kreso, "Sarajevska Operacija," 4:693.

99. Donia, *Sarajevo,* 199.

100. This event became an important part of the Partisans' wartime legacy, but I have not yet come across corroborating evidence in the wartime (German or NDH) documents to confirm it.

101. United States Holocaust Memorial Museum Archive, statement of Antun Fest, Freising, RG-49.005M, reel 4a (August 8, 1945).

Figure 11. Victims of the Luburić terror, March 28, 1945. Courtesy of the Historical Museum of Bosnia and Herzegovina.

and strung them up on trees. The next day, passersby found dozens of men and women hanging from trees with signs around their necks that read "Long Live the Poglavnik." The families of missing people searched through the corpses in hopes of identifying their loved ones. The wife of one Muslim police officer recounted the horror of finding her husband's body dangling there.[102]

Although the mass hanging at Marijin Dvor was the most infamous scene of the Ustasha regime's final days in Sarajevo, it was just one episode among many. Some Ustasha policemen locked two hundred Sarajevans in a tower and then blew it up. Others executed four people accused of setting mines on the train tracks. The police also targeted relatives of suspected Partisans. They deported an eighty-year-old woman, Esma, to a concentration camp because her son had allegedly joined the Partisans. When a Muslim man went missing—presumably to join the armed insurgents—they killed his pregnant wife and three-year-old son in retaliation. While most of those targeted were Muslims and Serbs, the Ustasha police did not discriminate by nationality. On March 29, they arrested Alojz, most likely a Volksdeutsche. When the prisoner took a few steps away from the police car (allegedly from losing his balance), the agents shot him dead on the spot. His wife, Berta,

---

102. On the hangings and the town's reaction, see postwar testimonies in ABiH, Zemaljska komisija za utvrđivanje ratnih zločina okupatora i njihovih pomagača za BiH, box 194, document 116 and document 218 (1946). See also Donia, *Sarajevo,* 197.

stood by watching. A Catholic woman described how the Ustasha police told her family that her brother-in-law, who was arrested on March 26, had been deported on the last train to the prisoner camps. But as the train passed through the nearby town of Visoko, the man's brother, a Franciscan monk in the local monastery, could not find him among the prisoners. Days later, the family received a pile of bloody clothes and the news that the man had committed suicide in his cell after being tortured.[103]

Many families never heard anything. The Ustasha police tried to hang posters around town listing the names of prisoners sentenced to death, but the Germans demanded that they remove them. The Wehrmacht had not approved terrorizing the population or arresting Communists because it was in negotiations with some Partisan units for a prisoner swap.[104] It was not until April 3 that the local papers published a list of many of those tried and executed by the court of Luburić.[105] But the exact number of individual victims would never be verified.

On March 30, as the German retreat neared completion and the Partisans reached the city's outskirts, the Ustasha army prepared to leave Sarajevo as well. To no effect, leaders of Napredak begged local commanders to release from duty a soldier who was running their charitable assistance division, no doubt hoping to protect their colleagues from being dragged into the mountains to fight for a losing cause.[106] On April 4, 1945, General Luburić left the city. But the terror he had started continued for two more days. Roughly 350 Ustasha policemen and 400 Ustasha soldiers stayed to defend the city.[107] On the evening of April 4, the soldiers set fire to barrels of gasoline and explosives in a factory, killing nine people.[108] On April 5, as the last German soldiers trickled out of the city with Ustasha troops guarding the rear, soldiers ransacked factories and buildings.[109] They also shot on sight any soldier who refused to leave the city with his unit.[110] Amid the retreat, street fighting intensified. Local Communist Party members took to the streets to lead the charge for liberation, hoping to time their uprising to coincide with the Partisan army's entry into the city. After waiting years for this moment, few of the party's leaders would live to greet the Partisan troops. In the final hours of occupation, the German and

103. In ABiH, Zemaljska komisija za utvrđivanje ratnih zločina okupatora i njihovih pomagača za BiH, see box 194, document 7 (1946); box 195, documents 489, 584, and 578 (1945–46); and box 196, document 46647 (1946).

104. Statement of Antun Fest.

105. *Sarajevski Novi List*, April 3, 1945, 3.

106. ABiH, Hrvatsko kulturno društvo Napredak, box 155, document 268 (March 26, 1945) and document 288 (March 30, 1945).

107. ABiH, Zbirka NOR-a Okružni Komitet KPJ Sarajevo, box 1, document 110 (1945).

108. ABiH, Zemaljska komisija za utvrđivanje ratnih zločina okupatora i njihovih pomagača za BiH, box 196, document 17665 (1945).

109. Schmidt-Richberg, *Der Endkampf auf dem Balkan*, 106.

110. *Oslobođenje*, April 12, 1945, 4.

Ustasha troops managed to kill twenty members of the city's small Communist core, including the party secretary, Vladimir Perić, a.k.a. Valter.[111]

Ruins and Red Stars

On April 6, 1945, four years to the day after the first German bomb struck Sarajevo, Partisan troops marched into the city. The date went down in history as the day of the city's liberation, although street fighting continued for days and a new local government did not form for two weeks.[112] Sarajevans slowly emerged from their homes to see what was in store for them next. Postwar Yugoslav histories described how jubilant Sarajevans flooded the streets to welcome their liberators. The Partisans sponsored a celebratory rally on April 8, during which thousands assembled to rejoice in the liberation and the beginning of a new "magnificent era."[113] However, while the townsmen welcomed the exit of the Axis troops and the end of the terror, firsthand Partisan reports paint a less glowing picture. The first Partisan officers on the scene noted the city's apprehensiveness as the Communists arrived and described a population stunned by the final weeks of the Ustasha terror. Although many Sarajevans were elated to be freed of the stranglehold of the Ustasha regime, the agonizing search for missing loved ones and the exhumation of freshly dug unmarked graves dampened spirits.[114] A Soviet military commission filmed a crew cleaning out Luburić's villa and unearthing corpses from the backyard garden. The father of eighteen-year-old Halid, a Muslim, discovered his son's remains there. The boy's head was deformed and missing an eye. His genitalia bore the scars of boiling water burns. The uncle of a Serb youth, Nikola, found his nephew in a pile of mutilated corpses. He identified the body by its toes, a number of which had been amputated earlier that year while the nephew was serving in a German labor battalion in the mountains. Such stories fill boxes of postwar testimony.[115] An American journalist, Landrum Bolling, who arrived in the city on April 7 with a group of Allied representatives, recalled in an interview with Robert Donia that he was led to a room of bodies "stacked like cordwood on top of one another" and told that these

111. Uzelac and Kreso, "Sarajevska Operacija," 4:703.
112. For descriptions of the transitional era, see David Davidović and Dragutin Kosovac, "Društveno i političko stanje u Sarajevu neposredno nakon oslobođenja," in *Sarajevo u socijalističkoj Jugoslaviji*, ed. Nisim Albahari et al. (Sarajevo: Istorijski Arhiv Sarajevo, 1988), 12–13.
113. Ahmet Djonlagić, "Kroz drevne vratničke kapije u Sarajevu," in Albahari et al., *Sarajevo u Revoluciji*, 4:717–724.
114. *Oslobođenje*, April 12, 1945, 4.
115. On the Soviet film commission, see ABiH, Zemaljska komisija za utvrđivanje ratnih zločina okupatora i njihovih pomagača za BiH, box 195, document 7061 (1945). On Halid, see in the same collection, box 195, document 5971/6 (1945). On Nikola, see box 197, document 53406 (1946).

were "Serbs whom the Ustasha had hanged by barbed wire from lamp posts in Sarajevo."[116]

In reality, the bodies likely included Orthodox Serbs, Catholics, Jews, and Muslims, since no community was left untouched by the terror. Indeed, photographs of the funerals of Luburić's victims reveal their confessional diversity; they were buried in separate cemeteries and mourned according to their own confessional traditions. While tradition thus prevailed, there was nevertheless a sense that profound change was occurring. For example, one photograph of a funeral shows a Muslim woman, wearing a veil and head scarf, standing among the mourners, an unusual sight since Muslim women did not traditionally attend burials.[117]

In addition to leaving the city's population in a state of shock, terror and total war had crippled local institutions, creating a vacuum of power. The Communists quickly established a complex local party apparatus and a new municipal government dominated by party sympathizers. On April 9 the party formed a new local committee (*mjesni komitet*) to fill the void left by the death of Secretary Vladimir Perić and other party members a few days before.[118] Tito appointed Vaso Miskin, a Serb Communist from southern Herzegovina, as secretary. Miskin had been active in Sarajevo's Communist Party since the 1930s, serving as the chapter's secretary in 1941.[119] He spent the wartime years fighting in other parts of Bosnia and Herzegovina, eventually becoming an important player in the party's education, cultural, and propaganda activities. Under his direction, the small local party began indoctrinating Sarajevans with Communist symbols and culture and introducing elements of the new order.

From April 9 to April 20, Tito appointed a dozen Communists to join Miskin on Sarajevo's municipal committee.[120] Despite the ongoing war, the Partisans used military planes to fly dedicated and loyal party members into Sarajevo. The city had been designated the capital of the Federation of Bosnia and Herzegovina, one of six republics that made up the new Yugoslav state. Tito found it imperative that savvy political leaders take over the city and integrate it into the state. Among those who arrived in early April were the city's wartime party activists Olga Marasović and Dane

---

116. Donia, *Sarajevo*, 198.

117. HM, Zbirke Fotografije, fond NOB, image 5795.

118. On the formation of the municipal committee, see Davidović and Kosovac, "Društveno i političko stanje u Sarajevu," 13.

119. For background on Vaso Miskin, see Danica Kurtović, "Vaso Miskin Crni," in Albahari et al., *Sarajevo u Revoluciji*, 4:449–462.

120. The group included Vaso Miskin, Novak Anđelić, Betika Romano, Ferid Čengić, Jovanka Čović, Mladen Knežević, Dragutin Kosovac, Marija Koš, Olga Marasović, Juraj Marek, Dane Olbina, Gojko Rodić, and Radovan Stijačić. See Davidović and Kosovac, "Društveno i političko stanje u Sarajevu," 13–14. On the arrival of the members of the *mjesni komitet*, see the accounts of Dane Olbina, "Povratak u Sarajevo," in Albahari et al., *Sarajevo u socijalističkoj Jugoslaviji*, 40, and Novak Anđelić, "Na Partijskom Radu u Sarajevu," in *Sarajevo u socijalističkoj Jugoslaviji*, 163.

Olbina. Within days of the Communists' arrival in the city, RadioSarajevo, a party-controlled program, dominated the airwaves. The Partisans' wartime newspaper for Bosnia, *Oslobodenje*, began to publish out of Sarajevo on April 12.[121] Together with local Communists, Sarajevans sympathetic to the Partisans draped balconies with pictures of Tito and decorated public buildings with Yugoslav, Communist Party, and Soviet flags. The Central Theatrical Company of Bosnia and Herzegovina arrived a week later; its premiere performance, *The Biography of Tito,* introduced the city to the new regime and its leader through the cosmopolitan medium that the townsmen had always enjoyed.[122]

Simultaneously party leaders organized small "national liberation" groups at city institutions, factories, and companies. Female party members assisted forty local women who had been involved in the Partisans' women's organization, the Anti-Fascist Front of Women (AFŽ), to reach out to women across the city.[123] Photographs of their first congress reveal crowded halls filled with a mix of women, including a handful wearing head scarves, their veils raised to reveal their faces to the cameras.[124] By late April at least a dozen party organizations and youth groups were up and running.

Commemorations, mass funerals, and public celebrations formed an important part of the transitional period. Among the Communists' first commemorative acts was a public funeral for Vladimir Perić Valter, held on April 10.[125] In history and public memory, the funeral is understood as a time of collective mourning for a great defender of the city; it solidified the notion of a cult of Valter as a symbol of Sarajevo heroism and Partisan solidarity. Yet photographs of the funeral procession and burial reveal a different picture: at the head of the procession were two Orthodox Serb priests and a deacon in traditional garb; behind them were several men carrying large crosses, a local Orthodox Christian tradition. Valter was then buried in a cemetery filled with crosses and decorated with banners written in Cyrillic.[126] Though one cannot determine from the available documents the exact confessions of those who attended his burial, one can infer from their participation in the rituals of the faith that many, if not most, were Orthodox Serbs. Similarly, parades for May Day featured children dressed in traditional attire, including a young Muslim boy dressed as a sheikh.[127] While banners of Tito decorated the town, the ceremonial aspects of the

121. Džemal Čelić, "Kulturne djelatnosti u našem gradu," in Albahari et al., *Sarajevo u socijalističkoj Jugoslaviji,* 443–463.

122. *Oslobodenje,* April 23, 1945, 3. See also Davidović and Kosovac, "Društveno i političko stanje u Sarajevu," 747.

123. *Oslobodenje,* April 17, 1945, 4. See also Davidović and Kosovac, "Društveno i političko stanje u Sarajevu," 18.

124. HM, Zbirke Fotografija, fond NOB, image 9386.

125. Davidović and Kosovac, "Društveno i političko stanje u Sarajevu," 736.

126. HM, Zbirke Fotografija, fond NOB, images 5597, 5495.

127. Ibid., images 19341, 19333.

Figure 12. Vladimir Perić (Valter) funeral procession, April 9, 1945. Courtesy of the Historical Museum of Bosnia and Herzegovina.

public celebration combined Partisan military displays with symbols of the town's confessional culture.

Despite these efforts to win over the city, Sarajevans remained wary of the new regime. On April 11, the municipal committee reported that when compared with people in other parts of Bosnia or Croatia: "The authority of our government is not at the highest level in this entire region . . . and relations with the nation have been weak and divided." The report emphasized that the city's political elite—specifically, Catholics who had belonged to the Croat Peasant Party, Muslims who had been in the Yugoslav Muslim Organization, and Serbs who had been involved in local politics—were suspicious of the new government. The committee was concerned because certain people seemed to be "trying to revive a peasant party [*zemljoradnička stranka*], in which all of the discontent could be included. Such a party would become a central place for dissatisfied people and reactionaries." Moreover, the report continued, Sarajevans continued to seek guidance from local Serb political leaders and their "old acquaintances"—a reference to the city's interwar political elite—instead of from the new Communist leadership. The committee warned headquarters, "[W]e need to strike back so that people hear our side rather than listen to these reactionaries. . . . [W]e need to try to raise our standing politically so that we are regarded by the masses as legitimate."[128]

128. ABiH Zbirka NOR-a Okružni Komitet KPJ Sarajevo, box 1, document 74 (April 11, 1945).

Figure 13. Celebrations for May Day, May 1, 1945. Courtesy of the Historical Museum of Bosnia and Herzegovina.

It is no wonder that Sarajevans—however exhilarated by liberation and worn out from the terror—were apprehensive about the new regime. Anti-Communist sentiment had been pervasive for years. Warnings of property confiscation, the annihilation of religious tradition, and the possibility of rural heathens' launching a revolution were proving accurate as the Communists put on a spectacle announcing the birth of a revolutionary era. Moreover, despite all the jubilant talk of liberation, the city was still caught in the throes of war. For most of April 1945, Sarajevo remained cut off from much of the surrounding region as Ustasha, Partisan, and German battalions continued fighting in the north. A few die-hard anti-Communists, like Father Božidar Bralo, the Catholic priest who served as an Ustasha deputy, refused to abandon the city. Bralo assembled a small force of about 145 Catholic men who hid in the mountains, fighting for several months until part of the unit was captured. Bralo stood trial in the fall of 1945; the rest of his "Catholic reactionary force," as it became known, went into hiding in Sarajevo for the next few years, stockpiling weapons and praying for reinforcements. About six hundred Ustasha officials continued fighting near Sarajevo for a few months as well.[129]

129. Smajo Mandžuka, "Odmetničke bande u Sarajevskom regionu i terorističke grupe u Sarajevu," in Albahari et al., *Sarajevo u Socialističkoj Jugoslaviji*, 117–119. On Bralo's trial, see *Oslobođenje*, September 9, 1945, 5.

For its part, the Communist party's central committee tried to suppress the counterinsurgency by enforcing strict curfews and ordering citizens to turn over radios and weapons. In its efforts to stabilize the city, the committee even created mandatory vegetarian days—during which eating meat in public or private was to be punished severely—in order to control the slaughter of valuable livestock needed for labor. Famine descended upon the city in the spring and hovered there for the next three years as the new Yugoslav state attempted to regulate food production and transportation.[130] Moreover, criminals roamed the streets pretending to belong to the Partisans so that they could demand entry to private homes and steal things.[131] Merchants hoarded food to sell on the black market, leaving store shelves as empty as they had been for the past year.[132] Much of the population remained in transit. Sarajevans who had fled the city began the journey home, while as early as April 19 the Communists began encouraging Muslim refugees to return to their villages.[133] One can assume that the refugees did not begin the long trek back through war-torn territory enthusiastically. Sarajevans, meanwhile, were put to work. The local Partisan command drafted townsmen for military service and labor battalions, rounding them up mahala by mahala to form special work brigades.[134] As compensation, laborers received nothing more than the dubious gratification of participating in building the new state. It would be months before the government would pay a single soldier, politician, or worker in money or food.[135]

Muslim religious leaders were especially concerned about the place that Islam would find in the new state. On April 15, 1945, the Ulema Medžlis sent a letter to the local Partisan command requesting that religious personnel, teachers, and imams be exempt from the military draft, as they had been exempted in the past, because without religious leaders, the city's mosques, madrassas, and mektebs would shut down, as would the religious council itself. This would be devastating, the Ulema Medžlis warned, because Muslims would be left without any religious leadership at a time

130. Husnija Kamberović, *Prema Modernom Društvu, Bosna i Hercegovina od 1945. do 1953. godine* (Tešanj, Bosnia and Herzegovina: Centar za kulturu i obrazovanje Tešanj, 2000) 18.
131. *Oslobođenje*, April 12, 1945, 7–8, and April 14, 1945, 3.
132. Dragutin Kosovac, "Uspostavljanje narodne vlasti u oslobođenom gradu," in Albahari et al., *Sarajevo u Revoluciji*, 4:743.
133. *Oslobođenje*, April 19, 1945, 3. I emphasize Muslim refugees because the name of the board was Veliki Zbor Muhadžira. *Muhadžiri* traditionally referred only to Muslim refugees, whereas *izbjeglici* was used to refer to all refugees.
134. Himzo Alić, "Radili smo bez naknade i sa zanosom," in Albahari et al., *Sarajevo u socijalističkoj Jugoslaviji*, 337–338.
135. It appears that salaries commenced at the request of the city government in late June. See Dušan Milidragović, "Organizovanje i izgradnja narodne vlasti u Sarajevu," in Albahari et al., *Sarajevo u socijalističkoj Jugoslaviji*, 78. See also Alić, "Radili smo bez naknade i sa zanosom," 337–340.

when they needed spiritual guidance.[136] Although the council wrote the letter in Cyrillic, a courtesy to the Serbs who dominated the local Partisan command, and signed it with the regime's new mantra, "Death to Fascism—Long live the nation," their request appears to have garnered no response. Religious leaders would receive no special treatment in the new order. On the contrary, within two years they would become "enemies of the people."

Recognizing local hostility and apprehension toward the new regime, the Communists tried to elicit support from local organizations to assuage fears and buttress their legitimacy as the official government. They invited nonparty elites to speak at public rallies and participate in political assemblies.[137] They also worked with the city's network of private societies, which had invaluable experience in handling local social service issues from the last months of the Ustasha period. On April 22 the city council appointed trustees for Napredak and other societies.[138] Under the trustees' oversight, the organizations were allowed to continue their humanitarian and cultural work. Many members of the Young Muslims remained active in Merhamet during these transitional weeks, preferring to focus on humanitarian work until the war ended and they could revisit their larger political and religious concerns.[139] The Communists also reestablished societies disbanded by the Ustasha—including Gajret, the Muslim Yugoslav society, and Prosvjeta, the Serb cultural society—using these groups to reach out to other segments of Sarajevo's Muslim and Serb communities.[140] All these societies acted as stabilizing agents between the new government and their communities, just as some of them had done under the Ustasha regime in the final months of the war. By working with Sarajevo's existing social structure, rather than dismantling it in favor of exclusively party organizations, the Communists began to cultivate ties with these communities through their own social and cultural networks. Allowing (and even encouraging) religious funerals and symbols contributed to a general feeling that Communism was not going to destroy their faiths.

A critical part of maintaining stability in the town in the transitional months was the restoration of a pluralist municipal government. On April 20 the presidency of the National Liberation Government of Bosnia and Herzegovina (ZAVNOBiH), the Partisans' wartime governing body for Bosnia, appointed a new city council for Sarajevo. The first council president—essentially a new name for mayor—was Husein Brkić, a Muslim who had been active in Sarajevo's underground Partisan movement. The party

136. ARIZBiH, Ulema Medžlis, document 960/45 (April 15, 1945).
137. Donia, *Sarajevo*, 207.
138. ABiH, Hrvatsko kulturno društvo Napredak, box 155, document 294 (April 22, 1945).
139. Mandžuka, "Odmetničke bande u Sarajevskom regionu," 121.
140. On Gajret's return, see the property discussion in IAS, Narodna Uzdanica, zapisnik, box 45 (May 28, 1945). On Prosvjeta, see ABiH, Prosvjeta kulturno društvo, box 32, document 55 (July 8, 1945).

appointed three vice presidents representing each of the city's surviving ethnoreligious groups. Although the party referred to the men only by profession, their ethnoreligious background is apparent from their names—Dušan Vasiljević (Serb), Mate Serka (Croat), and Ferid Čengić (Muslim). Twenty-five additional members were appointed, of whom all were party members or sympathizers.[141] The council thus served as a bridge between the city's prewar political traditions and the new socialist model: representatives came from every ethnoreligious community, but they shared a common political identity as socialists.

Under the direction of party leaders, the new city government launched an aggressive program to fix the city's wartime problems by importing food, repairing buildings and the transportation system, and vaccinating Sarajevans against typhoid fever. Disinfecting and repairing schools also became a priority. Several schools opened by mid-May, accommodating more than ten thousand children. Most had not attended school in years, if ever. The new government also started classes for illiterate adults, a gesture that had been a centerpiece of the Partisans' wartime educational efforts. The new curricula promoted the narrative of a city united by war, ignoring or rewriting the story of its divisive wartime experiences.[142]

Retribution was also an essential component of postwar reconstruction. From the moment the Communists arrived in the city, they hunted down and prosecuted war criminals. The government in Belgrade issued a list of Sarajevo's "most wanted," which included top figures from every community. Among the most important were the Catholic Church leaders Archbishop Ivan Šarić and Božidar Bralo, the Muslim Ustasha politician Hakija Hadžić, and the Serb lawyer Savo Besarović.[143] The regime established a special court in Sarajevo to prosecute the "enemies of the Serbs, Muslims, and Croats of the Federation of Bosnia and Herzegovina," a vague category that eventually was to target members of every Sarajevo community, even the Jewish community, which had barely survived the war.[144] The court began proceedings in May.[145] Whereas most of those tried in the first wave were Catholics and Muslims who had worked for the Ustasha regime, the Communists locked up men and women from every community for crimes like working for the Ustasha base or the Gestapo (even as a cook), buying

141. Donia, Sarajevo, 210–211.

142. Such a rewriting of history was not uncommon in Tito's Yugoslavia, especially in Bosnia. See, for example, Max Bergholtz, "The Strange Silence: Explaining the Absence of Monuments for Muslim Civilians Killed in Bosnia during the Second World War," East European Politics and Societies Online First, April 6, 2010: 1–27.

143. See a copy of a Belgrade leaflet entitled "Sarajevo je oslobodjeno" in HM, Ustaška Nadzorna Služba, document 3982 (April 6, 1945).

144. The court's foundation is discussed in Vera Katz, "Komunizam i represija: Sud Narodne Časti u Bosni i Hercegovini," in 60 Godine od završetka drugog svjetskog rata—kako se sjećati 1945. godine, ed. Husnija Kamberović (Sarajevo: Institut za Istoriju u Sarajevu, 2006), 145–166.

145. Oslobodenje, May 7, 1945, 4.

or overseeing Jewish property, being "intimate" with an Ustasha commander, and turning in Jewish neighbors.[146] Some wartime leaders, notably
Mayor Hasan Demirović and Mehmed Pandža, inaccurately believed that
the new government would welcome them into the fold.[147] Instead, they
were arrested for abetting the enemy. From May to July 1945, the court
tried an estimated 1,800 Sarajevans, with sentences ranging from dispos-
session of property to execution.[148] Of the three main wartime mayors, Atif
Hadžikadić was hanged, Hasan Demirović received five years of hard labor,
and Mustafa Softić had his property confiscated and received a five-year
sentence (although he was released after seven and a half months).[149] In
1946 and 1947, as the regime consolidated power, the police arrested hundreds of others, including the leaders of the Young Muslims and important
local Serbs.[150] Arrests and trials continued steadily until 1948 as the Communists consolidated state and society.

The trials became a keystone in the regime's plan to reduce the influence of Sarajevo's politicians, intelligentsia, and religious leaders and set
the stage for building the new social order. The Communists knew that
Sarajevans sought guidance from their old leaders and that they placed
little trust in the new regime. By starting the process of retributive justice
before the war even ended, the Communists could remove from public life
those elites who did not jump on board immediately and could also tie the
city's traditional elite to the murderous legacies of the Ustasha and Chetnik
armies. Moreover, the Communists prevented the possible emergence of a
viable political alternative during the transitional months by allowing only
those societies or individuals willing to participate in the socialist revolution
to remain in positions of power. Although Sarajevo's societies tried to preserve a semblance of the city's civic identity and social structure, without a
higher political authority and a viable postwar agenda they could maintain
some social services but not revive the city's prewar dynamic. The Communists quickly and successfully integrated themselves into Sarajevo's complex
social structure, which made it easier for them to begin to overhaul it. By
the fall of 1945 Communists and Communist sympathizers dominated local
cultural societies like Napredak and Preporod, a new Muslim society they
had created to merge Narodna Uzdanica and Gajret.[151]

146. Information on the trials can be found in ABiH, Zemaljska komisija za utvrđivanje
ratnih zločina okupatora i njihovih pomagača za BiH, box 8. See, for example, document 13
(September 18, 1945) and document 284 (December 1945). See also Katz, "Komunizam i
represija," 160–161.

147. Nametak, *Sarajevski Nekrologij*, 86 and 218.

148. Mandžuka, "Odmetničke bande u Sarajevskom regionu," 115.

149. Pajić, *Sarajevski Gradonačelniki*.

150. Mandžuka, "Odmetničke bande u Sarajevskom regionu,"122–125. For an example of
later trial proceedings, see ABiH, Zemaljska komisija za utvrđivanje ratnih zločina okupatora i
njihovih pomagača za BiH, box 13, document 929 (February 21, 1947).

151. Kamberović, *Prema modernom društvu*, 43–45.

Since most of the leading Ustasha perpetrators had abandoned Sarajevo by early April 1945, the new rulers found it fairly easy to forge a clear distinction between the foreign evil that had targeted the city and the local collective good that had stood in its defense. The postwar trials solidified this distinction. Everyone who was not judged a collaborator could share in the narrative of victims. By embracing the new regime and joining in the jubilation of victory, individuals could erase any record of dishonorable wartime activities and participate in the socialist revolution. Through state-controlled media, new history textbooks, films, and a postwar memorial culture, these foundational myths eventually became indistinguishable in many minds from the realities of the war. The Communist regime gradually anchored the Sarajevo identity to a new kind of multiculturalism, one rooted in socialism and a binary wartime legacy that all Sarajevans could share as victims of the foreign oppressors and heroes in the war of liberation.

Building socialism in Sarajevo also demanded the restoration of a demographic equilibrium. It is unclear whether the Communists engineered the demographic shifts or whether population changes occurred as a normal part of the chaos of postwar migration and refugee return, but from 1945 to 1948, the city's population changed dramatically. Whereas in 1945 Muslims had comprised around 60 percent of the population and Serbs less than 20 percent, by 1948 the city's 113,769 residents were a mix of 36 percent Serb, 35 percent Muslim, and 24 percent Croat.[152] A similar balance would be maintained for the next five decades. At the same time, Tito's regime set about transforming Sarajevo's society by forging a "new paradigm of common life," as Robert Donia fittingly describes it. The regime supplanted confessional identities with class and national frameworks. Sarajevans became indoctrinated through a complex system of new institutions that mirrored old ones, such as multiethnic sports teams, an expansive public education system, workers' collectives, and the volunteer "work brigades," which were largely in charge of rebuilding the city in the early postwar years. Once local construction had been completed, the regime expanded the program by sending youth work brigades on public service projects all around the country. This practice brought together children from every community, fostering a socialist youth culture within cities and across the country.

Marko Attila Hoare cogently argues that in the late wartime and immediate postwar period Communism became the great equalizer in Bosnia; it helped to override the nationalist ambitions of the wartime movements

152. See sections on Bosnia in *Konačni rezultati popisa stanovništva od 15 marta 1948 godine* (Belgrade: Savezni zavod za statistiku, 1951). The new census asked people to identify by national group rather than religion. An unofficial postwar census, from January 23, 1946, noted that Sarajevo had 97,144 residents, of which 58 percent were Muslim, 19 percent Orthodox, 21 percent Catholic, 1.5 percent Jewish, and 0.5 percent other. See IAS, ZV, Stanovništvo grada Sarajeva, document 94 (January 23, 1946).

and foster a supranational civic notion of community that reflected the region's tradition of multiethnic coexistence.[153] But the Communists, like the Ustashas, believed it was imperative to suppress a part of Sarajevo's traditional legacy in order to create the social order they envisioned. The ideological enemies disagreed on which part would be sacrificed—confessionalism or pluralism—but the two were one in Sarajevo, and negating either meant driving out local customs, dismantling social structures, and challenging Sarajevo's intangible essence, its civic consciousness.

• • •

The last act of German occupation and the NDH played out like a tragedy. Actors rehearsed scenes from a play depicting and honoring Sarajevo's everyday life, while ordinary Sarajevans spent their days awaiting the dreaded knock of Luburić's agents. Catholic leaders warned their parishes to fight the "uncivilized" Communists who threatened the moral order; but who could have been more beastly than the Ustasha interrogators torturing and murdering scores of Sarajevans? Muslim religious leaders encouraged their community to fight for a pluralist postwar solution, but the only group offering to do that was the Communists, their sworn enemy. The discrepancies between the terror of everyday life and the seemingly irrational goals of Sarajevo's leaders left the people of the city ideologically afloat. Yet the indiscriminate nature of the Luburić terror temporarily equalized Sarajevans; no community was left untouched by the cruel conclusion of the NDH. In a dark irony, rather than emboldening the city against the resistance, the gruesome public displays created mass support for the changing of the guard.

When the Partisans arrived in Sarajevo, they encountered a devastated city filled with starving, frightened people. Terror and total war had crippled local institutions. The new Communist leaders cleverly manipulated the chaos, uncertainty, and lack of leadership. They quickly established a complex local party apparatus, arrested unsympathetic community leaders, and commenced postwar trials, conveniently eliminating their competition. They also set about creating a new unifying culture that could win over the town. On the mountains above Sarajevo, in one of the loveliest hillside parks, a memorial museum to victims and heroes became the place to take children on a weekend afternoon. In the center of town, right off Marshal Tito Street (the former Ante Pavelić Street), the new socialist government erected a large plaque to remember the victims of the war and commemorate the city's heroic struggle against evil. At its base a small fire, known as the "Eternal Fire" (colloquially referred to as "Tito's fire"), burns day and night. Built in 1946, the memorial served as an immediate and constant

153. Hoare, *History of Bosnia*, 308.

reminder of the war and of Sarajevans' "unity and brotherhood"—the ideology behind Tito's Yugoslavism.

After initially looking to their traditional political leaders for guidance in April and May 1945, within a year the Sarajevo masses enthusiastically embraced their new socialist community and idolized their new leader, Tito. Through the collapse of the local government, the trauma of the occupation, and especially the Ustasha terror, Sarajevans had searched for something to believe in. Tito gave them hope for Sarajevo again.

THE SYMPATHETIC CITY

Community and Identity in Wartime Sarajevo

In reports on her trip to Sarajevo before the war, Rebecca West witnessed and commented on a noteworthy political spectacle: at the bequest of the Yugoslav government, Turkey's prime minister and minister of war descended on Sarajevo and publicly addressed the town. "Thousands of men with fezes and women with veils" took to the streets eagerly awaiting nostalgic speeches about their common Ottoman Muslim past. But much to the townspeople's visible dismay, the Kemalist ministers made no reference to shared legacies of empire, nor did they hint at a brotherhood of Muslims; instead, the Turks touted the secular, liberal South Slavic government that had come to rule over Bosnia.[1] According to West, the audience was crushed; they "[turned] away in desolation because the representatives of the New Turkey had looked on them coldly and had told them that the old Turkey, which had been their mother, was dead and buried."[2] West believed that she had witnessed the end of an historical era: "We had seen the end of a story that had taken five hundred years to tell. We had seen the final collapse of the old Ottoman Empire."[3]

She could not have known, of course, that this "final collapse" was still to come; at the time, what seemed like one world coming to an end was, in fact, that world *beginning* its steady and violent decline. The Turkish ministers' visit was part of a long process, one that had begun amid Ottoman reforms in the early nineteenth century and played out its critical concluding act only in the 1940s. For many observant Muslims, the Ottoman era would

---

1. Mustafa Kemal, also known as Ataturk, founded the Republic of Turkey and was its first president from 1923 to 1938. During his time in office, he introduced arguably radical modernizing and secularizing measures that aimed to reduce the presence of Islam and turn Turkey into a European-style nation-state.
2. West, *Black Lamb, Grey Falcon*, 1059.
3. Ibid., 317.

end with the banning of head scarves and veils in the late 1940s. For most Sarajevans, however, there was no single event that marked the profound transformation that occurred during the Second World War. Rather, as they gradually settled into the political and social structures of postwar Yugo-slavia, they slowly came to grasp that the war had done more than decimate Sarajevo's material infrastructure; it had also torn the city's social fabric thread by thread until only the barest of stitching remained.

In piecing together the stories of Sarajevo during the Second World War, I have introduced a framework that favors local community relation-ships over ideology. This narrative structure has emphasized local agendas, motives, and loyalties as the key components to understanding the pro-cesses of state transition, mass violence, ethnic conflict, civil war, military occupation, and nation building. By narrowing the investigation to one city in crisis, I have shown that wartime Sarajevo, and presumably other similar localities, can profitably be understood in terms of four central themes: (1) the breakdown of confessional institutions in modern Europe and their replacement by civic bodies as the custodians of community; (2) loyalty to place and the quest for local autonomy in perilous times; (3) the ways in which local stories reframe national narratives; and (4) the reciprocal effects of local, national, and international policy.

Multiconfessionalism: A Casualty of War?

Confessional politics remained salient in Sarajevo through the Second World War. To the frustration of foreign movements—the Nazis, Ustashas, radical nationalists, and Communists—multiple pre-ideological (or anti-ideological) approaches to identity and community had to be navigated when making policy in Sarajevo. Every policy debate had a confessional angle, be it refugee care, deportation exemptions, the composition of the municipal government, or women's recruitment in the Ustasha move-ment. National and international players seeking power in the city—from high-ranking leaders like Himmler, Pavelić, and Tito to the lower-ranking German, Ustasha, and Communist bureaucrats—recognized that ignoring Sarajevo's confessional politics would make it impossible to secure viable local alliances. Consequently, the Germans took seriously Muslim dietary restrictions, the Ustasha regime adapted its national ideology to under-score local confessional distinctions, and the Partisans included religious leaders at the funeral processions of Communist heroes.

Yet the pressures of racial policies and civil war weakened confessional ties. This process occurred gradually from 1941 to 1945, driven by three interrelated processes: the loss of moral capital among religious leaders, the convergence of the public and private spheres in the Independent State of Croatia, and the internal disputes within religious groups over the relationship between race, religion, nation, and community. By the end of the war, the custodianship of the community had been transferred from the domain of religious institutions to other sources.

The deportations of Sarajevo's Jews in the fall of 1941 marked the opening scene of the turn from a multicultural system rooted in confessionalism to one rooted in nationalism, a process that drew upon ongoing secularizing trends but was propelled forward by the war. The deportations destroyed Sarajevo's centuries-old Jewish community, a pillar of the confessional system, and impoverished the town's heterogeneous demographic. Less obviously, they also challenged two aspects of Sarajevo's culture: deference to religious institutions and leaders in matters pertaining to their congregations and, closely related, the long-established separation of the public, civic sphere and the private socioreligious one. As Jews who had converted to Islam and Catholicism were carted off in the night, religious leaders recognized that in Hitler's "New Order," religion would not only be relegated to the private sphere but also be subjugated to the will of the political leader. Controversy surrounded the numerous race disputes that involved professed Catholics and Muslims because civilians expected their religious leaders to do something. Džemal's hopeless plea to Reis-ul-ulema Fehim Spaho seeking an expedited conversion for his Jewish fiancée not only affected the young betrothed but spoke to the waning trust that younger generations came to place in religious leaders. When the leaders lost the power to determine membership in the community, they ceased to be viewed as its moral guardians.

Historians conventionally understand the Communist era as the time when the position of religion in east European society came under attack. Indeed, Tito's government, like most Marxist regimes, limited the practice of faith by shutting down religious schools, discouraging participation in religious groups, outlawing veils and head scarves, and trying and executing prominent religious leaders like Archbishop Stepinac.[4] But the implosion of traditional religious structures was intensified by the ascension of the radical Right Ustasha regime—a regime remembered as having morally questionable ties to the Catholic Church. The regime's policies on religious appointments and financing, as well as those on property, marriage, inheritance, custody, and education, subverted the long-standing custom limiting government interference in the private practices of religion. Whereas the frameworks of some religious institutions survived the NDH, the social and trust networks that gave them life were slowly dismantled. Thus, while

4. On religion and the state in Titoist Yugoslavia, see Stella Alexander, *Church and State in Yugoslavia since 1945* (Cambridge: Cambridge University Press, 1979). Alexander examines in detail the immediate postwar attacks on the Catholic and Orthodox Christian communities. For the Partisans' approach to Muslims and the Islamic Religious Community, see Jelena Batinić, "Gender, Revolution, and War: The Mobilization of Women in the Yugoslav Partisan Movement during World War II" (PhD diss., Stanford University, 2009).

confessional identity retained its role as a lens for understanding oneself and one's background, and perhaps one's responsibility to others, the confessional community surrendered its role as a moral compass and as a necessary adjunct to practices that signified and reinforced religious conviction.

The breakdown of confessional structures and the transfer of power to new centers happened differently in each community. The few hundred Sarajevo Jews who survived the Holocaust as Sarajevo Jews (i.e., unconverted and remaining in or returning to the town) confronted the annihilation of their institutional structures of religion and community. Gradually they sought to repair and rebuild their local networks with a new Jewish movement, one influenced by the modern ideologies of Zionism, socialism, and secular thought.[5] Shell-shocked, Sarajevo's Orthodox Serbs emerged from the war having lost far more than their icons, churches, and priests: the strategies of genocide against Serbs divested the Orthodox community of its confessional foundations. Although the Ustashas allowed "Orthodox Croats" to return to public life during the war, the regime had unhinged their community's internal network. Individual survival may have been an option, but the preservation of a public community was not. Thus like the Jews, Orthodox Serbs in Sarajevo faced the difficult task of rebuilding their community, a process that took place amid socialist state building, ongoing civil conflict, and postwar tension between Serb returnees and the Muslim refugees who occupied their apartments and their town.[6]

In the Catholic and Muslim communities, the integration of religion and nationalism undermined central premises of faith, contributing to secularization and the breakdown of confessional ties and trust networks. Ironically, while many prominent Catholic and Muslim religious leaders supported the NDH as the means of resurrecting religiously rooted systems of ethics, their gradual complicity in the Ustasha regime's wartime agenda ultimately undermined the very ethical system that they had hoped the new order would produce. After the war, the stigma of collaboration, together with the arrest of prominent religious leaders, shook Catholic and Muslim religious institutions and left those communities without leadership. Yet one cannot look merely at postwar stigmas in explaining the implosion of confessional networks. Also critical was the dissension within these communities during the war, a friction complicated by the severed communication lines between central religious institutions and rural parishes. The internal conflicts that plagued both the Muslim and Catholic communities reached a crescendo just as the survival of the NDH was growing most tenuous. The surge of Catholic participation in resistance activities after 1943 underscored the widening rift between the goals of ordinary Catholics

5. Emil Kerenji, "Jewish Citizens of Socialist Yugoslavia: Politics of Jewish Identity in a Socialist State, 1944–1974" (PhD diss., University of Michigan, 2008).

6. On this tension, see Kamberović, *Prema modernom društvu*, 63.

and those of the church leaders, many of whom refused to sever the link between Catholicism and Croat nationalism. For the Muslim leadership in Sarajevo during the war, the goals of protecting Islam as a system of law and ethics and protecting Muslims as people proved incompatible. The former required ideological purity; the latter meant compromising certain tenets of the faith to meet the demands of the political leadership and the appeal of secular lifestyles among Muslim youth. Heated debates about women's participation in youth groups and the representation of Islam in theatrical productions—which continued into 1945—revealed the deep divisions among Muslims over the relationship of Islam to the nation-state.

As religious institutions became less important as mechanisms for unifying the confessional communities in Sarajevo, private secular organizations filled the void. In his analysis of trust networks, Charles Tilly favors the notion that trust is "a relationship with practices attached" rather than just "an attitude."[7] In other words, trust requires action. Tilly notes that trust networks could traditionally be found in "public religious solidarities, lineages, trade diasporas, patron-client chains, credit networks, societies of mutual aid . . . and some kinds of local communities." Among the most effective, he suggests, were networks that limited participation and where local leaders had access to and the responsibility for distributing resources.[8] These kinds of networks are more manageable on an everyday basis, particularly in times of crisis.

Tilly's model would predict precisely what seems to have occurred in Sarajevo: as the responsibilities for distributing social welfare and providing education shifted to lay organizations, they became the crux of community trust networks. Societies like Merhamet, Narodna Uzdanica, and Napredak advocated for the communities that they served, working as liaisons between civilians and government bodies. They maintained a stock of resources such as food, fuel, and medical supplies, and they determined how best to distribute them. Through their work with schools, libraries, youth groups, soup kitchens, refugee camps, and so on, they perpetuated and strengthened local rituals and contributed to a sense of connectedness within each group. In so doing, they cultivated concepts of community that were not dependent on religious institutions; however, despite their institutional independence, many of these private organizations maintained underlying religious agendas and informal affiliations with religious institutions. These relationships allowed them to protect aspects of the prewar, confessionally based communities and thus to counter the new trust networks being forged by the socialist regime.

As private societies became more powerful during the war, they sought to redefine their local communities according to their own visions, resisting

7. Charles Tilly, *Trust and Rule* (Cambridge University Press, 2005), 12.
8. Ibid., 6, 57–58.

agendas being imposed by external actors. The executive council of Merhamet, for example, used its charity work to assert a particular political agenda, one steeped in a conservative, exclusive understanding of Muslim identity. The council called on Muslims to abandon their national and political affiliations—that is, to cease identifying as Muslim Croats or Muslim Serbs—and instead to see themselves simply as Muslims. Religious identity thus crystallized in a way that conformed to (and sought to compete with) secular models. The Croat cultural society Napredak used its standing at the center of educational and cultural life as the basis for its intervention on behalf of local Catholic Croat students who were snatched by the Ustasha in 1945. In filling basic material, cultural, and security needs, Napredak and similar institutions gradually assumed and subtly revised the trust networks, cultural roles, and boundaries of community that had been previously administered by religious organizations. In this way, local leaders sustained elements of the multiconfessional system while simultaneously helping it to conform to the practices and ideas required of the modern political state.

Autonomy and Uncertainty

Prior to the war, Sarajevans had derived some sense of belonging, heritage, and social norms through the cultural bonds of their confessional communities and through the multicultural character of their *civitas* that enveloped the mosaic of confessions. As each of the confessional communities adopted a more secular, national basis of collective identity, the overarching civic community adapted, and the meaning and practices of being a *Sarajlija* changed with it. This process began before the war and ended after it, but it is through a close analysis of the wartime era that we can best understand how, within a generation, the confessional mosaic could be transformed into a melting pot of multinationalism.

Post-Ottoman multiconfessional social systems, like the one that had persisted in Sarajevo, do not subsist merely on mutual respect for different faiths or large communities of observant people. They depend on a combination of institutional, infrastructural, social, and cultural connections and networks that cement the larger community. Sarajevo's civic consciousness was based on patterns of communal behavior and activity. It was not just a mentality but a way of living, offering concrete solutions to real problems. I have argued in this work that Sarajevo's local leaders responded to the challenges of occupation, civil war, and state-sponsored genocide by carefully guarding the values and unspoken codes deemed vital to the sustenance of a pluralist community while simultaneously compromising with the occupying authorities on political and ideological matters that the leaders felt would bear less significantly on the codes of the local community. Central to this argument has been my contention that loyalty to *place*, or to home-town, persisted through the modern era and, in many instances, trumped other loyalties and affiliations. In different ways and to different degrees, city leaders integrated elements of their local culture—its values, ethics, and institutional practices—into the new political order, simultaneously accommodating and resisting the imposition of externally imposed ide-ologies. Not only did Sarajevo develop a high-minded civic consciousness, but in a more practical sense, the particular set of traditional relationships among its inhabitants helped get things done and problems solved. These *Lokalpatriotismus* traditions of intellect and emotion were based on efficacy and action. If it had not worked in the city's interest to be civically conscious and multicultural, different ideologies and different sets of practices would have been developed to secure autonomy and survive the war.

Although there is no reason why similar local loyalties could not have persisted in provincial or rural towns, one can expect this dynamic to have been stronger in urban locales, which were better able to maintain the bureaucratic and institutional frameworks needed to preserve local govern-ment despite the chaos of war. By contrast, rural areas often dissolved into anarchy or fell to armed insurgencies, which left local administrators with significantly less power to shape law and policy. Sarajevo's administrators controlled or influenced a variety of programs during the war, including education, social welfare, humanitarian relief, housing requests, refugee transportation, and unemployment; they had to develop networks between the local markets and the state and international economies—as in negotia-tions over the production of factory goods for the Wehrmacht. Throughout the war, the municipal government aimed to provide political continuity, seeking not only to keep the city running but also to preserve intangible but essential codes of neighborliness embedded in the town's bureaucratic traditions and public life. When the city government and public institutions shut down in 1944 and 1945, local organizations stepped in, using their influence to chaperone the city's transition through the terror and into the next political era. Well into 1945 members of Sarajevo's traditional elite remained hopeful that they could still play a role in shaping the postwar political order. When they accepted that this would not be the case, they tried to foster a durable civic culture that might bind the city as a unit regardless of what political entity prevailed.

Yet throughout this process, a tension existed in wartime Sarajevo, as in many parts of the region, between duty to the nation and duty to the neighborhood, or, in local terms, between who was the *narod* and who was *naši*. For example, when the Ustasha regime began to implement discrimi-natory laws and a campaign of mass murder against the town's Serbs, Jews, and Roma, local leaders from a range of religious and civic organizations rejected aspects of the state's agenda that they perceived as attacks on their community and culture. Religious clergy who had welcomed regime change and embraced the NDH nevertheless ignored Ustasha laws that placed racial above religious identity. Local judges and politicians appointed by the regime often governed by custom and precedent, challenging intrusions into the city's self-management and ignoring laws not in line with local codes of conduct. From the mayor's office to the city's museums, bureaucrats refused to follow through with mandatory job purges when doing so targeted individuals or groups deemed vital to the Sarajevo community. Defining the boundaries of the local community was a key to claiming a stake in the war.

There are two larger points I seek to make here. First, local responses to Ustasha policies reveal an awareness of the unfinished political process within which Sarajevo maneuvered. Sarajevo's leaders held no presumptions that today's social order would exist tomorrow. Although local leaders across Hitler's Europe recognized the fragility of the system, especially late in the war, such concerns were particularly prevalent in the NDH, a state under the constant threat of extinction. Moreover, Sarajevo's leaders accepted that their city had always been part of some state and that it required affiliation with an outside power in order to survive and prosper. The reactions of Sarajevo's Muslim and Catholic elite to extreme nationalism and genocide may have spanned a broad political, ideological, and even moral spectrum, but their motives were consistent. They neither despised Fascism nor sought to overthrow the occupying power. Rather, they hoped to keep enough freedom to preserve certain values regardless of who became the new imperial boss. Unfortunately, the political latitude that they envisioned had no place in twentieth-century Europe, let alone in Hitler's expanding empire.

Second, I suggest that existing social codes and administrative and legal practices necessarily include social, logistical, and psychological barriers to change, and extreme movements like Nazism can institute radical change only through periods of acclimation, as well as by tolerating trial and error. Understanding how Sarajevo's leaders navigated this process helps us better understand the complicated relationship between neighborhood and national politics in Hitler's Europe. Administrative confusion often plagues new governments, and Sarajevo's failure to comply with NDH initiatives can be understood in part through the lens of regime change. It takes time for new regimes to integrate the periphery into the state, during which time local leaders can be left, temporarily, to govern themselves. However, there were many instances in which Sarajevo bureaucrats were not unclear about their responsibilities but rather exploited inefficiencies that were occurring at the higher, more remote levels of the regime's government. From property confiscation to linguistic reform, local responses to state policy underscored a profound uncertainty about the state's political future and a skepticism about the permanence (and irreversibility) of its genocidal and nationalizing agendas.

Histories and Memories of Sarajevo's Wartime Dynamics

During the Bosnian war of the 1990s, the Sarajevan poet Semezdin Mehmedinović penned the following verse:

> A shell hit one of the facades on Marshal Tito Street. The plaster poured down, and with it, a sheet metal sign. The sign read: Ante Pavelić 11. Until then I had no idea, but now I knew: the central street of Sarajevo had a different name fifty years ago, and that name was hidden for years behind the plaster, like in a geological diagram of different ages.[9]

As the shelling of Sarajevo slowly picked away at the plaster, the hidden stories of the city's past were uncovered. To the surprise of many, these stories were not the ones that they had learned growing up. The 1990s thus brought to the city a new era of questioning and truth seeking.

This book has aimed to dig deeper into the rubble of Yugoslavia's ruins, beyond the Communist and nationalist accounts of the Second World War and into a historical territory with which few are familiar. Many Bosnians who have heard me speak about the stories and people in these chapters do not know how to respond. Not only does this narrative often feel like "a geological diagram of [a] different age," but it often seems to belong to a different city altogether. Part of the difficulty of discerning this story is the nature of the narrative itself. The local elite in Sarajevo were fighting a war different from the one being fought around them, a war better suited to another era. They were, in many ways, creatures of a different age, an age of empire and monarchs, an age when confessional ties and codes of neighborliness and civility were understood to be the foundations of coexistence. While deeply embroiled in the multifaceted war raging across the Balkans, Sarajevo did not engage with the war in a way that conforms to established historical narratives. Sarajevo's story, like many local histories that encourage scholars to transcend nationcentric models of historical writing, reveals the deep inadequacies in the history and memory of the Second World War in the Balkans.[10]

For example, the infamous rivalry between the Chetniks, Partisans, and Ustashas—prolifically covered by Yugoslav and Western scholars—influenced strategies and dictated the military outcome of the war. But the victory sought by each side was political in nature, and in this political war, there were more than three sides. Thus far, historical studies that have challenged

9. Semezdin Mehmedinović, *Sarajevo Blues*, trans. Ammiel Alcalay (San Francisco: City Light Books, 1998), 88. Verse set in original format of translation.

10. On the ways that silence shaped the memory and history of the war, see Max Bergholtz, "The Strange Silence: Explaining the Absence of Monuments for Muslim Civilians Killed in Bosnia during the Second World War," *East European Politics and Societies Online First*, April 6, 2010.

the three-sided paradigm have usually done so not by questioning the entire model but rather by reevaluating the objectives, alliances, and internal divisions within the three major factions.[11] However, members of Sarajevo's local elite felt disconnected from all the factions, with their rural character and strong peasant bases.[12] Mass movements had little appeal to city notables, who were accustomed (and preferred) explicitly non-mass forms of elite politics. Thus none of the warring rivals ever won great support in Bosnia's capital city, although each of them hoped to conquer it. A majority of Sarajevo's Serbs rejected extreme Serb nationalism and the Chetnik resistance, while a number of the city's Croats eventually worked to undermine the Ustasha regime. The Partisans, meanwhile, faced great difficulty in rallying support because of the city's strong religious culture, cosmopolitan character, and the pervasive fear of Communism among the local elite.

The Muslim story, a largely understudied chapter of the civil conflict, underscores the complexity of the regional political struggle.[13] Caught in a cycle of violence with no obvious ally, Sarajevo's Muslim leaders sought to protect their community from the dangers posed by each of the warring factions: the Ustasha regime sought to subjugate Islam to the state and make Muslims second-class citizens, the Communist forces threatened to extinguish religious Islam, and the Chetniks aimed to ethnically cleanse Muslims from Bosnia. In other words, the warring factions targeted different aspects of Islam as a religion and Muslims as citizens, but they all, in some way, used Muslim-ness as a marker of pathology. In their quest to survive politically, Muslim leaders allied themselves with the various groups during the war, harnessing the community's political identity so as to retain an element of their own autonomy. Consequently, Islam was subject to constant reinterpretation, which left the core movement fragmented. Although Muslim leaders disagreed on the best political framework for the state—an ongoing debate since at least the 1920s—they gradually recognized that in order to compete in a European war among nation-states backed by armies, they had to develop a centralized army and a long-term political plan. This goal aligned with the German army's need for foot soldiers to combat the indefatigable insurgents, and after lengthy deliberations, multiple Muslim factions joined the Germans in supporting the creation of the Bosnian Muslim Waffen SS unit in the spring of 1943. But while the Germans provided Muslims with a structure for a military, they failed to provide any meaningful political reform. Furthermore, the Waffen SS unit failed to rally the Muslim

11. Dulić, *Utopias of Nation*, and Hoare, *Genocide and Resistance in Hitler's Bosnia*.
12. On the rural character of the Partisan movement and how this affected its policies, see the first chapter in Melissa K. Bokovoy, *Peasants and Communists: Politics and Ideology in the Yugoslav Countryside, 1941–1953* (Pittsburgh: University of Pittsburgh Press, 1988).
13. The Muslim dimension of the war is addressed in Redžić, *Bosnia and Hercegovina in the Second World War*, Hasanbegović, *Muslimani u Zagrebu*, and Imamović, *Historija Bošnjaka*, which focus on particular aspects of the Muslim movements but do not connect those stories to international movements.

community, let alone serve as an effective military force. The inability of Muslims to develop a competitive military machine assured their absence in postwar narratives, which largely emphasized the military conflict. In popular memory and local historical narratives, Muslims were categorized simply as "good" (those who joined the Partisan resistance) or "bad" (those who collaborated with the Ustashas or Nazis). The majority, however, fell somewhere in between these ideological extremes and spent much of the war trying to avoid the violence of both.

Civil conflict in Sarajevo engendered complex, ambiguous affiliations, affected by local, national, and international concerns. Hitler's Europe produced many such complicated urban settings. The Wehrmacht's march across the continent unleashed a host of civil conflicts from Ukraine to Greece, as dissatisfied groups tried to carve out countries on Europe's new map. The ensuing local and regional conflicts underscored the ambiguity in both the concept and realization of the new order.[14] Many of Hitler's supporters had incompatible goals. Holly Case's work on Transylvania, for example, illuminates the competing agendas of Axis partners Hungary and Romania: though they were technically on the same side of the war, their goals of territory and power often made them each other's primary enemy.[15] In the NDH, the Nazis and Ustashas won support from such diverse groups as Muslims who sought the revival of Sharia law, Catholic reactionaries who detested Islam and wanted to convert Muslims, and secular, ideologically driven Croat nationalists who hoped to install a race-based order similar to that of Nazi Germany. All these groups used the rhetoric of National Socialism and Croat nationalism in their quests for power. Yet their goals, like their power, were often conspicuously local.

Civil war, Stathys Kalyvas argues, "privatizes politics," and it was this mode of private politics that most directly shaped wartime behavior in Sarajevo when local leaders realized that they had not made adequate alliances in order to have a hand in building a postwar order.[16] Forging a state, not fighting the war, was often the local priority. It was partly for this reason that few of Sarajevo's leaders supported the armed insurgencies, even though they grew to detest the Ustasha regime. In examining the spectrum of passive and active forms of politics employed by Sarajevans in the late stages of the war, I have shown how Sarajevo's leaders tried to transcend the dominant political-military programs in order to further their own religious, civic, and political agendas. Tied to specific cultural or humanitarian groups (e.g., the Red Cross or Merhamet), religious societies (e.g., the Islamic organization El-Hidaje), or places of employment (e.g., the munitions warehouse), these local movements tended to sever connections to

14. Mazower, *Hitler's Empire*.
15. Case, *Between States*.
16. Stathys Kalyvas, *The Logic of Violence in Civil War* (New York: Cambridge University Press, 2006), 389.

broader national and international programs and focus instead on matters that directly affected the city and assured their continued local agency. Only in 1945 would some of these movements be integrated into the grander narrative of the resistance, a narrative that local leaders would have rejected at the time since participation in resistance activities would have meant collaborating with their Chetnik or Communist enemies.

Civil conflict continued in various forms after the Partisans marched victoriously into Sarajevo in April 1945. "Rebels" and "bandits," as they became known, roamed the hills for months and even years, hiding out in villages, hoarding weapons and food, and preparing for the next stage of war. That the Communists would be a permanent fixture had not yet been determined, and fringe groups, such as the Catholic militias, still hoped to influence the postwar order. They did not yet realize that the Allies had grown tired of war, much less that they had already colored Yugoslavia red in the new map of Europe. With no assistance forthcoming, the bandits gradually fled the region or were arrested; some just disappeared into their old communities. Local loyalties ran deep; Bosnia's mountainous terrain was filled with hideouts; identities were easily transferable.[17] In time, the bandits disappeared, and so too did many of their stories.

As the members of the various groups vying for prominence in the coming regime found their way, piecemeal, back into the obscurity of the social fabric, the postwar order gradually found form and acceptance. As resistance to Communism petered out, Sarajevans confronted the same harsh reality facing many Europeans: the world in which they lived was a different world from the one they wanted. The challenge that the city would face over the next half century would be to integrate the ideal with the reality, a challenge that meant actively and collectively forgetting many aspects of the wartime battles, particularly those of a confessional nature and those that implied an incompatibility between civic consciousness and socialism. These lost chapters of the war—the voluntary conversions of Jews, the Islamist movements, the Serb presence in local political life—were the essence of Sarajevo's civil conflict. It is precisely the unresolved and under-the-surface conflicts of these lost chapters, rather than the openly acknowledged and familiar war between Chetniks, Partisans, and Ustashas, that Mehmedonović's generation now confronts.

Reading Wartime through a Local Lens

Analyzing local stories allows us to break from the constraints of the predominant nationcentric model and test ways that events in one place mirror

---

17. Such a story is well known in Bosnia, where war criminals evaded capture for decades after the Bosnian war of the 1990s. At the time of writing this book, the war criminal Ratko Mladić was still at large, presumably in Bosnia or Serbia.

or challenge historical assumptions. In this regard, Sarajevo's story is not exceptional: it is not just a Balkan story, a Bosnian story, or a Sarajevan story, but a European story, one that took place within the transnational space of Hitler's Europe. It emphasizes how the idea and practice of policies in Hitler's Europe reflected a combination of local, national, and international agendas. In creating the Handžar Division, for example, the Germans contributed to the shifting dynamics of civil war in Yugoslavia while integrating Bosnia's Muslims into the ideological army of Hitler's Europe. Debates between the Ustasha regime and Muslim leaders about the jurisdiction of Sharia law led directly to the passage of state civil marriage laws in 1944.[18] German frustrations with Ustasha ineptitude created opportunities for Sarajevo's leaders to assert their own agendas. Reciprocity and negotiation occurred on all sides.

Even more striking is the reciprocity exhibited between Sarajevo and the Ustasha regime, whereby local identities could and did affect state policies. For example, the town's refusal to condone the racial categorization of Roma as non-Aryans sent the Ustashas back to the drawing board—for two years city and state leaders negotiated both the abstract language and concrete means of targeting Roma. When the regime sought to cleanse Sarajevo of its Serb population, the Bosnian capital put pressure on the regime—at times openly defying national directives—which in turn contributed to a shifting discourse on the meaning of Serb and the Ustasha regime's discriminatory policies. Although local challenges did not single-handedly change state policy, they helped to undermine the legitimacy of the Ustasha regime's policies and even its foundational ideology.[19]

Sarajevo's story also sheds light on the ways that local loyalties can shape the reception of new ideologies. One of the clearest examples of this dynamic was in the town's diverse approaches to Croat nationhood. The leaders of the local Roman Catholic Church projected a clerical understanding of nation rooted in faith. They aimed to use the Croat nation as a means to strengthen and promulgate conservative, Catholic values in a region they viewed to be dominated by Orthodox Serbs and Muslims. In a different approach, progressive Muslim politicians, while espousing discrete notions of Muslim autonomy, tended to adopt a broad, secular understanding of the Croat nation that left room for the practice of Islam in the private realm. By contrast, Islamists hoped the Croat national movement would give them space to revive a religious-based culture and promote a political relationship that allowed for religious self-government.

18. HDA, Ministarstvo pravosuđa i bogoštovlja NDH, Odjel za Pravosuđe, box 1, no document number (August 7, 1944). On the response of the Sharia courts, see ABiH, Vrhovni Šerijatski Sud, box 198, document 87 (Summer 1944).
19. Balić, "When Croatia Needed Serbs."

In yet another variation on the theme of the Croat nation, members of Sarajevo's cultural milieu often conflated the Croat national project with their loyalty to Sarajevo's urban, cosmopolitan culture rather than adopting the Ustasha national program in toto. They anticipated that the nation would be a framework through which they would respect, confirm, and perpetuate the city's tradition of high cultural standards, erudition, and strong civic (and "civilized") values, which they then hoped to spread deep into the provinces. From their discrete vantage points, Sarajevo's Croats confronted a paradox of modernism eloquently described by Kenneth Frampton— "how to become modern and to return to sources; how to revive an old, dormant civilization and take part in universal civilization."[20] They were at once seeking to join new political and ideological movements and to reflect, respect, and rehabilitate the local culture they cherished. Nationalism was not just a way of seeing the world; it was a way of enabling the coexistence of the local Sarajevo community and a universalizing modern ideology. Whereas the above-noted modernist paradox is often analyzed on a theoretical level, Sarajevo's story offers empirical evidence of how local communities sought to integrate the local into the universal and the universal into the local.

Members of Sarajevo's Muslim and Catholic elite had thrown their support to the NDH because of expectations of autonomy, promises of cultural renewal, and a desire to combat interwar secular liberalism with a new political culture strongly rooted in some combination of conservative, reactionary, and religious values. None of these expectations were met. The Ustasha regime had its own model for political transition and state building, its own visions for the culture of a new order, and its own plan for the relationship between religion and the state. Though an uneasy partnership had developed between the Ustasha regime and Sarajevo's various Croats, the incongruity between local and national goals was apparent almost immediately. Sarajevan Croats looked the nation-state squarely in the face, recognized its flaws, and decided that it was neither a viable nor a desirable option. Their turn to pluralism was thus not merely a revival of past traditions, but a direct response to modern mass politics and a rejection of the nation-state.

There is another lesson to be learned from an evaluation of these disconnected local interpretations of nation: in some urban areas, cultural and psychological resistance to state ideology could be far more effective than traditional violent means. While certainly not the only reason for the failure of the NDH—which involved a combination of poor leadership, defective policies, bad alliances, and civil conflict—the inability to forge a coherent, accessible, universal identity in the peripheries did play a role in the state's implosion.

20. Kenneth Frampton, "Prospects for a Critical Regionalism," *Perspecta* 20 (1983): 148.

Circuitous explanations of the way that local, national, and international politics played out on the ground in Sarajevo reveal the shortcomings of the models most often employed in framing war and Yugoslavia—particularly the lens of ethnic conflict and the dichotomy of collaboration and resistance. While useful in distilling general themes and patterns of the war, these frameworks, like many other analytical frameworks, tend to obscure local dynamics. Indeed, the big picture hides the details that often tell a very different story. Ethnic conflict fails to capture the political infighting within groups, as well as the divergent concepts of ethnicity and community addressed at length throughout this work. The many variants of local nationalism underscore the ambiguity and insufficiency of ethnicity as a framework, which make ethnic conflict a slippery concept in the study of the Second World War and the Balkans.

The classic dichotomy of collaboration and resistance—the analytical model used to examine some types of behavior in Hitler's Europe—poses a different methodological problem. In seeking to categorize acts rather than explain what drove such behavior, we miss the complexities and interconnections of the local agendas and local histories at work. In other words, such categories conscript evidence of local behavior to the service of a grand narrative rather than parsing that behavior to elucidate a unique regional dynamic. In analyzing the local responses to the Ustasha genocidal agenda, I have shown that, overwhelmingly, Sarajevo's leaders disagreed with a central tenet of the Nazi "New Order": that biology could determine an individual's identity. Consequently, they fought for exemptions for individuals—and at times for entire groups such as Muslim Roma, Jewish converts, and Sarajevo Serbs—who they believed belonged to *their* community because of a shared religious, ethnic, or civic connection. Yet resistance as a category was not normative: there were many different reasons why people acted as they did. Acquiring power, property, goods, or services could be a motive for assisting a Serb coworker or visiting a Jewish hairdresser, just as it could be a motive for undermining corrupt Ustasha officials or assisting the Germans. Moreover, while rejecting externally imposed definitions of belonging, local communities had their own means of "othering." Sarajevo's responses to refugees, beggars, and political enemies all indicated that town officials were relatively amenable to proscription by social or political category, which they employed to serve the practical maintenance and general well-being of the community.

It is difficult to escape the simplistic binaries that are embedded in popular understandings of the history of the war, and analyzing the local allows us to investigate the subtleties beneath the dichotomy of resistance and complicity. Discussions of Muslim resistance, for example, typically highlight the Muslim resolutions in the fall of 1941, an important public stand against Ustasha violence and genocide. By contrast, the formation of the Bosnian Muslim Waffen SS unit is the evidence of choice in arguments depicting Muslims as brutal Nazi collaborators. What is often overlooked, however, is that many of *the same men* were involved in the development of both. Whereas specific acts might be classified as collaboration or resistance, applying the same labels to the individuals who undertook those acts is far trickier. Any given individual made many decisions during the war, and in the case of Sarajevo, those decisions do not cohere under the established binary standards. Read in terms of local motive, however, these individuals can be seen as having consistent, personal goals.[21] In each of the examples above, Muslim leaders sought a solution that would protect the Muslim community, safeguard Islamic institutions, and stifle the escalating violence toward Muslims. Such an analysis by no means diminishes the moral or ethical responsibility associated with the decision to join the Nazi war effort. Rather, it indicates the necessity of understanding local motives in the process of evaluating national and international processes.

Synthesizing these elements, we begin to understand how Sarajevo's society and civic culture persevered in the face of crisis, its multicultural character shifting from one rooted in confessional traditions to one grounded in the secular bonds of social and political culture. At a time when other multicultural towns imploded under the pressures of war and nationalism, Sarajevo avoided the discontinuities of the modern state and retained a multicultural fabric that, one may argue, is not possible even in modern liberal democracy. The multiculturalism that endures in Sarajevo today has been built atop these very layers of community that, at a time of severe crisis and deprivation, did not coalesce in any romantic sense, but nonetheless eluded the prevalent fate of dissolution.

21. Timothy Snyder's *Red Prince* makes a similar argument in examining the character and lifetime acts of Wilhelm von Habsburg, whose alliances and activities during the 1930s and 1940s appeared ideologically contradictory but whose central goals—Ukrainian independence and his own political leadership—remained consistent. *The Red Prince: The Secret Lives of a Habsburg Archduke* (New York: Basic Books, 2008).

BIBLIOGRAPHY

Archival Sources

The archives of the former Yugoslavia have had as complicated a history as the region itself. After World War II, Tito's government encouraged each republic (Serbia, Bosnia and Herzegovina, Croatia, Slovenia, Montenegro, and Macedonia) to maintain and develop its own archives, which meant that records pertaining to the war landed in various institutions. The state divided documents on the Ustasha government between archives in Croatia and Bosnia, and it created new archives to collect materials related to the country's socialist origins, such as Sarajevo's Muzej Revolucije (Museum of the Revolution), which is today called Historijski Muzej Bosne i Hercegovine (Historical Museum of Bosnia and Herzegovina). Similarly, German wartime documents did not end up in one place but can instead be found in Yugoslavia, Germany, and the United States.

After the breakup of Yugoslavia in 1991, there was another reshuffling of archival materials as each of the successor states claimed records that belonged to its history. Documents pertaining to Sarajevo also became victims of the war. During the devastating siege of Sarajevo (1992–95), many of the city's libraries, museums, and archives were destroyed by heavy shelling and fires. A handful of dedicated archivists collected and hid as much as they could in basements and warehouses across the city. After the war these collections (or parts of them) remained scattered because the archives did not have adequate funds or space to relocate them. Luckily for researchers, the archivists have an uncanny recollection of where they put things a decade ago. One archivist led me to the minute books of Narodna Uzdanica's women's committee, which were "filed" on the second floor of a warehouse next door to the home of refugee squatters. Another led me through dark basement tunnels with low ceilings to a tiny room with unmarked boxes that contained entire World War II collections. Research on Bosnia would be impossible without these dedicated servants of history, and I am deeply indebted to them all.

Because of the region's complicated history, in my investigation of Sarajevo's past I worked with more than fifty archival collections (fonds) in seven major archives. Each archive has its own method of categorizing and collecting materials, which at times creates the appearance of an unsystematic approach to footnotes. For instance, the Croatian National Archives in Zagreb have been organized according to West European norms: collections have detailed inventories and are arranged by document number and date. Some Bosnian archives aim to follow this model; however, because of the constraints of war and funding, there is great diversity in both the quality and quantity of materials in each collection. Some collections have just one box, while others have thousands. The majority of those surveyed for this study had five to eleven boxes of materials related to the war. A few have detailed inventories, with documents organized by number and arranged in boxes. Unfortunately, some of the large collections remain uncataloged, and I can refer only to a box number and date in my notes (e.g., Gradsko Poglavarstvo, the records of Sarajevo's mayor's office). Still other collections, such as those of the local courts (Sudbeni Stol) were temporarily held together by string. I offer as precise information as possible whenever citing materials.

ABiH—Arhiv Bosne i Hercegovine (Archives of Bosnia and Herzegovina)
Društvo Crveni Križ (Society of the Red Cross)
Državno Ravnateljstvo za Gospodarstvenu Ponovu (State Department for Economic Regeneration)
Državno Zastupništvo u Sarajevu (State Attorney's Office in Sarajevo)
Hrvatsko Kulturno Društvo Napredak (Croat Cultural Society Napredak)
Javni Ured Rada Sarajevo (Office of Labor and Employment, Sarajevo)
Narodno Pozorište Sarajevo (National Theater of Sarajevo)
Poglavnikovo Povjereništvo Sarajevo (Office of the Poglavnik's Deputies for Sarajevo)
Povjerenstvo za Radnje Drž. Hrv.—Sarajevo (Commission of Stores for the State of Croatia, Sarajevo)
Prosvjeta Kulturno Društvo (Prosvjeta Cultural Society)
Riznično Upraviteljstvo Ured za podržavljeni Imetak (Department of Treasury, Office for State Confiscated Property)
Sudbeni Stol (Local courts; records also include documents from the county courts, *kotarski sud*)
Ured za kolonizaciju—Sarajevo (Office for Colonization, Sarajevo)
Veliki Župan Vrhbosna (County Executive of Vrhbosna)
Vrhovni Šerijatski Sud (High Sharia Court)
Zbirka NOR-a Okružni Komitet KPJ Sarajevo (Regional Committee of the Communist Party of Yugoslavia)
Zemaljska komisija za utvrđivanje ratnih zločina okupatora i njihovih pomagača za BiH (Land Commission for the Establishment of War Crimes of the Occupiers and Their Collaborators in Bosnia and Herzegovina)
Zemaljski Muzej Bosne i Hercegovine (Land Museum of Bosnia and Herzegovina)

ARIZBiH—Arhiv Rijaseta Islamske Zajednice Bosne i Hercegovine (Archives of the Islamic Religious Community of Bosnia and Herzegovina)
Ulema Medžlis (Council of Advisers to the Reis-ul-ulema)

HDA—Hrvatski državni arhiv (Croatian State Archives), Žagreb
Ministarstvo Narodne Prosvjete NDH (Ministry of National Education of the Independent State of Croatia)

Ministarstvo pravosuđa i bogoštovlja NDH (Ministry of Law and Religion of the Independent State of Croatia)
Ministarstvo Unutrašnjih Poslova NDH (Ministry of the Interior of the Independent State of Croatia)

HM—*Historijski Muzej Bosne i Hercegovine (Historical Museum of Bosnia and Herzegovina)*
Četnička građa (Chetnik Documents)
Ustaška građa (Ustasha Documents)
Ustaška Nadzorna Služba (Ustasha Surveillance Service)
Zbirka Fotografija, fond NOB [Narodne Oslobodilačke Borbe] (Photograph collection, National Liberation Struggle)

Hoover Institution Archives
Heinrich Himmler Papers
Jozo Tomasevich Papers

IAS—*Istorijski Arhiv Sarajevo (Historical Archives of the City of Sarajevo)*
Društvo Hrvatskih Katoličkih Žena u Sarajevu (Society of Croat Catholic Women of Sarajevo)
Društvo Hrvatskih Katoličkih Muževa (Society of Croat Catholic Men)
Državno Ravnateljstvo za Gospodarstvenu Ponovu (State Department for Economic Regeneration)
Gradsko Poglavarstvo (City Hall/Municipal Government)
Hrvatski Crveni Križ (Croatian Red Cross)
Hurijet
Kotarsko Nadzorničtvo Narodne Zaštite u Sarajevu (Regional Office for National Security in Sarajevo)
Muslimansko Društvo "Jediler" (Muslim Society Jediler)
Muslimansko Kulturno i Humanitarstvo Društvo "Bratstvo" (Muslim Cultural and Humanitarian Society Bratstvo)
Muslimansko Humanitarno Društvo "Merhamet" (Muslim Humanitarian Society Merhamet)
Muslimansko Kulturno Društvo "Narodna Uzdanica" (Muslim Cultural Society Narodna Uzdanica)
Ostavština Abdullah Bušatlića (Personal collection of Abdullah Bušatlić)
Ostavština Borivoja Jevtića (Personal collection of Borivoje Jevtić)
Ostavština Fehima Spaha (Personal collection of Fehim Spaho)
Ostavština Hamdije Kreševljakovića (Personal collection of Hamdija Kreševljaković)
Riznično Upraviteljstvo Ured za podržavljeni imetak (Department of Treasury, Office for State Confiscated Property)
Ured za upravu židovskim nekretninama (Office for the Administration of Jewish Property)
Zbirka Varia (Miscellaneous Collection)

USHMM—*Archives of the United States Holocaust Memorial Museum*

Newspapers and Periodicals

Bratstvo
El-Hidaje
Gajret Kalendar
Glasnik Islamske Vjerske Zajednice
Glas Pravoslavlja
Hrvatska Misao
Jugoslovenska Pošta
Kalendar Bratstvo
Kalendar Svetog Ante
Katolički Tjednik
Napredak—Kalendar
Narodna Uzdanica—Kalendar
Narodno Jedinstvo
Novi Behar
Novi Istočnik
Oslobođenje
Osvit
Pregled
Sarajevski Novi List
Službeni List
Vrhbosna

Published Primary Sources

Almirli, Jaša, ed. *Živi i Mrtvi: Razgovori sa Jevrejima*. Belgrade: S. Mešić, 2002.
The Cetniks, A Survey of Cetnik Activity in Yugoslavia, April 1941–July 1944. Allied Forces Head Quarters, September 1944.
Danon, I. Cadik "Braco." *Sasečeno stablo Danonovih, sećanje na Jasenovac*. Belgrade: S. Mesić, 2000.
Dedijer, Vladimir. *The War Diaries of Vladimir Dedijer*. Vol. 2. Ann Arbor: University of Michigan Press, 1990.
Dedijer, Vladimir, and Antun Miletić, eds. *Genocid nad Muslimanima, 1941–1945: zbornik dokumenata i svedočenja*. Sarajevo: Svjetlost, 1990.
——, eds. *Proterivanje Srba sa ognjišta 1941–1944, Svedočanstva*. Belgrade: Prosveta, 1990.
Gaon, Aleksandar, ed. *Mi smo preživeli: Jevreji o Holokaustu*. Belgrade: Jevrejski Istorijski Muzej, 2001.
Horvat, Joža, and Štambuk, Zdenko. *Dokumenti o protunarodnom radu i zločinima jednog dijela katoličkog klera*. Zagreb: Štamparija Rozankowski, 1946.
Huseinović, I., and Dž Babić. *Svjetlost Evrope u Bosni i Hercegovini*. Sarajevo: Buybook, 2004.
Jevtić, Borivoje. *Izabrana Djela*. Vols. 1–3. Sarajevo: Svjetlost, 1982.
——. *Sarajevski Atentat*. Sarajevo: Štamparija i izd. Petra N. Gakovića, 1924.
Konačni rezultati popisa stanovništva od 15 marta 1948 godine. Belgrade: Savezni zavod za statistiku, 1951.
Korkut-Spaho, Muniba, and Safija Šiljak, eds. *Mlade muslimanke, Svjedočenja i Sjećanja*. Sarajevo: Mladi Muslimani, 1999.

Krišto, Jure, ed. *Katolička Crkva i Nezavisna Država Hrvatska, Dokumenti.* Zagreb: Hrvatski Institut za Povijest, 1998.

Nametak, Alija. *Sarajevski Nekrologij.* Zurich: Bošnjački Institut and Nakladni Zavod Globus, 1994.

Popis Stanovnišva, 31. Marta 1931. Belgrade: Opšta državna statistika, 1931.

Sindik, Dušan, ed. *Sećanja Jevreja na logor Jasenovac.* Belgrade: Savez Jevrejskih opština, 1972.

Spomenica pravoslavnih sveštenika—zrtava fašističkog terora i palih u narodnooslobodilačkoj borbi. Belgrade: Savez udruženja pravoslavnog sveštenstva FNRJ, 1960.

Vukmanović-Tempo, Svetozar. *Revolucija koja teče, Memoari.* Zagreb: Globus, 1982.

West, Rebecca. *Black Lamb, Grey Falcon: A Journey through Yugoslavia.* New York: Viking, 1941.

Zbornik dokumenata i podataka o narodnooslobodilačkom ratu jugoslovenskih naroda. Belgrade: Vojnoistorijski Institut, 1949–72.

Zbornik zakona i naredaba Nezavisne Države Hrvatske. Zagreb: Narodne novina, 1941–44.

Zločini na jugoslovenskim prostorima u prvom i drugom svetskom ratu, Zbornik Dokumenata. Belgrade: Vojnoistorijski Institut, 1993.

Cited Secondary Sources

Ademović, Fadil. *Novinstvo i Ustaška Propaganda u Nezavisnoj Državi Hrvatskoj.* Sarajevo: Media Centar, 2000.

Albahari, Nisim et al., eds. *Sarajevo u Revoluciji.* Vols. 1–4. Sarajevo: Istorijski Arhiv Sarajevo, 1976–81.

——, eds. *Sarajevo u socijalističkoj Jugoslaviji.* Vol. 1. Sarajevo: Istorijski Arhiv Sarajevo, 1988.

Alexander, Stella. *Church and State in Yugoslavia since 1945.* Cambridge: Cambridge University Press, 1979.

Alić, Dijana, and Maryam Gusheh. "Reconciling Nationalist Narratives in Socialist Bosnia and Herzegovina: The Baščaršija Project, 1948–1953." *Journal of the Society of Architectural Historians* 58, no. 1 (March 1999): 6–25.

Allcock, John. *Explaining Yugoslavia.* New York: Columbia University Press, 2000.

Anderson, Benedict. *Imagined Communities: Reflections on the Origin and Spread of Nationalism.* New York: Verso, 1991.

Anderson, Margaret Lavinia. "Historiographical Review: The Limits of Secularization: On the Problem of the Catholic Revival in Nineteenth-Century Germany." *Historical Journal* 38, no. 3 (1995): 647–670.

Antonić, Zdravko et al., eds. *Pokrajinsko savjetovanje KPJ za Bosnu i Hercegovinu.* Sarajevo: Institut za Istoriju, 1983.

Auty, Phyllis. *Tito: A Biography.* Harmondsworth, U.K.: Penguin, 1974.

Balić, Emily Greble. "When Croatia Needed Serbs: Nationalism and Genocide in Sarajevo (1941–1942)." *Slavic Review* 68, no. 1 (Spring 2009): 116–137.

Banac, Ivo. *The National Question in Yugoslavia: Origins, History, Politics.* Ithaca: Cornell University Press, 1984.

Banac, Ivo, and Katherine Verdery, eds. *National Character and National Ideology in Interwar Eastern Europe.* New Haven: Yale Center for International and Area Studies, 1995.

Bartov, Omer. "The Roots of Modern Genocide: On the Macro- and Microhistory of Mass Murder." In *The Specter of Genocide: Mass Murder in Historical Perspective,* edited by Robert Gellately and Ben Kiernan. New York: Cambridge University Press, 2003.

Barun, Anđelko. *Svjedoci i učitelji, povijest franjevaca Bosne Srebrene.* Sarajevo: Svjetlo Riječi, 2003.

Batinić, Jelena. "Gender, Revolution, and War: The Mobilization of Women in the Yugoslav Partisan Movement during World War II." PhD diss., Stanford University, 2009.

Bavčič, Uzeir. *"Merhamet" (1913–2003).* Sarajevo: Muslimansko Dobrotvorno Društvo, "Merhamet" Sarajevo, 2003.

Behmen, Omer, ed. *Mladi Muslimani 1939–1999.* Vol 1. Sarajevo: Mladi Muslimani, 2001.

Bejtić, Alija. "Ali-pašina Mahala u Sarajevu." *Prilozi Instituta za Istoriju* 2 (1966): 19–58.

Biondich, Mark. "Religion and Nation in Wartime Croatia: Reflections on the Ustaša Policy of Forced Religious Conversions, 1941–1942." *Slavonic and East European Review* 83, no. 1 (January 1995): 71–116.

———. *Stjepan Radić, the Croatian Peasant Party, and the Politics of Mass Mobilization, 1918–1928.* Toronto: University of Toronto, 2000.

Bjork, James. *Neither German nor Pole: Catholicism and National Indifference in a Central European Borderland.* Ann Arbor: University of Michigan Press, 2008.

Blackbourn, David, and James Retallack, eds. *Localism, Landscape, and the Ambiguities of Place: German-Speaking Central Europe, 1860–1930.* Toronto: University of Toronto Press, 2007.

Bojić, Mehmedalija. *Historija Bosne i Bošnjaka (VII–XX vijeka).* Sarajevo: TKD Šahinpašić, 2001.

Bokovoy, Melissa K. *Peasants and Communists: Politics and Ideology in the Yugoslav Countryside, 1941–1953.* Pittsburgh: University of Pittsburgh Press, 1988.

Boym, Svetlana. *The Future of Nostalgia.* New York: Basic Books, 2001.

Braude, Benjamin. "Foundation Myths of the *Millet* System." In *Christians and Jews in the Ottoman Empire: The Functioning of a Plural Society,* edited by Benjamin Braude and Bernard Lewis. New York: Holmes and Meyer, 1982.

Breuilly, John. *Nationalism and the State.* Chicago: University of Chicago Press, 1994.

Bringa, Tone. *Being Muslim the Bosnian Way.* Princeton: Princeton University Press, 1995.

Brint, Steven. "Gemeinschaft Revisited: A Critique and Reconstruction of the Community Concept." *Sociological Theory* 19, no. 1 (March 2001): 1–23.

Brubaker, Rogers. *Ethnicity without Groups.* Cambridge, Mass.: Harvard University Press, 2004.

———. *Nationalism Reframed: Nationhood and the National Question in the New Europe.* New York: Cambridge University Press, 1996.

Brubaker, Rogers, Margit Feischmidt, Jon Fox, and Liana Grancea. *Nationalist Politics and Everyday Ethnicity in a Transylvanian Town.* Princeton: Princeton University Press, 2006.

Bryant, Chad. "Either German or Czech: Fixing Nationality in Bohemia and Moravia, 1939–1946." *Slavic Review* 61, no. 4 (Winter 2002).

———. *Prague in Black: Nazi Rule and Czech Nationalism.* Cambridge, Mass.: Harvard University Press, 2007.

Brynjar, Lia. *The Society of the Muslim Brothers in Egypt: The Rise of an Islamic Mass Movement 1928–1942.* Ithaca: Ithaca Press, 2006.

Bugge, Peter. "The Making of a Slovak City: The Czechoslovak Renaming of Pressburg/Pozsony/Prešporok, 1918–1919." *Austrian History Yearbook* 35 (2004): 205–227.

Burrin, Phillipe. *France under the Germans: Collaboration and Compromise.* Translated by Janet Lloyd. New York: New Press, 1993.

Case, Holly. *Between States: The Transylvanian Question and the European Idea during WWII.* Stanford: Stanford University Press, 2009.

Clark, Christopher, and Wolfram Kaiser, eds. *Culture Wars: Secular-Catholic Conflict in Nineteenth-Century Europe.* Cambridge: Cambridge University Press, 2003.

Colić, Mladen. *Takozvana Nezavisna Država Hrvatska 1941.* Belgrade: Delta-Pres, 1973.

Deák, István, Jan T. Gross, and Tony Judt, eds. *The Politics of Retribution in Europe: World War II and Its Aftermath.* Princeton: Princeton University Press, 2000.

Djilas, Milovan. *Tito: The Story from Inside.* New York: Harcourt Brace Jovanovich, 1980.

Donia, Robert. *Islam under the Double Eagle: The Muslims of Bosnia and Hercegovina, 1878–1914.* Boulder: East European Monographs, 1981.

——. *Sarajevo: A Biography.* Ann Arbor: University of Michigan Press, 2006.

Donia, Robert, and John Fine. *Bosnia and Hercegovina: A Tradition Betrayed.* New York: Columbia University Press, 1994.

Dragostinova, Theodora. "Speaking National: Nationalizing the Greeks of Bulgaria, 1900–1939." *Slavic Review* 67, no. 1 (Spring 2008): 154–181.

Dulić, Tomaslav. *Utopias of Nation, Local Mass Killing in Bosnia and Herzegovina, 1941–1942.* Stockholm: Elanders Gotab, 2005.

Etzioni, Amitai. "Creating Good Communities and Good Societies." *Contemporary Sociology* 29, no. 1 (January 2000) 188–195.

Filandra, Šaćir. *Bošnjačka politika.* Sarajevo: IP Sejtarija, 1998.

Finci, Moni. "O hapšenju komunista i otkrivanju tehnike pokrajinskog komiteta u Sarajevu, krajem Juna 1941. Godine." *Prilozi institut za Istoriju* 19 (1982).

——. "O socijalnoj i političkoj diferencijaciji među sarajevskim jevrejima u razdoblje 1918–1941." *Prilozi Institut za Istoriju* 18 (1981).

Fine, John V. A. *When Ethnicity Did Not Matter in the Balkans: A Study of Identity in Prenationalist Croatia, Dalmatia, and Slavonia in the Medieval and Early Modern Periods.* Ann Arbor: University of Michigan Press, 2006.

Ford, Kirk. *OSS and the Yugoslav Resistance, 1943–1945.* College Station: Texas A&M University Press, 1992.

Fox, Edward Whiting. *History in Geographic Perspective, the Other France.* New York: Norton, 1971.

Frampton, Kenneth. "Prospects for a Critical Regionalism." *Perspecta* 20 (1983): 147–162.

Freidenreich, Harriet Pass. *The Jews of Yugoslavia: A Quest for Community.* Philadelphia: Jewish Publication Society of America, 1979.

Friedman, Francine. *The Bosnian Muslims, Denial of a Nation.* Boulder: Westview, 1996.

Gavran, Ignacije. *Lucerna Lucens? Odnos vrhbosanskog ordinarijata prema Bosanskim Franjevcima (1881–1975).* Visoko: Nadlada pisceva, 1978.

Gavranović Berislav. *Uspostava redovite katoličke hijerarhije u Bosni i Hercegovini 1881. godine.* Belgrade: Popović, 1935.

Gellner, Ernest. *Nations and Nationalism.* Oxford: Blackwell, 1982.

Gigova, Irina. "Writers of the Nation: Intellectual Identity in Bulgaria, 1939–1953." PhD diss., University of Illinois, 2005.

Gildea, Robert. *Marianne in Chains: Daily Life in the Heart of France during the German Occupation.* New York: Metropolitan Books, 2002.

Glenny, Misha. *The Balkans, Nationalism, War, and the Great Powers, 1804–1999.* New York: Penguin, 1999.

Goldstein, Ivo, ed. *Antisemitizam, Holokaust, Antifašizam.* Zagreb: Židovska općina Zagreb, 1996.

Grijak, Zoran. *Politička djelatnost vrhbosanskog nadbiskupa Josipa Stadlera.* Zagreb: Hrvatski Institut za Povijest and Vrhbosanska nadbiskupija, 2001.

Gross, Jan. *Neighbors: The Destruction of the Jewish Community in Jedwabne, Poland.* Princeton: Princeton University Press, 2001.

Gumz, Jonathan. "German Counterinsurgency Policy in Independent Croatia, 1941–1944." *Historian* 61 (Fall 1998): 33–50.

Hadžiahmetović, Ismail. *Narodna Uzdanica u kulturnome i društvenome životu Muslimana Bosne i Hercegovine.* Tuzla: Historijski Arhiv, 1998.

Hadžibegović, Iljas. *Bosanskohercegovački gradovi na razmeđu 19. i 20. stoljeća.* Sarajevo: Institut za Istoriju u Sarajevu, 2004.

Hadžijahić, Muhamed. "Bosanski Romi 1941–1942." *Naše teme* 7–8 (1984): 1313–1323.

——. *Od tradicije do identiteta.* Zagreb: Islamska Zajednica Zagreb, 1990.

Hanebrink, Paul. *In Defense of Christian Hungary: Religion, Nationalism, and Antisemitism, 1890–1944.* Ithaca: Cornell University Press, 2006.

Hasanbegović, Zlatko. *Jugoslavenska muslimanska organizacija u političkom životu Kraljevine Jugoslavije 1929.–1941.* PhD diss., University of Zagreb, 2009.

——. *Muslimani u Zagrebu, 1878–1945.* Zagreb: Institut društvenih znanosti Ivo Pilar, 2007.

——. "O pokušajima donošenja Ustava Islamske Vjerske Zajednice u Nezavisnoj Državi Hrvatskoj." *Časopis za suvremenu povijest* 27, no. 3 (1995): 75–90.

Hawkesworth, Celia, Muriel Heppell, and Harry Norris, eds. *Religious Quest and National Identity in the Balkans.* London: Palgrave, 2001.

Hehn, Paul N. *The German Struggle against Yugoslav Guerillas in World War II.* Boulder: East European Monographs, 1979.

Herzfeld, Michael. *Cultural Intimacy: Social Poetics in the Nation-State.* 2nd ed. New York: Routledge, 2005.

Hnilicka, Karl. *Das Ende auf dem Balkan: 1944–45.* Musterschmidt: Gottingen, 1970.

Hoare, Marko Attila. *Genocide and Resistance in Hitler's Bosnia: The Partisans and the Chetniks, 1941–1943.* Oxford: Oxford University Press, 2007.

——. *The History of Bosnia from the Middle Ages to the Present Day.* London: Saqi, 2007.

——. "Whose Is the Partisan Movement? Serbs, Croats, and the Legacy of a Shared Resistance." *Journal of Slavic Military Studies* 15, no. 4 (December 2002): 24–41.

Hobsbawm, Eric, and Terence Ranger, eds. *The Invention of Tradition.* New York: Cambridge University Press, 1992.

Hory, Ladislaus, and Martin Broszat. *Der Kroatische Ustascha-Staat 1941–1945.* Stuttgart: Deutsche Verlags-anstalt, 1964.

Imamović, Mustafa. *Historija Bošnjaka*. Sarajevo: Preporod, 1998.

——. *Historija države i prava Bosne i Hercegovine*. Sarajevo: Magistrat, 2003.

Išek, Tomislav. *Mjesto i uloga HKD Napredak u kulturnom životu Hrvata Bosne i Herce-govine*. Sarajevo: Institut za Istoriju, 2004.

Ivanov, Pavle Dželetović. *Jevreji Kosova i Metohije*. Belgrade: Panpublik, 1988.

Jareb, Mario. *Ustaško-domobranski pokret: Od nastanska do travnja 1941. Godine.* Zagreb: Školska Knjiga, 2006.

Jelić-Butić, Fikreta. *Ustaše i Nezavisna Država Hrvatska 1941–1945*. Zagreb: Sveučilišana naklada Liber, 1978.

Jelinek, Yeshayahu A. "Bosnia-Herzegovina at War: Relations between Moslems and non-Moslems." *Holocaust and Genocide Studies* 5, no. 3 (1990): 275–292.

——. "Nationalities and Minorities in the Independent State of Croatia." *Nationalities Papers* 8, no. 2 (Fall 1980): 195–206.

Jelinović, Zvonimir. "Hrvatska vojska (domobranstvo) i obrana." *Časopis za suvremenu povijesti* 27, no. 3 (1995), 569–583.

Judson, Pieter. *The Guardians of the Nation: Activists on the Language Frontiers of Imperial Austria*. Cambridge, Mass.: Harvard University Press, 2006.

Judt, Tony. *Postwar: Europe Since 1945*. New York: Penguin, 2005.

Kalyvas, Stathys. *The Logic of Violence in Civil War*. New York: Cambridge University Press, 2006.

Kamberović, Husnija. *Prema modernom društvu. Bosna i Hercegovina od 1945. do 1953. godine*. Tešanj: Centar za kulturu i obrazovanje Tešanj, 2000.

Kamhi, Samuel, ed. *Spomenica, 400 godina od dolaska Jevreja u Bosnu i Hercegovinu*. Sarajevo: Oslobodenje, 1966.

Karić, Enes, ed. *Reis Džemaludin Čaušević: Prosvjetitelj i reformator*. Sarajevo: Ljiljan, 2002.

Karpat, Kemal. "An Enquiry into the Social Foundations of Nationalism in the Ottoman State: From Social Estates to Classes, From Millets to Nations." Princeton University Center of International Studies Research Monograph no. 39, July 1973.

Katz, Vera. "Komunizam i represija: Sud Narodne Časti u Bosni i Hercegovini." In *60 Godine od završetka drugog svjetskog rata—kako se sjećati 1945. Godine*, edited by Husnija Kamberović, 145–166. Sarajevo: Institut za Istoriju u Sarajevu, 2006.

Kemura, Ibrahim. *Uloga "Gajreta" u društvenom životu Muslimana Bosne i Hercegovine (1903–1941)*. Sarajevo: Veselin Masleša, 1986.

——. *Značaj i uloga "Narodne Uzdanice" u društvenom životu Bošnjaka (1923–1945)*. Sarajevo: Bošnjački Institut i Institut za Istoriju, 2002.

Kerenji Emil. "Jewish Citizens of Socialist Yugoslavia: Politics of Jewish Identity in a Socialist State, 1944–1974." PhD diss., University of Michigan, 2008.

King, Jeremy. *Budweisers into Czechs and Germans: A Local History of Bohemian Politics, 1848–1948*. Princeton: Princeton University Press, 2002.

——. "The Nationalization of East Central Europe: Ethnicism, Ethnicity, and Beyond." In *Staging the Past: The Politics of Commemoration in Habsburg Central Europe, 1848 to the Present*, edited by Maria Bucur and Nancy M. Wingfield. West Lafayette, Ind.: Purdue University Press, 2001.

Kisić-Kolanović, Nada. "Muslimanska inteligencija i islam u Nezavisnoj Državi Hrvatskoj." *Časopis za suvremenu povijesti* 36, no. 3 (2004): 895–1322.

——. "Povijest NDH kao predmet istraživanja," *Časopis za suvremenu povijest* 34, no. 3 (2002): 679–712.

Ključanin, Zilhad, ed. *Mladi Muslimani.* Sarajevo: Biblioteka Ključanin, 1991.

Kohn,Hans. *The Ideal of Nationalism: A Study in Its Origins and Background.* New York: Collier Books, 1944.

Koller, Markus. *Bosnien an der Schwelle zur Neuzeit: Eine Kulturgeschicthe der Gewalt, 1747–1798.* Munich: R. Oldenbourg, 2004.

Koller, Markus, and Kemal Karpat, eds. *Ottoman Bosnia: A History of Peril.* Madison: University of Wisconsin Press, 2004.

Koonz, Claudia. *Mothers in the Fatherland: Women, the Family, and Nazi Politics.* New York: St. Martin's, 1987.

Korb, Alexander. "The Drina Border, Nationalizing Civil War, and the Holocaust in the Independent State of Croatia, 1941–43." Paper presented at the Institute for Global Studies at the University of Minnesota, 2007.

Kostić, Cvetko. "Postanak i razvitak 'čaršije' (Primer čaršije Bajine Bašte)." *Glasnik etnografskog instituta SAN-u,* 4–6 (1955–57): 123–149.

Kreso, Muharem. "Sarajevo-Sjedište Okupacionog sistema u drugom svjetskom ratu." In *Prilozi historiji Sarajeva,* edited by Dževad Juzbašić, 357–366. Sarajevo: Institut za istoriju and Orijentalni institut, 1997.

Krišto, Jure. *Katolička Crkva i Nezavisna Država Hrvatska: 1941–1945.* Zagreb: Hrvatski Institut za Povijest, 1998.

Krizman, Bogdan. *Pavelić i ustaša.* Zagreb: Globus, 1978.

——. *Ustaše i Treći Reich.* Zagreb: Globus, 1983.

Lampe, John. *Yugoslavia as History: Twice There Was a Country.* Cambridge: Cambridge University Press, 2000.

Lampe, John, and Alan Jackson. *Balkan Economic History, 1550–1950: From Imperial Borderlands to Developing Nations.* Bloomington: Indiana University Press, 1982.

Lebl, Ženi. *Do "Konačnog Rešenja": Jevreji u Beogradu 1521–1942.* Belgrade: Čigoja štampa, 2001.

——. *Do Konačnog Rešenja: Jevreji u Srbiji.* Belgrade: Čigoja štampa, 2002.

——. *Jevreji u Pirotu.* Belgrade: Privredni pregled Biblioteka Svedoćanstva, 1990.

Lederer, Ivo. *Yugoslavia at the Paris Peace Conference: A Study in Frontiermaking.* New Haven: Yale University Press, 1963.

Les Systemes d'occupation en Yougoslavie 1941–1945: Reports from the 3rd International Congress on the History of European Resistance in Karlovy Vary, 1963. Belgrade: L'Institute pour l'Etude du Mouvement Ouvrier, 1963.

Levi, Isak. *Jevrejska Opština, Jewish Community in Sarajevo.* Sarajevo: Jevrejska Opština, 1984.

Levi, Pavle. *Disintegration in Frames, Aesthetics and Ideology in the Yugoslav and Post-Yugoslav Cinema.* Stanford: Stanford University Press, 2007.

Levntal, Zdenko, ed. *Zločini fašističkih okupatora i njihovih pomagača protiv Jevreja u Jugoslaviji.* Belgrade: Savez jevrejskih opština Jugoslavije, 1952.

Levy, Moritz. *Die Sephardim in Bosnien.* Klagenfurt, Aus.: Wieser Verlag, 1996.

Malcolm, Noel. *Bosnia: A Short History.* New York: NYU Press, 1996.

Marjanović, Jovan. *Draža Mihailović između Britanaca i Nemaca.* Zagreb: Globus, 1979.

Mazower, Mark. *Hitler's Empire: How the Nazis Ruled Europe.* New York: Penguin, 2008.

——. *Salonica, City of Ghosts: Christians, Muslims and Jews, 1430–1950.* New York: Knopf, 2005.

McConville, Michael. *A Small War in the Balkans: British Military Involvement in Wartime Yugoslavia, 1941–1945*. London: Macmillan, 1986.

Mehmedinović, Semezdin. *Sarajevo Blues*. Translated by Ammiel Alcalay. San Francisco: City Light Books, 1998.

Miličić, Budimir. *Radnička klasa Sarajeva 1919–1941*. Sarajevo: Institut za Istoriju, 1985.

Milton, Giles. *Paradise Lost: Smyrna, 1922*. New York: Basic Books, 2007.

Milošević, Slobodan D. *Izbeglice i preseljenici na teritoriji okupirane Jugoslavije, 1941–1945*. Belgrade: Institut za savremenu istoriju, 1981.

Minić, Miloš. *Oslobodilački ili građanski rat u Jugoslaviji 1941–1945*. Novi Sad: Agencija "Mir," 1993.

Mujić, Muhamed A. "Položaj cigana u jugoslovenskim zemljama pod osmanskom vlašću." *Prilozi za orijentalnu filologiju* 3–4 (1952–53): 137–93.

Murdoch, Caitlin. "The Leaky Boundaries of Manmade States: National Identity, State Policy, and Everyday Life in the Saxon-Bohemian Borderlands, 1870–1938." PhD diss., Stanford University, 2003.

Musabegović, Jasmina. *Kultura španskih Jevreja na Jugoslovenskom tlu*. Sarajevo: Svjetlost, 1990.

Mušović, Ejub. "Nešto o Novopazarskim Jevrejima i njihovoj sudbini u drugom svjetskom ratu." *Jevrejski Almanah* (1965–1967): 149–156.

Naimark, Norman, and Holly Case, eds. *Yugoslavia and Its Historians*. Stanford: Stanford University Press, 2001.

Narodno Pozorište u Sarajevu. Sarajevo: Muzej književnosti i pozorišne umjetnosti BiH, 1998.

Novak, Viktor. *Magnum Krimen, pola vijeka klerikalizma u Hrvatskoj*. 2nd ed. Belgrade: Nova Knjiga, 1986.

Okey, Robin. *Taming Balkan Nationalism. The Habsburg 'Civilizing Mission' in Bosnia, 1878–1914*. Oxford: Oxford University Press, 2007.

Pajić, Milenko. *Sarajevski gradonačelnici*. Sarajevo: Večernje Novine, 1998.

Palavestra, Predrag. *Književnost Mlade Bosne*. Sarajevo: Svjetlost, 1965.

Pavelić, Ante. *Hrvatska Pravoslavna Crkva*. Madrid: Domovina, 1984.

Pavlowitch, Stevan. *Hitler's New Disorder: The Second World War in Yugoslavia*. New York: Columbia University Press, 2008.

Pavlowitch, Stevan. *Tito—Yugoslavia's Great Dictator: A Reassessment*. London: C. Hurst, 1992.

Pelesić, Muhidin. "Prilog istraživanjima propagande i kulturne politike NDH u BiH." *Prilozi institut za Istoriju* 32 (2003): 231–247.

Petešić, Ćiril. *Katoličko svećenstvo u NOB-u 1941–1945*. Zagreb: Vjesnikova Press Agencija, 1982.

Pinson, Mark, ed. *The Muslims of Bosnia-Herzegovina: Their Historic Development from the Middle Ages to the Dissolution of Yugoslavia*. Cambridge, Mass.: Distributed for the Center for Middle Eastern Studies of Harvard University by Harvard University Press, 1996.

Pinto, Avram. *Jevreji Sarajeva i Bosne i Hercegovine*. Sarajevo: Veselin Masleša, 1987.

Porter, Brian. *When Nationalism Began to Hate*. New York: Oxford University Press, 2000.

Požar, Petar. *Hrvatska Pravoslavna Crkva u prošlosti i budućnosti*. Zagreb: Naklada Pavičić, 1996.

Prlenda Sandra. "Young, Religious, and Radical: The Croat Catholic Youth Organizations, 1922–1945." In *Ideologies and National Identities*, edited by John Lampe and Mark Mazower (Budapest: Central European University Press, 2004).

Purivatra, Atif. *Jugoslovenska Muslimanska Organizacija u političkom životu Kraljevine Srba, Hrvata, i Slovenaca*. Sarajevo: Preporod, 1987.

Ramet, Sabrina P. "The NDH—An Introduction." *Totalitarian Movements and Political Religions* 7, no. 4 (December 2006): 399–408.

Redlich, Shimon. *Together and Apart in Brzezany: Poles, Jews and Ukrainians, 1919–1945*. Bloomington: Indiana University Press, 2002.

Redžić, Enver. *Bosnia and Hercegovina in the Second World War*. Translated by Aida Vidan. London: Frank Cass, 2005.

——. *Muslimansko autonomaštvo i 13. SS divizija: Autonomija Bosne i Hercegovine i Hitlerov Treći Rajh*. Sarajevo: Svjetlost, 1987.

Ristović, Milan. *U potrazi za Utočištem: Jugoslovenski Jevreji u Bekstvu od Holokausta 1941–1945*. Belgrade: Službeni list SRJ, 1998.

Roberts, Walter R. *Tito, Mihailović, and the Allies, 1941–1945*. Durham, NC: Duke University Press, 1987.

Rodogno, Davide. *Fascism's European Empire, Italian Occupation during the Second World War*. Translated by Adrian Belton. New York: Cambridge University Press, 2006.

Romano, Jaša. *Jevreji Jugoslavije 1941–1945. Žrtve genocida i učesnici u Narodnooslobodilačkom Ratu*. Belgrade: Savez jevrejskih opština Jugoslavije, 1980.

Šabanović, Hazim. *Bosanski pašaluk*. Sarajevo: Svjetlost, 1982.

Samardžić, Miloslav. *General Draža Mihailović i opšta istorija četničkog pokreta*. Kragujevac: Novi pogledi, 2005.

Sarić, Sajma. "Arhivski fond velika župa Vrhbosna." *Glasnik Arhiva i društva arhivskih radnika Bosne i Hercegovine* 14–15 (1974–75).

Schmidt-Richberg, Erich. *Der Endkampf auf dem Balkan, Die Operationen der Heeresgruppe E von Griechenland bis zu den Alpen*. Heidelberg: Kurt Vowinckel Verlag, 1955.

Serbian Orthodox Church, Its Past and Present. Belgrade: Serbian Orthodox Church, 1965.

Šeta, Ferhat. *Reis-ul-ulema u Bosni i Hercegovini i Jugoslaviji od 1882. do 1991. godine*. Sarajevo: Islamska Vjerska Zajednica, 1991.

Smith, Anthony D. *The Ethnic Origins of Nations*. New York: B. Blackwell, 1987.

Snyder, Timothy. *The Reconstruction of Nations: Poland, Ukraine, Lithuania, Belarus, 1569–1999*. New Haven: Yale University Press, 2003.

——. *The Red Prince: The Secret Lives of a Habsburg Archduke*. New York: Basic Books, 2008.

Steinberg, Jonathan. *All or Nothing: The Axis and the Holocuast, 1941–43*. London: Routledge, 1990.

Straus, Scott. *The Order of Genocide: Race, Power, and War in Rwanda*. Ithaca: Cornell University Press, 2006.

Sugar, Peter. *Industrialization of Bosnia-Hercegovina, 1878–1918*. Seattle: University of Washington Press, 1963.

Tihić Esad S. "Jedinice domobranske dobrovoljačke pukovnije (Domdo) na teritoriji Trebave, Ratiša i Posavine (1942–1943)." *Glasnik Gračanica* 2 (November 1996).

Tilly, Charles. *Trust and Rule.* New York: Cambridge University Press, 2005.

——. *The Vendée.* Cambridge, Mass.: Harvard University Press, 1964.

Timišišić, H. *The Measure of Sarajevo.* Sarajevo: Zavod za izdavanje udžbenika, 1970.

Todorov, Nikolai. *The Balkan City 1400–1900.* Seattle: University of Washington Press, 1983.

Todorova, Maria. *Imagining the Balkans.* New York: Oxford University Press, 1997.

Tomasevich, Jozo. *The Chetniks: War and Revolution in Yugoslavia, 1941–1945.* Stanford: Stanford University Press, 1975.

——. *War and Revolution in Yugoslavia, 1941–1945: Occupation and Collaboration.* Stanford: Stanford University Press, 2001.

Tönnes, Ferdinand. *Community and Civil Society.* Translated by Jose Harris and Margaret Hollis. Cambridge: Cambridge University Press, 2001.

Traljić, Mahmud. *Istaknuti Bošnjaci.* Sarajevo: Rijaset Islamske Zajednice BiH, 1998.

Trew, Simon. *Britain, Mihailovic and the Chetniks, 1941–42.* New York: St. Martin's, 1998.

Trhulj, Sead. *Mladi Muslimani.* Zagreb: Globus, 1992.

Trubeta, Sevasti. "'Gypsiness,' Racial Discourse and Persecution: Balkan Roma during the Second World War." *Nationalities Papers* 31, no. 4 (December 2003): 495–514.

Velikonja, Mitja. *Religious Separation and Political Intolerance in Bosnia-Herzegovina.* Austin: University of Texas Press, 2003.

Vucinich, Wayne. "Modern Yugoslav Drama." *American Slavic and East European Review,* 5, nos. 1 and 2 (May 1946): 1–18.

Wachtel, Andrew. *Making a Nation, Breaking a Nation: Literature and Cultural Politics in Yugoslavia.* Stanford: Stanford University Press, 1998.

Walker, Mack. *German Home Towns.* Ithaca: Cornell University Press, 1971, pb. ed. 1998 with a new foreword by James J. Sheehan.

Weber, Eugen. *Peasants into Frenchmen: The Modernization of Rural France, 1870–1914.* Stanford: Stanford University Press, 1976.

Williams, Heather. *Parachutes, Patriots and Partisans: The Special Operations Executive and Yugoslavia, 1941–1945.* London: Hurst, 2003.

Winter, Jay, and Jean-Louis Robert. *Capital Cities at War: Paris, London, Berlin (1914–1919).* Vol. 2. Cambridge: Cambridge University Press, 2007.

Zahra, Tara. *Kidnapped Souls: National Indifference and the Battle for Children in Bohemia, 1900–1948.* Ithaca: Cornell University Press, 2008.

INDEX